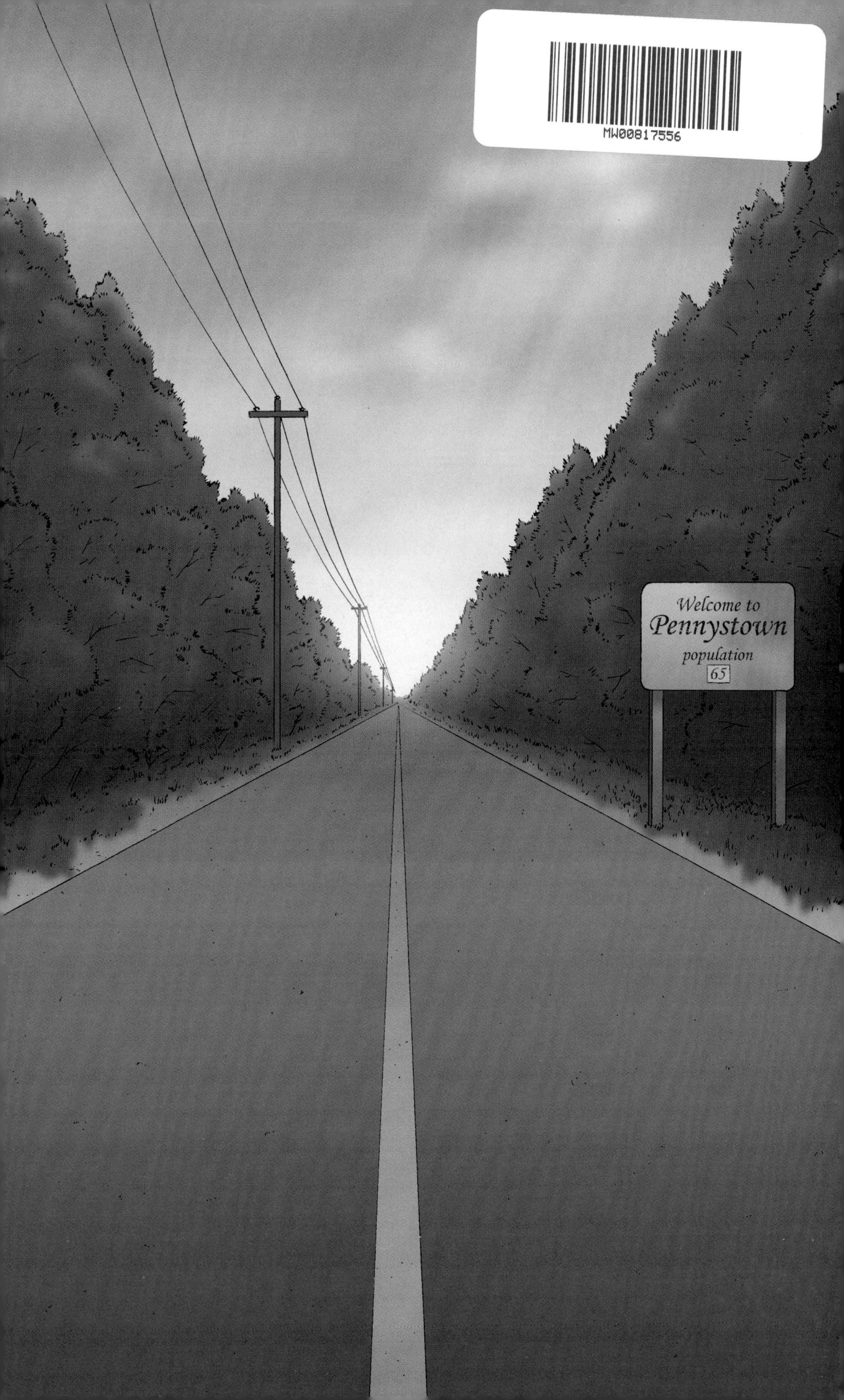
Welcome to
Pennystown
population
65

GIRLS™

Volume 2
EMERGENCE

www.ImageComics.com

www.LunaBrothers.com

GIRLS, VOL. 2: EMERGENCE. 2006. Published by Image Comics, Inc., Office of publication: 1942 University Avenue, Suite 305, Berkeley, California 94704.

Joshua Luna
Plot, Script, Layouts, Letters

Jonathan Luna
Plot, Art, Colors

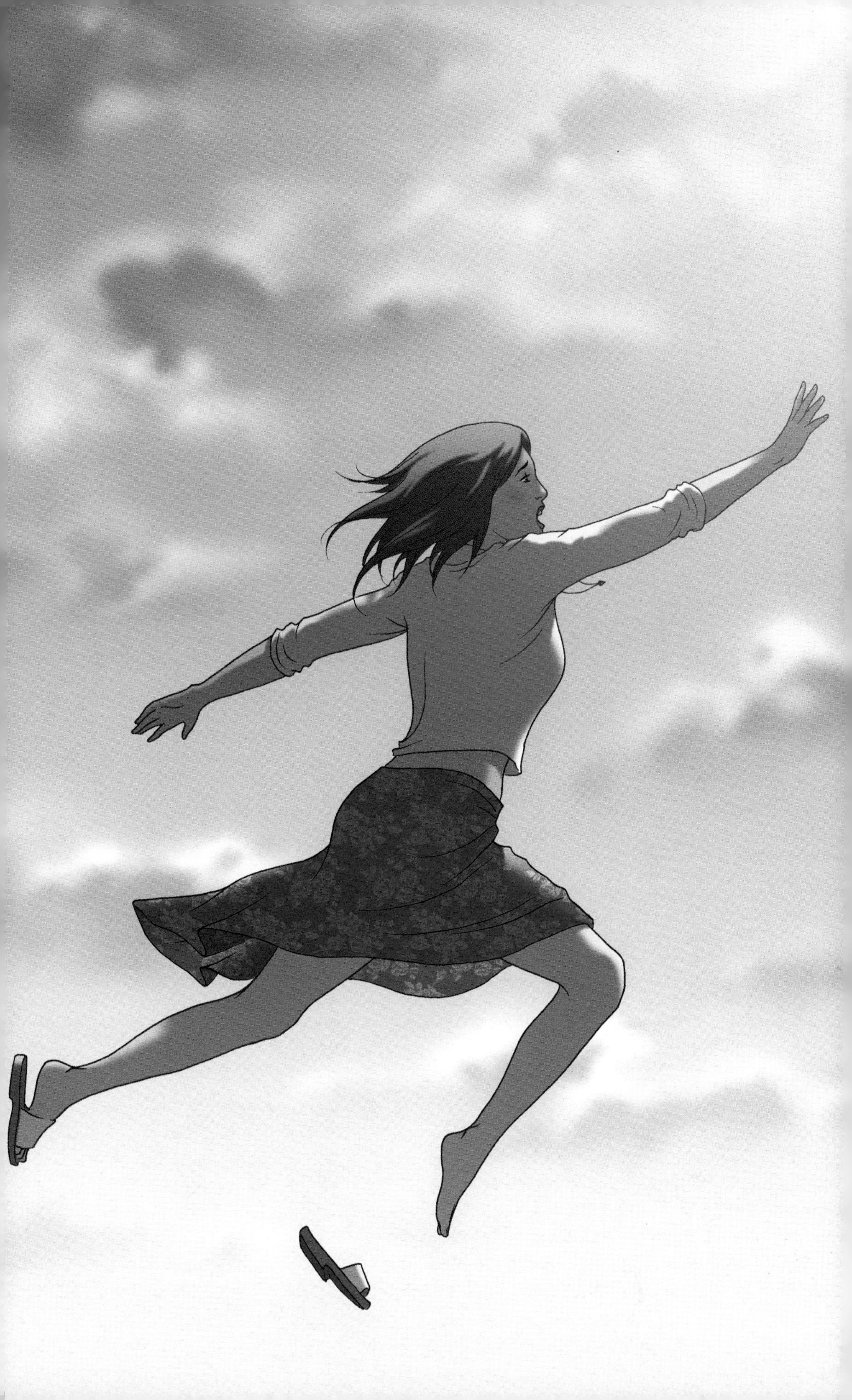

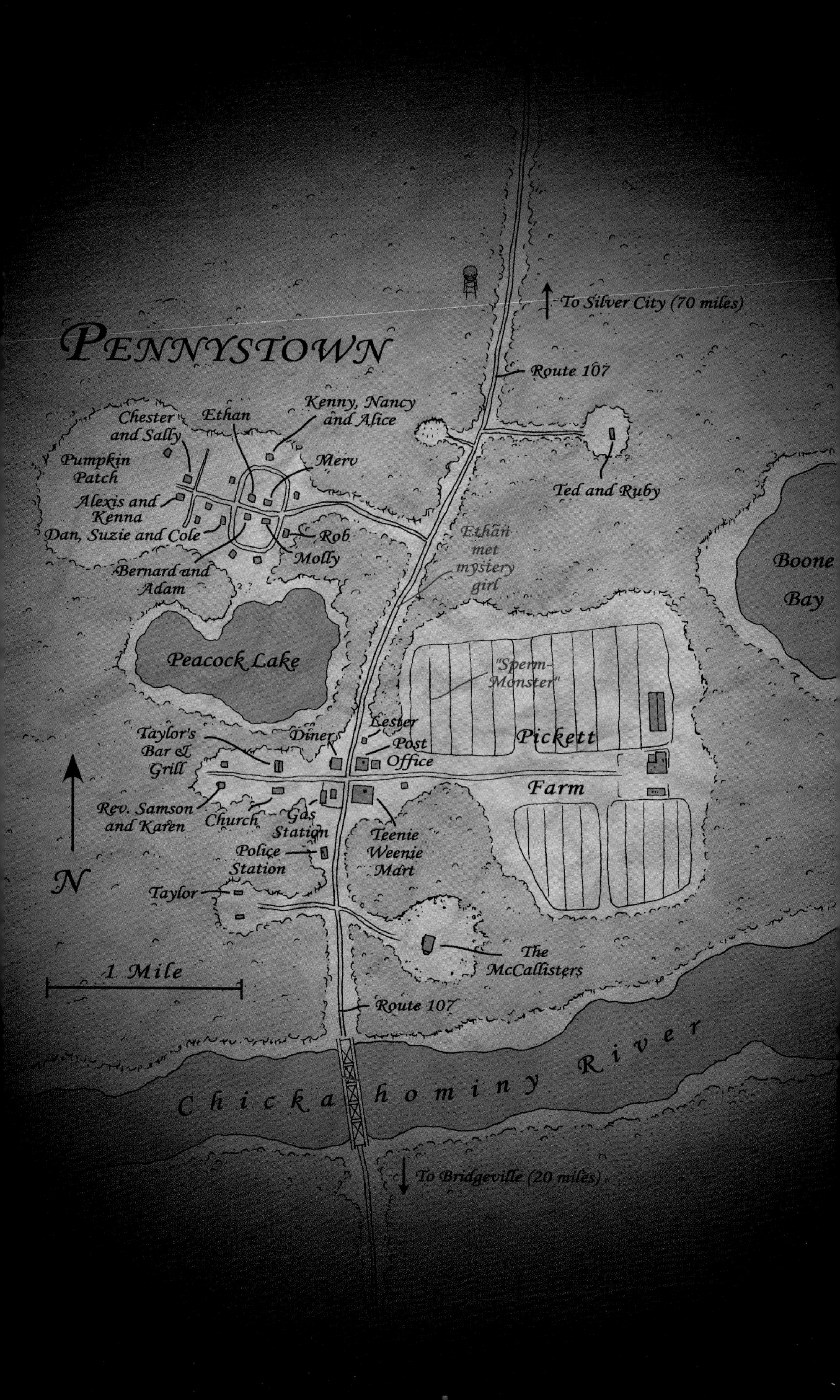

Pennystown
To Silver City (70 miles)
Route 107
Kenny, Nancy and Alice
Chester and Sally
Ethan
Pumpkin Patch
Merv
Ted and Ruby
Alexis and Kenna
Dan, Suzie and Cole
Rob
Molly
Bernard and Adam
Ethan met mystery girl
Boone Bay
Peacock Lake
"Sperm-Monster"
Lester
Taylor's Bar & Grill
Diner
Post Office
Pickett
Farm
Rev. Samson and Karen
Church
Gas Station
Teenie Weenie Mart
Police Station
N
Taylor
The McCallisters
1 Mile
Route 107
Chickahominy River
To Bridgeville (20 miles)

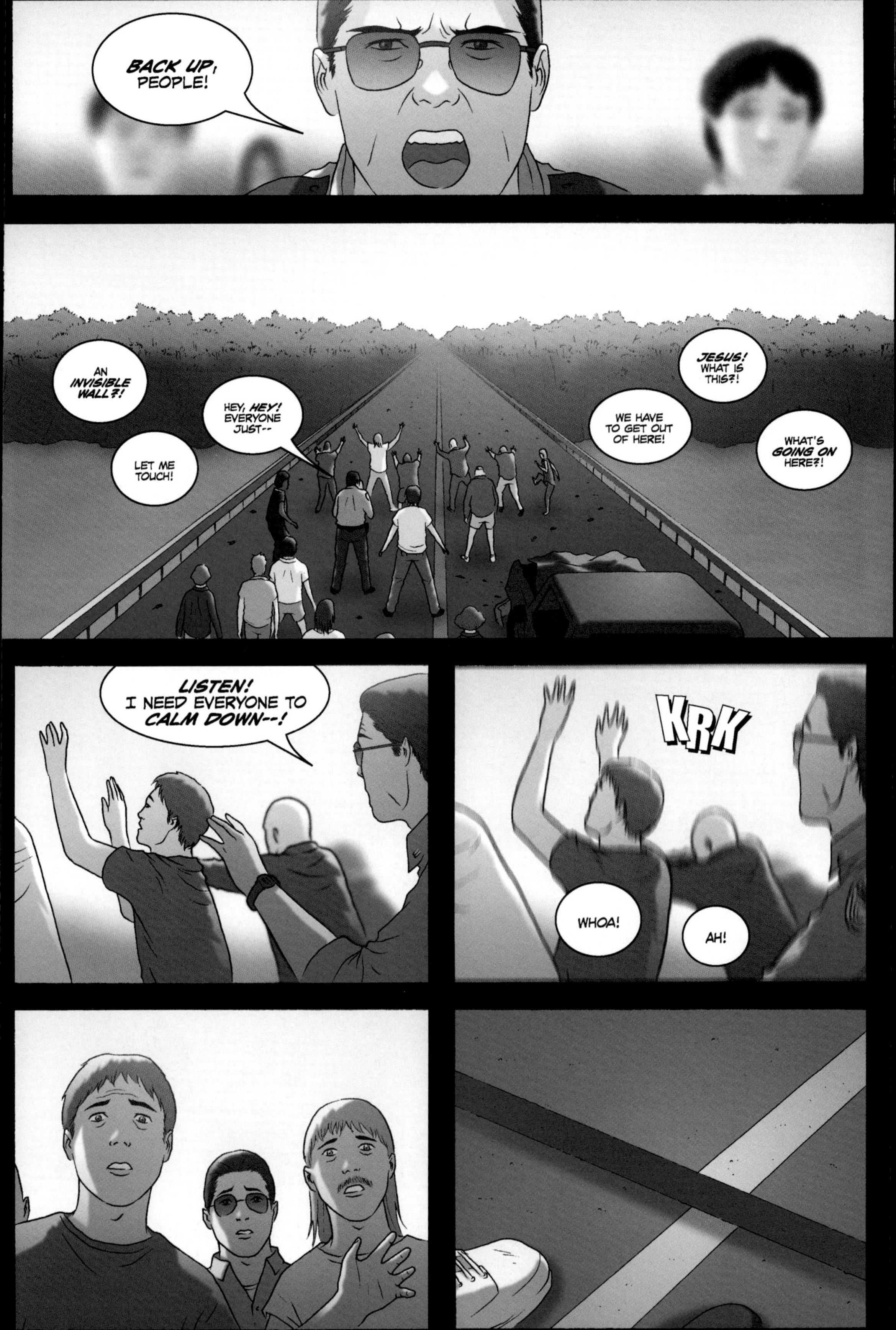
BACK UP, PEOPLE!
AN INVISIBLE WALL?!
LET ME TOUCH!
HEY, HEY! EVERYONE JUST--
WE HAVE TO GET OUT OF HERE!
JESUS! WHAT IS THIS?!
WHAT'S GOING ON HERE?!
LISTEN! I NEED EVERYONE TO CALM DOWN--!
KRK
WHOA!
AH!

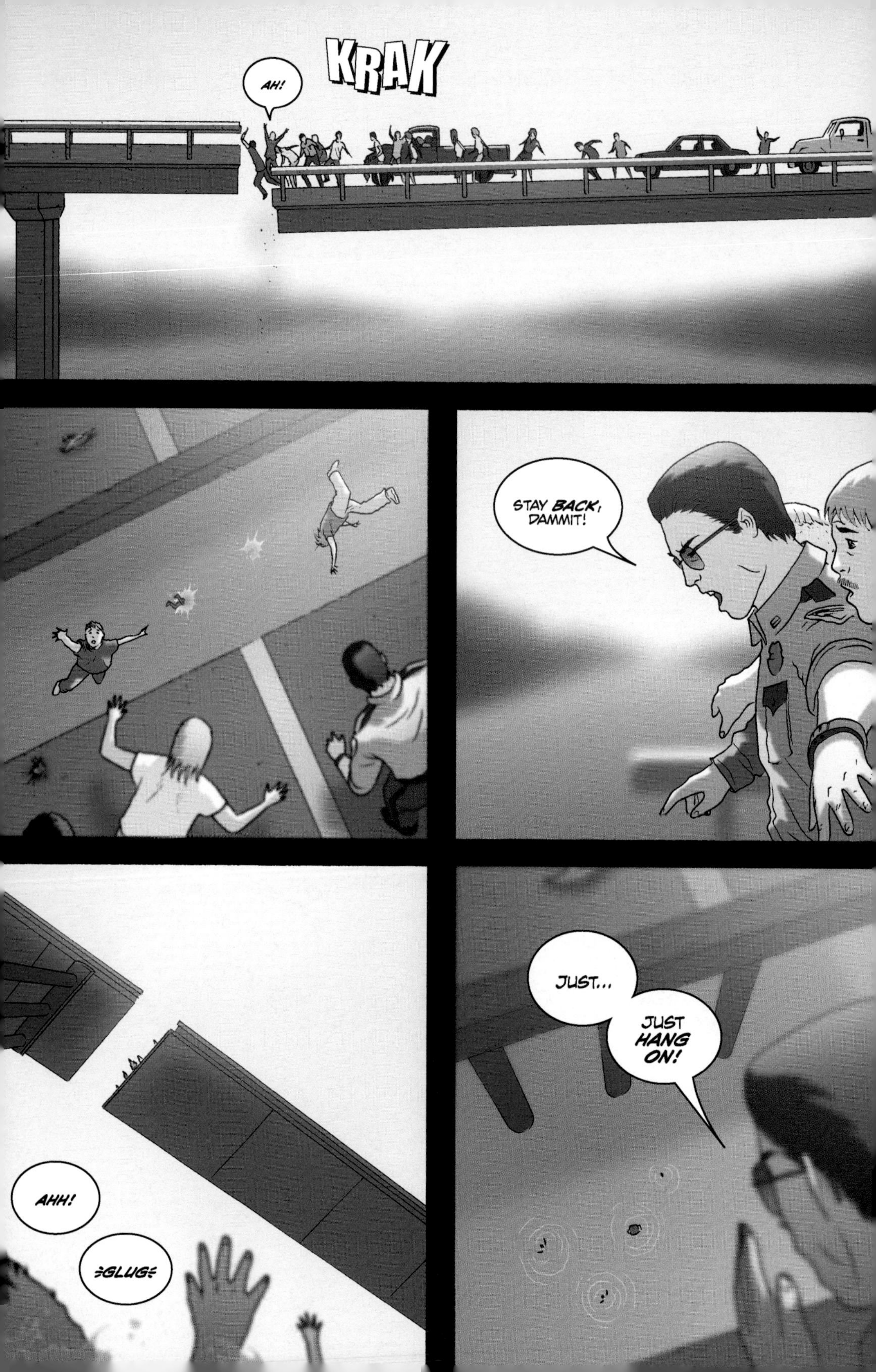
AH!
KRAK
STAY BACK, DAMMIT!
AHH!
≈GLUG≈
JUST...
JUST HANG ON!

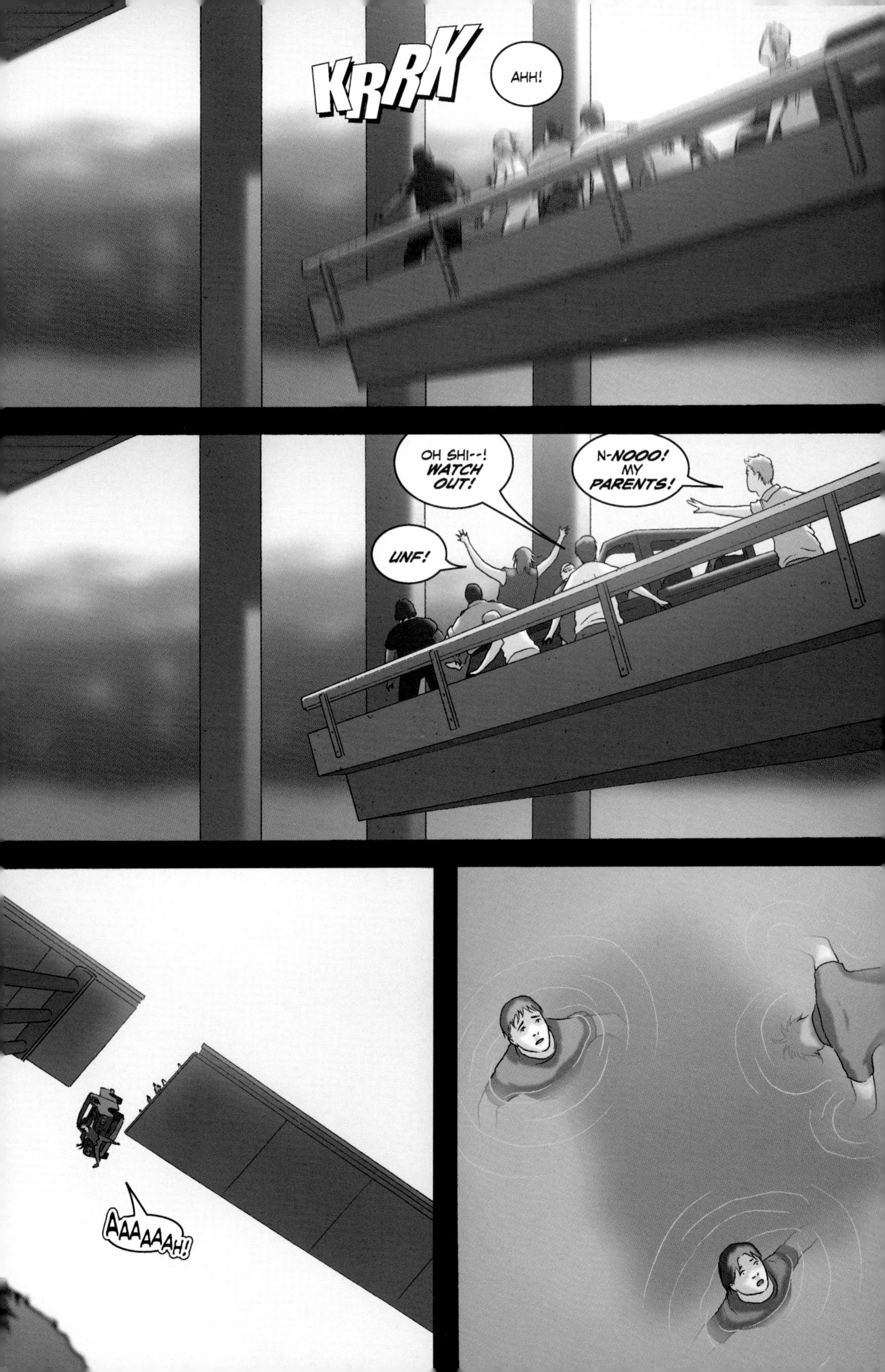
KRRK
AHH!
OH SHI--! WATCH OUT!
N-NOOO! MY PARENTS!
UNF!
AAAAAAH!

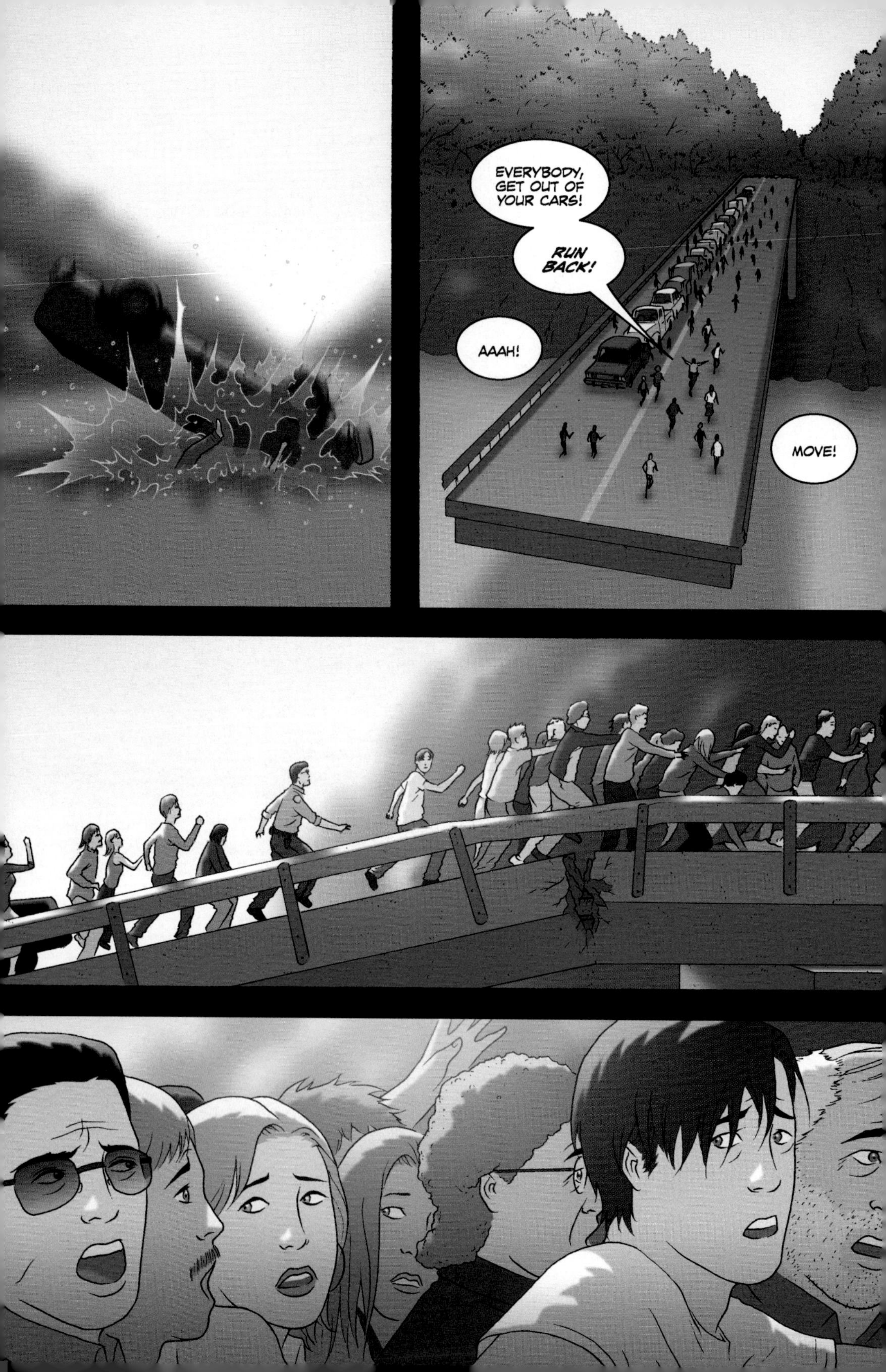

EVERYBODY, GET OUT OF YOUR CARS!
RUN BACK!
AAAH!
MOVE!

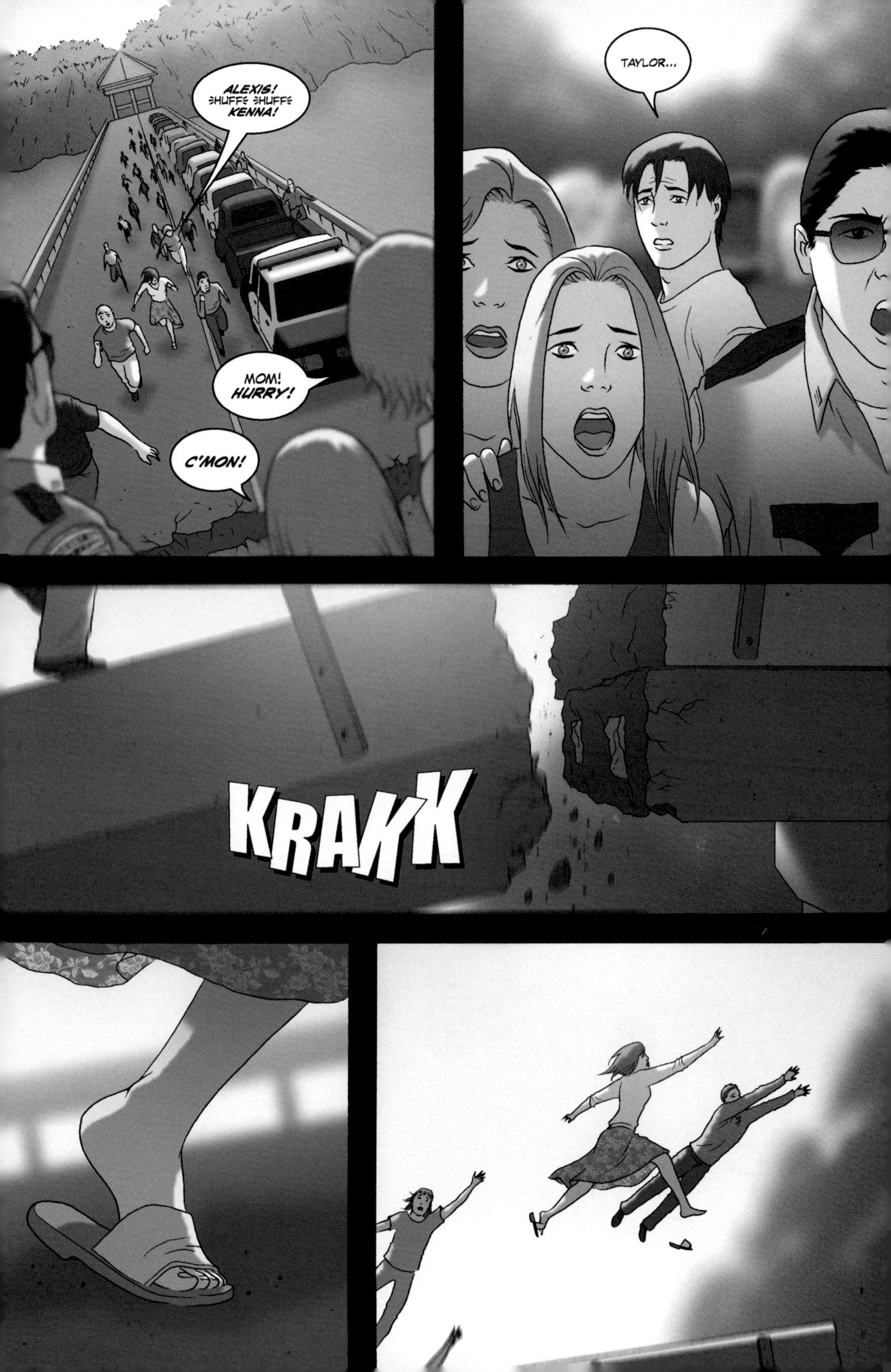
ALEXIS! ≋HUFF≋ ≋HUFF≋ KENNA!
MOM! HURRY!
C'MON!
TAYLOR...
KRAKK

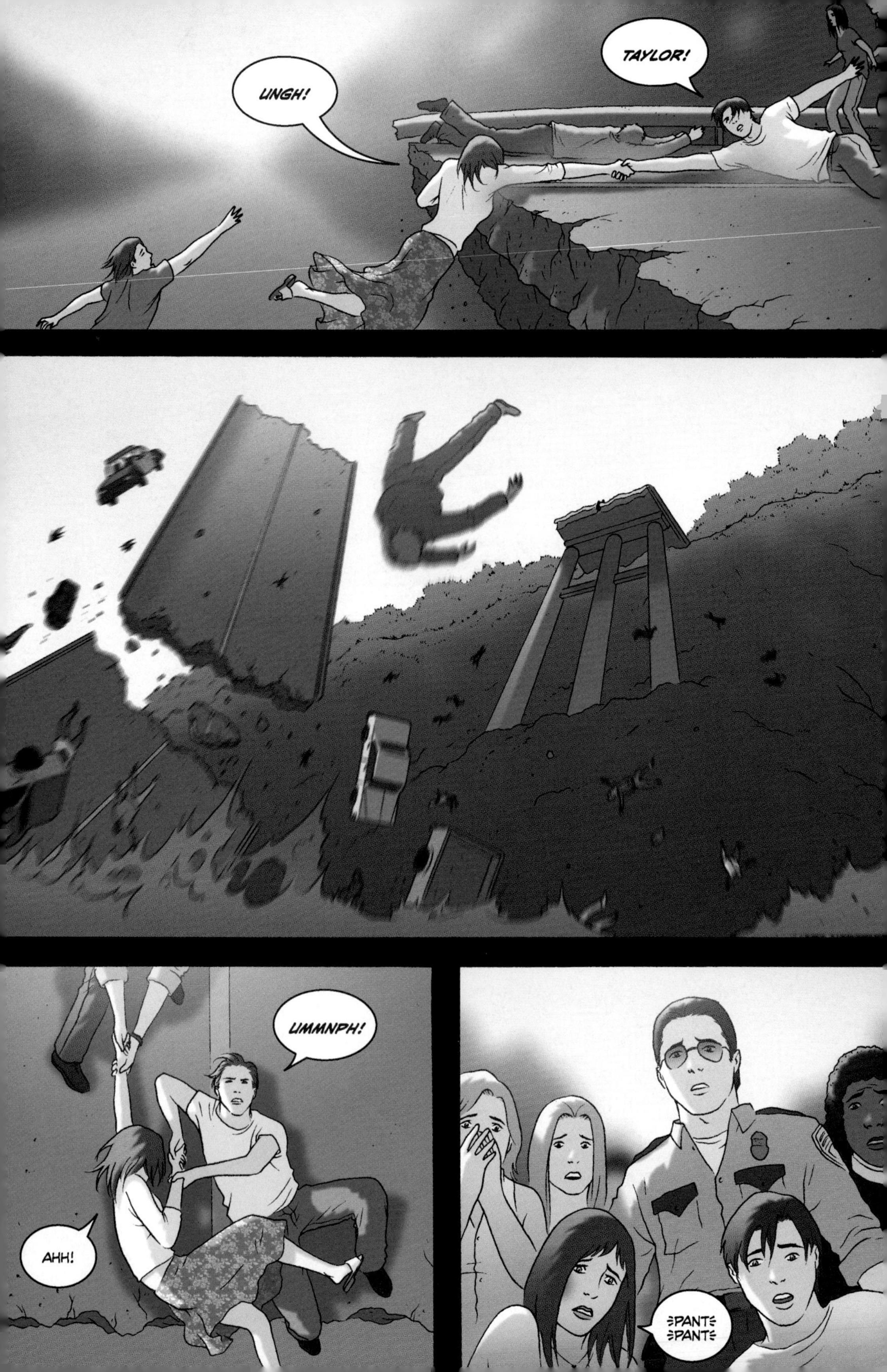
UNGH!
TAYLOR!
UMMNPH!
AHH!
PANT
PANT

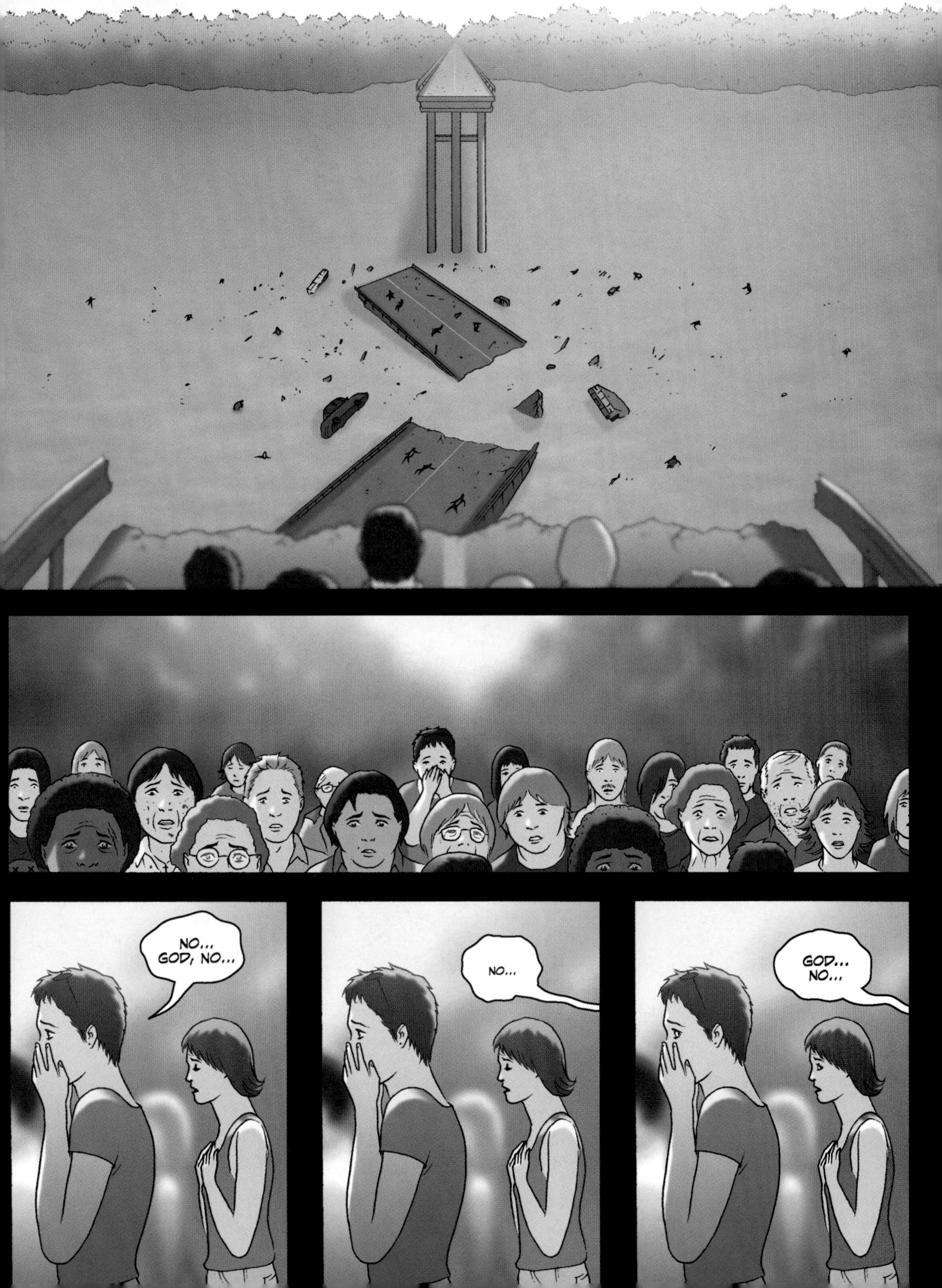
NO...
GOD, NO...
NO...
GOD...
NO...

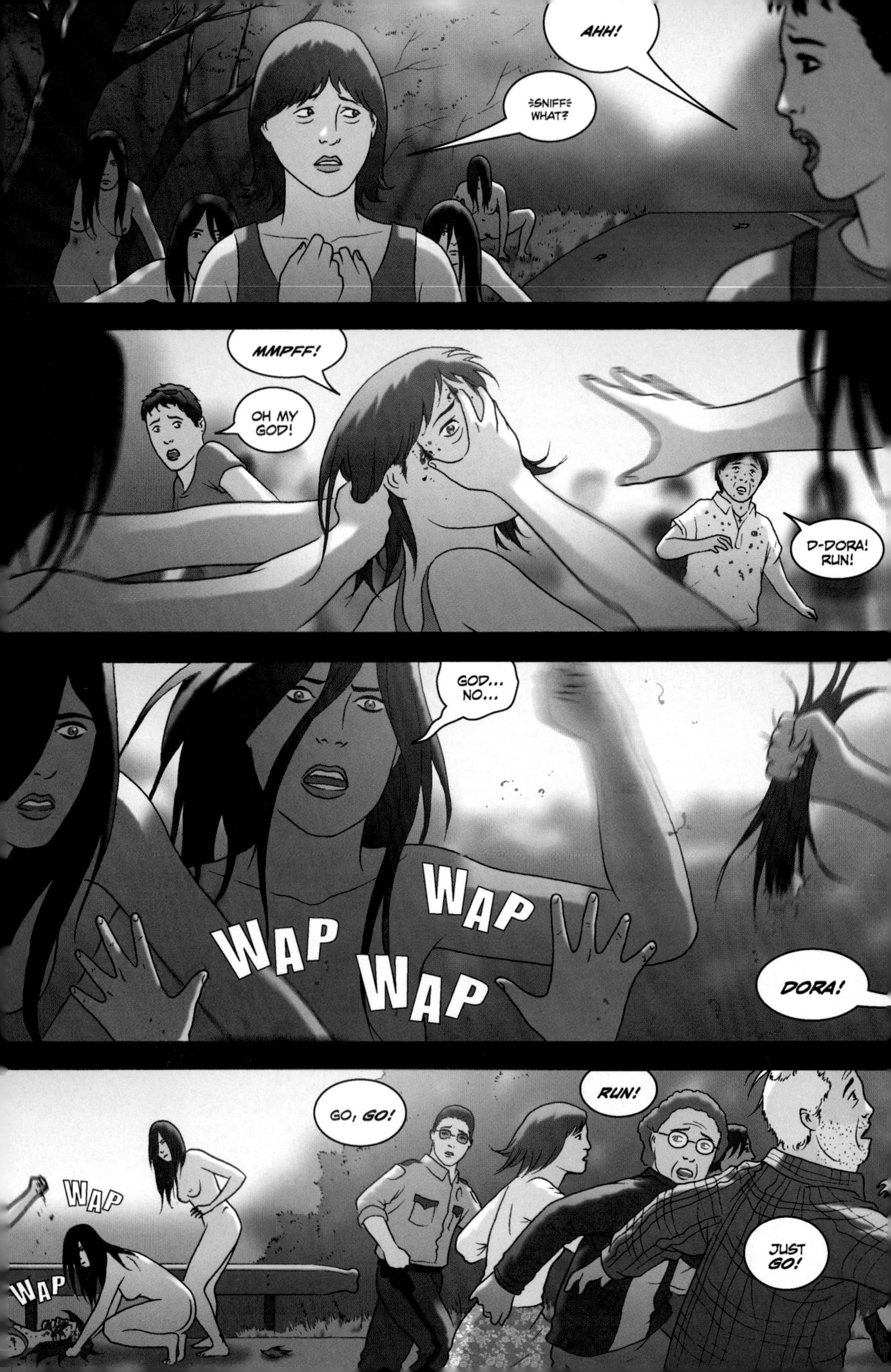

AHH!
=SNIFF= WHAT?
MMPFF!
OH MY GOD!
D-DORA! RUN!
GOD... NO...
WAP
WAP
WAP
DORA!
RUN!
GO, GO!
WAP
WAP
JUST GO!

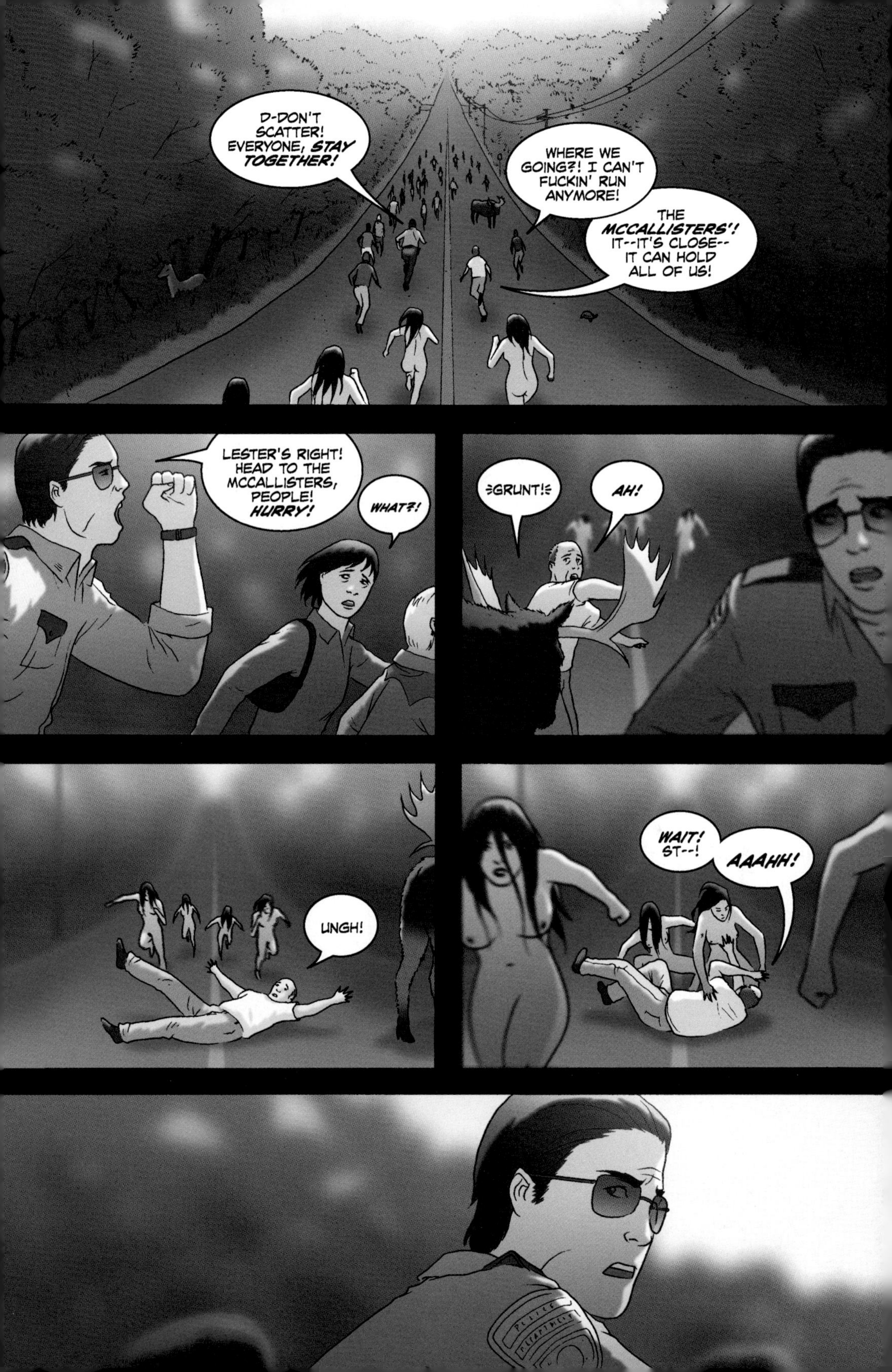
D-DON'T SCATTER! EVERYONE, STAY TOGETHER!
WHERE WE GOING?! I CAN'T FUCKIN' RUN ANYMORE!
THE MCCALLISTERS'! IT--IT'S CLOSE-- IT CAN HOLD ALL OF US!
LESTER'S RIGHT! HEAD TO THE MCCALLISTERS, PEOPLE! HURRY!
WHAT?!
GRUNT!
AH!
UNGH!
WAIT! ST--!
AAAHH!

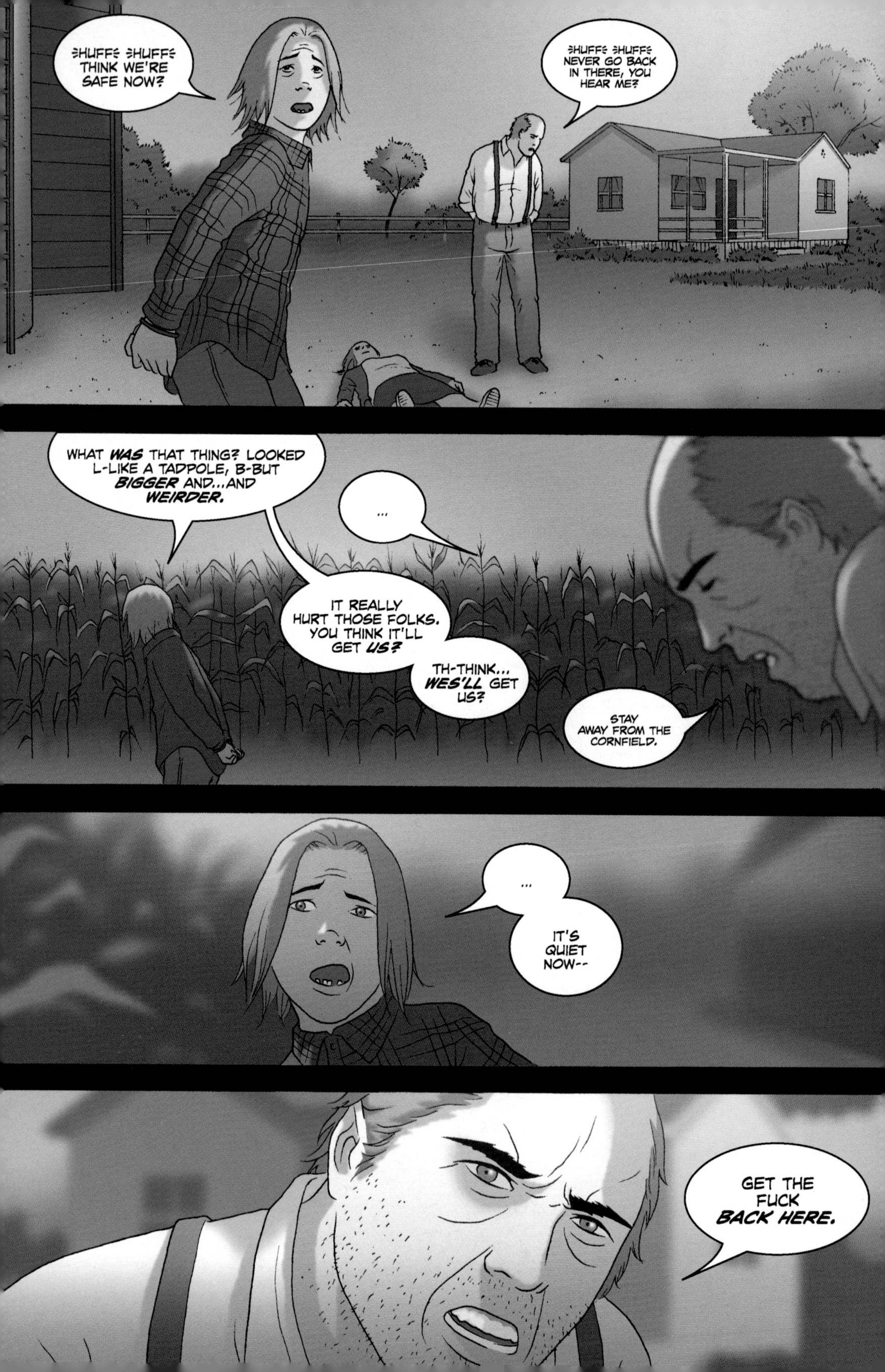

≶HUFF≶ ≶HUFF≶ THINK WE'RE SAFE NOW?
≶HUFF≶ ≶HUFF≶ NEVER GO BACK IN THERE, YOU HEAR ME?
WHAT **WAS** THAT THING? LOOKED L-LIKE A TADPOLE, B-BUT **BIGGER** AND...AND **WEIRDER.**
...
IT REALLY HURT THOSE FOLKS. YOU THINK IT'LL GET **US?**
TH-THINK... **WES'LL** GET US?
STAY AWAY FROM THE CORNFIELD.
...
IT'S QUIET NOW--
GET THE FUCK **BACK HERE.**

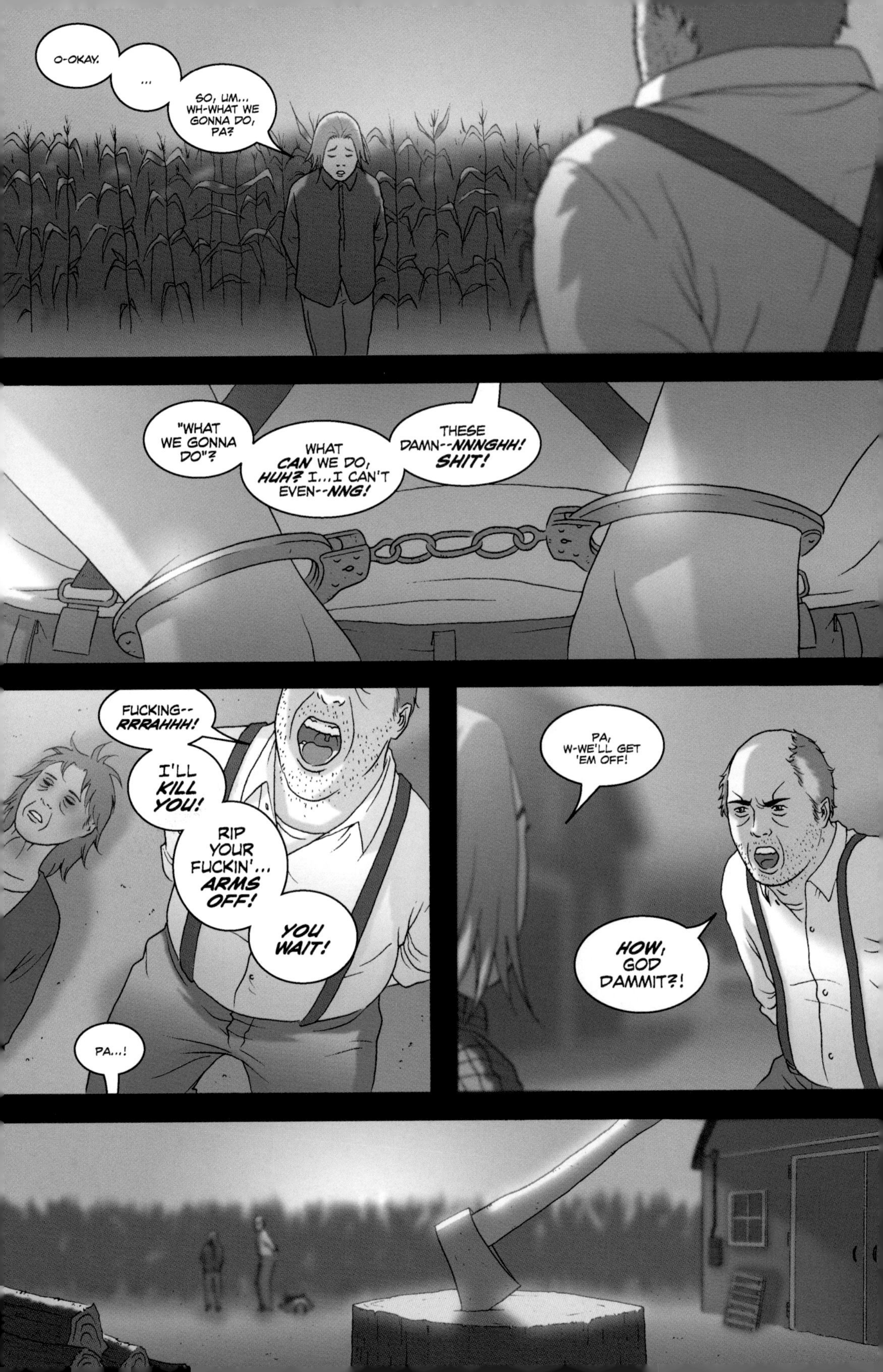
O-OKAY.
...
SO, UM... WH-WHAT WE GONNA DO, PA?
"WHAT WE GONNA DO"?
WHAT CAN WE DO, HUH? I...I CAN'T EVEN--NNG!
THESE DAMN--NNNGHH! SHIT!
FUCKING--RRRAHHH!
I'LL KILL YOU!
RIP YOUR FUCKIN'... ARMS OFF!
YOU WAIT!
PA...!
PA, W-WE'LL GET 'EM OFF!
HOW, GOD DAMMIT?!

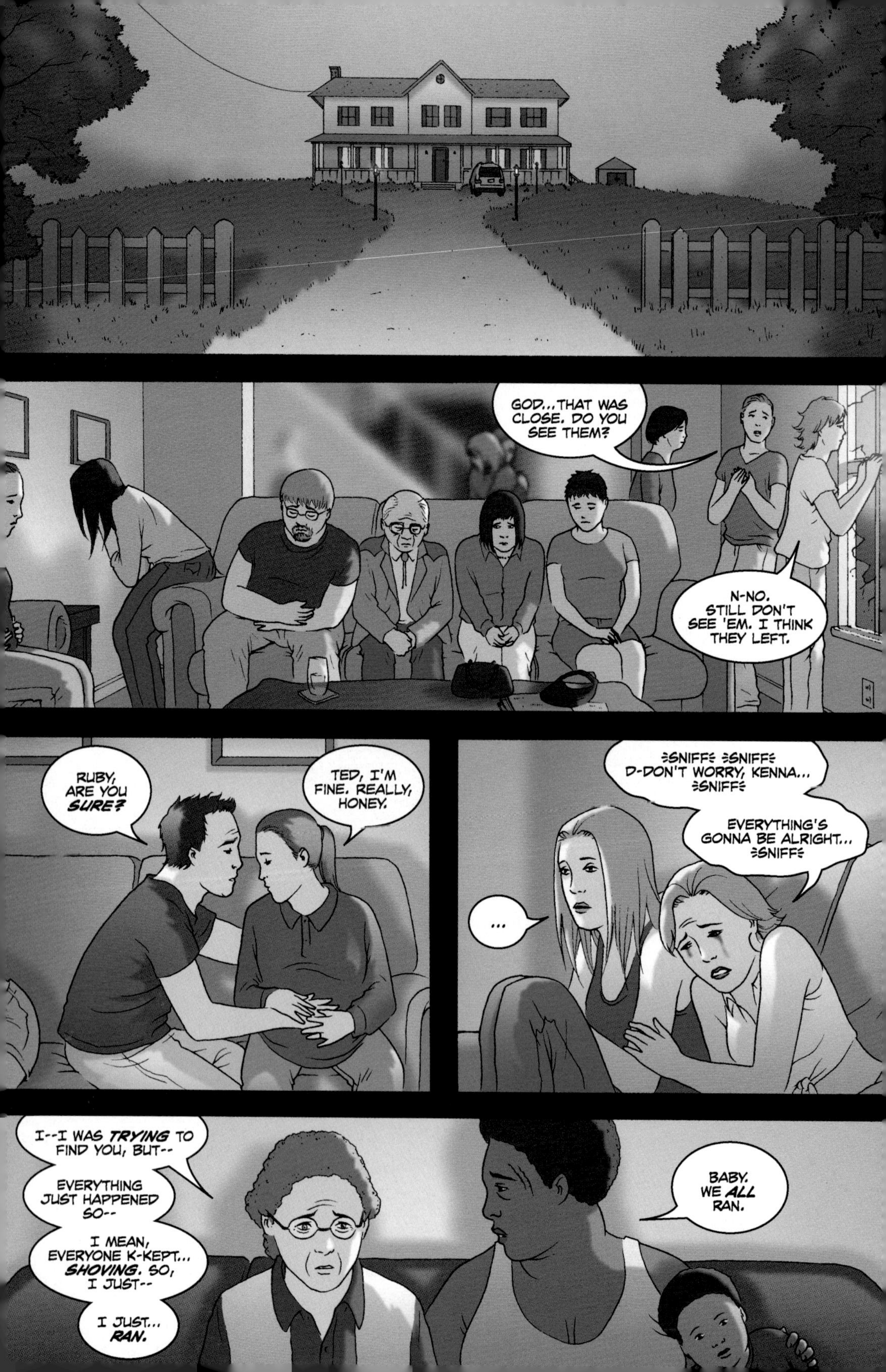
GOD...THAT WAS CLOSE. DO YOU SEE THEM?
N-NO. STILL DON'T SEE 'EM. I THINK THEY LEFT.
RUBY, ARE YOU *SURE?*
TED, I'M FINE. REALLY, HONEY.
≷SNIFF≶ ≷SNIFF≶ D-DON'T WORRY, KENNA... ≷SNIFF≶
EVERYTHING'S GONNA BE ALRIGHT... ≷SNIFF≶
...
I--I WAS *TRYING* TO FIND YOU, BUT--
EVERYTHING JUST HAPPENED SO--
I MEAN, EVERYONE K-KEPT... *SHOVING*. SO, I JUST--
I JUST... *RAN.*
BABY. WE *ALL* RAN.

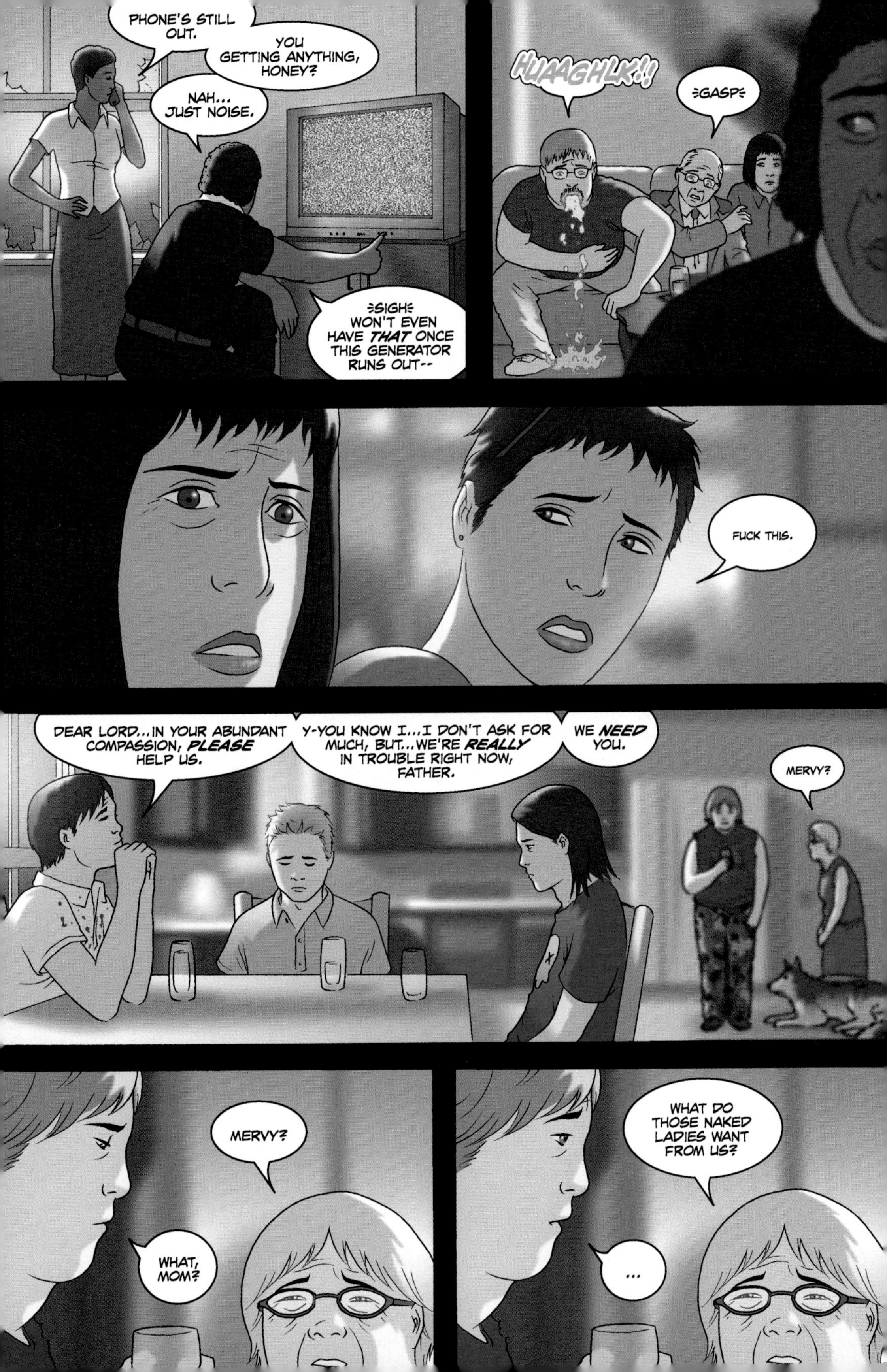
PHONE'S STILL OUT.
YOU GETTING ANYTHING, HONEY?
NAH... JUST NOISE.
⁼SIGH⁼ WON'T EVEN HAVE *THAT* ONCE THIS GENERATOR RUNS OUT--
HUAAGHLK!!
⁼GASP⁼
FUCK THIS.
DEAR LORD...IN YOUR ABUNDANT COMPASSION, *PLEASE* HELP US.
Y-YOU KNOW I...I DON'T ASK FOR MUCH, BUT...WE'RE *REALLY* IN TROUBLE RIGHT NOW, FATHER.
WE *NEED* YOU.
MERVY?
MERVY?
WHAT, MOM?
WHAT DO THOSE NAKED LADIES WANT FROM US?
...

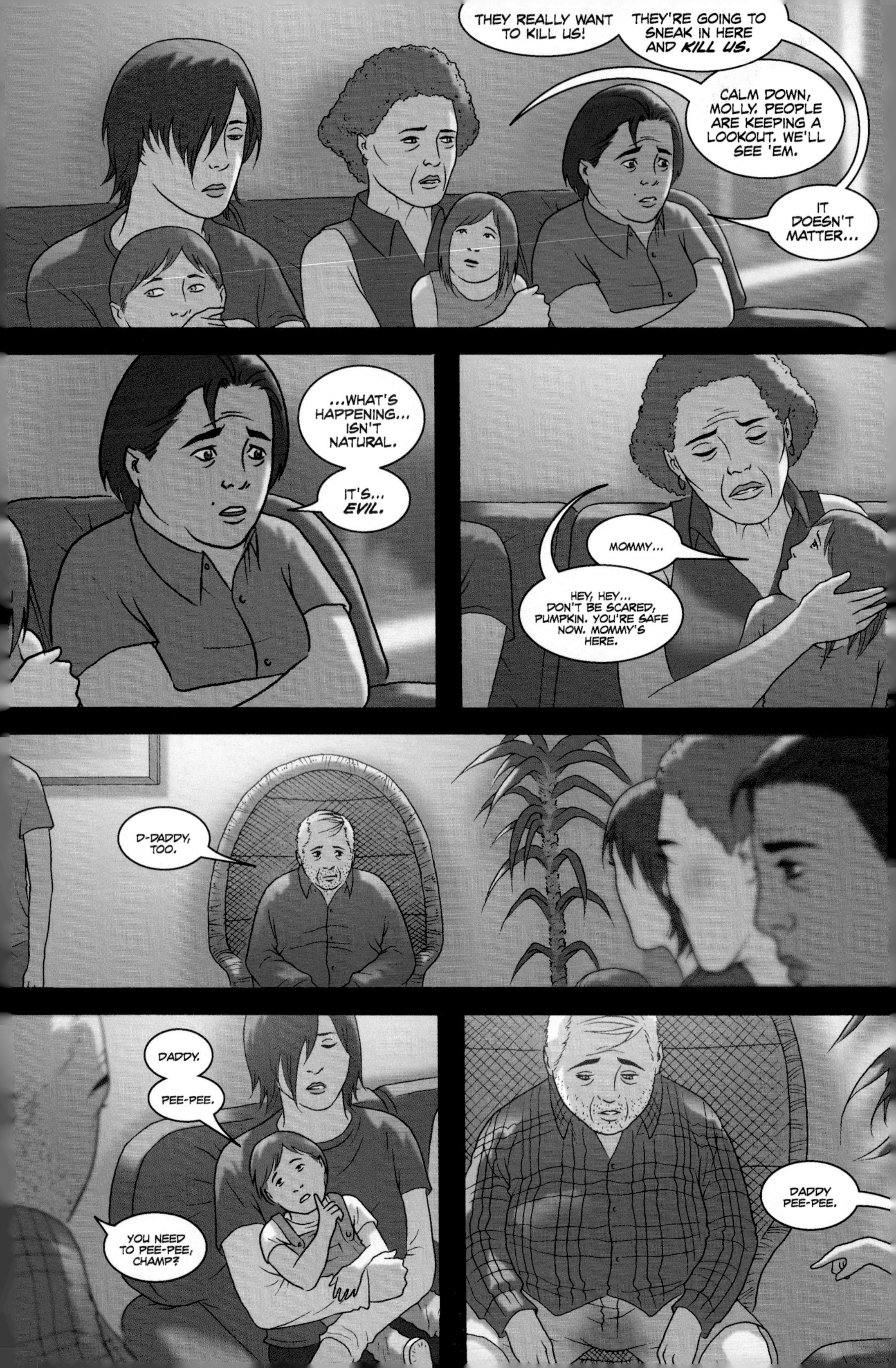
THEY REALLY WANT TO KILL US!
THEY'RE GOING TO SNEAK IN HERE AND *KILL US.*
CALM DOWN, MOLLY. PEOPLE ARE KEEPING A LOOKOUT. WE'LL SEE 'EM.
IT DOESN'T MATTER...
...WHAT'S HAPPENING... ISN'T NATURAL.
IT'S... *EVIL.*
MOMMY...
HEY, HEY... DON'T BE SCARED, PUMPKIN. YOU'RE SAFE NOW. MOMMY'S HERE.
D-DADDY, TOO.
DADDY.
PEE-PEE.
YOU NEED TO PEE-PEE, CHAMP?
DADDY PEE-PEE.

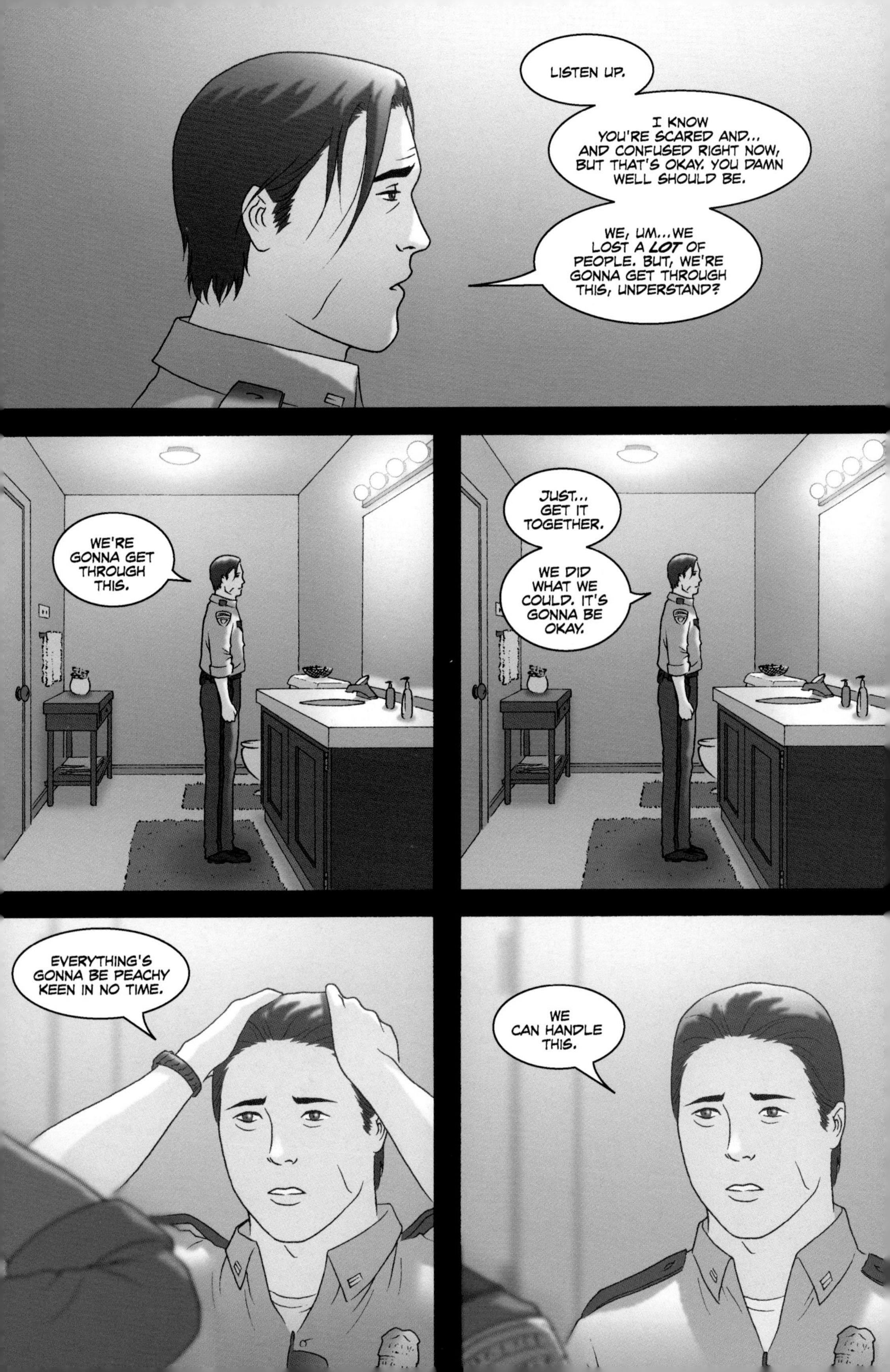
LISTEN UP.
I KNOW YOU'RE SCARED AND... AND CONFUSED RIGHT NOW, BUT THAT'S OKAY. YOU DAMN WELL SHOULD BE.
WE, UM...WE LOST A *LOT* OF PEOPLE. BUT, WE'RE GONNA GET THROUGH THIS, UNDERSTAND?
WE'RE GONNA GET THROUGH THIS.
JUST... GET IT TOGETHER.
WE DID WHAT WE COULD. IT'S GONNA BE OKAY.
EVERYTHING'S GONNA BE PEACHY KEEN IN NO TIME.
WE CAN HANDLE THIS.

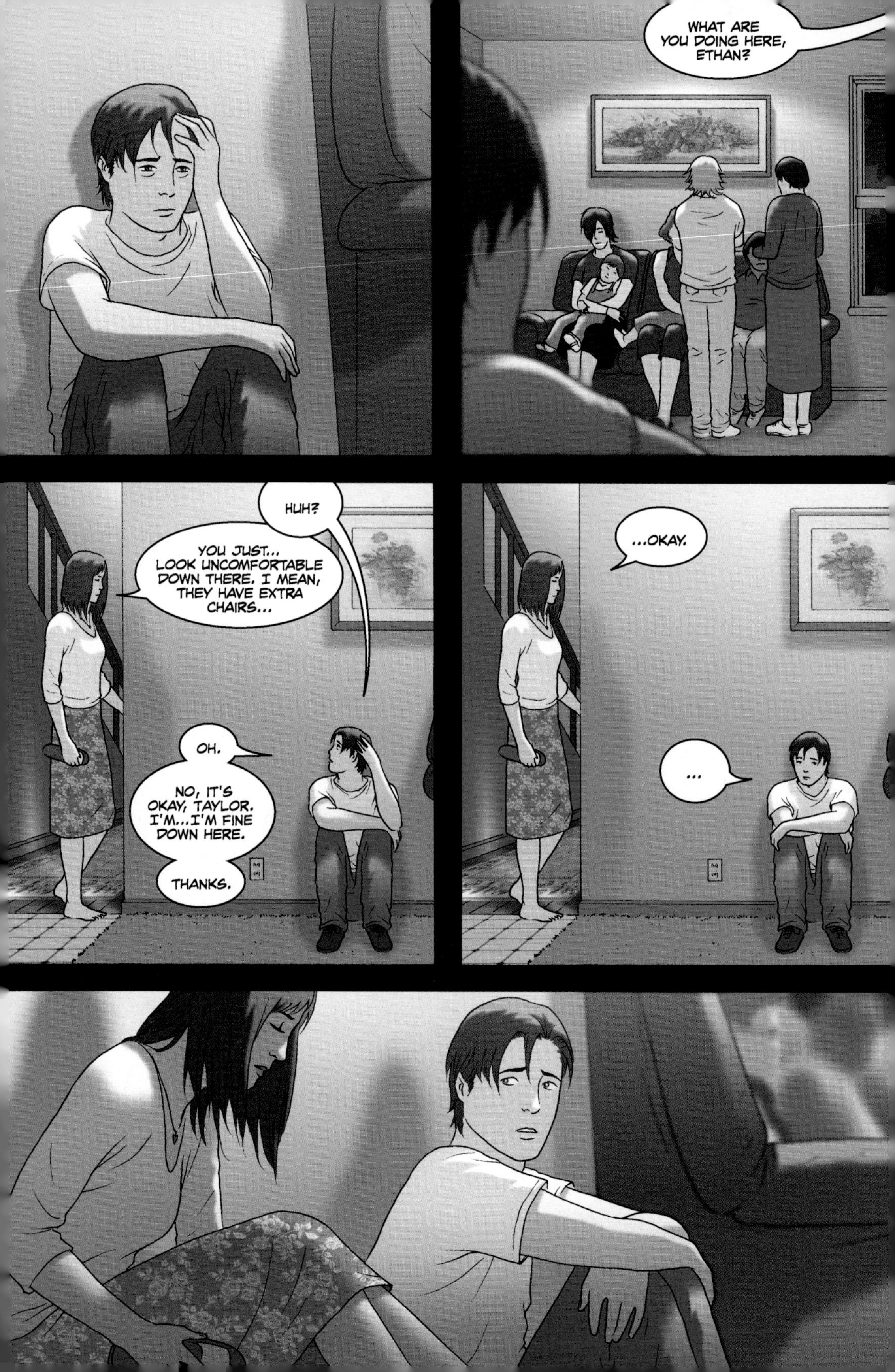
WHAT ARE YOU DOING HERE, ETHAN?
HUH?
YOU JUST... LOOK UNCOMFORTABLE DOWN THERE. I MEAN, THEY HAVE EXTRA CHAIRS...
OH.
NO, IT'S OKAY, TAYLOR. I'M...I'M FINE DOWN HERE.
THANKS.
...OKAY.
...

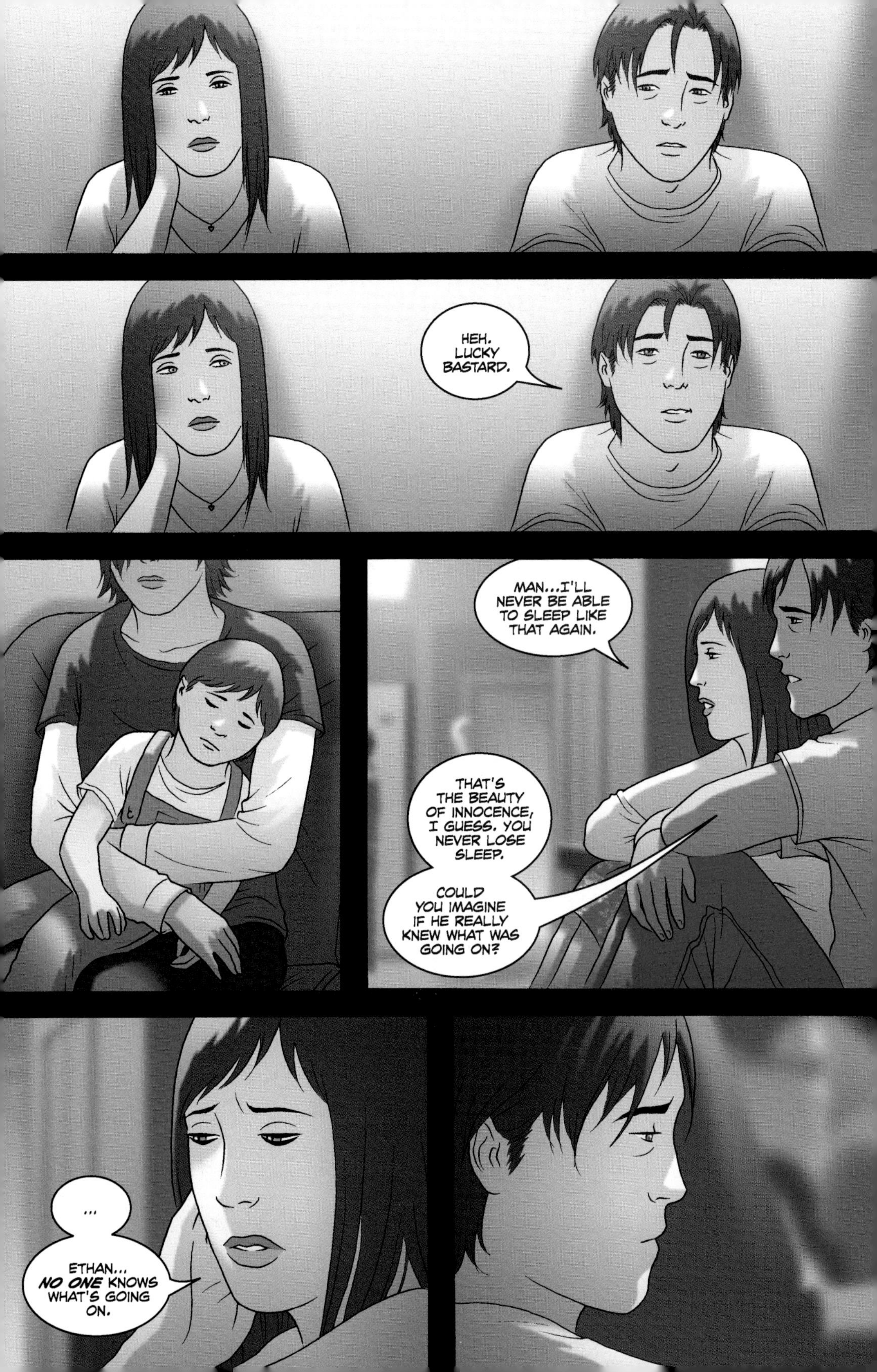
HEH. LUCKY BASTARD.
MAN...I'LL NEVER BE ABLE TO SLEEP LIKE THAT AGAIN.
THAT'S THE BEAUTY OF INNOCENCE, I GUESS. YOU NEVER LOSE SLEEP.
COULD YOU IMAGINE IF HE REALLY KNEW WHAT WAS GOING ON?
...
ETHAN... NO ONE KNOWS WHAT'S GOING ON.

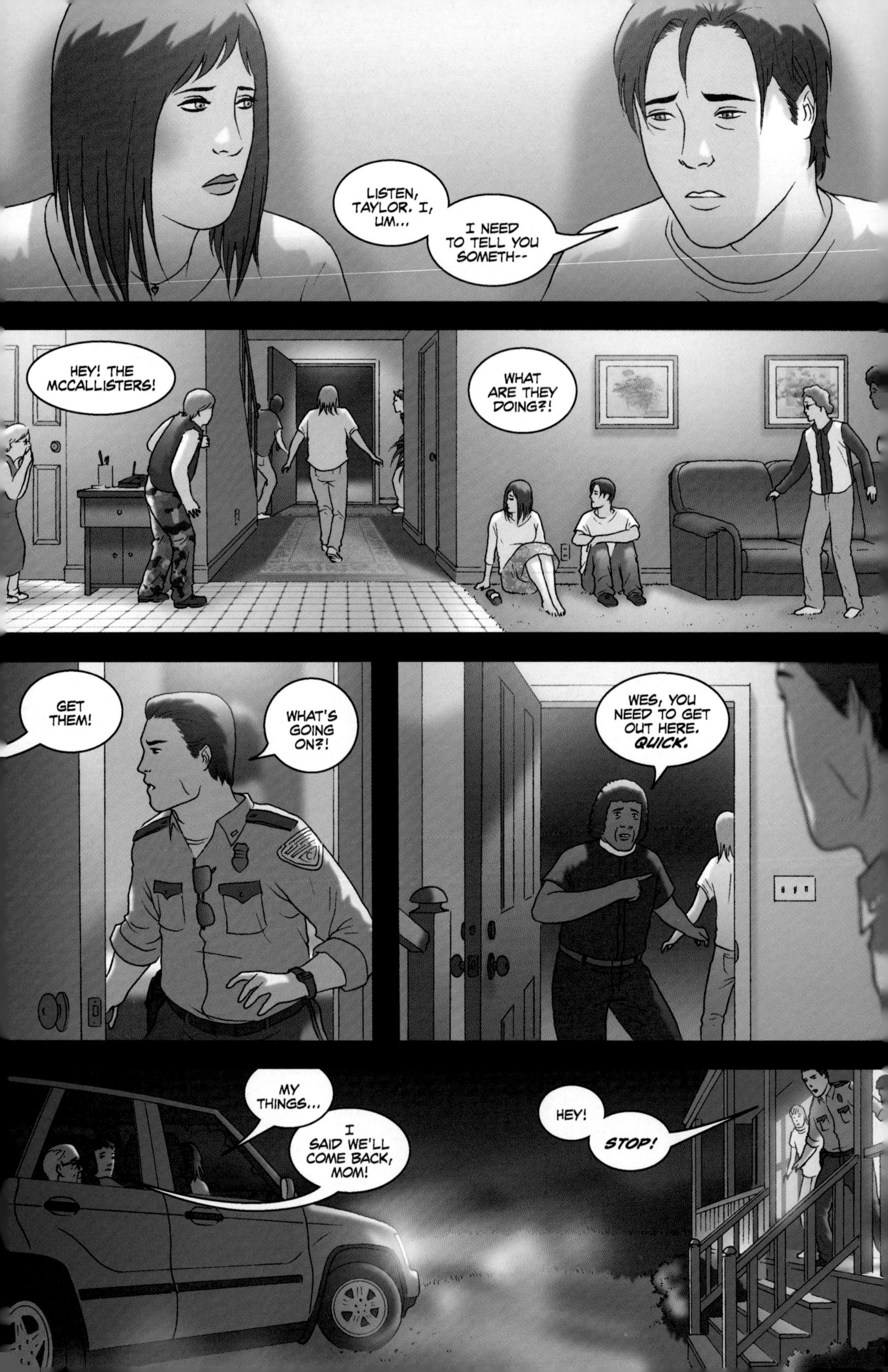
LISTEN, TAYLOR. I, UM...
I NEED TO TELL YOU SOMETH--
HEY! THE MCCALLISTERS!
WHAT ARE THEY DOING?!
GET THEM!
WHAT'S GOING ON?!
WES, YOU NEED TO GET OUT HERE. *QUICK.*
MY THINGS...
I SAID WE'LL COME BACK, MOM!
HEY!
STOP!

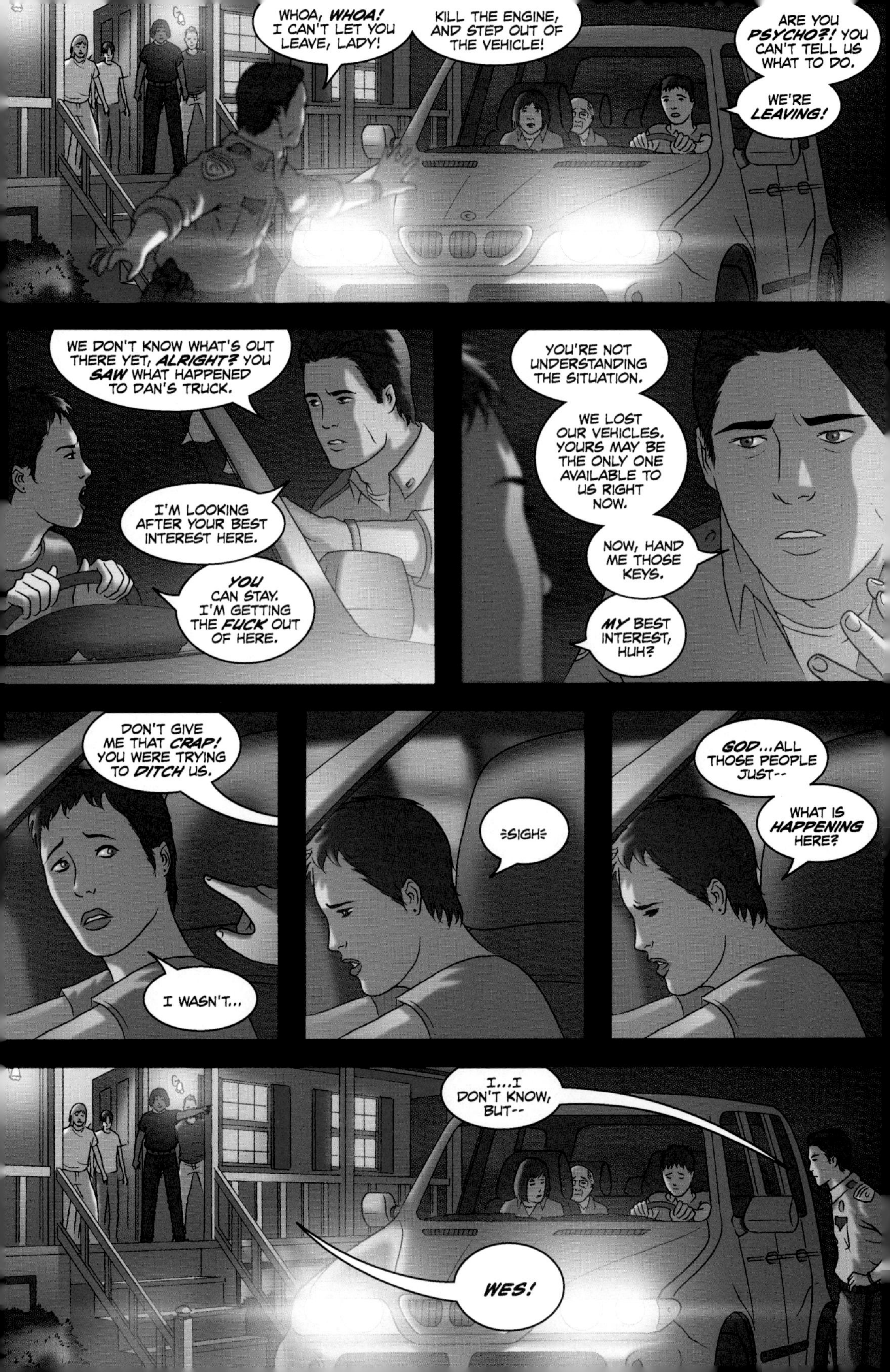
WHOA, WHOA! I CAN'T LET YOU LEAVE, LADY!
KILL THE ENGINE, AND STEP OUT OF THE VEHICLE!
ARE YOU PSYCHO?! YOU CAN'T TELL US WHAT TO DO.
WE'RE LEAVING!
WE DON'T KNOW WHAT'S OUT THERE YET, ALRIGHT? YOU SAW WHAT HAPPENED TO DAN'S TRUCK.
I'M LOOKING AFTER YOUR BEST INTEREST HERE.
YOU CAN STAY. I'M GETTING THE FUCK OUT OF HERE.
YOU'RE NOT UNDERSTANDING THE SITUATION.
WE LOST OUR VEHICLES. YOURS MAY BE THE ONLY ONE AVAILABLE TO US RIGHT NOW.
NOW, HAND ME THOSE KEYS.
MY BEST INTEREST, HUH?
DON'T GIVE ME THAT CRAP! YOU WERE TRYING TO DITCH US.
I WASN'T...
SIGH
GOD...ALL THOSE PEOPLE JUST--
WHAT IS HAPPENING HERE?
I...I DON'T KNOW, BUT--
WES!

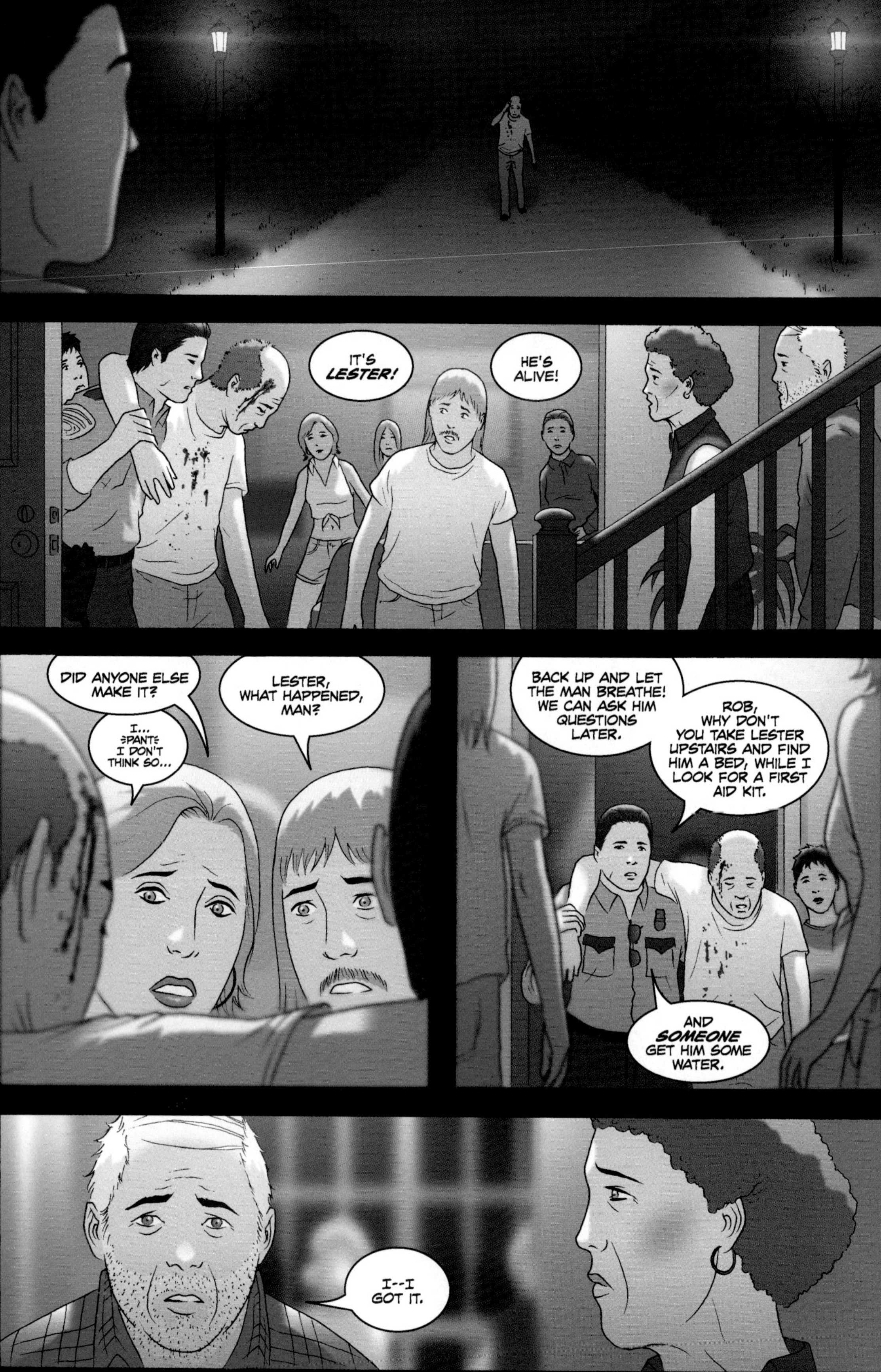
IT'S LESTER!
HE'S ALIVE!
DID ANYONE ELSE MAKE IT?
I... PANT I DON'T THINK SO...
LESTER, WHAT HAPPENED, MAN?
BACK UP AND LET THE MAN BREATHE! WE CAN ASK HIM QUESTIONS LATER.
ROB, WHY DON'T YOU TAKE LESTER UPSTAIRS AND FIND HIM A BED, WHILE I LOOK FOR A FIRST AID KIT.
AND SOMEONE GET HIM SOME WATER.
I--I GOT IT.

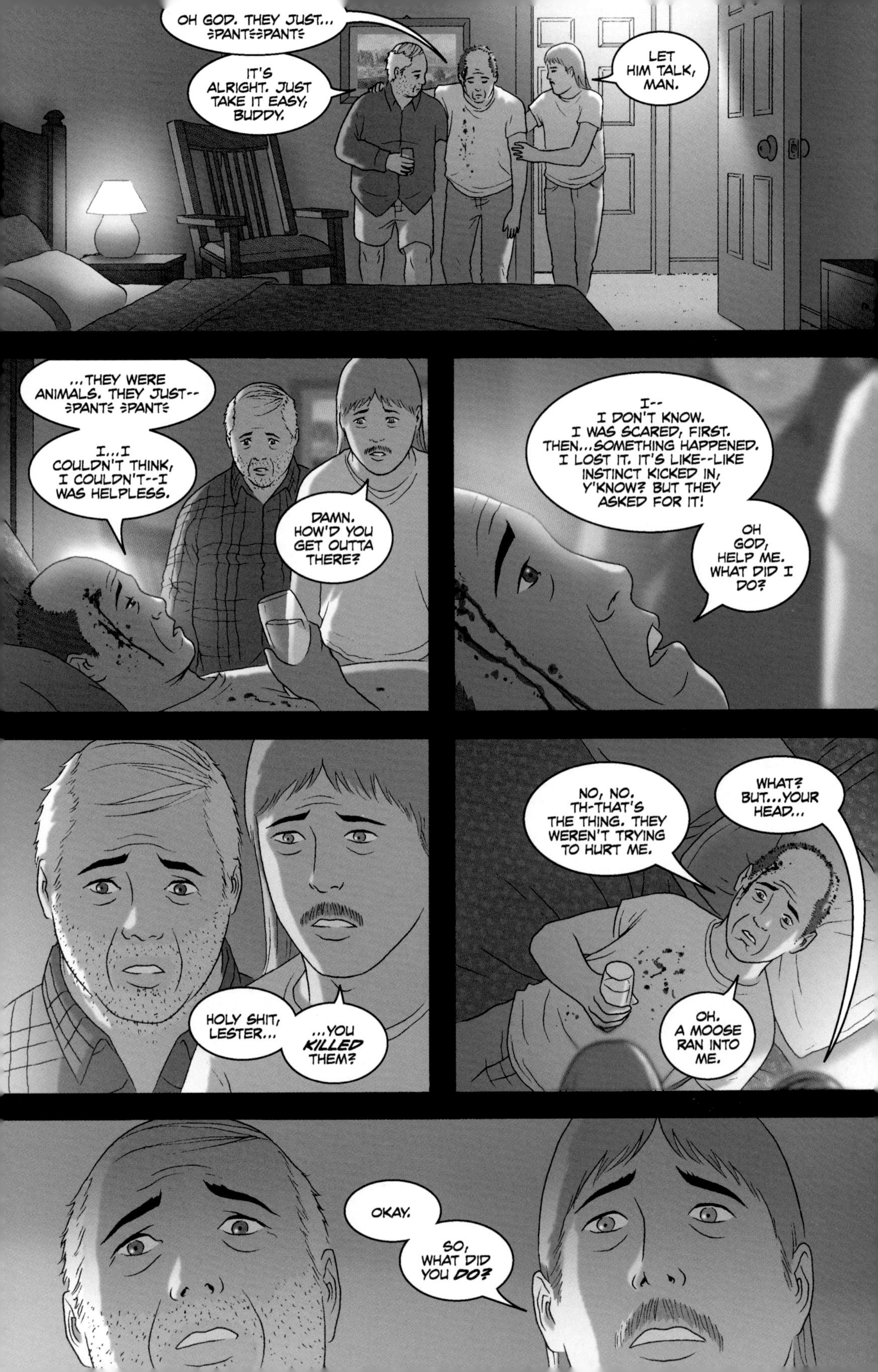
OH GOD. THEY JUST... ≑PANT≑≑PANT≑
IT'S ALRIGHT. JUST TAKE IT EASY, BUDDY.
LET HIM TALK, MAN.
...THEY WERE ANIMALS. THEY JUST-- ≑PANT≑ ≑PANT≑
I...I COULDN'T THINK, I COULDN'T--I WAS HELPLESS.
DAMN. HOW'D YOU GET OUTTA THERE?
I-- I DON'T KNOW. I WAS SCARED, FIRST. THEN...SOMETHING HAPPENED. I LOST IT. IT'S LIKE--LIKE INSTINCT KICKED IN, Y'KNOW? BUT THEY ASKED FOR IT!
OH GOD, HELP ME. WHAT DID I DO?
HOLY SHIT, LESTER...
...YOU *KILLED* THEM?
NO, NO. TH-THAT'S THE THING. THEY WEREN'T TRYING TO HURT ME.
WHAT? BUT...YOUR HEAD...
OH. A MOOSE RAN INTO ME.
OKAY.
SO, WHAT DID YOU *DO?*

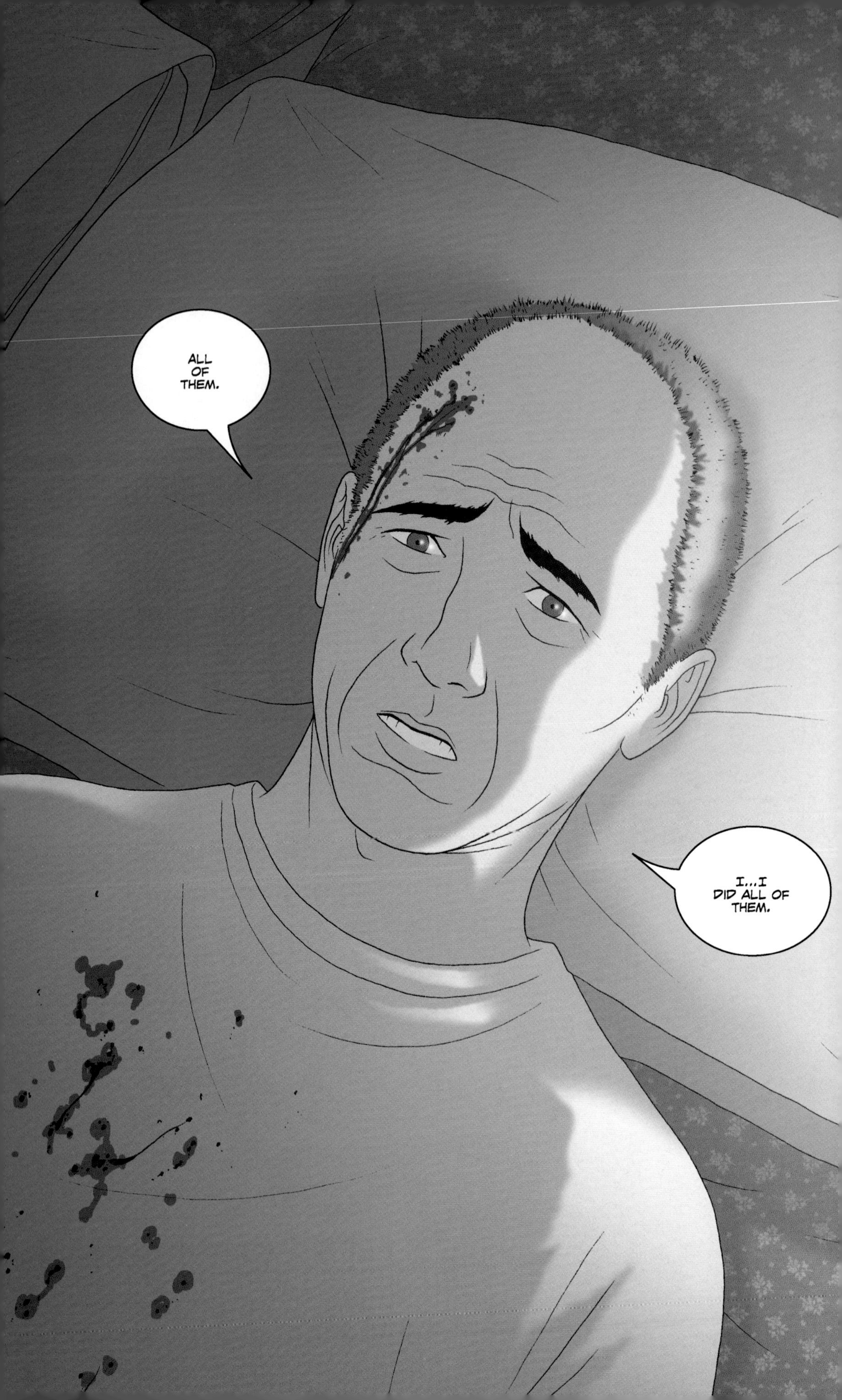
ALL OF THEM.
I...I DID ALL OF THEM.

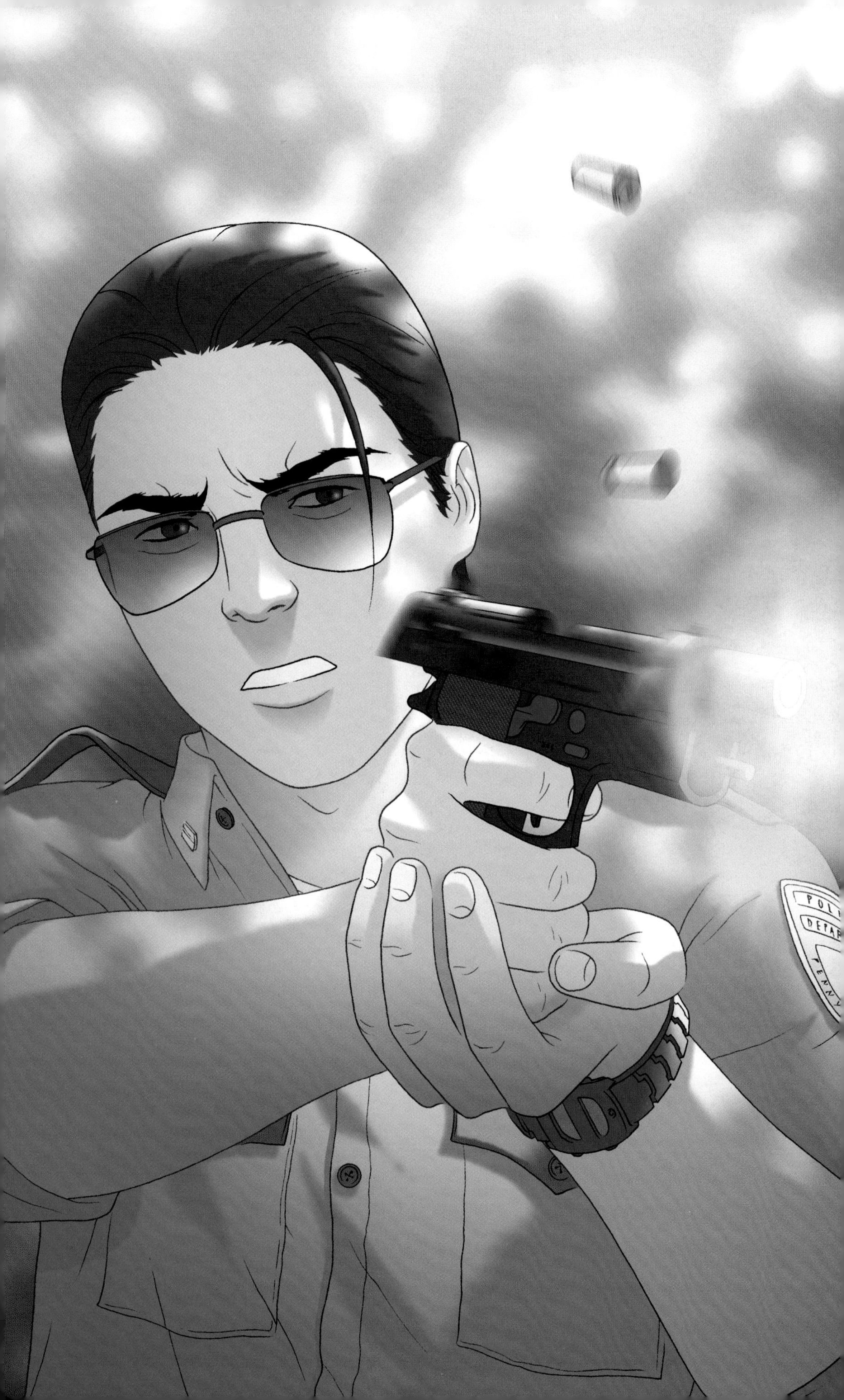

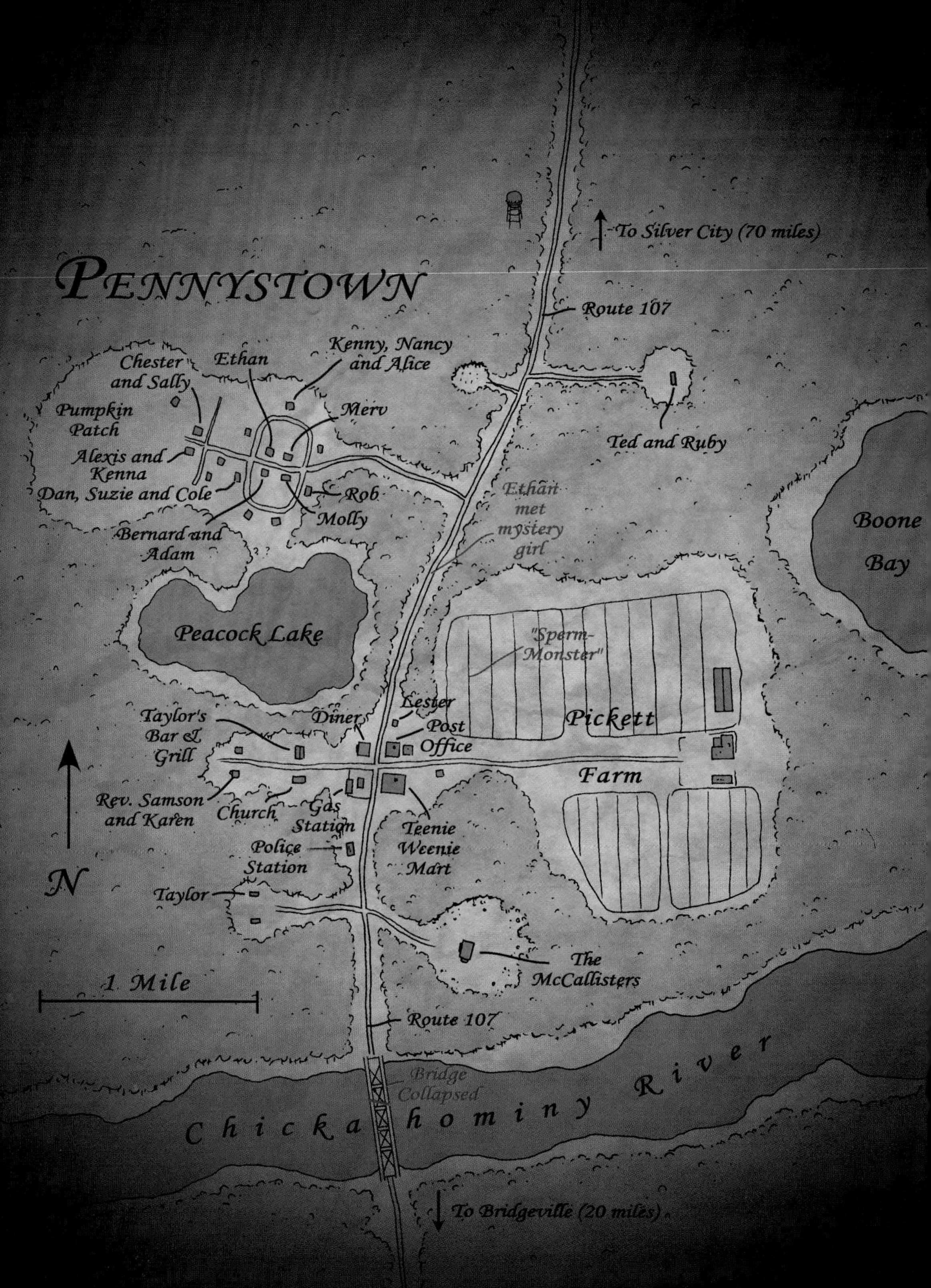
Pennystown
To Silver City (70 miles)
Route 107
Kenny, Nancy and Alice
Chester and Sally
Ethan
Pumpkin Patch
Merv
Ted and Ruby
Alexis and Kenna
Dan, Suzie and Cole
Rob
Molly
Bernard and Adam
Ethan met mystery girl
Boone Bay
Peacock Lake
"Sperm-Monster"
Lester
Taylor's Bar & Grill
Diner
Post Office
Pickett Farm
Rev. Samson and Karen
Church
Gas Station
Teenie Weenie Mart
Police Station
N
Taylor
The McCallisters
1 Mile
Route 107
Bridge Collapsed
Chickahominy River
To Bridgeville (20 miles)

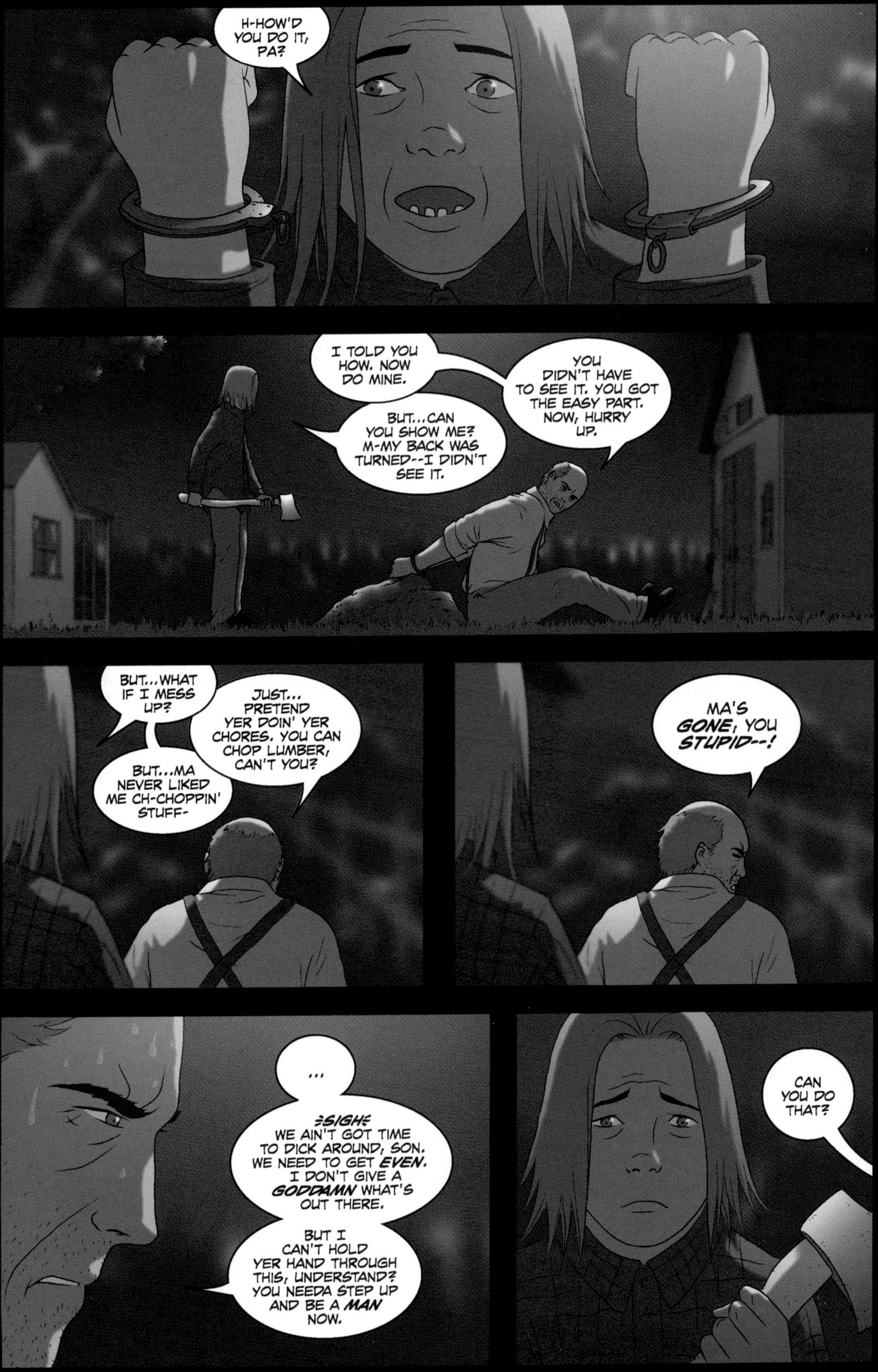
H-HOW'D YOU DO IT, PA?
I TOLD YOU HOW. NOW DO MINE.
BUT...CAN YOU SHOW ME? M-MY BACK WAS TURNED--I DIDN'T SEE IT.
YOU DIDN'T HAVE TO SEE IT. YOU GOT THE EASY PART. NOW, HURRY UP.
BUT...WHAT IF I MESS UP?
JUST... PRETEND YER DOIN' YER CHORES. YOU CAN CHOP LUMBER, CAN'T YOU?
BUT...MA NEVER LIKED ME CH-CHOPPIN' STUFF-
MA'S GONE, YOU STUPID--!
...
SIGH WE AIN'T GOT TIME TO DICK AROUND, SON. WE NEED TO GET EVEN. I DON'T GIVE A GODDAMN WHAT'S OUT THERE.
BUT I CAN'T HOLD YER HAND THROUGH THIS, UNDERSTAND? YOU NEEDA STEP UP AND BE A MAN NOW.
CAN YOU DO THAT?

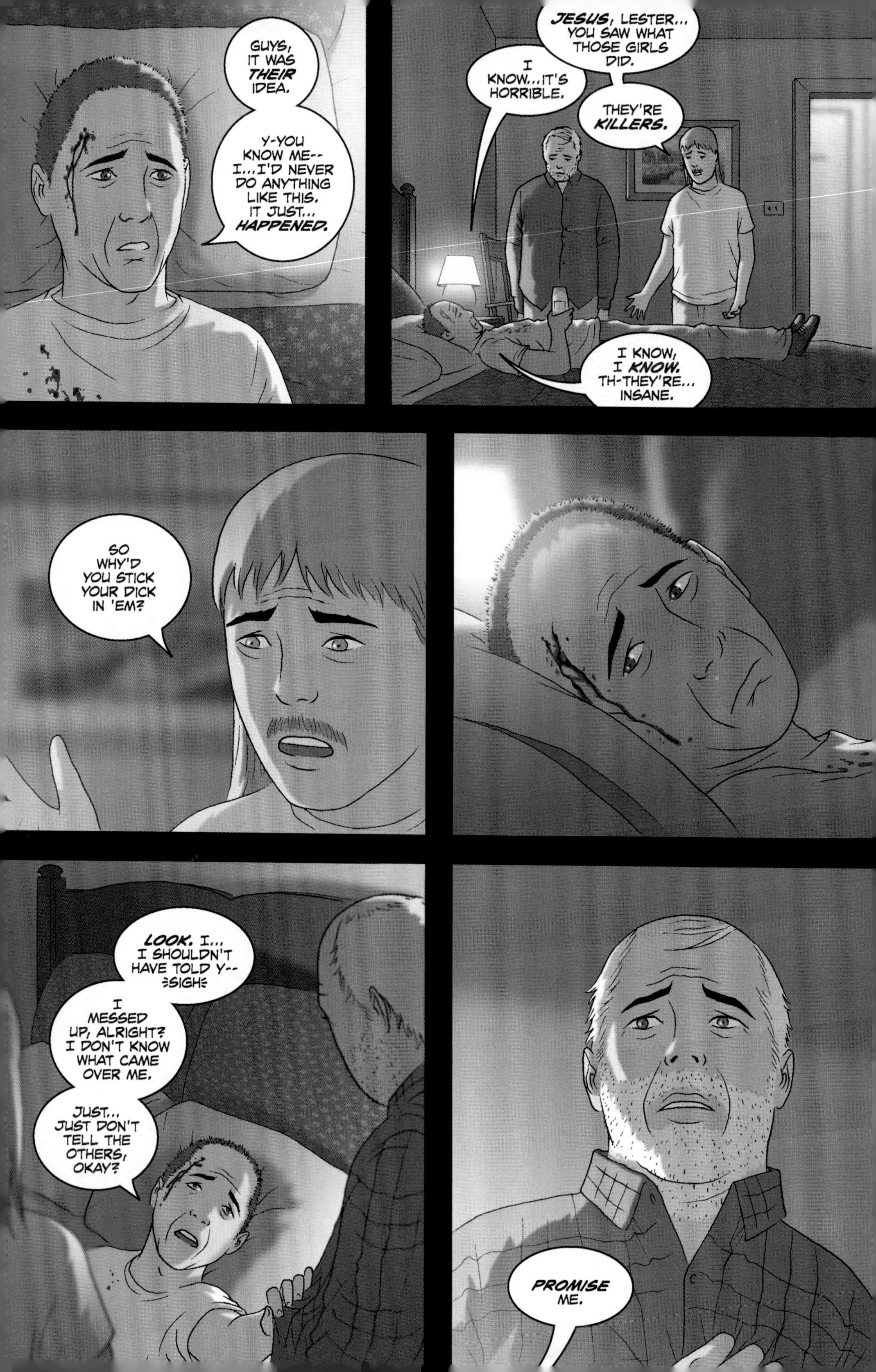

GUYS, IT WAS THEIR IDEA.
Y-YOU KNOW ME-- I...I'D NEVER DO ANYTHING LIKE THIS. IT JUST... HAPPENED.
JESUS, LESTER... YOU SAW WHAT THOSE GIRLS DID.
I KNOW...IT'S HORRIBLE.
THEY'RE KILLERS.
I KNOW, I KNOW. TH-THEY'RE... INSANE.
SO WHY'D YOU STICK YOUR DICK IN 'EM?
LOOK. I... I SHOULDN'T HAVE TOLD Y-- =SIGH=
I MESSED UP, ALRIGHT? I DON'T KNOW WHAT CAME OVER ME.
JUST... JUST DON'T TELL THE OTHERS, OKAY?
PROMISE ME.

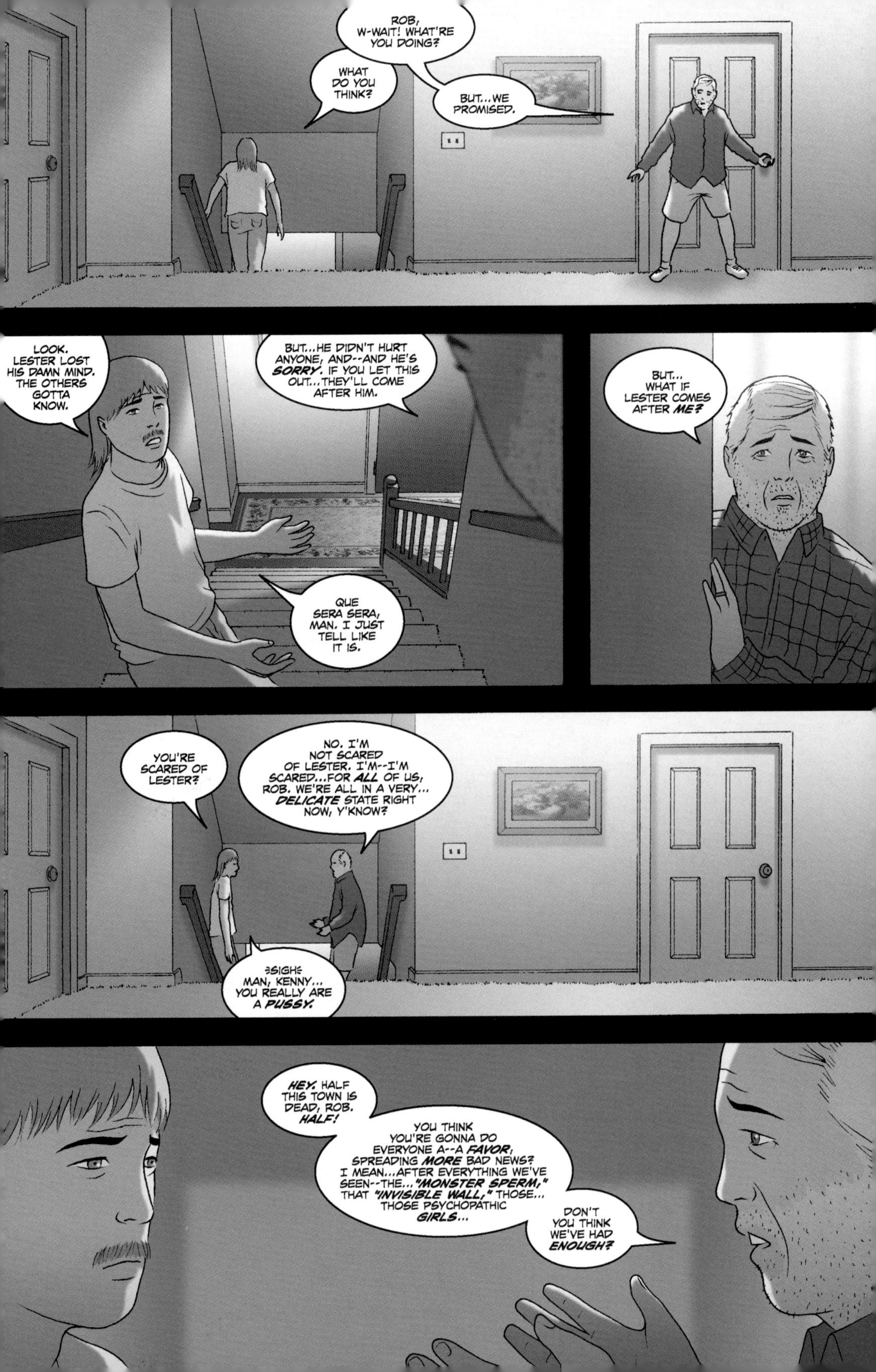

ROB, W-WAIT! WHAT'RE YOU DOING?
WHAT DO YOU THINK?
BUT...WE PROMISED.
LOOK. LESTER LOST HIS DAMN MIND. THE OTHERS GOTTA KNOW.
BUT...HE DIDN'T HURT ANYONE, AND--AND HE'S SORRY. IF YOU LET THIS OUT...THEY'LL COME AFTER HIM.
QUE SERA SERA, MAN. I JUST TELL LIKE IT IS.
BUT... WHAT IF LESTER COMES AFTER ME?
YOU'RE SCARED OF LESTER?
NO. I'M NOT SCARED OF LESTER. I'M--I'M SCARED...FOR ALL OF US, ROB. WE'RE ALL IN A VERY... DELICATE STATE RIGHT NOW, Y'KNOW?
≠SIGH≠ MAN, KENNY... YOU REALLY ARE A PUSSY.
HEY. HALF THIS TOWN IS DEAD, ROB. HALF!
YOU THINK YOU'RE GONNA DO EVERYONE A--A FAVOR, SPREADING MORE BAD NEWS? I MEAN...AFTER EVERYTHING WE'VE SEEN--THE..."MONSTER SPERM," THAT "INVISIBLE WALL," THOSE... THOSE PSYCHOPATHIC GIRLS...
DON'T YOU THINK WE'VE HAD ENOUGH?

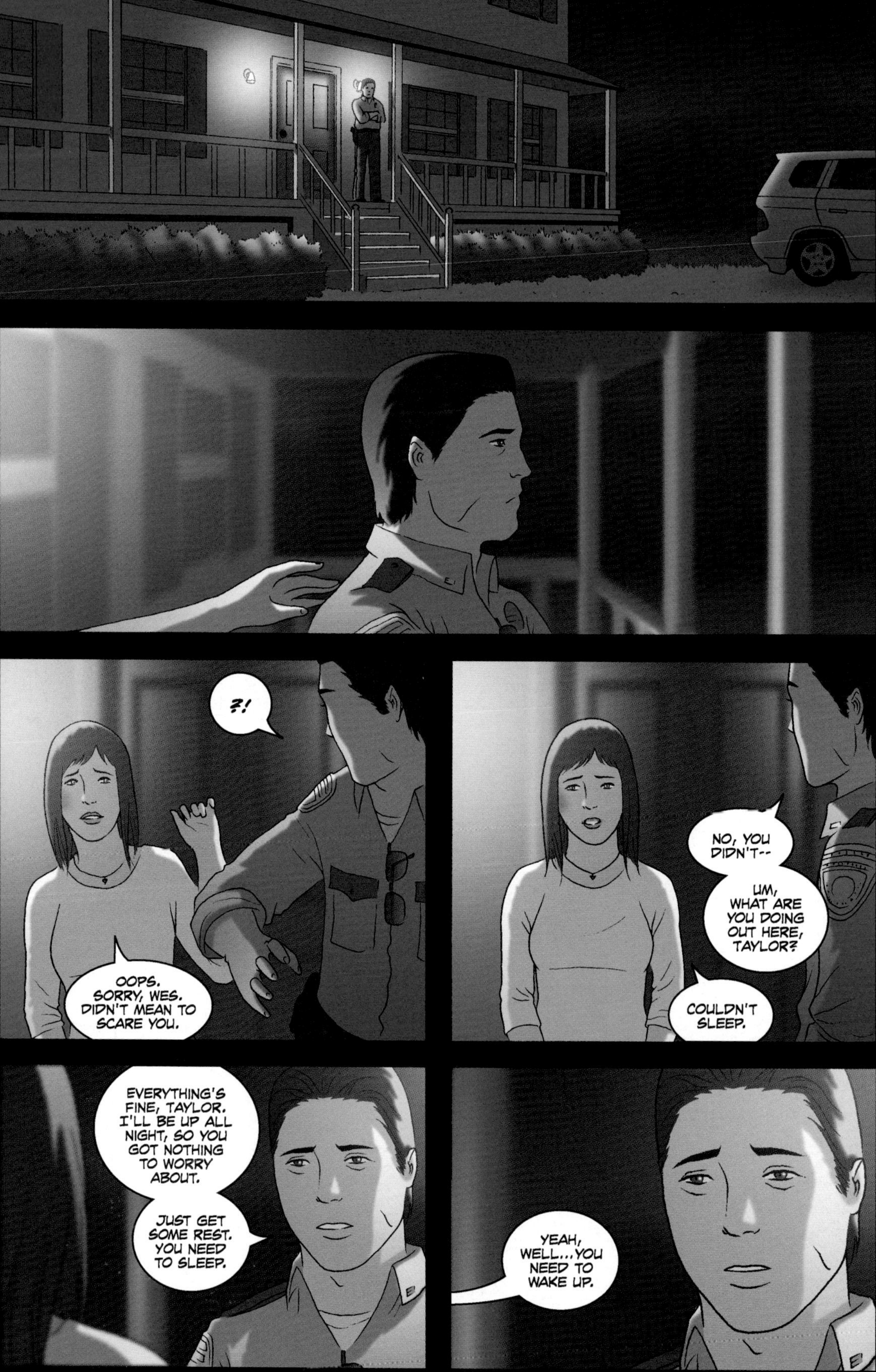
?!
OOPS. SORRY, WES. DIDN'T MEAN TO SCARE YOU.
NO, YOU DIDN'T--
UM, WHAT ARE YOU DOING OUT HERE, TAYLOR?
COULDN'T SLEEP.
EVERYTHING'S FINE, TAYLOR. I'LL BE UP ALL NIGHT, SO YOU GOT NOTHING TO WORRY ABOUT.
JUST GET SOME REST. YOU NEED TO SLEEP.
YEAH, WELL...YOU NEED TO WAKE UP.

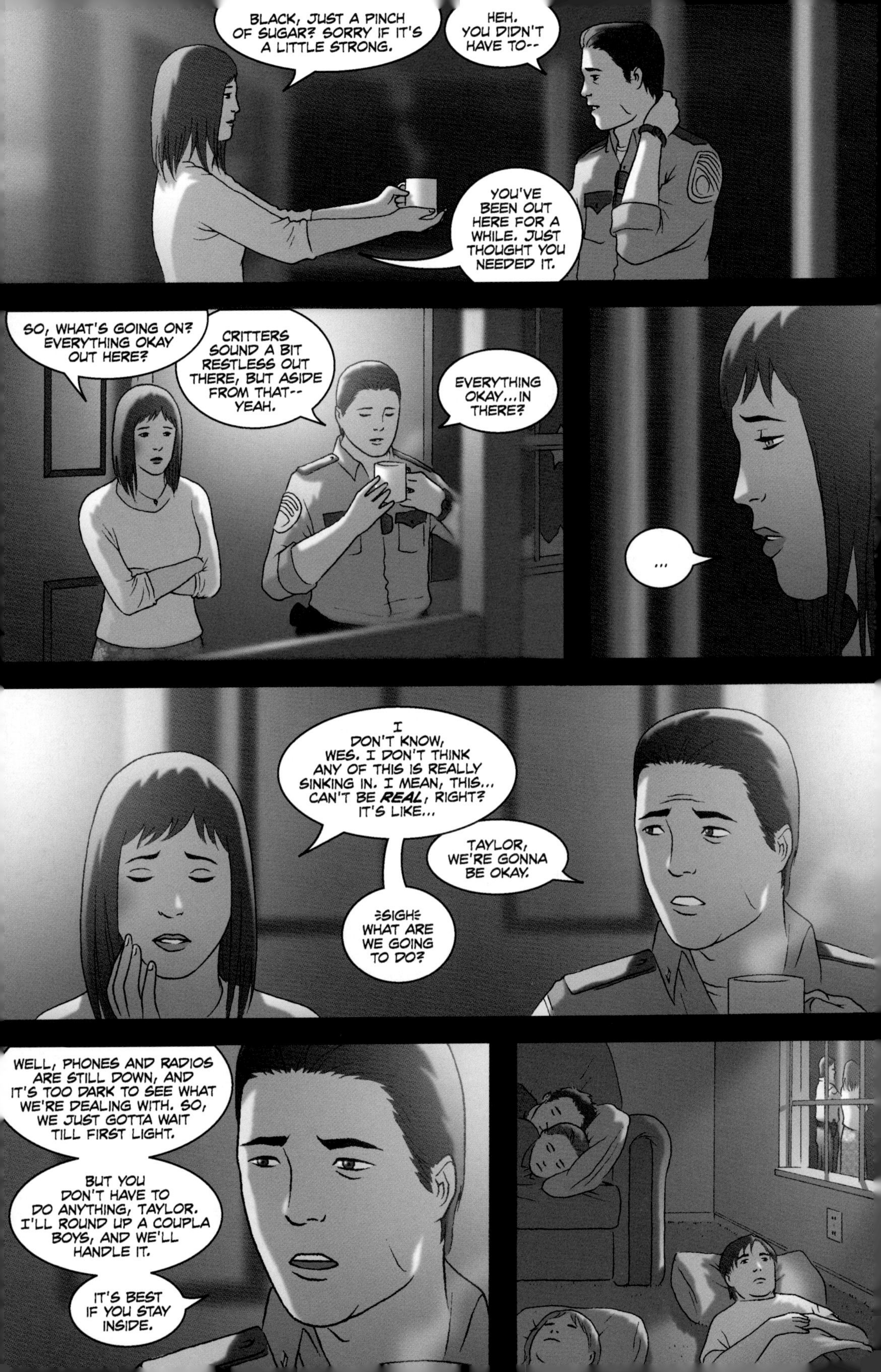
BLACK, JUST A PINCH OF SUGAR? SORRY IF IT'S A LITTLE STRONG.
HEH. YOU DIDN'T HAVE TO--
YOU'VE BEEN OUT HERE FOR A WHILE. JUST THOUGHT YOU NEEDED IT.
SO, WHAT'S GOING ON? EVERYTHING OKAY OUT HERE?
CRITTERS SOUND A BIT RESTLESS OUT THERE, BUT ASIDE FROM THAT-- YEAH.
EVERYTHING OKAY... IN THERE?
...
I DON'T KNOW, WES. I DON'T THINK ANY OF THIS IS REALLY SINKING IN. I MEAN, THIS... CAN'T BE ***REAL***, RIGHT? IT'S LIKE...
=SIGH= WHAT ARE WE GOING TO DO?
TAYLOR, WE'RE GONNA BE OKAY.
WELL, PHONES AND RADIOS ARE STILL DOWN, AND IT'S TOO DARK TO SEE WHAT WE'RE DEALING WITH. SO, WE JUST GOTTA WAIT TILL FIRST LIGHT.
BUT YOU DON'T HAVE TO DO ANYTHING, TAYLOR. I'LL ROUND UP A COUPLA BOYS, AND WE'LL HANDLE IT.
IT'S BEST IF YOU STAY INSIDE.

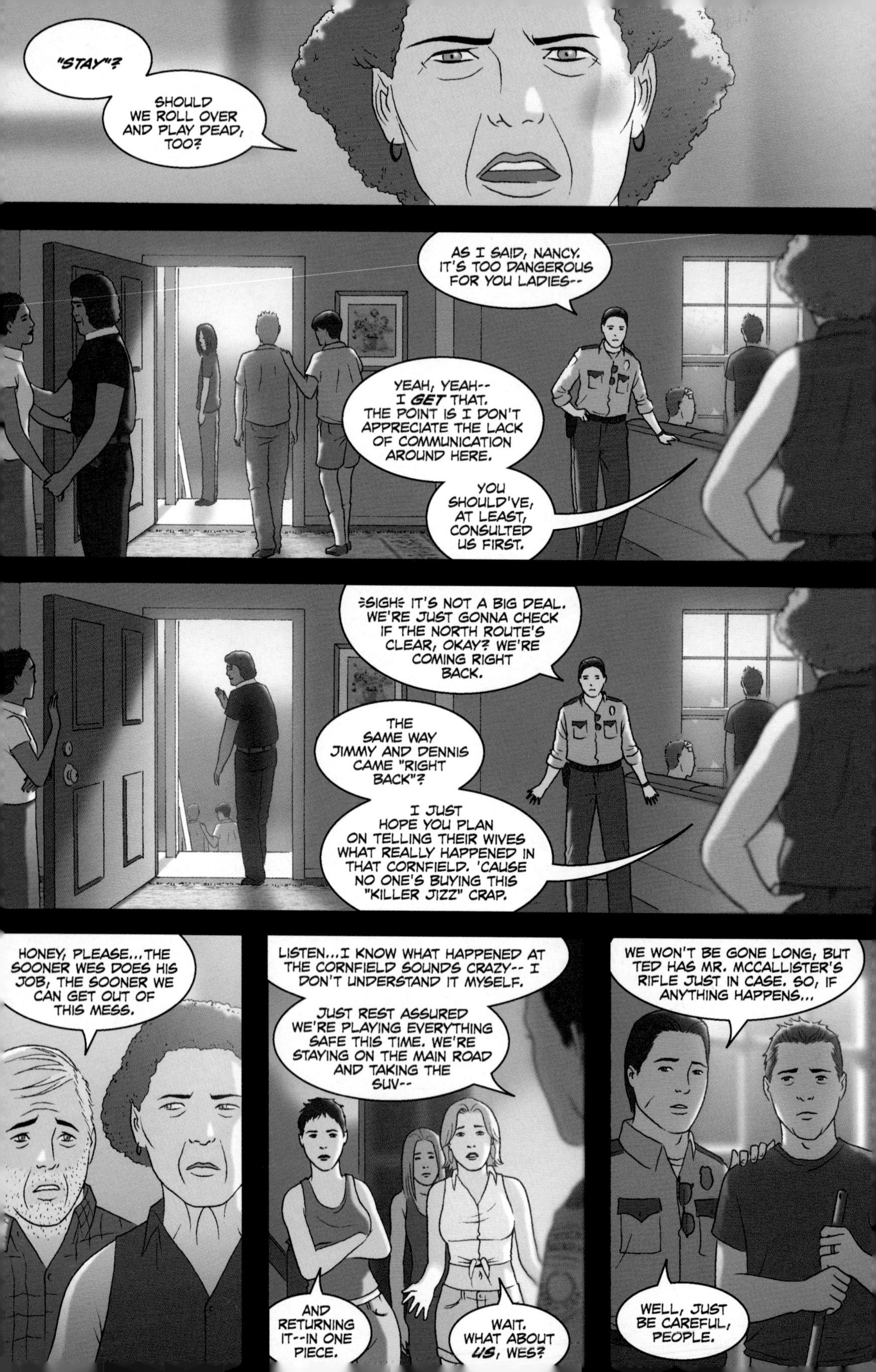
"STAY"?
SHOULD WE ROLL OVER AND PLAY DEAD, TOO?
AS I SAID, NANCY. IT'S TOO DANGEROUS FOR YOU LADIES--
YEAH, YEAH-- I GET THAT. THE POINT IS I DON'T APPRECIATE THE LACK OF COMMUNICATION AROUND HERE.
YOU SHOULD'VE, AT LEAST, CONSULTED US FIRST.
=SIGH= IT'S NOT A BIG DEAL. WE'RE JUST GONNA CHECK IF THE NORTH ROUTE'S CLEAR, OKAY? WE'RE COMING RIGHT BACK.
THE SAME WAY JIMMY AND DENNIS CAME "RIGHT BACK"?
I JUST HOPE YOU PLAN ON TELLING THEIR WIVES WHAT REALLY HAPPENED IN THAT CORNFIELD. 'CAUSE NO ONE'S BUYING THIS "KILLER JIZZ" CRAP.
HONEY, PLEASE...THE SOONER WES DOES HIS JOB, THE SOONER WE CAN GET OUT OF THIS MESS.
LISTEN...I KNOW WHAT HAPPENED AT THE CORNFIELD SOUNDS CRAZY-- I DON'T UNDERSTAND IT MYSELF.
JUST REST ASSURED WE'RE PLAYING EVERYTHING SAFE THIS TIME. WE'RE STAYING ON THE MAIN ROAD AND TAKING THE SUV--
AND RETURNING IT--IN ONE PIECE.
WAIT. WHAT ABOUT US, WES?
WE WON'T BE GONE LONG, BUT TED HAS MR. MCCALLISTER'S RIFLE JUST IN CASE. SO, IF ANYTHING HAPPENS...
WELL, JUST BE CAREFUL, PEOPLE.

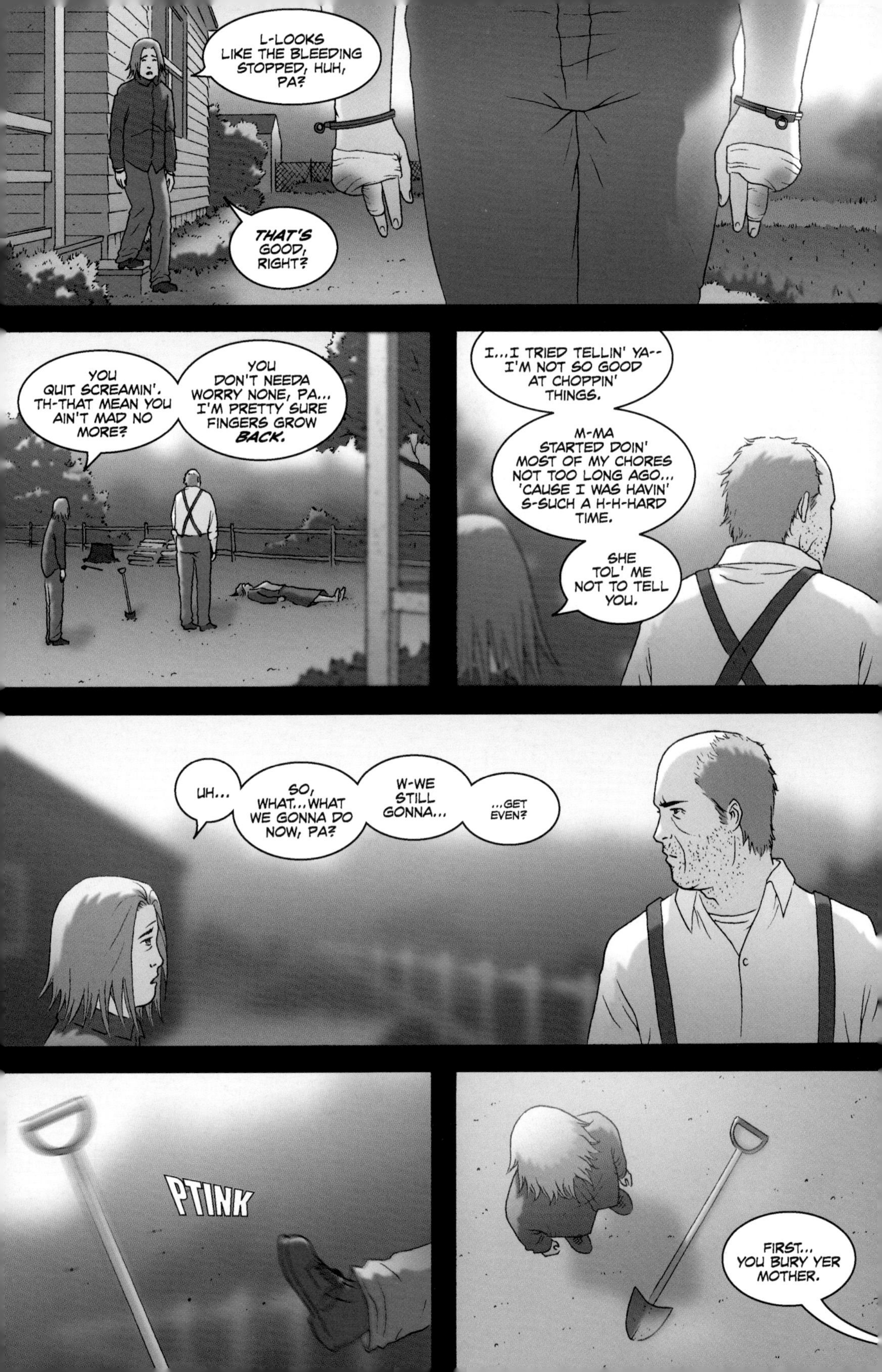

L-LOOKS LIKE THE BLEEDING STOPPED, HUH, PA?
THAT'S GOOD, RIGHT?
YOU QUIT SCREAMIN'. TH-THAT MEAN YOU AIN'T MAD NO MORE?
YOU DON'T NEEDA WORRY NONE, PA... I'M PRETTY SURE FINGERS GROW BACK.
I...I TRIED TELLIN' YA-- I'M NOT SO GOOD AT CHOPPIN' THINGS.
M-MA STARTED DOIN' MOST OF MY CHORES NOT TOO LONG AGO... 'CAUSE I WAS HAVIN' S-SUCH A H-H-HARD TIME.
SHE TOL' ME NOT TO TELL YOU.
UH...
SO, WHAT...WHAT WE GONNA DO NOW, PA?
W-WE STILL GONNA...
...GET EVEN?
PTINK
FIRST... YOU BURY YER MOTHER.

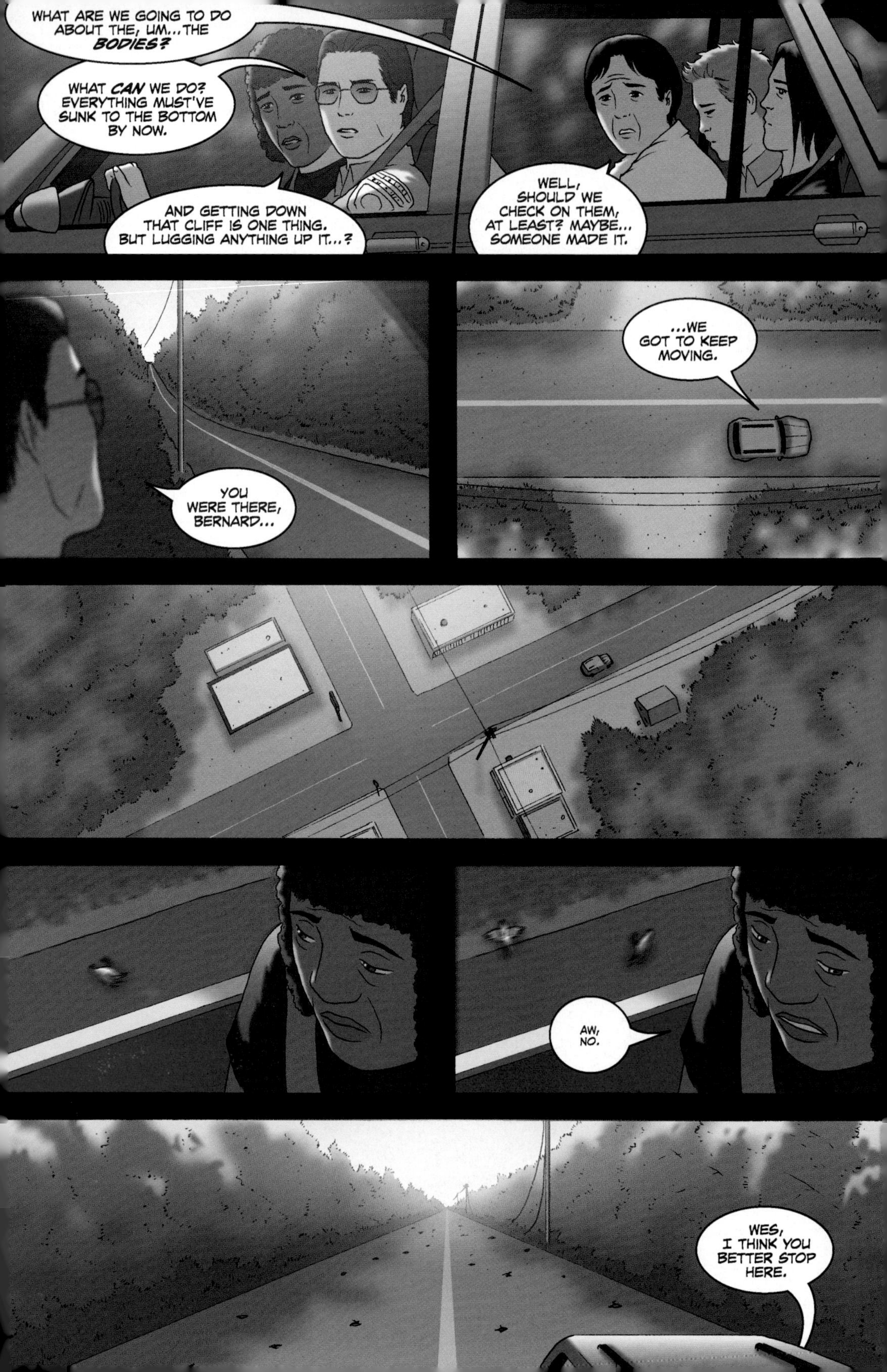

WHAT ARE WE GOING TO DO ABOUT THE, UM... THE BODIES?
WHAT CAN WE DO? EVERYTHING MUST'VE SUNK TO THE BOTTOM BY NOW.
AND GETTING DOWN THAT CLIFF IS ONE THING. BUT LUGGING ANYTHING UP IT...?
WELL, SHOULD WE CHECK ON THEM, AT LEAST? MAYBE... SOMEONE MADE IT.
YOU WERE THERE, BERNARD...
...WE GOT TO KEEP MOVING.
AW, NO.
WES, I THINK YOU BETTER STOP HERE.

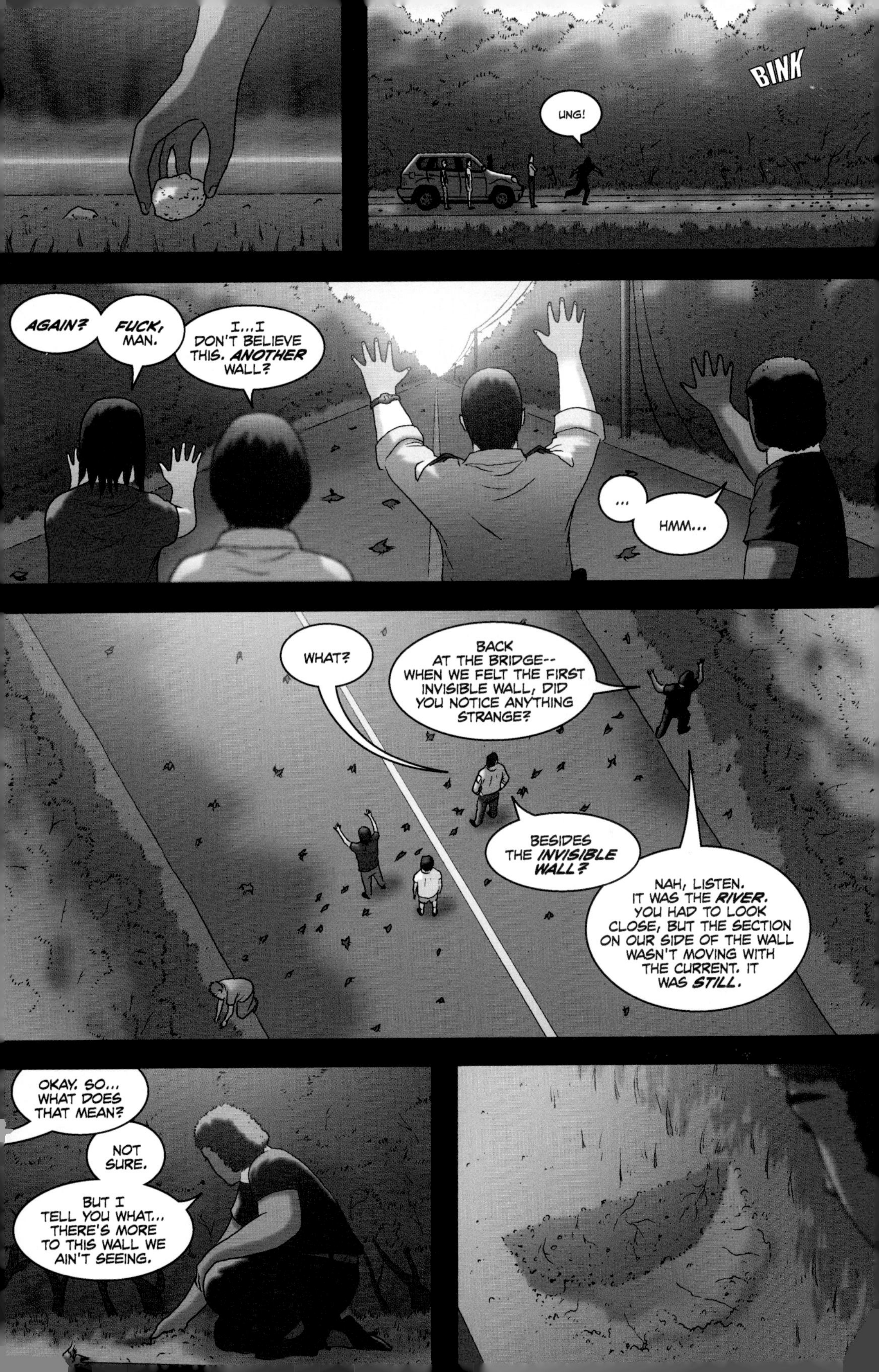
BINK
UNG!
AGAIN?
FUCK, MAN.
I...I DON'T BELIEVE THIS. ANOTHER WALL?
...
HMM...
WHAT?
BACK AT THE BRIDGE-- WHEN WE FELT THE FIRST INVISIBLE WALL, DID YOU NOTICE ANYTHING STRANGE?
BESIDES THE INVISIBLE WALL?
NAH, LISTEN. IT WAS THE RIVER. YOU HAD TO LOOK CLOSE, BUT THE SECTION ON OUR SIDE OF THE WALL WASN'T MOVING WITH THE CURRENT. IT WAS STILL.
OKAY. SO... WHAT DOES THAT MEAN?
NOT SURE.
BUT I TELL YOU WHAT... THERE'S MORE TO THIS WALL WE AIN'T SEEING.

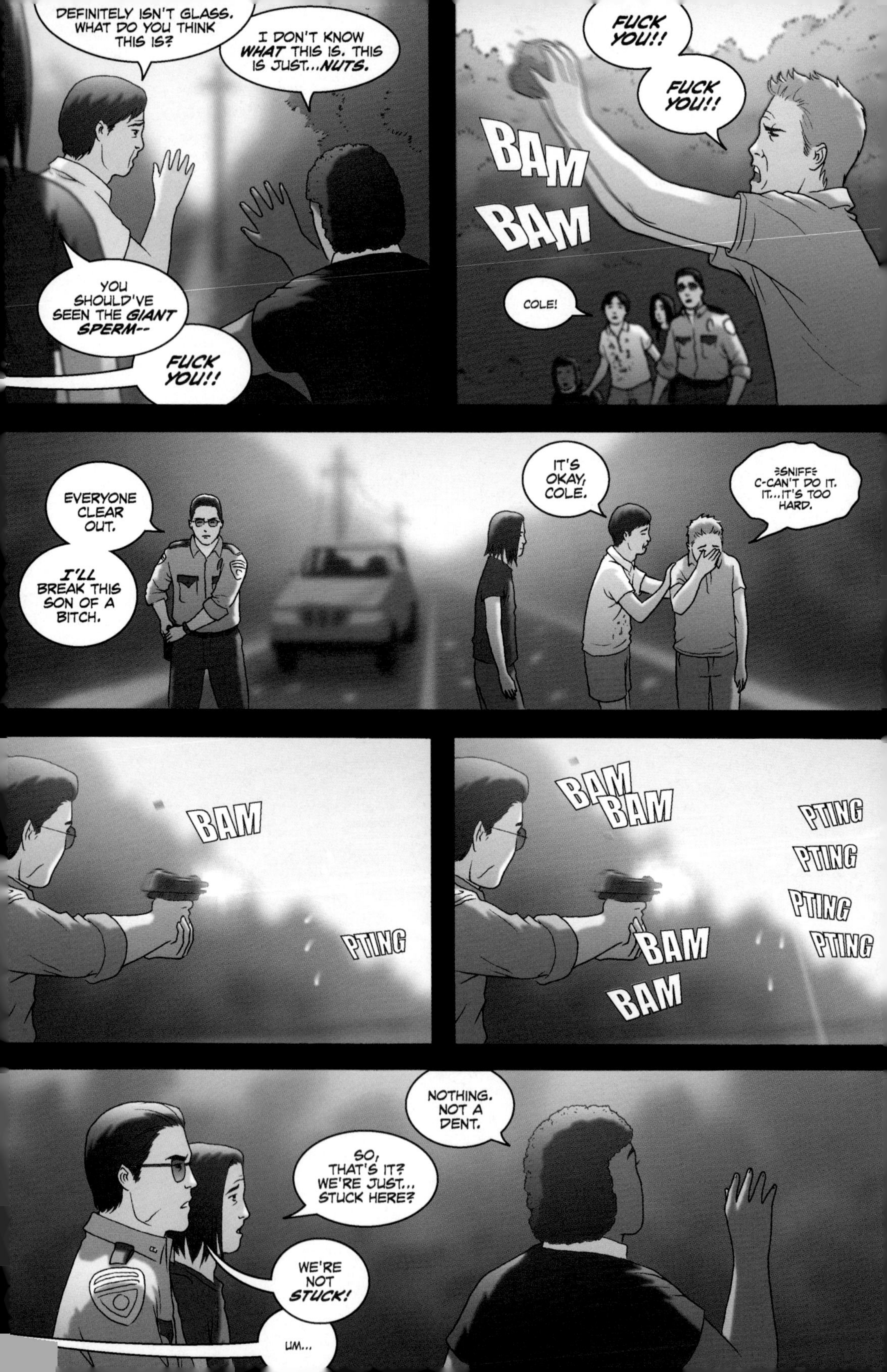
DEFINITELY ISN'T GLASS. WHAT DO YOU THINK THIS IS?
I DON'T KNOW WHAT THIS IS. THIS IS JUST...NUTS.
YOU SHOULD'VE SEEN THE GIANT SPERM--
FUCK YOU!!
FUCK YOU!!
FUCK YOU!!
BAM
BAM
COLE!
EVERYONE CLEAR OUT.
I'LL BREAK THIS SON OF A BITCH.
IT'S OKAY, COLE.
SNIFF C-CAN'T DO IT. IT...IT'S TOO HARD.
BAM
PTING
BAM
BAM
PTING
PTING
PTING
BAM
PTING
BAM
NOTHING. NOT A DENT.
SO, THAT'S IT? WE'RE JUST... STUCK HERE?
WE'RE NOT STUCK!
UM...

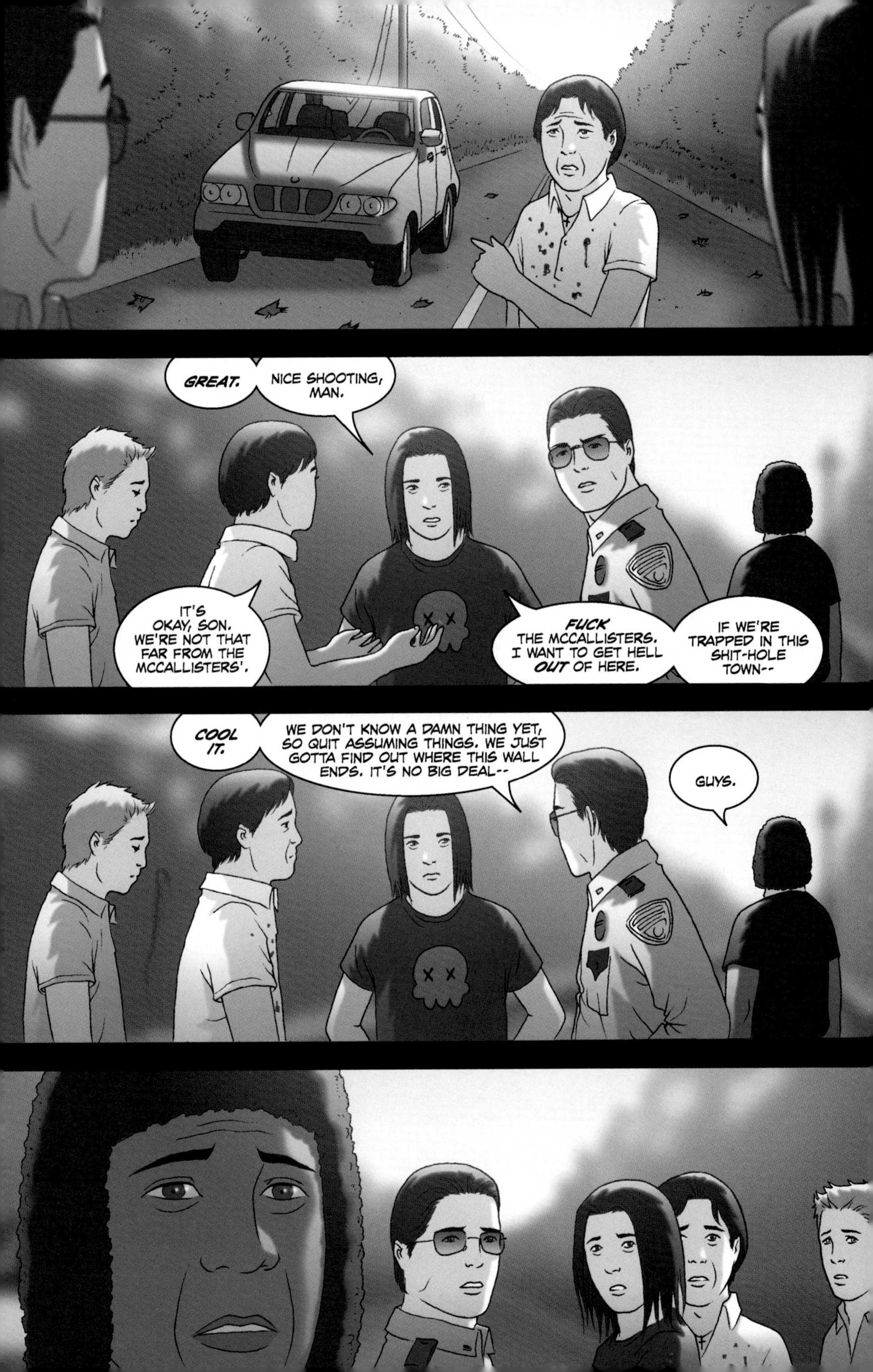
GREAT.
NICE SHOOTING, MAN.
IT'S OKAY, SON. WE'RE NOT THAT FAR FROM THE MCCALLISTERS'.
FUCK THE MCCALLISTERS. I WANT TO GET HELL OUT OF HERE.
IF WE'RE TRAPPED IN THIS SHIT-HOLE TOWN--
COOL IT.
WE DON'T KNOW A DAMN THING YET, SO QUIT ASSUMING THINGS. WE JUST GOTTA FIND OUT WHERE THIS WALL ENDS. IT'S NO BIG DEAL--
GUYS.

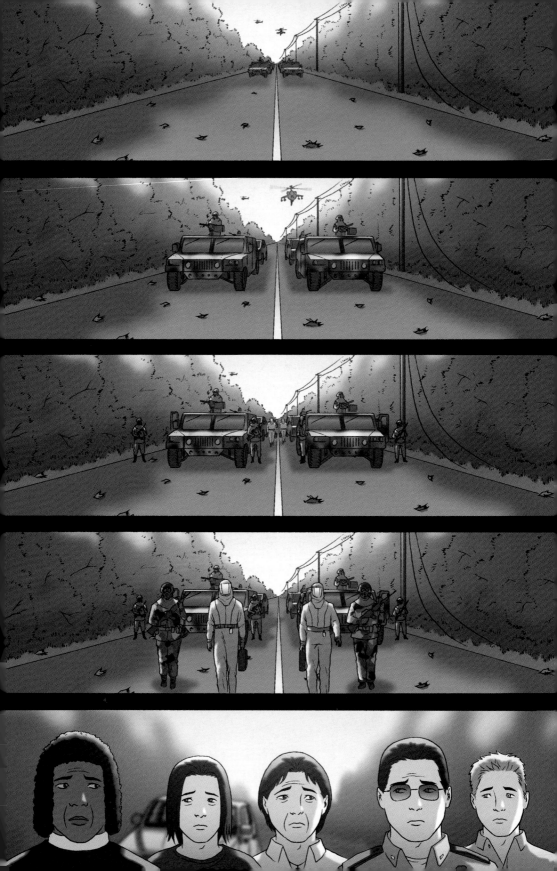

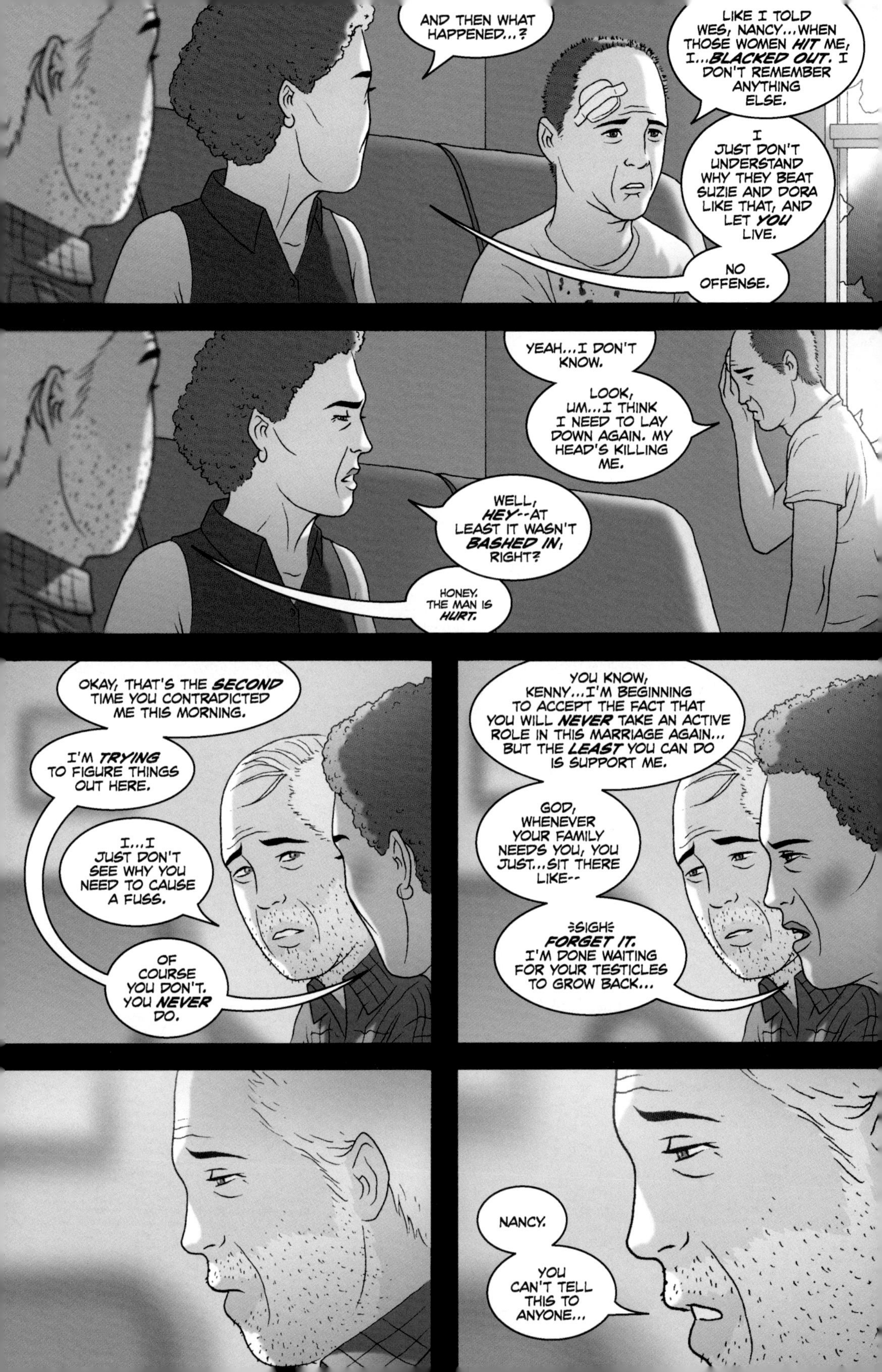
AND THEN WHAT HAPPENED...?
LIKE I TOLD WES, NANCY...WHEN THOSE WOMEN HIT ME, I...BLACKED OUT. I DON'T REMEMBER ANYTHING ELSE.
I JUST DON'T UNDERSTAND WHY THEY BEAT SUZIE AND DORA LIKE THAT, AND LET YOU LIVE.
NO OFFENSE.
YEAH...I DON'T KNOW.
LOOK, UM...I THINK I NEED TO LAY DOWN AGAIN. MY HEAD'S KILLING ME.
WELL, HEY--AT LEAST IT WASN'T BASHED IN, RIGHT?
HONEY. THE MAN IS HURT.
OKAY, THAT'S THE SECOND TIME YOU CONTRADICTED ME THIS MORNING.
I'M TRYING TO FIGURE THINGS OUT HERE.
I...I JUST DON'T SEE WHY YOU NEED TO CAUSE A FUSS.
OF COURSE YOU DON'T. YOU NEVER DO.
YOU KNOW, KENNY...I'M BEGINNING TO ACCEPT THE FACT THAT YOU WILL NEVER TAKE AN ACTIVE ROLE IN THIS MARRIAGE AGAIN... BUT THE LEAST YOU CAN DO IS SUPPORT ME.
GOD, WHENEVER YOUR FAMILY NEEDS YOU, YOU JUST...SIT THERE LIKE--
SIGH
FORGET IT. I'M DONE WAITING FOR YOUR TESTICLES TO GROW BACK...
NANCY.
YOU CAN'T TELL THIS TO ANYONE...

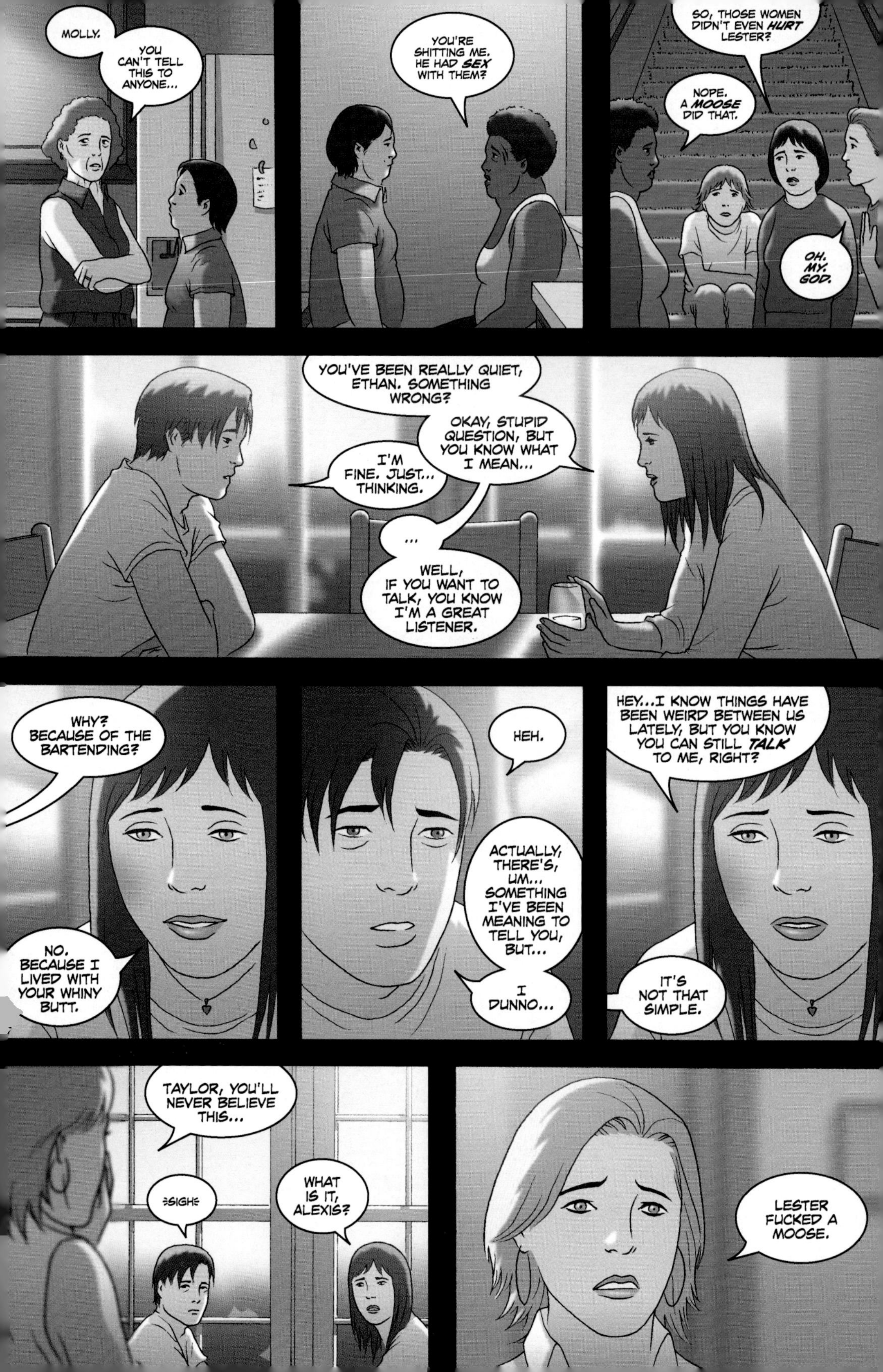
MOLLY.
YOU CAN'T TELL THIS TO ANYONE...
YOU'RE SHITTING ME. HE HAD SEX WITH THEM?
SO, THOSE WOMEN DIDN'T EVEN HURT LESTER?
NOPE. A MOOSE DID THAT.
OH. MY. GOD.
YOU'VE BEEN REALLY QUIET, ETHAN. SOMETHING WRONG?
OKAY, STUPID QUESTION, BUT YOU KNOW WHAT I MEAN...
I'M FINE. JUST... THINKING.
...
WELL, IF YOU WANT TO TALK, YOU KNOW I'M A GREAT LISTENER.
WHY? BECAUSE OF THE BARTENDING?
NO. BECAUSE I LIVED WITH YOUR WHINY BUTT.
HEH.
ACTUALLY, THERE'S, UM... SOMETHING I'VE BEEN MEANING TO TELL YOU, BUT...
I DUNNO...
HEY...I KNOW THINGS HAVE BEEN WEIRD BETWEEN US LATELY, BUT YOU KNOW YOU CAN STILL TALK TO ME, RIGHT?
IT'S NOT THAT SIMPLE.
TAYLOR, YOU'LL NEVER BELIEVE THIS...
SIGH
WHAT IS IT, ALEXIS?
LESTER FUCKED A MOOSE.

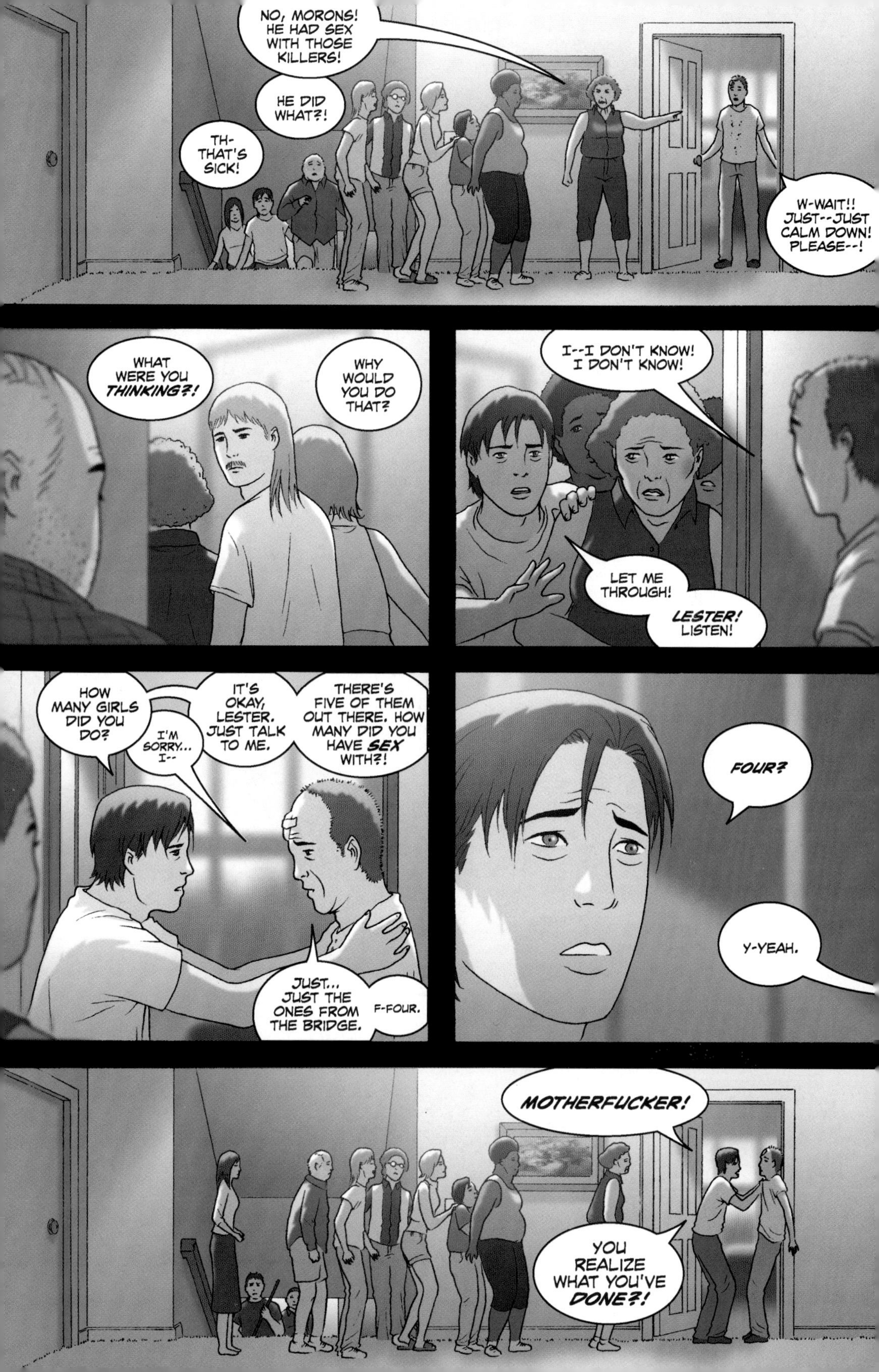
NO, MORONS! HE HAD SEX WITH THOSE KILLERS!
HE DID WHAT?!
TH- THAT'S SICK!
W-WAIT!! JUST--JUST CALM DOWN! PLEASE--!
WHAT WERE YOU THINKING?!
WHY WOULD YOU DO THAT?
I--I DON'T KNOW! I DON'T KNOW!
LET ME THROUGH!
LESTER! LISTEN!
HOW MANY GIRLS DID YOU DO?
I'M SORRY... I--
IT'S OKAY, LESTER. JUST TALK TO ME.
THERE'S FIVE OF THEM OUT THERE. HOW MANY DID YOU HAVE SEX WITH?!
JUST... JUST THE ONES FROM THE BRIDGE.
F-FOUR.
FOUR?
Y-YEAH.
MOTHERFUCKER!
YOU REALIZE WHAT YOU'VE DONE?!

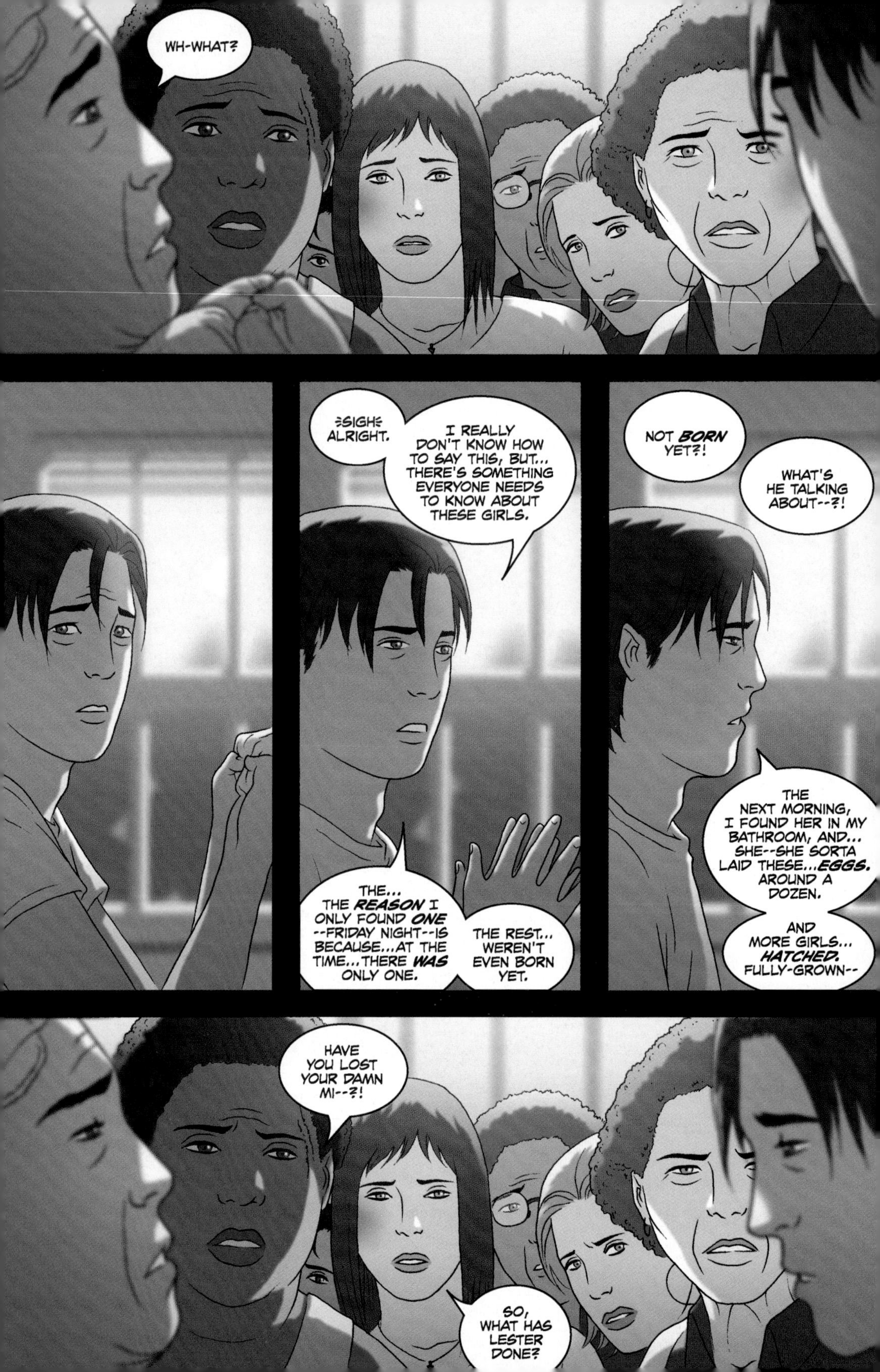
WH-WHAT?
=SIGH= ALRIGHT.
I REALLY DON'T KNOW HOW TO SAY THIS, BUT... THERE'S SOMETHING EVERYONE NEEDS TO KNOW ABOUT THESE GIRLS.
THE... THE REASON I ONLY FOUND ONE --FRIDAY NIGHT--IS BECAUSE...AT THE TIME...THERE WAS ONLY ONE.
THE REST... WEREN'T EVEN BORN YET.
NOT BORN YET?!
WHAT'S HE TALKING ABOUT--?!
THE NEXT MORNING, I FOUND HER IN MY BATHROOM, AND... SHE--SHE SORTA LAID THESE...EGGS. AROUND A DOZEN.
AND MORE GIRLS... HATCHED. FULLY-GROWN--
HAVE YOU LOST YOUR DAMN MI--?!
SO, WHAT HAS LESTER DONE?

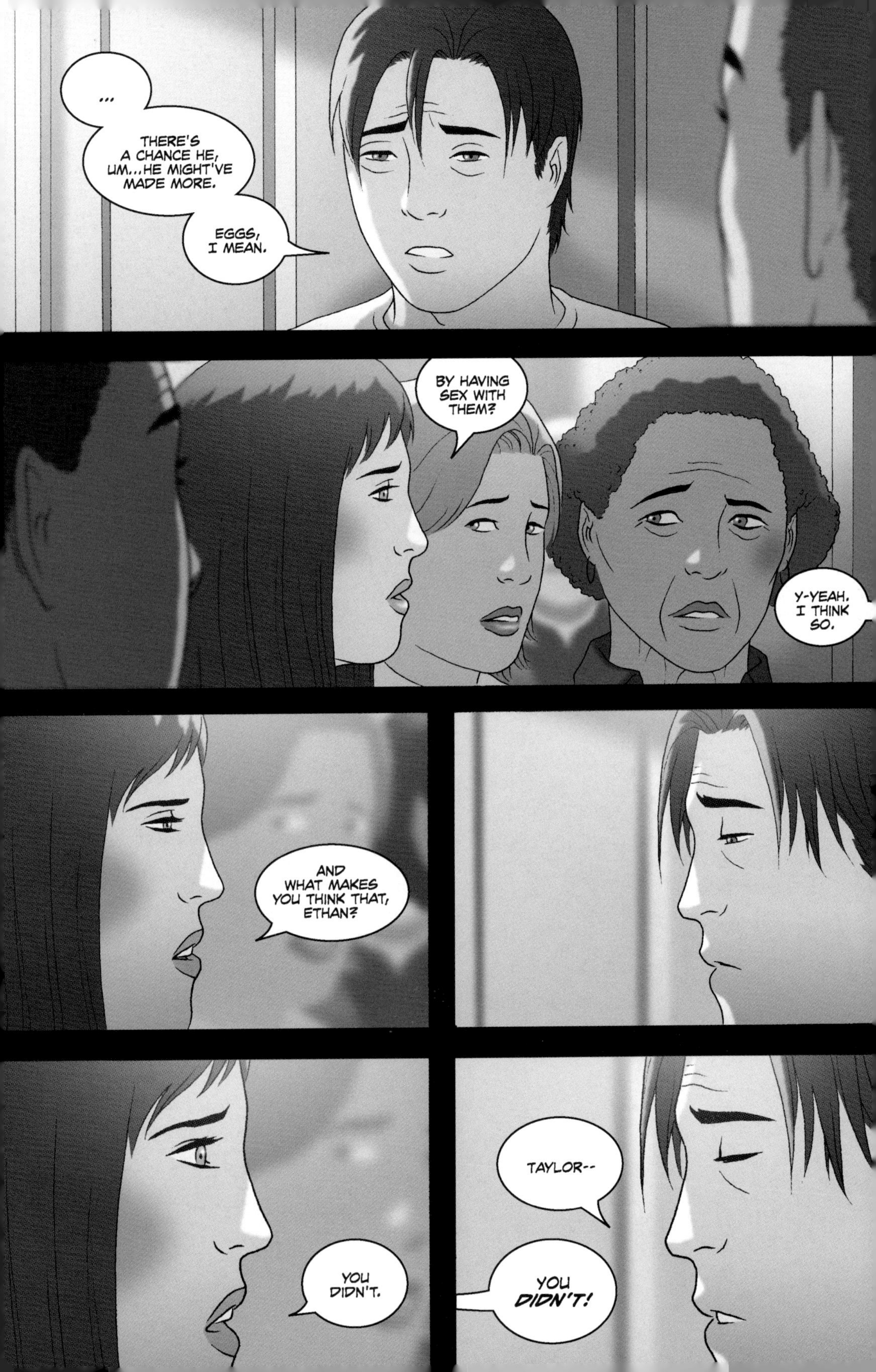
...
THERE'S A CHANCE HE, UM...HE MIGHT'VE MADE MORE.
EGGS, I MEAN.
BY HAVING SEX WITH THEM?
Y-YEAH. I THINK SO.
AND WHAT MAKES YOU THINK THAT, ETHAN?
TAYLOR--
YOU DIDN'T.
YOU *DIDN'T!*

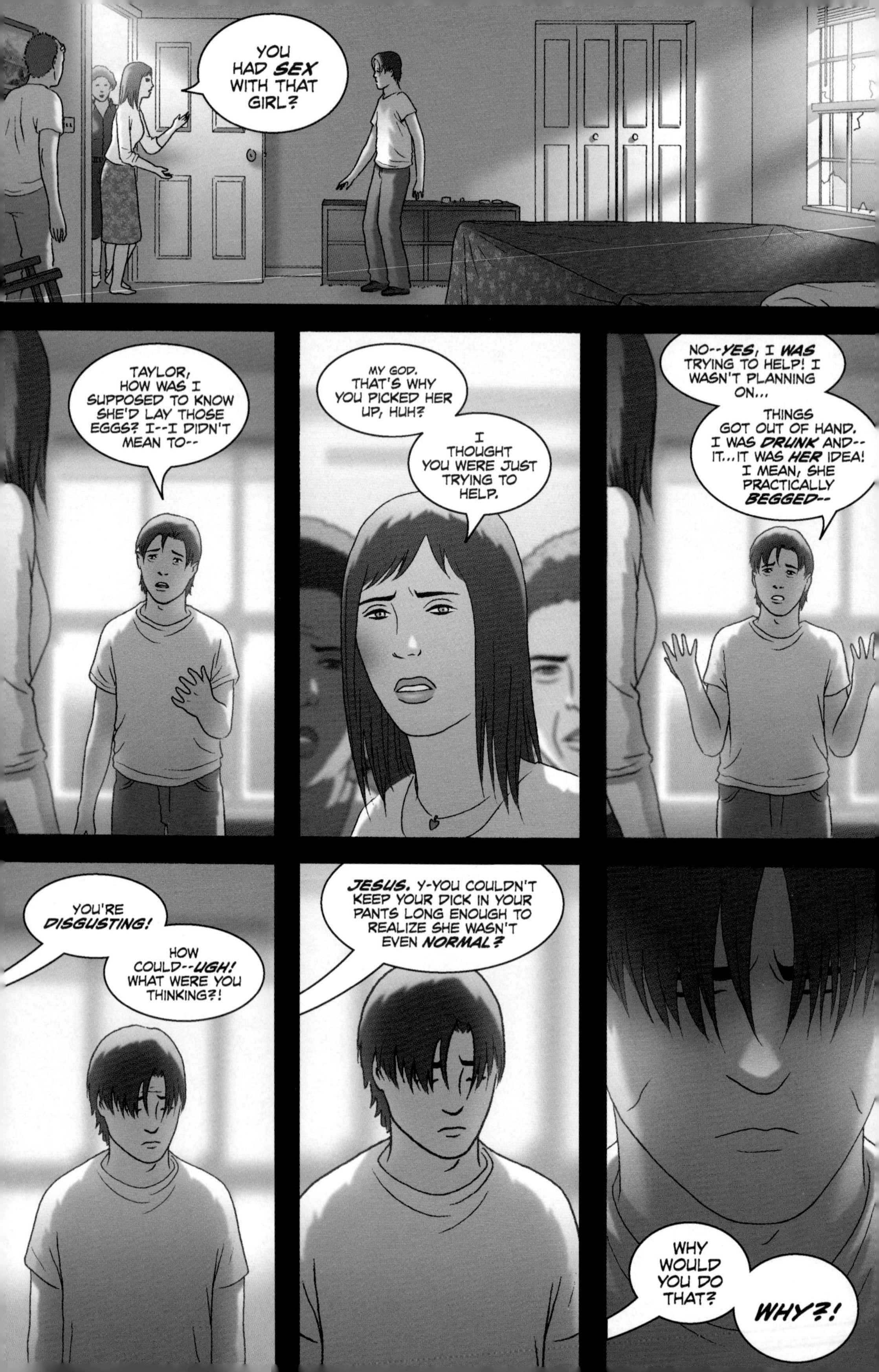
YOU HAD SEX WITH THAT GIRL?
TAYLOR, HOW WAS I SUPPOSED TO KNOW SHE'D LAY THOSE EGGS? I--I DIDN'T MEAN TO--
MY GOD. THAT'S WHY YOU PICKED HER UP, HUH?
I THOUGHT YOU WERE JUST TRYING TO HELP.
NO--YES, I WAS TRYING TO HELP! I WASN'T PLANNING ON...
THINGS GOT OUT OF HAND. I WAS DRUNK AND-- IT...IT WAS HER IDEA! I MEAN, SHE PRACTICALLY BEGGED--
YOU'RE DISGUSTING!
HOW COULD--UGH! WHAT WERE YOU THINKING?!
JESUS. Y-YOU COULDN'T KEEP YOUR DICK IN YOUR PANTS LONG ENOUGH TO REALIZE SHE WASN'T EVEN NORMAL?
WHY WOULD YOU DO THAT?
WHY?!

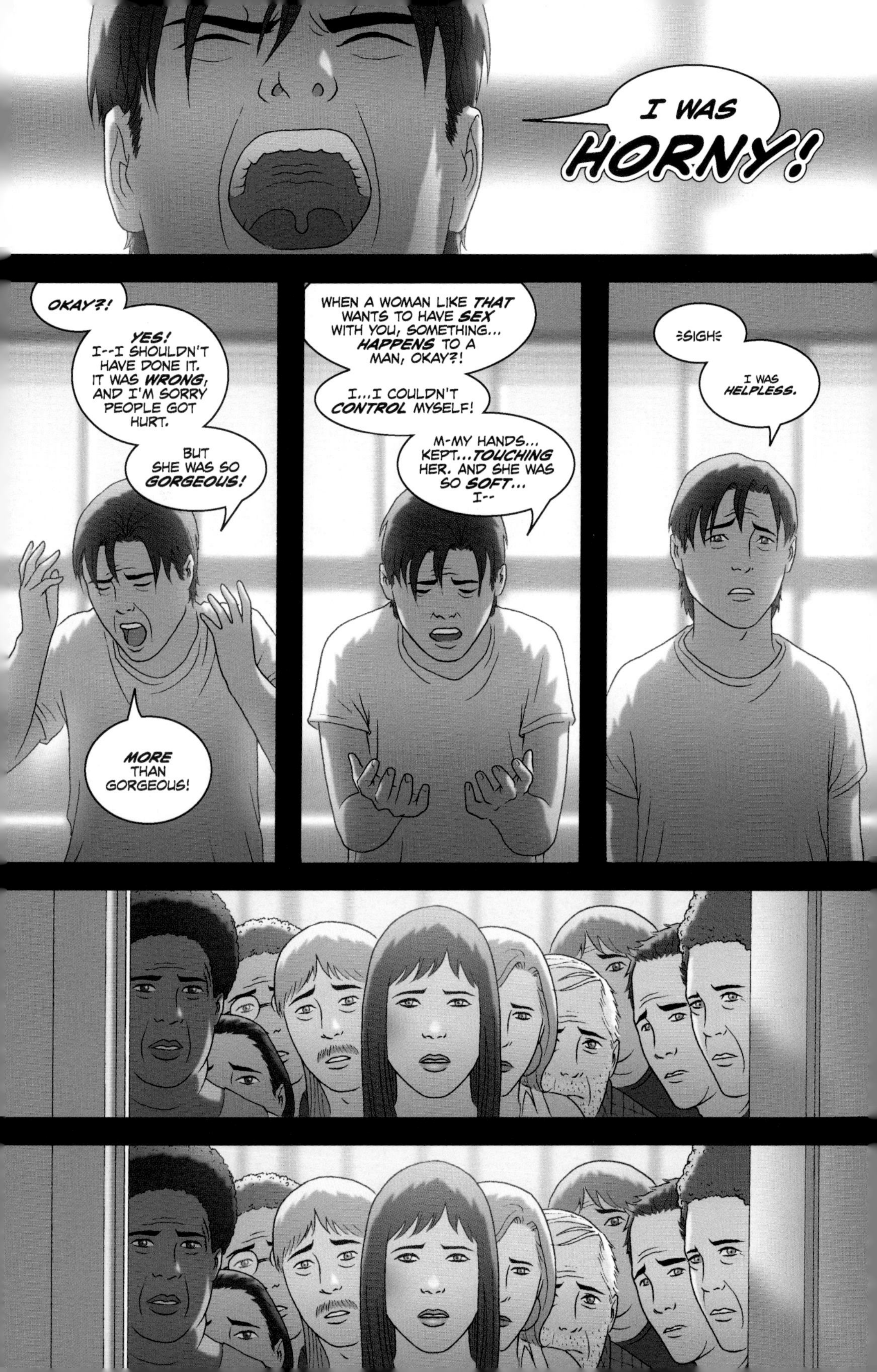
I WAS HORNY!
OKAY?!
YES! I--I SHOULDN'T HAVE DONE IT. IT WAS WRONG, AND I'M SORRY PEOPLE GOT HURT.
BUT SHE WAS SO GORGEOUS!
MORE THAN GORGEOUS!
WHEN A WOMAN LIKE THAT WANTS TO HAVE SEX WITH YOU, SOMETHING... HAPPENS TO A MAN, OKAY?!
I...I COULDN'T CONTROL MYSELF!
M-MY HANDS... KEPT...TOUCHING HER. AND SHE WAS SO SOFT... I--
SIGH
I WAS HELPLESS.

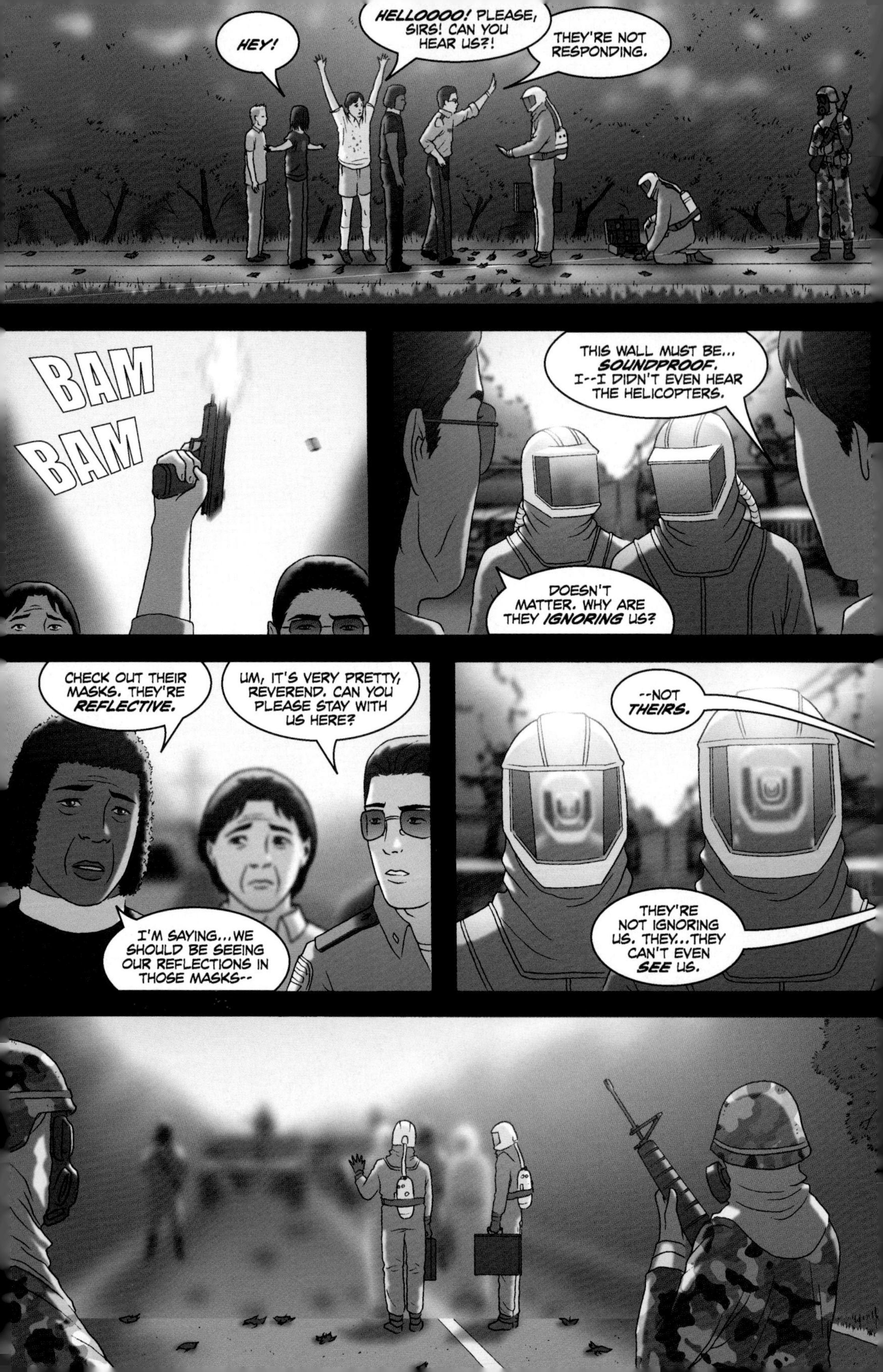
HEY!
HELLOOOO! PLEASE, SIRS! CAN YOU HEAR US?!
THEY'RE NOT RESPONDING.
BAM
BAM
THIS WALL MUST BE... SOUNDPROOF. I--I DIDN'T EVEN HEAR THE HELICOPTERS.
DOESN'T MATTER. WHY ARE THEY IGNORING US?
CHECK OUT THEIR MASKS. THEY'RE REFLECTIVE.
UM, IT'S VERY PRETTY, REVEREND. CAN YOU PLEASE STAY WITH US HERE?
I'M SAYING...WE SHOULD BE SEEING OUR REFLECTIONS IN THOSE MASKS--
--NOT THEIRS.
THEY'RE NOT IGNORING US. THEY...THEY CAN'T EVEN SEE US.

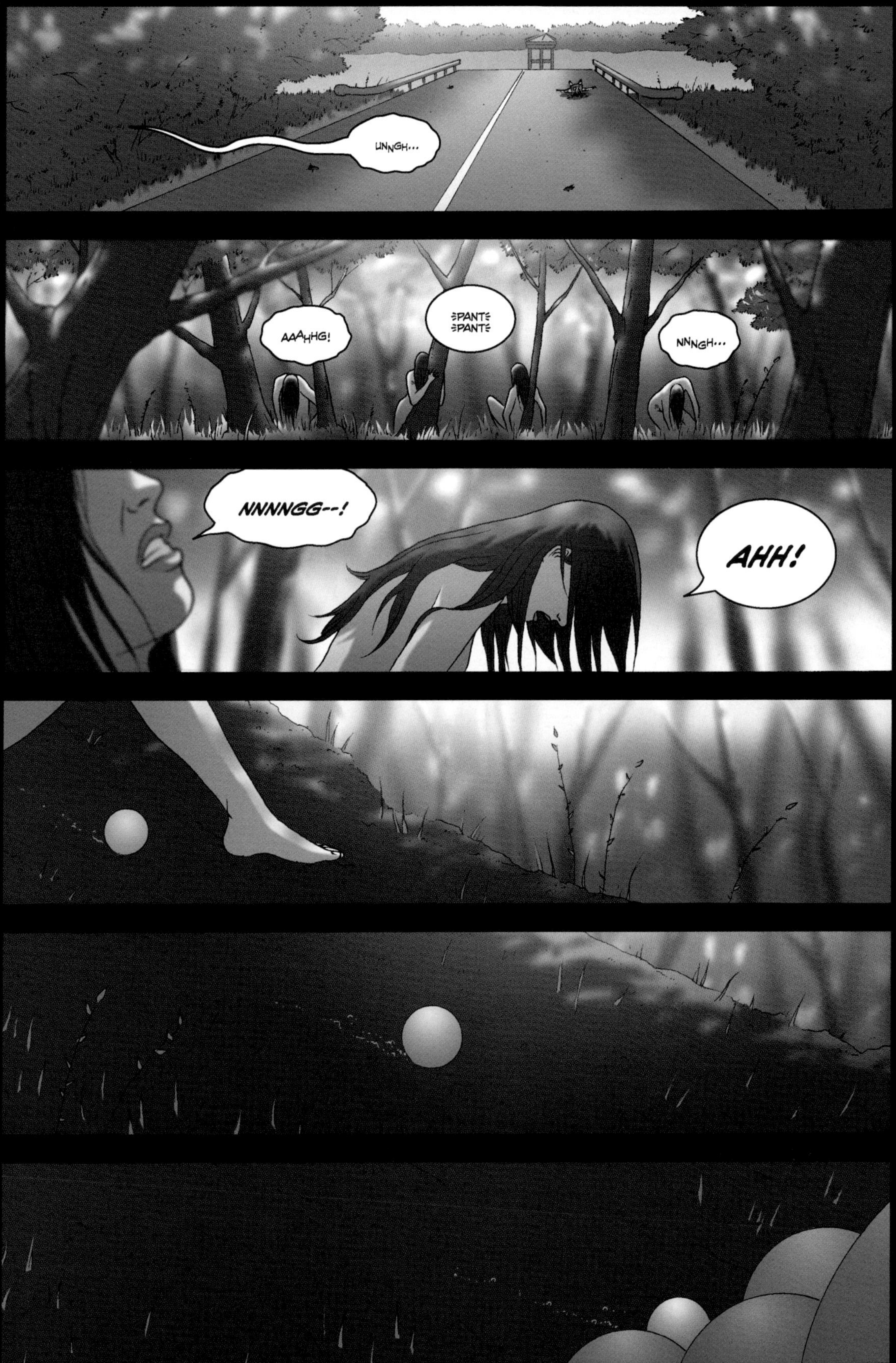
UNNGH...
AAAHHG!
=PANT=
=PANT=
NNNGH...
NNNNGG--!
AHH!

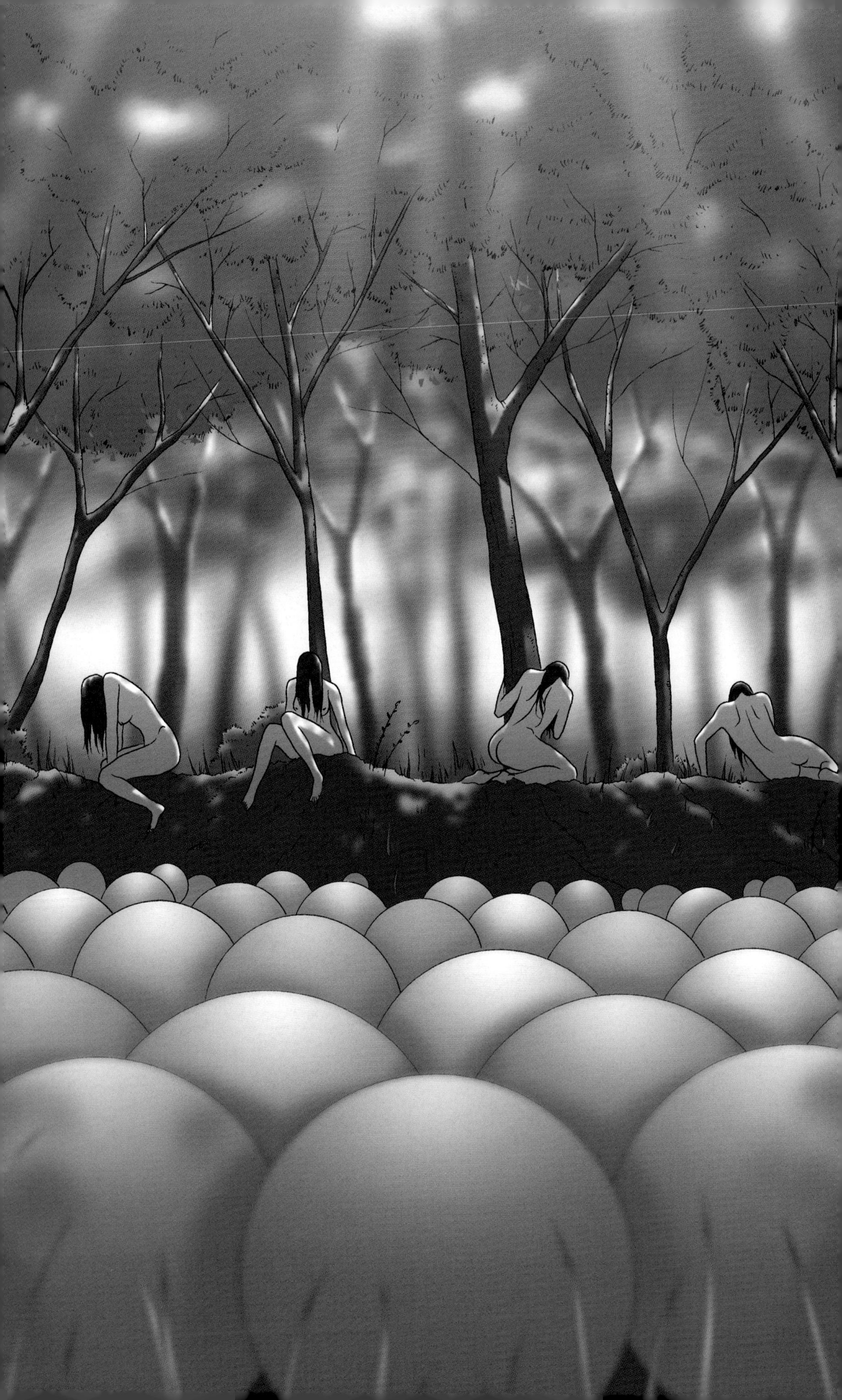

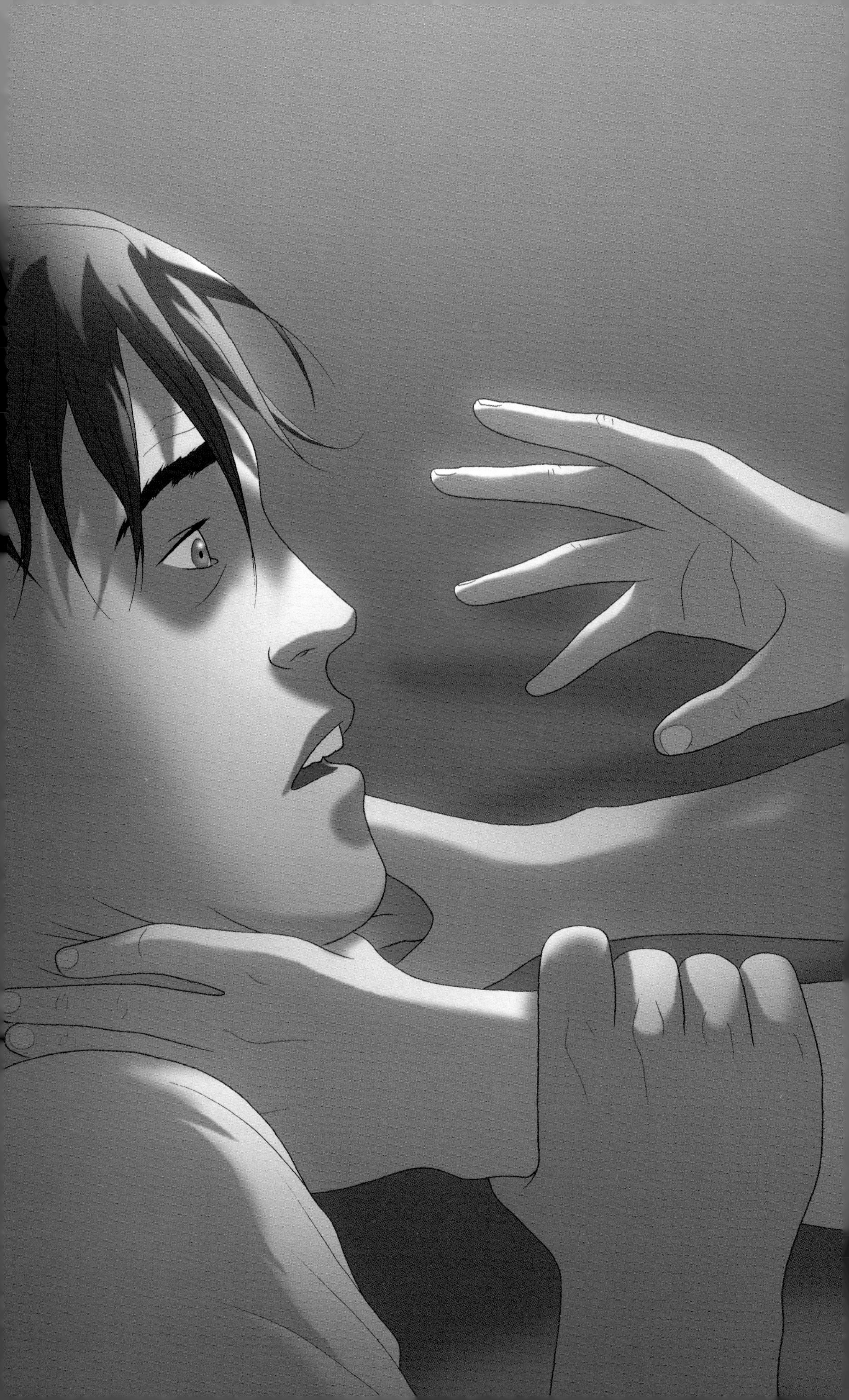

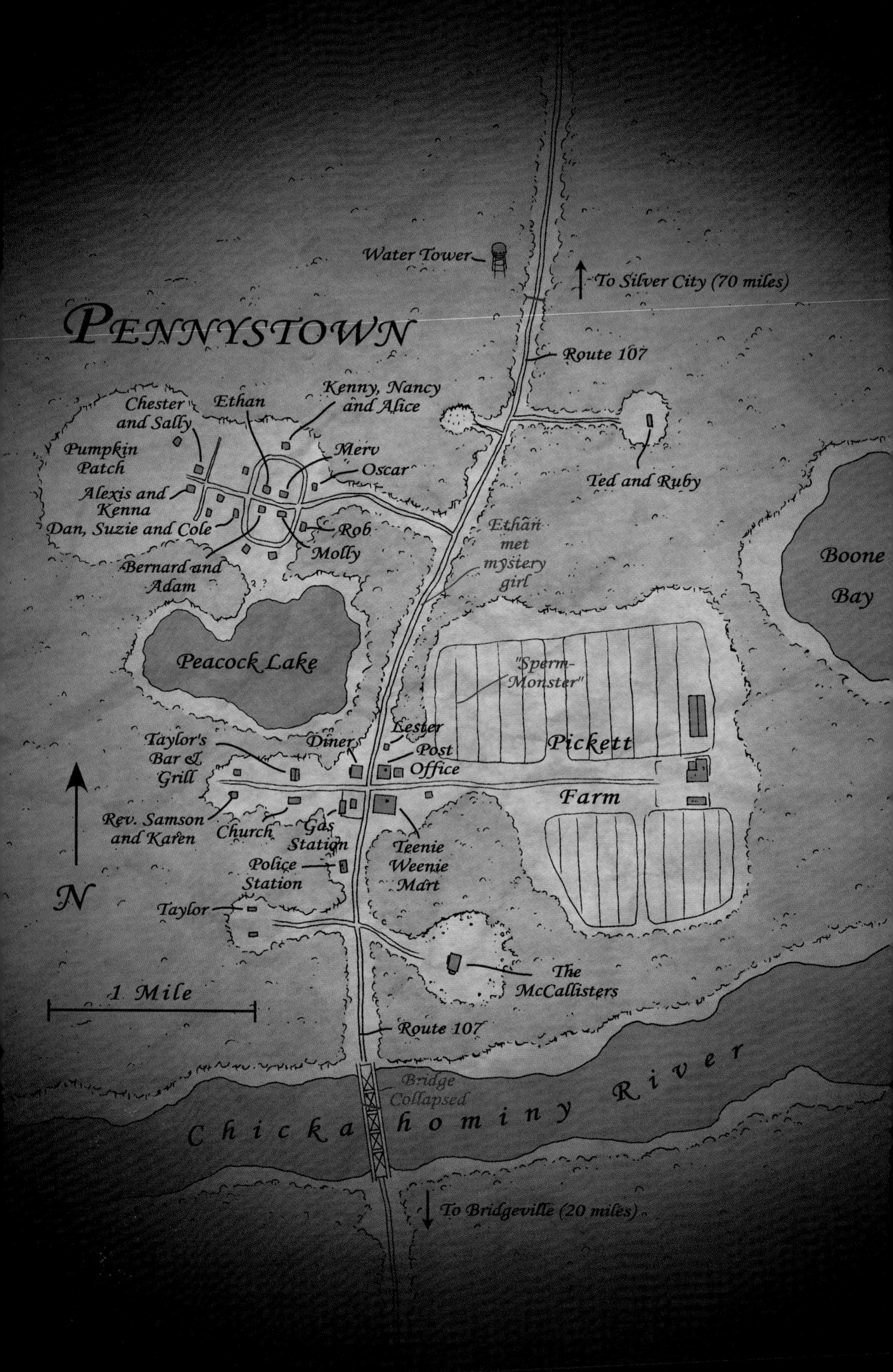
Pennystown
Water Tower
To Silver City (70 miles)
Route 107
Kenny, Nancy and Alice
Chester and Sally
Ethan
Pumpkin Patch
Merv
Oscar
Ted and Ruby
Alexis and Kenna
Dan, Suzie and Cole
Rob
Molly
Bernard and Adam
Ethan met mystery girl
Boone Bay
Peacock Lake
"Sperm-Monster"
Taylor's Bar & Grill
Diner
Lester
Post Office
Pickett
Farm
Rev. Samson and Karen
Church
Gas Station
Teenie Weenie Mart
Police Station
N
Taylor
1 Mile
The McCallisters
Route 107
Bridge Collapsed
Chickahominy River
To Bridgeville (20 miles)

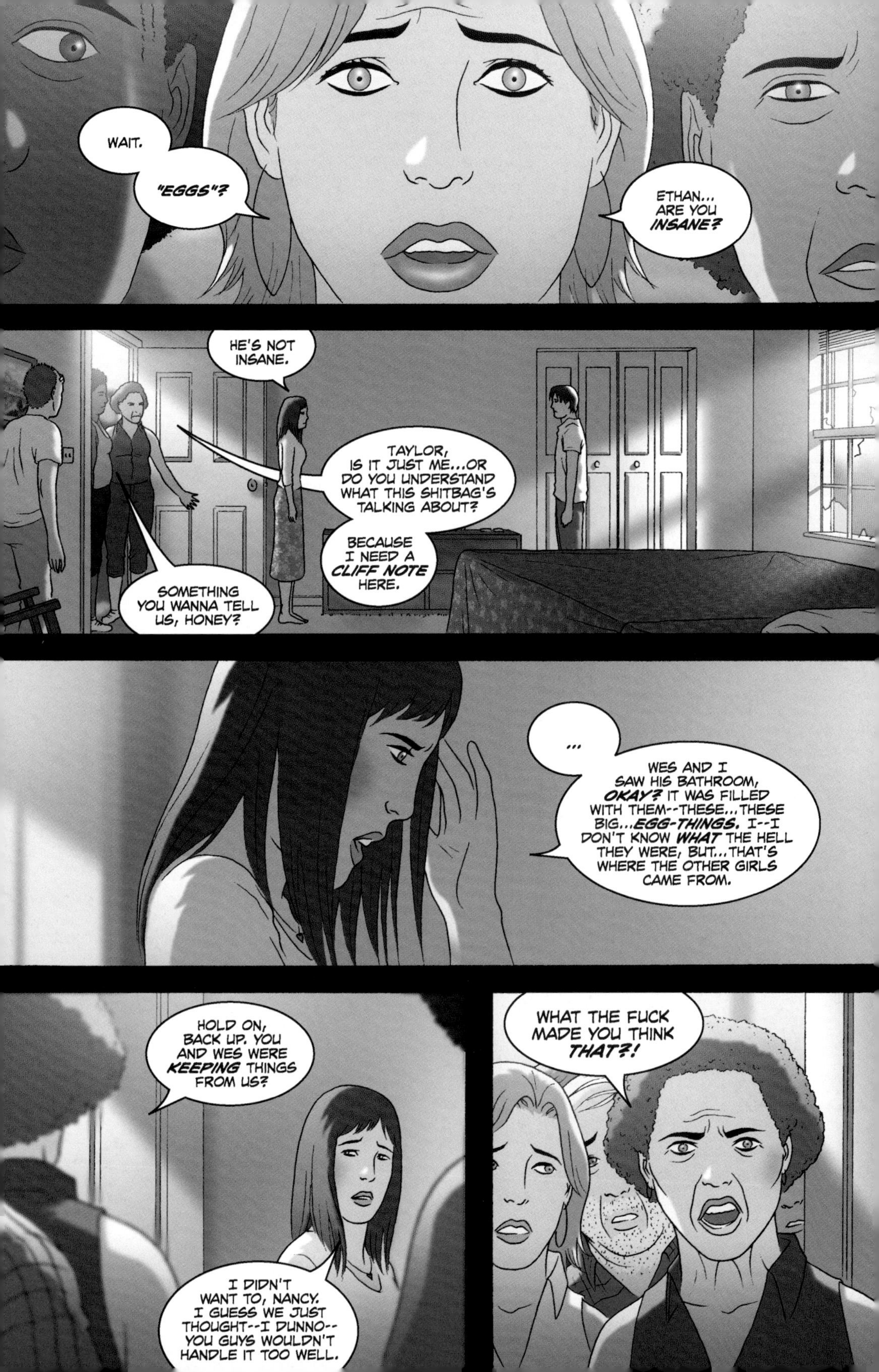
WAIT.
"EGGS"?
ETHAN... ARE YOU INSANE?
HE'S NOT INSANE.
TAYLOR, IS IT JUST ME...OR DO YOU UNDERSTAND WHAT THIS SHITBAG'S TALKING ABOUT?
BECAUSE I NEED A CLIFF NOTE HERE.
SOMETHING YOU WANNA TELL US, HONEY?
...
WES AND I SAW HIS BATHROOM, OKAY? IT WAS FILLED WITH THEM--THESE...THESE BIG...EGG-THINGS. I--I DON'T KNOW WHAT THE HELL THEY WERE, BUT...THAT'S WHERE THE OTHER GIRLS CAME FROM.
HOLD ON, BACK UP. YOU AND WES WERE KEEPING THINGS FROM US?
I DIDN'T WANT TO, NANCY. I GUESS WE JUST THOUGHT--I DUNNO--YOU GUYS WOULDN'T HANDLE IT TOO WELL.
WHAT THE FUCK MADE YOU THINK THAT?!

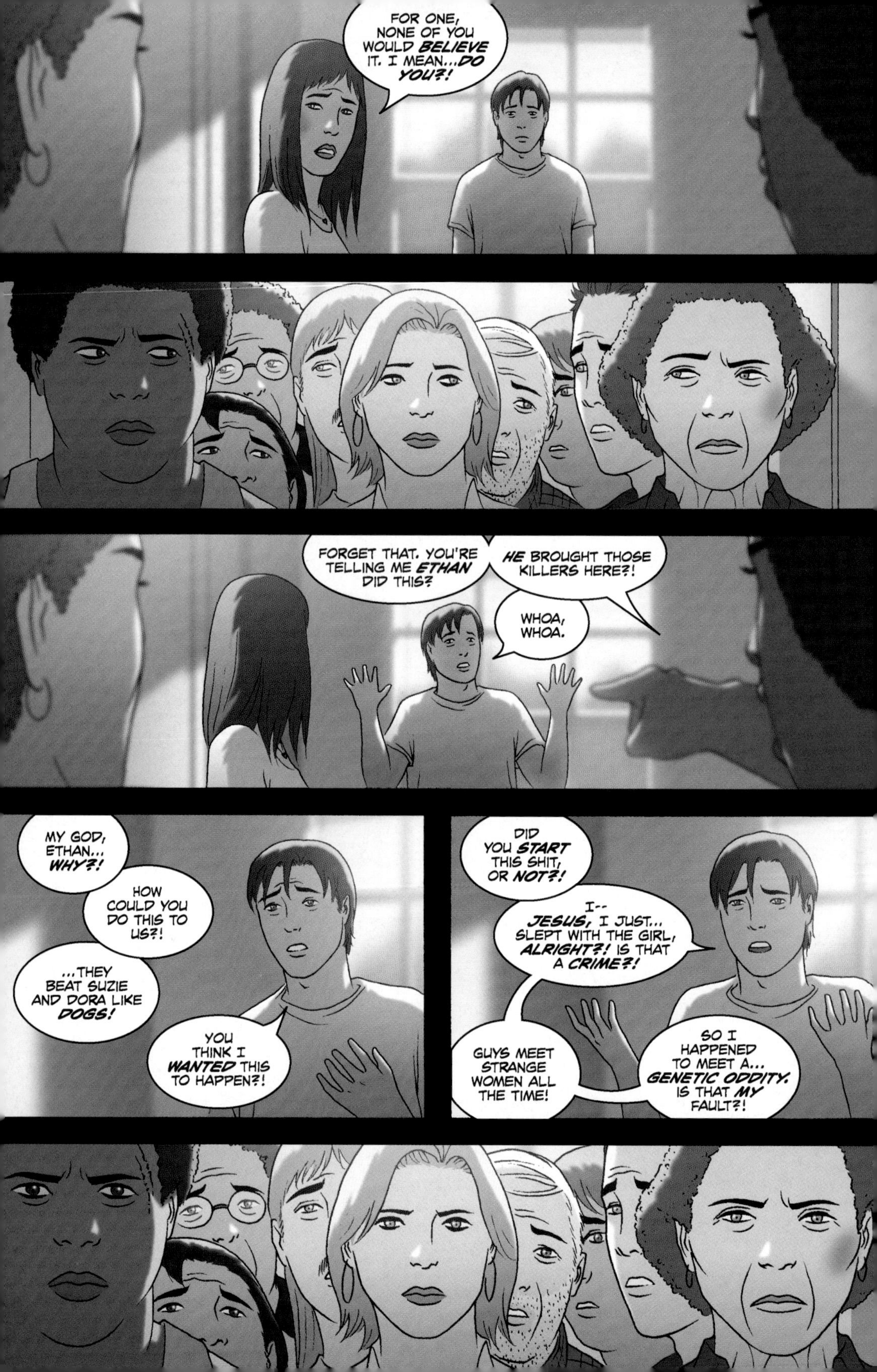
FOR ONE, NONE OF YOU WOULD BELIEVE IT. I MEAN...DO YOU?!
FORGET THAT. YOU'RE TELLING ME ETHAN DID THIS?
HE BROUGHT THOSE KILLERS HERE?!
WHOA, WHOA.
MY GOD, ETHAN... WHY?!
HOW COULD YOU DO THIS TO US?!
...THEY BEAT SUZIE AND DORA LIKE DOGS!
YOU THINK I WANTED THIS TO HAPPEN?!
DID YOU START THIS SHIT, OR NOT?!
I-- JESUS, I JUST... SLEPT WITH THE GIRL, ALRIGHT?! IS THAT A CRIME?!
GUYS MEET STRANGE WOMEN ALL THE TIME!
SO I HAPPENED TO MEET A... GENETIC ODDITY. IS THAT MY FAULT?!

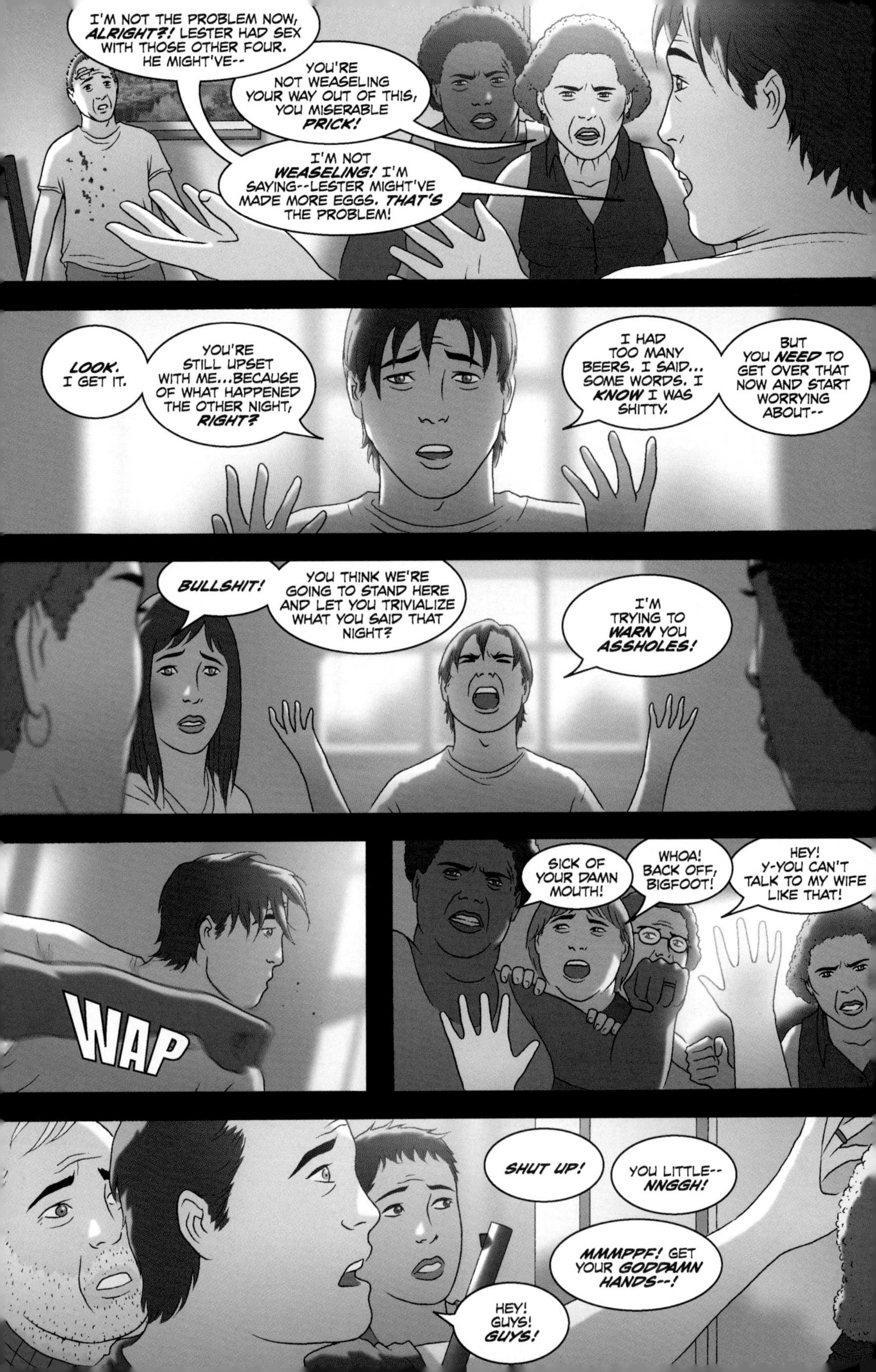
I'M NOT THE PROBLEM NOW, ALRIGHT?! LESTER HAD SEX WITH THOSE OTHER FOUR. HE MIGHT'VE--
YOU'RE NOT WEASELING YOUR WAY OUT OF THIS, YOU MISERABLE PRICK!
I'M NOT WEASELING! I'M SAYING--LESTER MIGHT'VE MADE MORE EGGS. THAT'S THE PROBLEM!
LOOK. I GET IT.
YOU'RE STILL UPSET WITH ME...BECAUSE OF WHAT HAPPENED THE OTHER NIGHT, RIGHT?
I HAD TOO MANY BEERS. I SAID... SOME WORDS. I KNOW I WAS SHITTY.
BUT YOU NEED TO GET OVER THAT NOW AND START WORRYING ABOUT--
BULLSHIT!
YOU THINK WE'RE GOING TO STAND HERE AND LET YOU TRIVIALIZE WHAT YOU SAID THAT NIGHT?
I'M TRYING TO WARN YOU ASSHOLES!
WAP
SICK OF YOUR DAMN MOUTH!
WHOA! BACK OFF, BIGFOOT!
HEY! Y-YOU CAN'T TALK TO MY WIFE LIKE THAT!
SHUT UP!
YOU LITTLE-- NNGGH!
MMMPPF! GET YOUR GODDAMN HANDS--!
HEY! GUYS! GUYS!

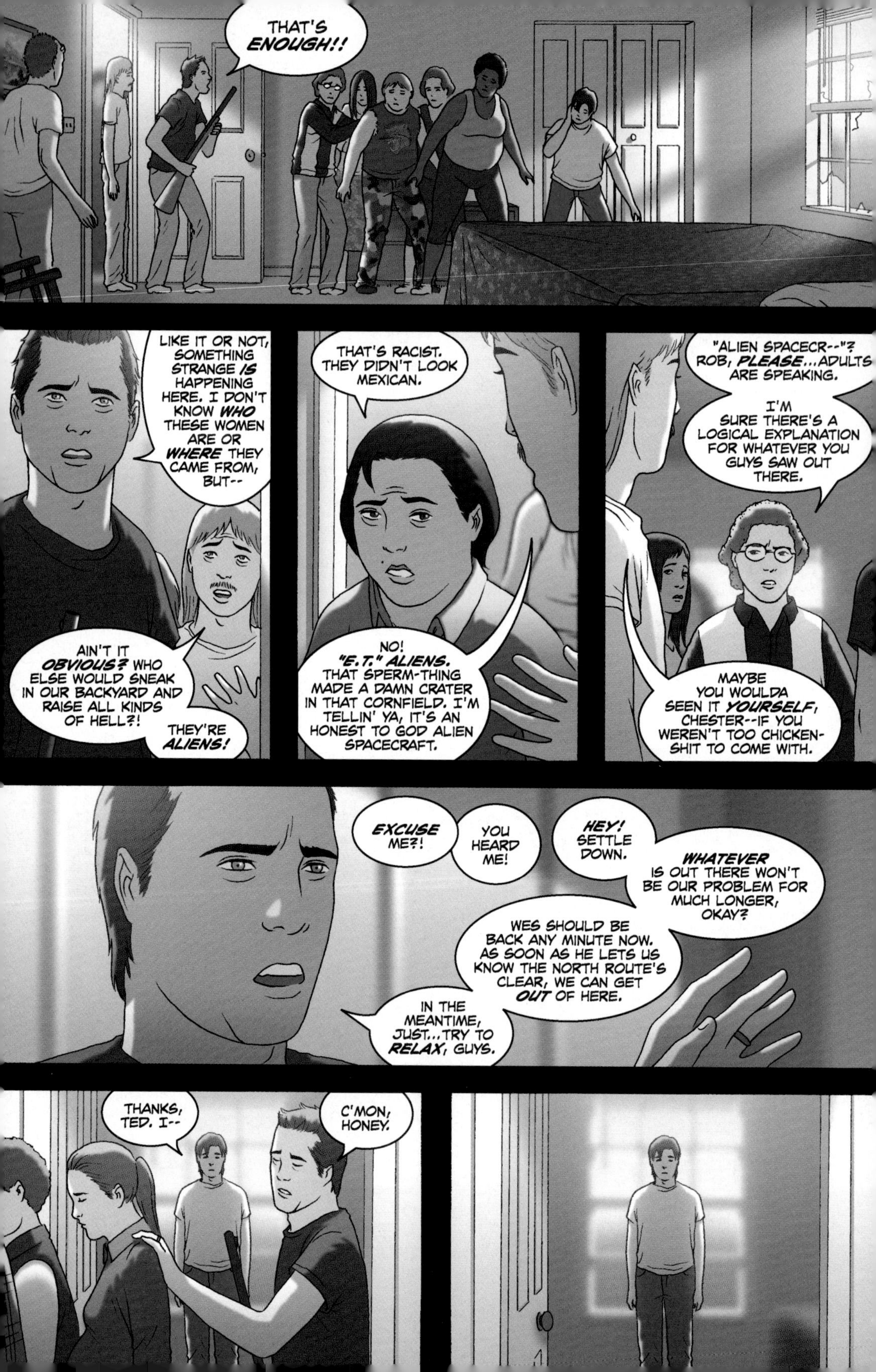
THAT'S ENOUGH!!
LIKE IT OR NOT, SOMETHING STRANGE IS HAPPENING HERE. I DON'T KNOW WHO THESE WOMEN ARE OR WHERE THEY CAME FROM, BUT--
AIN'T IT OBVIOUS? WHO ELSE WOULD SNEAK IN OUR BACKYARD AND RAISE ALL KINDS OF HELL?!
THEY'RE ALIENS!
THAT'S RACIST. THEY DIDN'T LOOK MEXICAN.
NO! "E.T." ALIENS. THAT SPERM-THING MADE A DAMN CRATER IN THAT CORNFIELD. I'M TELLIN' YA, IT'S AN HONEST TO GOD ALIEN SPACECRAFT.
"ALIEN SPACECR--"? ROB, PLEASE...ADULTS ARE SPEAKING.
I'M SURE THERE'S A LOGICAL EXPLANATION FOR WHATEVER YOU GUYS SAW OUT THERE.
MAYBE YOU WOULDA SEEN IT YOURSELF, CHESTER--IF YOU WEREN'T TOO CHICKEN-SHIT TO COME WITH.
EXCUSE ME?!
YOU HEARD ME!
HEY! SETTLE DOWN.
WHATEVER IS OUT THERE WON'T BE OUR PROBLEM FOR MUCH LONGER, OKAY?
WES SHOULD BE BACK ANY MINUTE NOW. AS SOON AS HE LETS US KNOW THE NORTH ROUTE'S CLEAR, WE CAN GET OUT OF HERE.
IN THE MEANTIME, JUST...TRY TO RELAX, GUYS.
THANKS, TED. I--
C'MON, HONEY.

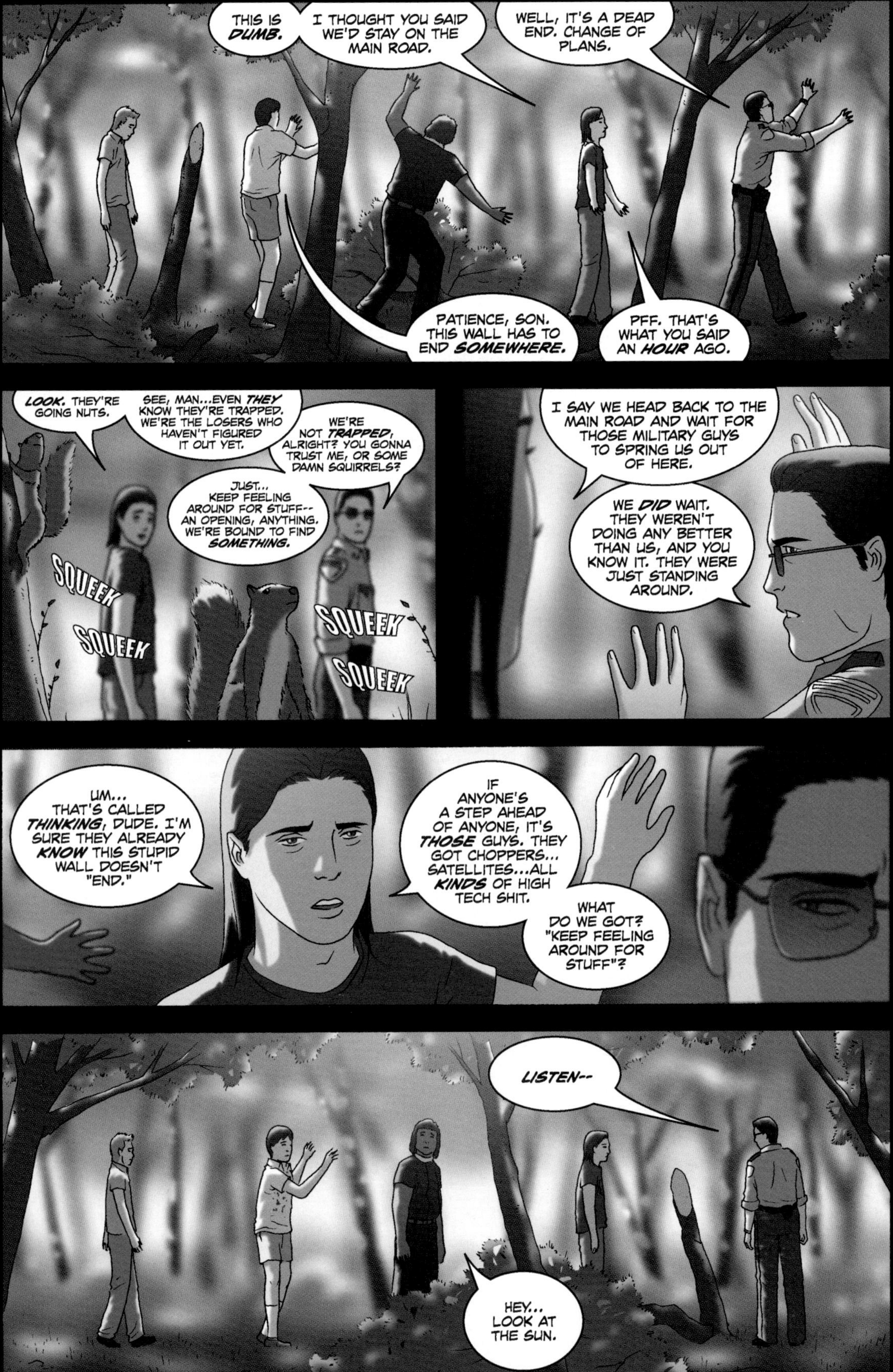
THIS IS DUMB.
I THOUGHT YOU SAID WE'D STAY ON THE MAIN ROAD.
WELL, IT'S A DEAD END. CHANGE OF PLANS.
PATIENCE, SON. THIS WALL HAS TO END SOMEWHERE.
PFF. THAT'S WHAT YOU SAID AN HOUR AGO.
LOOK. THEY'RE GOING NUTS.
SEE, MAN...EVEN THEY KNOW THEY'RE TRAPPED. WE'RE THE LOSERS WHO HAVEN'T FIGURED IT OUT YET.
WE'RE NOT TRAPPED, ALRIGHT? YOU GONNA TRUST ME, OR SOME DAMN SQUIRRELS?
JUST... KEEP FEELING AROUND FOR STUFF-- AN OPENING, ANYTHING. WE'RE BOUND TO FIND SOMETHING.
SQUEEK
SQUEEK
SQUEEK
SQUEEK
I SAY WE HEAD BACK TO THE MAIN ROAD AND WAIT FOR THOSE MILITARY GUYS TO SPRING US OUT OF HERE.
WE DID WAIT. THEY WEREN'T DOING ANY BETTER THAN US, AND YOU KNOW IT. THEY WERE JUST STANDING AROUND.
UM... THAT'S CALLED THINKING, DUDE. I'M SURE THEY ALREADY KNOW THIS STUPID WALL DOESN'T "END."
IF ANYONE'S A STEP AHEAD OF ANYONE, IT'S THOSE GUYS. THEY GOT CHOPPERS... SATELLITES...ALL KINDS OF HIGH TECH SHIT.
WHAT DO WE GOT? "KEEP FEELING AROUND FOR STUFF"?
LISTEN--
HEY... LOOK AT THE SUN.

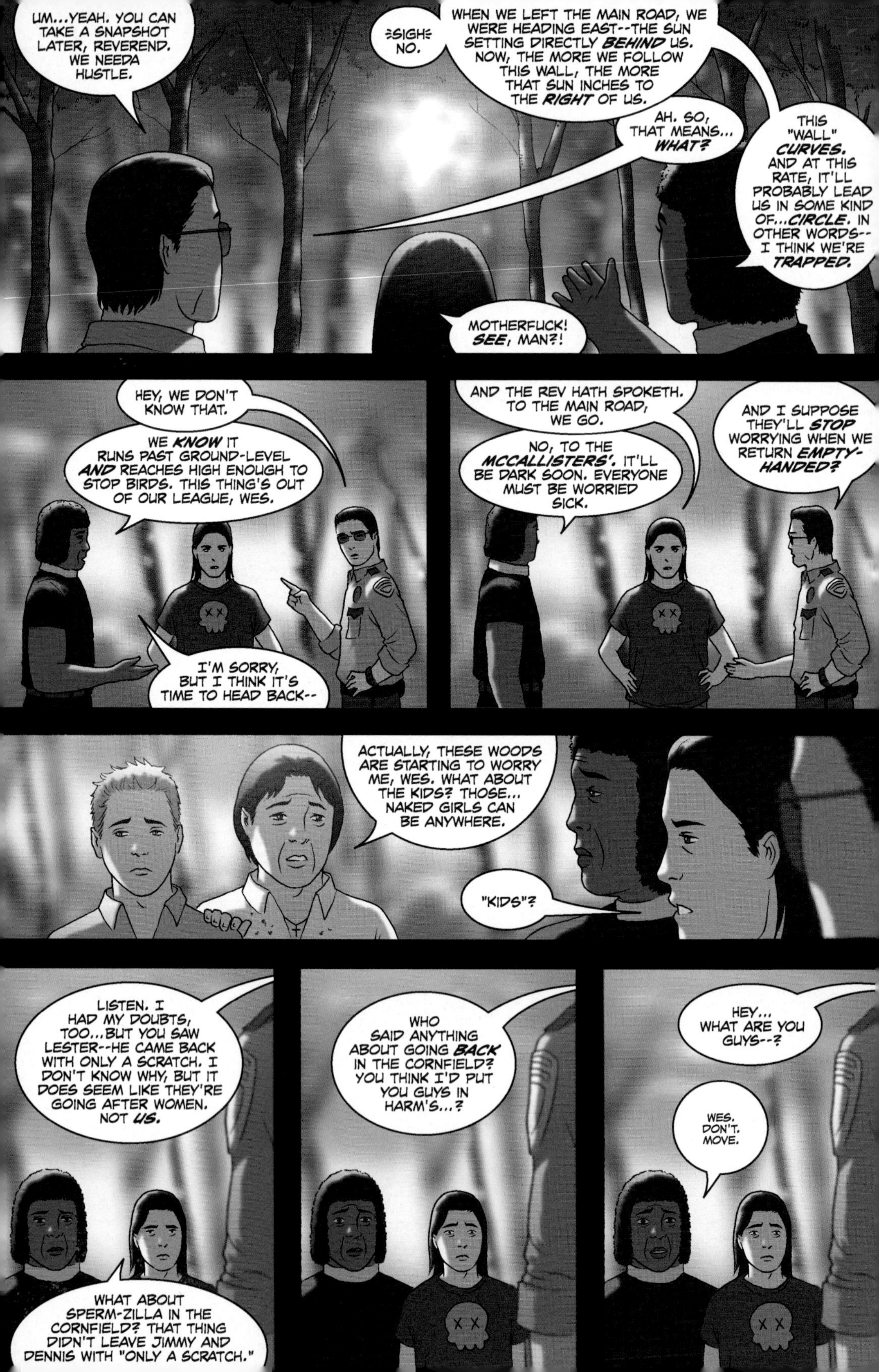
UM...YEAH. YOU CAN TAKE A SNAPSHOT LATER, REVEREND. WE NEEDA HUSTLE.
≶SIGH≷ NO.
WHEN WE LEFT THE MAIN ROAD, WE WERE HEADING EAST--THE SUN SETTING DIRECTLY BEHIND US. NOW, THE MORE WE FOLLOW THIS WALL, THE MORE THAT SUN INCHES TO THE RIGHT OF US.
AH. SO, THAT MEANS... WHAT?
THIS "WALL" CURVES. AND AT THIS RATE, IT'LL PROBABLY LEAD US IN SOME KIND OF...CIRCLE. IN OTHER WORDS--I THINK WE'RE TRAPPED.
MOTHERFUCK! SEE, MAN?!
HEY, WE DON'T KNOW THAT.
WE KNOW IT RUNS PAST GROUND-LEVEL AND REACHES HIGH ENOUGH TO STOP BIRDS. THIS THING'S OUT OF OUR LEAGUE, WES.
I'M SORRY, BUT I THINK IT'S TIME TO HEAD BACK--
AND THE REV HATH SPOKETH. TO THE MAIN ROAD, WE GO.
NO, TO THE MCCALLISTERS'. IT'LL BE DARK SOON. EVERYONE MUST BE WORRIED SICK.
AND I SUPPOSE THEY'LL STOP WORRYING WHEN WE RETURN EMPTY-HANDED?
ACTUALLY, THESE WOODS ARE STARTING TO WORRY ME, WES. WHAT ABOUT THE KIDS? THOSE... NAKED GIRLS CAN BE ANYWHERE.
"KIDS"?
LISTEN. I HAD MY DOUBTS, TOO...BUT YOU SAW LESTER--HE CAME BACK WITH ONLY A SCRATCH. I DON'T KNOW WHY, BUT IT DOES SEEM LIKE THEY'RE GOING AFTER WOMEN. NOT US.
WHAT ABOUT SPERM-ZILLA IN THE CORNFIELD? THAT THING DIDN'T LEAVE JIMMY AND DENNIS WITH "ONLY A SCRATCH."
WHO SAID ANYTHING ABOUT GOING BACK IN THE CORNFIELD? YOU THINK I'D PUT YOU GUYS IN HARM'S...?
HEY... WHAT ARE YOU GUYS--?
WES. DON'T. MOVE.

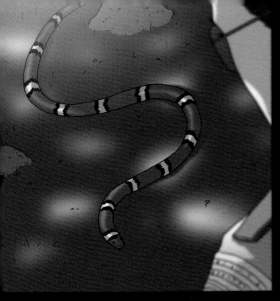

ALRIGHT. NOBODY PANIC. JUST... TAKE IT EASY.

...

OKAY, UM...RED ON YELLOW, KILL A FELLOW...RED ON BLACK, VENOM LACK--

GUYS, IT'S OKAY. THIS SNAKE ISN'T POISONOUS. HEH. ≶PHEW≶

HEY. *LADIES.* I SAID IT'S OKAY. YOU CAN RELAX NOW.

WES...

...*BEHIND* YOU.

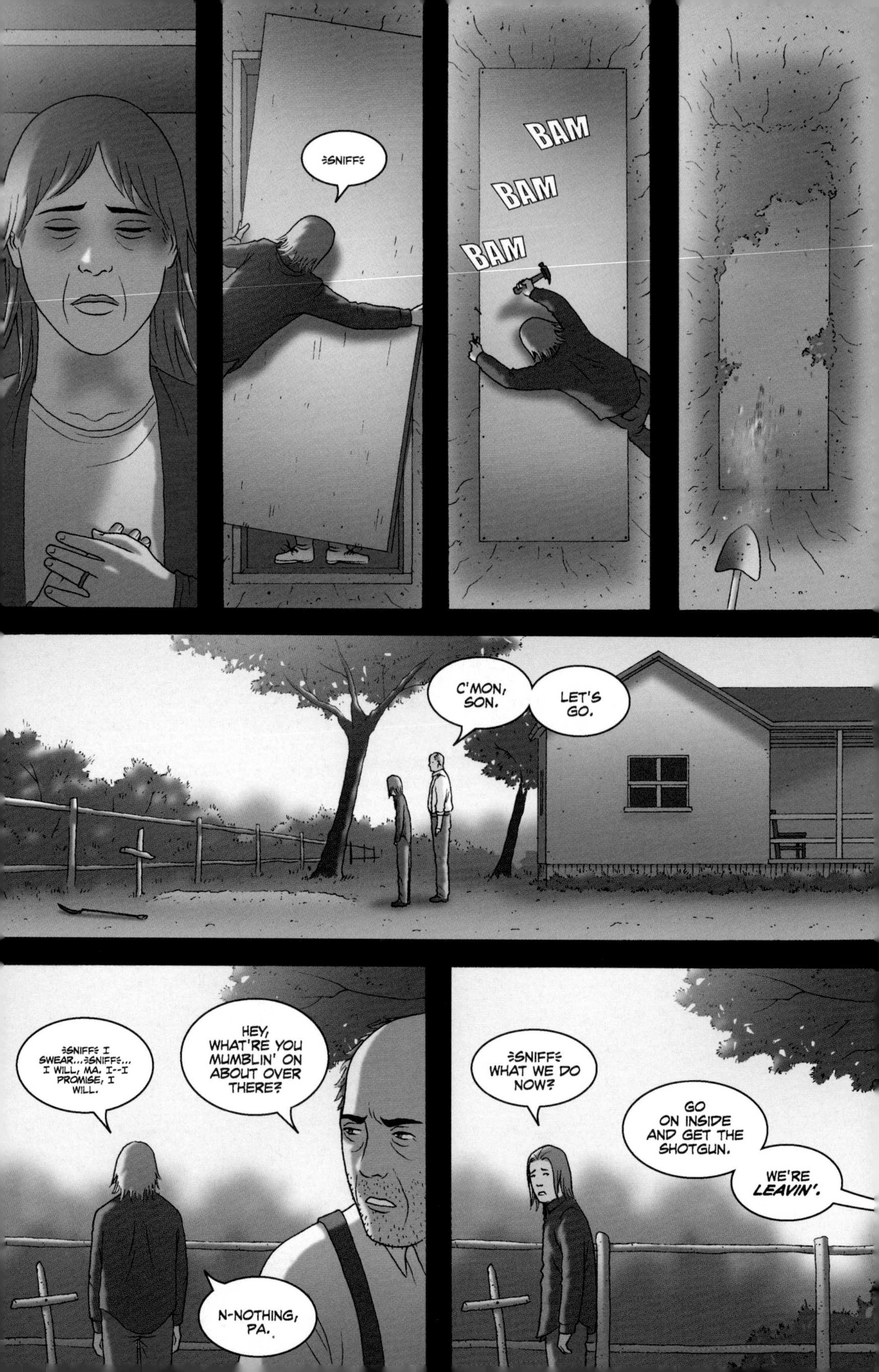

=SNIFF=
BAM
BAM
BAM
C'MON, SON.
LET'S GO.
=SNIFF= I SWEAR... =SNIFF=... I WILL, MA. I--I PROMISE, I WILL.
HEY, WHAT'RE YOU MUMBLIN' ON ABOUT OVER THERE?
N-NOTHING, PA.
=SNIFF= WHAT WE DO NOW?
GO ON INSIDE AND GET THE SHOTGUN.
WE'RE *LEAVIN'.*

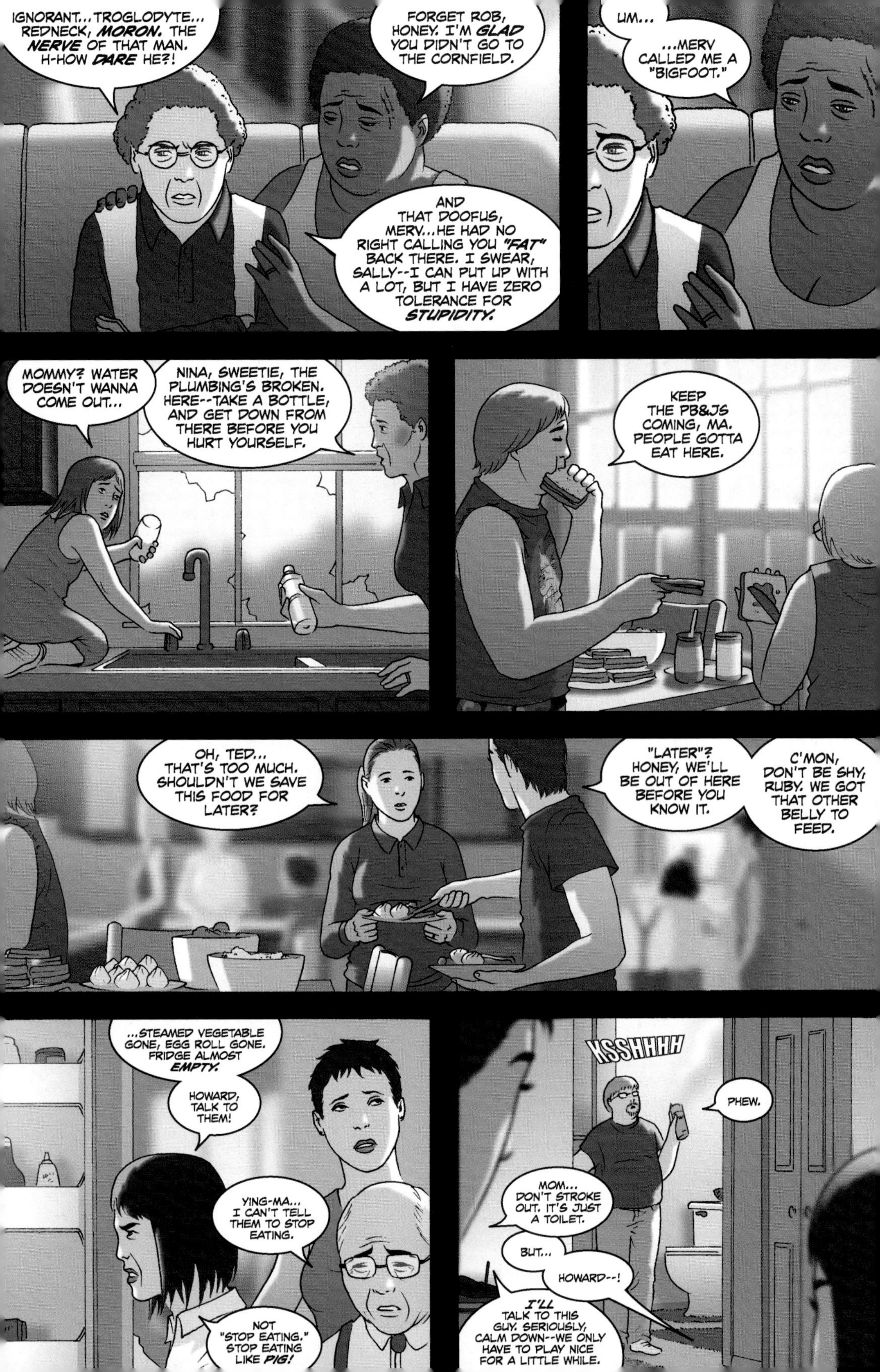
IGNORANT...TROGLODYTE... REDNECK, MORON. THE NERVE OF THAT MAN. H-HOW DARE HE?!
FORGET ROB, HONEY. I'M GLAD YOU DIDN'T GO TO THE CORNFIELD.
AND THAT DOOFUS, MERV...HE HAD NO RIGHT CALLING YOU "FAT" BACK THERE. I SWEAR, SALLY--I CAN PUT UP WITH A LOT, BUT I HAVE ZERO TOLERANCE FOR STUPIDITY.
UM...
...MERV CALLED ME A "BIGFOOT."
MOMMY? WATER DOESN'T WANNA COME OUT...
NINA, SWEETIE, THE PLUMBING'S BROKEN. HERE--TAKE A BOTTLE, AND GET DOWN FROM THERE BEFORE YOU HURT YOURSELF.
KEEP THE PB&JS COMING, MA. PEOPLE GOTTA EAT HERE.
OH, TED... THAT'S TOO MUCH. SHOULDN'T WE SAVE THIS FOOD FOR LATER?
"LATER"? HONEY, WE'LL BE OUT OF HERE BEFORE YOU KNOW IT.
C'MON, DON'T BE SHY, RUBY. WE GOT THAT OTHER BELLY TO FEED.
...STEAMED VEGETABLE GONE, EGG ROLL GONE. FRIDGE ALMOST EMPTY.
HOWARD, TALK TO THEM!
YING-MA... I CAN'T TELL THEM TO STOP EATING.
NOT "STOP EATING." STOP EATING LIKE PIG!
KSSHHHH
PHEW.
MOM... DON'T STROKE OUT. IT'S JUST A TOILET.
BUT...
HOWARD--!
I'LL TALK TO THIS GUY. SERIOUSLY, CALM DOWN--WE ONLY HAVE TO PLAY NICE FOR A LITTLE WHILE.

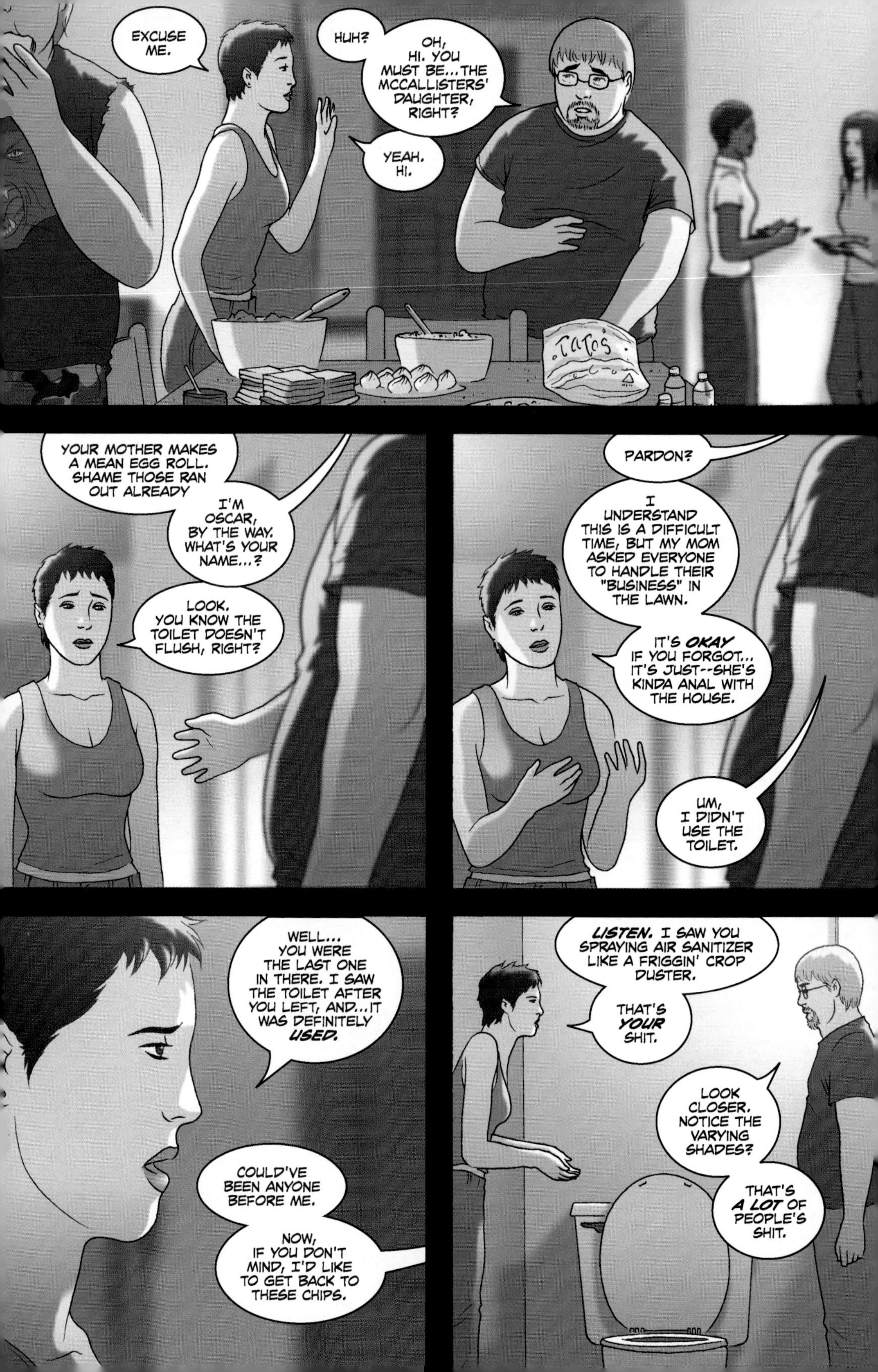
EXCUSE ME.
HUH?
OH, HI. YOU MUST BE...THE MCCALLISTERS' DAUGHTER, RIGHT?
YEAH. HI.
TATOS
YOUR MOTHER MAKES A MEAN EGG ROLL. SHAME THOSE RAN OUT ALREADY
I'M OSCAR, BY THE WAY. WHAT'S YOUR NAME...?
LOOK. YOU KNOW THE TOILET DOESN'T FLUSH, RIGHT?
PARDON?
I UNDERSTAND THIS IS A DIFFICULT TIME, BUT MY MOM ASKED EVERYONE TO HANDLE THEIR "BUSINESS" IN THE LAWN.
IT'S OKAY IF YOU FORGOT... IT'S JUST--SHE'S KINDA ANAL WITH THE HOUSE.
UM, I DIDN'T USE THE TOILET.
WELL... YOU WERE THE LAST ONE IN THERE. I SAW THE TOILET AFTER YOU LEFT, AND...IT WAS DEFINITELY USED.
COULD'VE BEEN ANYONE BEFORE ME.
NOW, IF YOU DON'T MIND, I'D LIKE TO GET BACK TO THESE CHIPS.
LISTEN. I SAW YOU SPRAYING AIR SANITIZER LIKE A FRIGGIN' CROP DUSTER.
THAT'S YOUR SHIT.
LOOK CLOSER. NOTICE THE VARYING SHADES?
THAT'S A LOT OF PEOPLE'S SHIT.

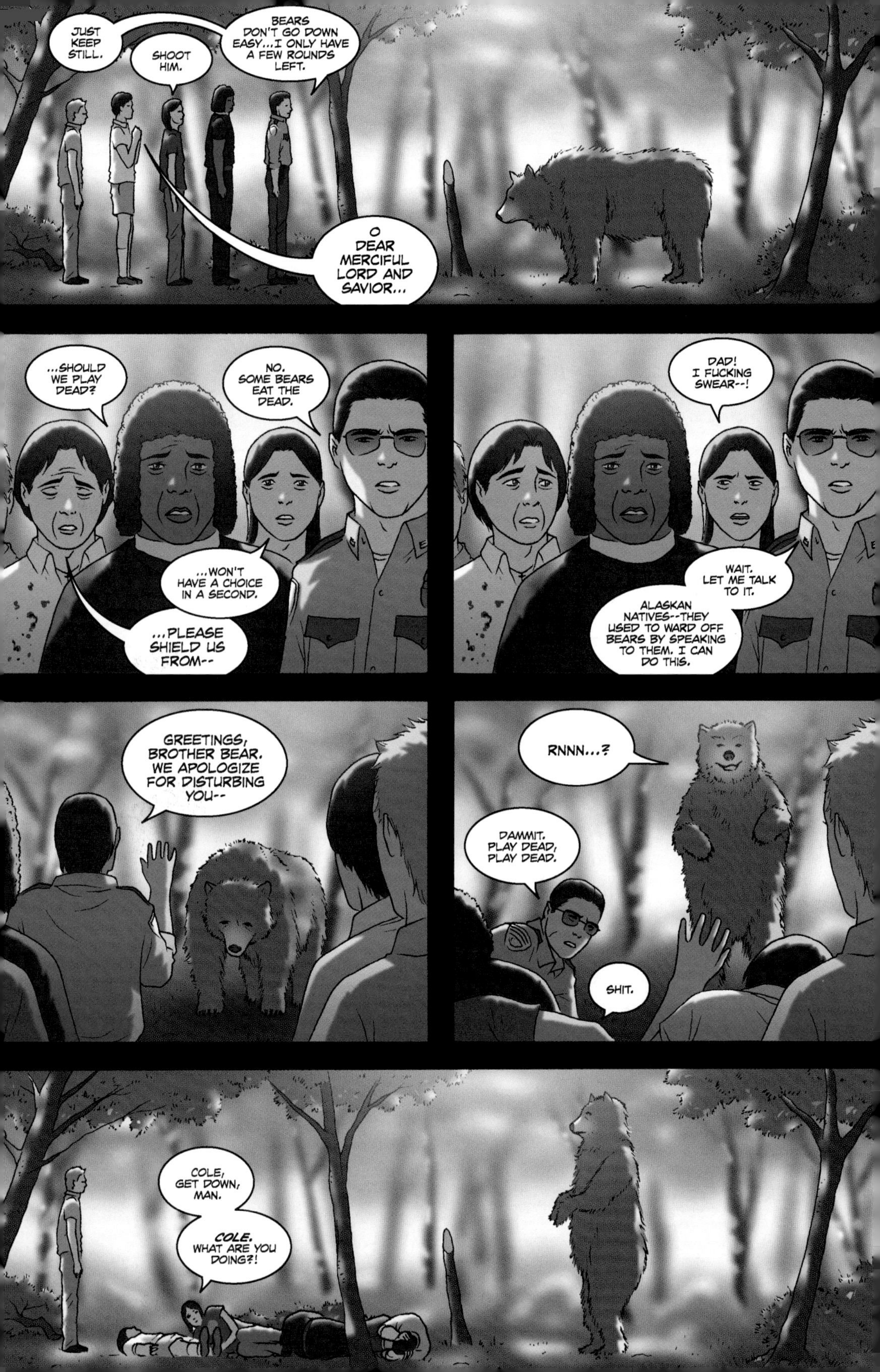
JUST KEEP STILL.
BEARS DON'T GO DOWN EASY...I ONLY HAVE A FEW ROUNDS LEFT.
SHOOT HIM.
O DEAR MERCIFUL LORD AND SAVIOR...
...SHOULD WE PLAY DEAD?
NO. SOME BEARS EAT THE DEAD.
...WON'T HAVE A CHOICE IN A SECOND.
...PLEASE SHIELD US FROM--
DAD! I FUCKING SWEAR--!
WAIT. LET ME TALK TO IT.
ALASKAN NATIVES--THEY USED TO WARD OFF BEARS BY SPEAKING TO THEM. I CAN DO THIS.
GREETINGS, BROTHER BEAR. WE APOLOGIZE FOR DISTURBING YOU--
RNNN...?
DAMMIT. PLAY DEAD, PLAY DEAD.
SHIT.
COLE, GET DOWN, MAN.
COLE. WHAT ARE YOU DOING?!

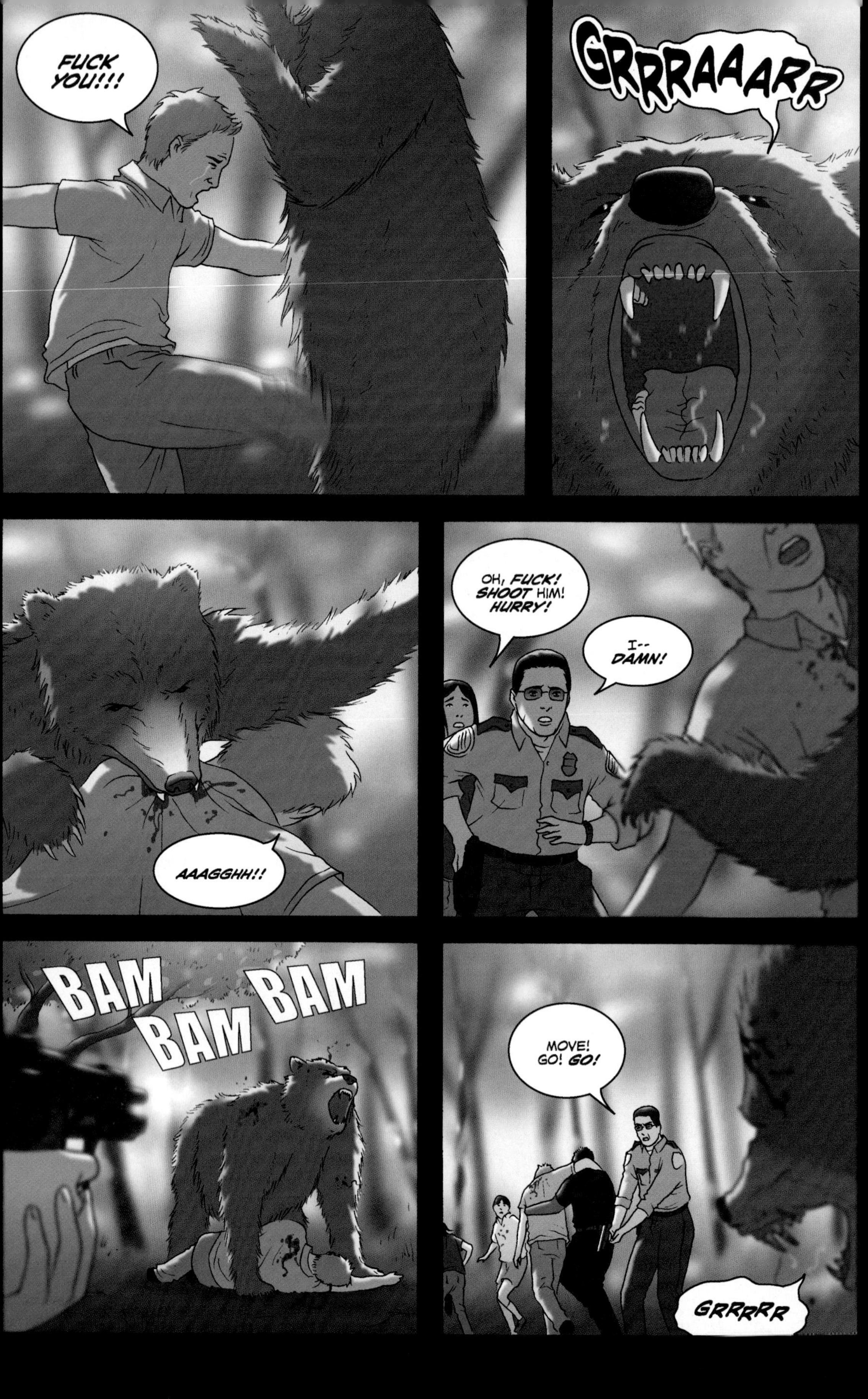
FUCK YOU!!!
GRRRAAARR
AAAGGHH!!
OH, FUCK! SHOOT HIM! HURRY!
I-- DAMN!
BAM
BAM
BAM
MOVE! GO! GO!
GRRRRR

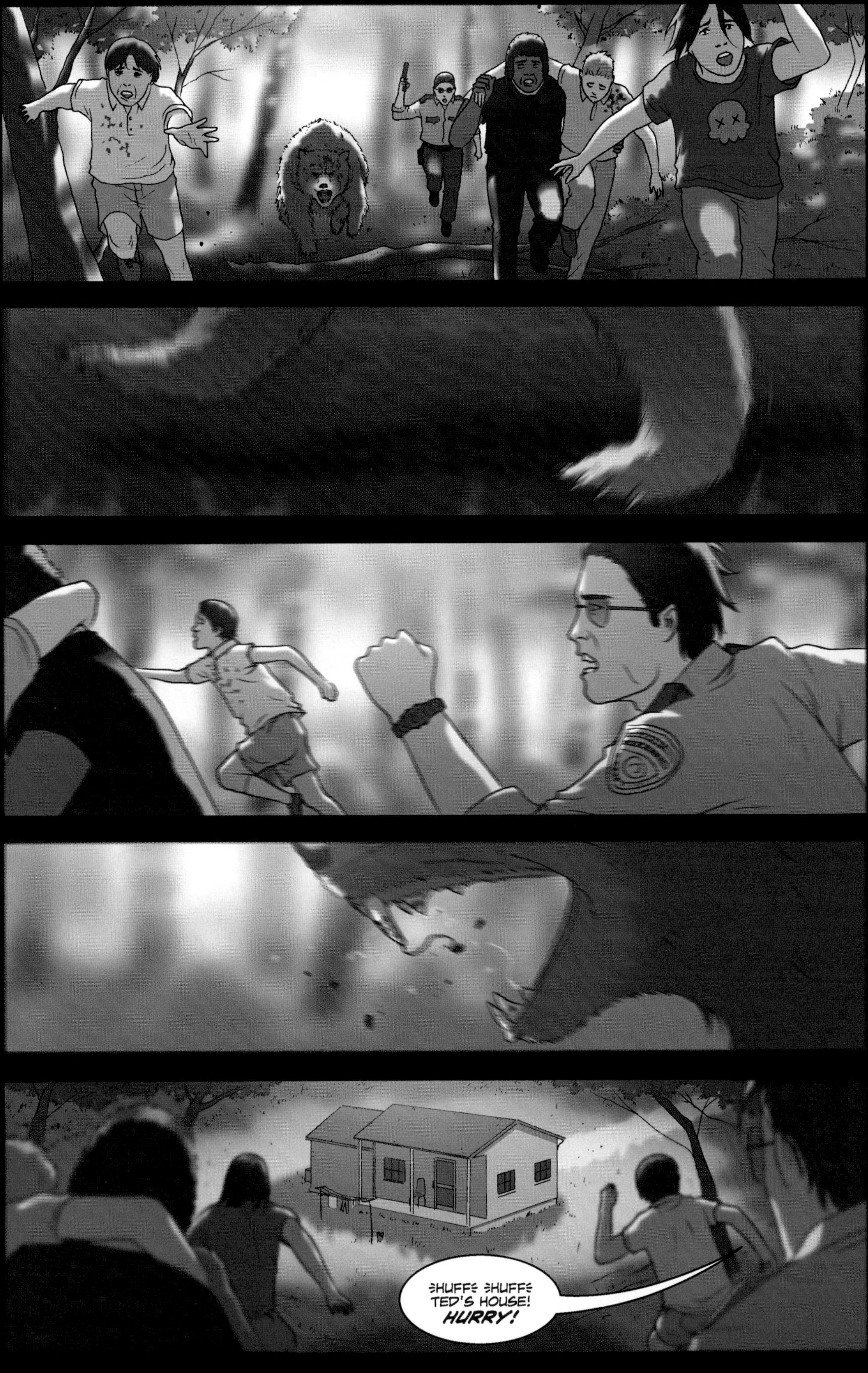
HUFF HUFF TED'S HOUSE! HURRY!

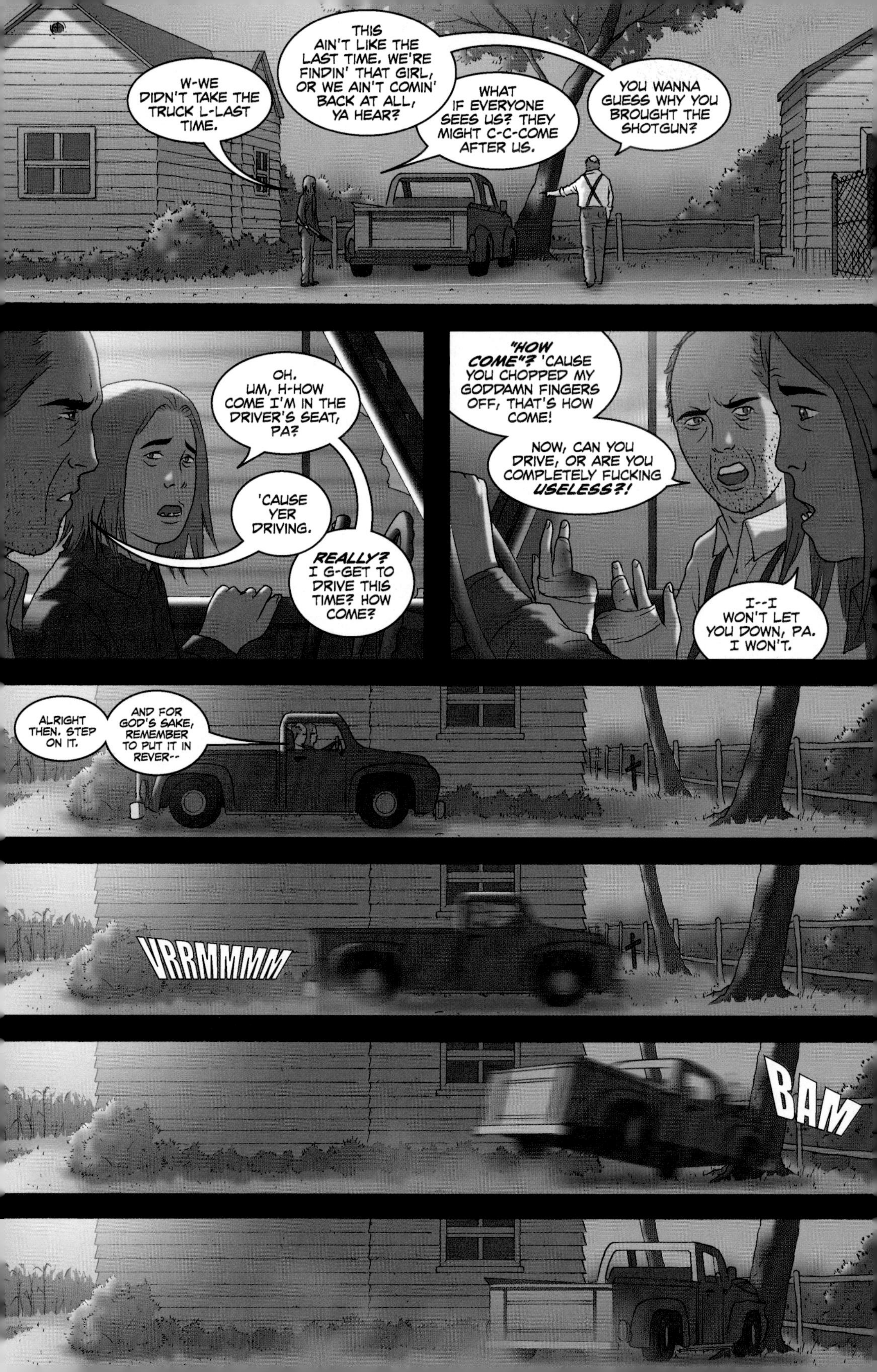

W-WE DIDN'T TAKE THE TRUCK L-LAST TIME.
THIS AIN'T LIKE THE LAST TIME. WE'RE FINDIN' THAT GIRL, OR WE AIN'T COMIN' BACK AT ALL, YA HEAR?
WHAT IF EVERYONE SEES US? THEY MIGHT C-C-COME AFTER US.
YOU WANNA GUESS WHY YOU BROUGHT THE SHOTGUN?
OH. UM, H-HOW COME I'M IN THE DRIVER'S SEAT, PA?
'CAUSE YER DRIVING.
REALLY? I G-GET TO DRIVE THIS TIME? HOW COME?
"HOW COME"? 'CAUSE YOU CHOPPED MY GODDAMN FINGERS OFF, THAT'S HOW COME!
NOW, CAN YOU DRIVE, OR ARE YOU COMPLETELY FUCKING USELESS?!
I--I WON'T LET YOU DOWN, PA. I WON'T.
ALRIGHT THEN. STEP ON IT.
AND FOR GOD'S SAKE, REMEMBER TO PUT IT IN REVER--
VRRMMMM
BAM

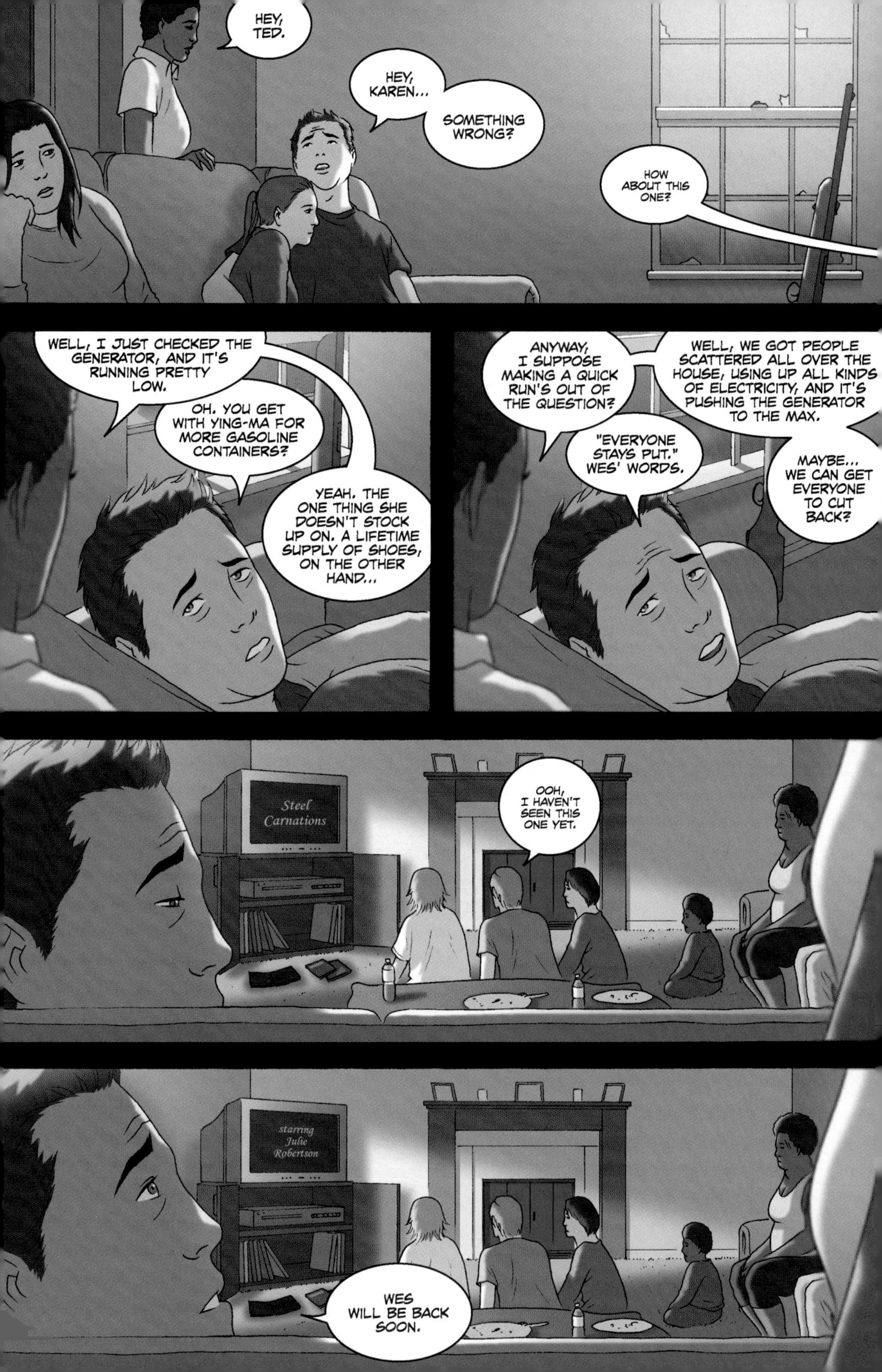
HEY, TED.
HEY, KAREN...
SOMETHING WRONG?
HOW ABOUT THIS ONE?
WELL, I JUST CHECKED THE GENERATOR, AND IT'S RUNNING PRETTY LOW.
OH. YOU GET WITH YING-MA FOR MORE GASOLINE CONTAINERS?
YEAH. THE ONE THING SHE DOESN'T STOCK UP ON. A LIFETIME SUPPLY OF SHOES, ON THE OTHER HAND...
ANYWAY, I SUPPOSE MAKING A QUICK RUN'S OUT OF THE QUESTION?
"EVERYONE STAYS PUT." WES' WORDS.
WELL, WE GOT PEOPLE SCATTERED ALL OVER THE HOUSE, USING UP ALL KINDS OF ELECTRICITY, AND IT'S PUSHING THE GENERATOR TO THE MAX.
MAYBE... WE CAN GET EVERYONE TO CUT BACK?
Steel Carnations
OOH, I HAVEN'T SEEN THIS ONE YET.
starring Julie Robertson
WES WILL BE BACK SOON.

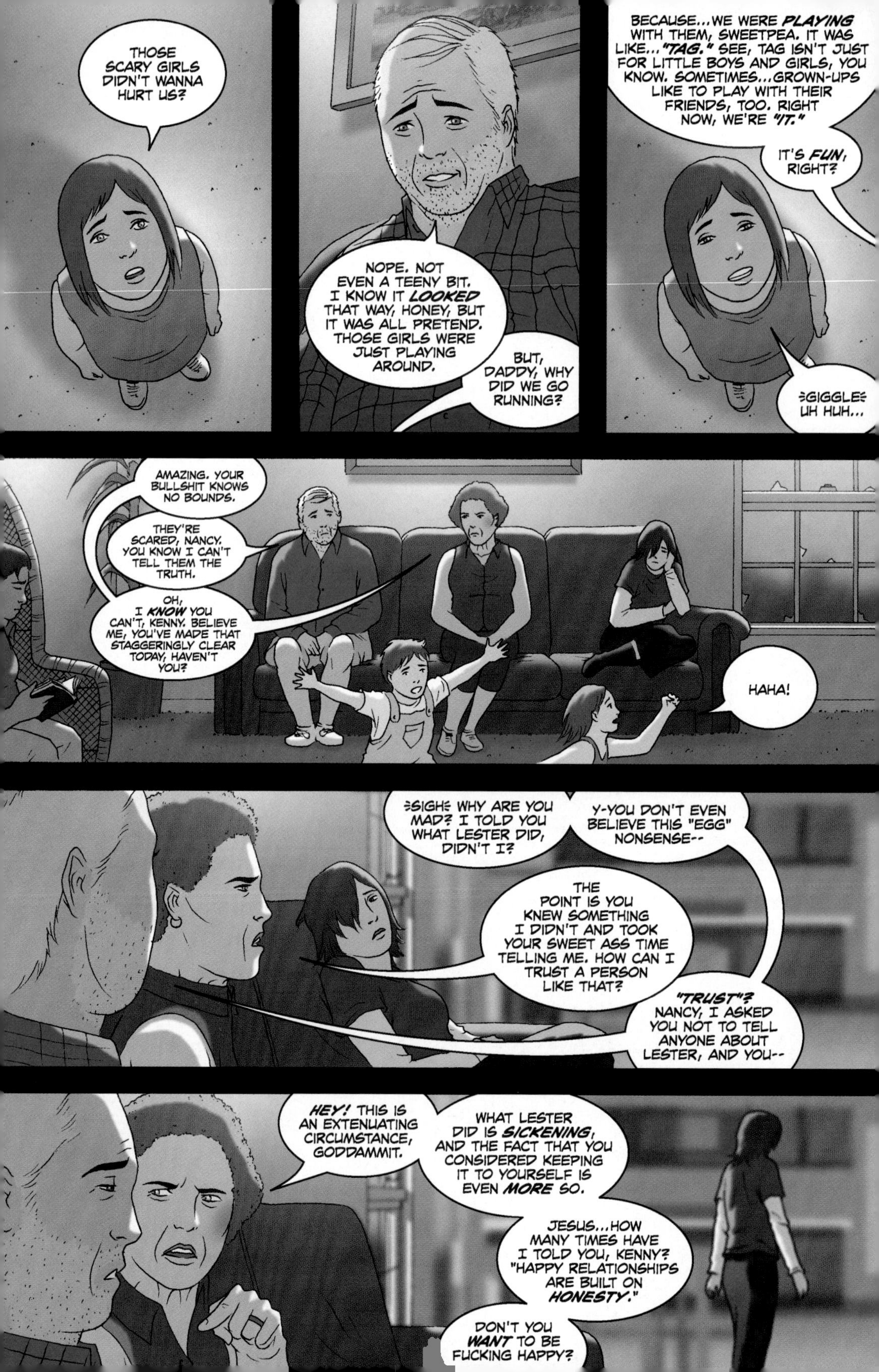

THOSE SCARY GIRLS DIDN'T WANNA HURT US?
NOPE. NOT EVEN A TEENY BIT. I KNOW IT *LOOKED* THAT WAY, HONEY, BUT IT WAS ALL PRETEND. THOSE GIRLS WERE JUST PLAYING AROUND.
BUT, DADDY, WHY DID WE GO RUNNING?
BECAUSE...WE WERE *PLAYING* WITH THEM, SWEETPEA. IT WAS LIKE..."*TAG.*" SEE, TAG ISN'T JUST FOR LITTLE BOYS AND GIRLS, YOU KNOW. SOMETIMES...GROWN-UPS LIKE TO PLAY WITH THEIR FRIENDS, TOO. RIGHT NOW, WE'RE "*IT.*"
IT'S *FUN*, RIGHT?
=GIGGLE= UH HUH...
AMAZING. YOUR BULLSHIT KNOWS NO BOUNDS.
THEY'RE SCARED, NANCY. YOU KNOW I CAN'T TELL THEM THE TRUTH.
OH, I *KNOW* YOU CAN'T, KENNY. BELIEVE ME, YOU'VE MADE THAT STAGGERINGLY CLEAR TODAY, HAVEN'T YOU?
HAHA!
=SIGH= WHY ARE YOU MAD? I TOLD YOU WHAT LESTER DID, DIDN'T I?
Y-YOU DON'T EVEN BELIEVE THIS "EGG" NONSENSE--
THE POINT IS YOU KNEW SOMETHING I DIDN'T AND TOOK YOUR SWEET ASS TIME TELLING ME. HOW CAN I TRUST A PERSON LIKE THAT?
"*TRUST*"? NANCY, I ASKED YOU NOT TO TELL ANYONE ABOUT LESTER, AND YOU--
HEY! THIS IS AN EXTENUATING CIRCUMSTANCE, GODDAMMIT.
WHAT LESTER DID IS *SICKENING*, AND THE FACT THAT YOU CONSIDERED KEEPING IT TO YOURSELF IS EVEN *MORE* SO.
JESUS...HOW MANY TIMES HAVE I TOLD YOU, KENNY? "HAPPY RELATIONSHIPS ARE BUILT ON *HONESTY*."
DON'T YOU *WANT* TO BE FUCKING HAPPY?

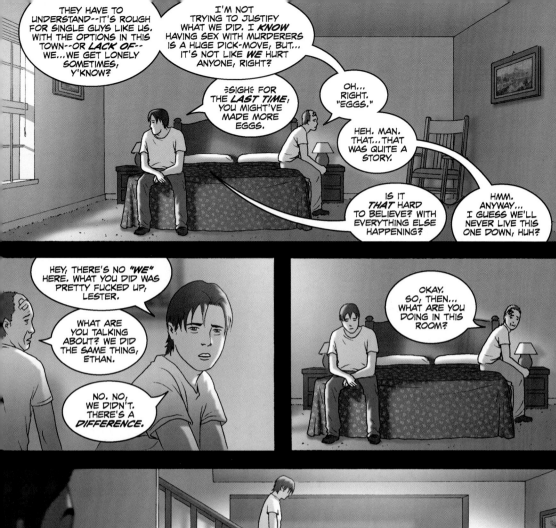

THEY HAVE TO UNDERSTAND--IT'S ROUGH FOR SINGLE GUYS LIKE US, WITH THE OPTIONS IN THIS TOWN--OR *LACK OF*-- WE...WE GET LONELY SOMETIMES, Y'KNOW?

I'M NOT TRYING TO JUSTIFY WHAT WE DID. I *KNOW* HAVING SEX WITH MURDERERS IS A HUGE DICK-MOVE, BUT... IT'S NOT LIKE *WE* HURT ANYONE, RIGHT?

≶SIGH≷ FOR THE *LAST TIME*, YOU MIGHT'VE MADE MORE EGGS.

OH... RIGHT. "EGGS."

HEH. MAN. THAT...THAT WAS QUITE A STORY.

IS IT *THAT* HARD TO BELIEVE? WITH EVERYTHING ELSE HAPPENING?

HMM. ANYWAY... I GUESS WE'LL NEVER LIVE THIS ONE DOWN, HUH?

HEY, THERE'S NO *"WE"* HERE. WHAT YOU DID WAS PRETTY FUCKED UP, LESTER.

WHAT ARE YOU TALKING ABOUT? WE DID THE SAME THING, ETHAN.

NO. NO, WE DIDN'T. THERE'S A *DIFFERENCE*.

OKAY. SO, THEN... WHAT ARE YOU DOING IN THIS ROOM?

TAYLOR?

CAN WE TALK FOR A SECOND?

JUST GO AWAY.

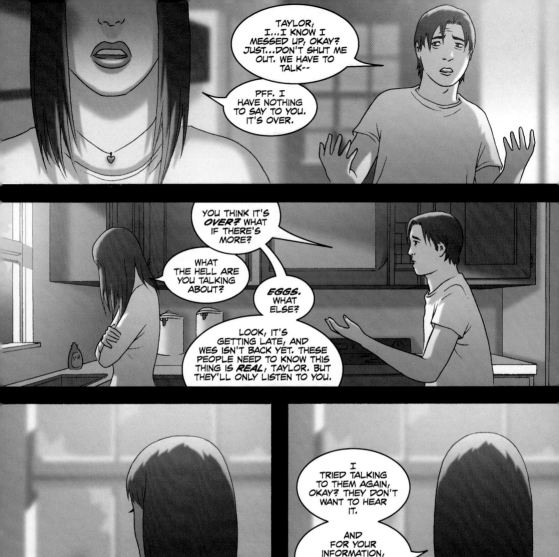

TAYLOR, I...I KNOW I MESSED UP, OKAY? JUST...DON'T SHUT ME OUT. WE HAVE TO TALK--

PFF. I HAVE NOTHING TO SAY TO YOU. IT'S OVER.

YOU THINK IT'S *OVER?* WHAT IF THERE'S MORE?

WHAT THE HELL ARE YOU TALKING ABOUT?

EGGS. WHAT ELSE?

LOOK, IT'S GETTING LATE, AND WES ISN'T BACK YET. THESE PEOPLE NEED TO KNOW THIS THING IS *REAL*, TAYLOR. BUT THEY'LL ONLY LISTEN TO YOU.

I TRIED TALKING TO THEM AGAIN, OKAY? THEY DON'T WANT TO HEAR IT.

AND FOR YOUR INFORMATION, I'M NOT EXACTLY TRUSTWORTHY RIGHT NOW.

HMM. OKAY, WELL... YOU AND I NEED TO PUT OUR HEADS TOGETHER AND THINK THIS OUT THEN--

ARE YOU FOR REAL?

YOU EXPECT US TO JUST...PARTNER UP? AFTER YOU SCREWED THAT GIRL?

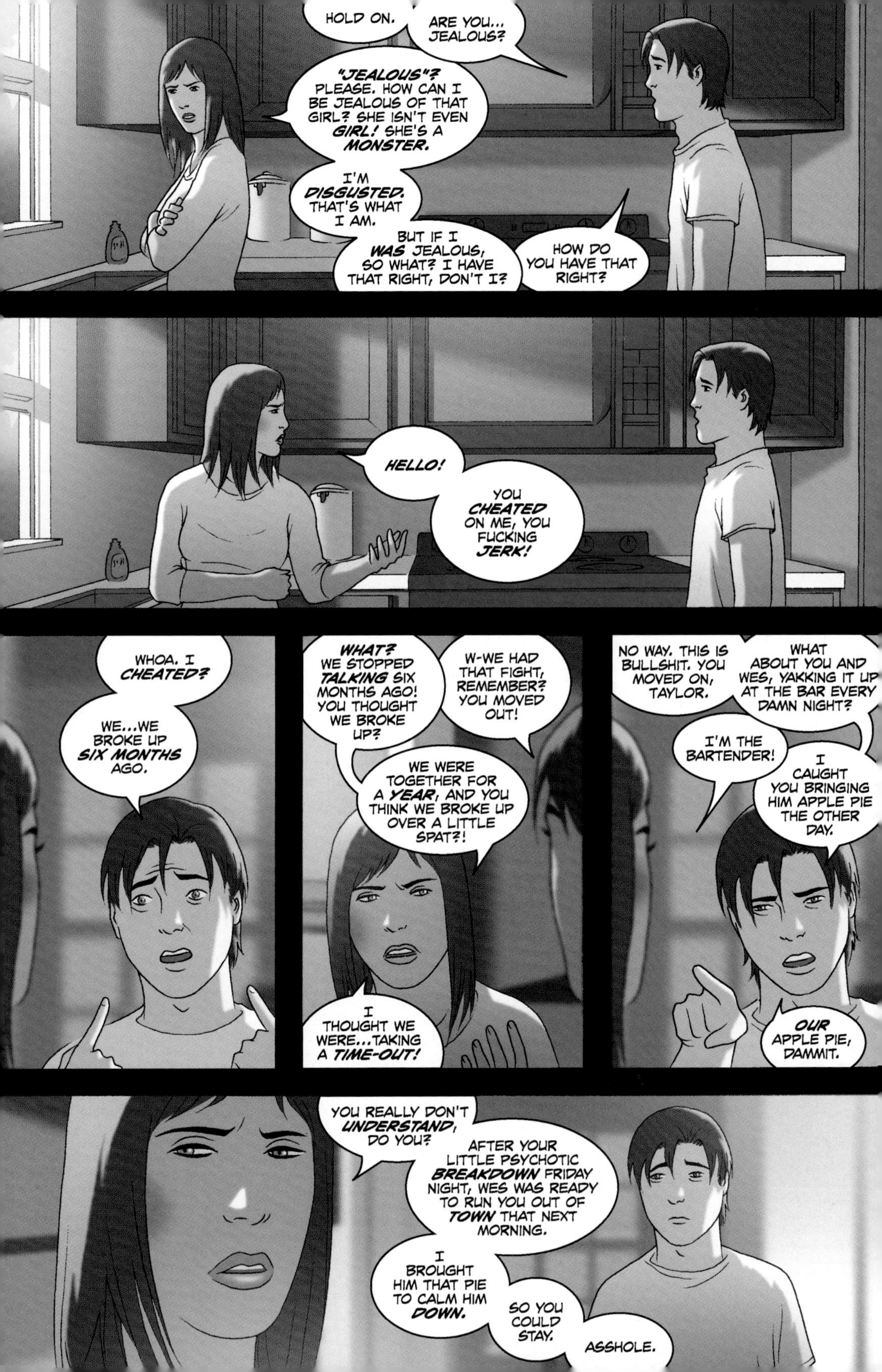
HOLD ON.
ARE YOU... JEALOUS?
"JEALOUS"? PLEASE. HOW CAN I BE JEALOUS OF THAT GIRL? SHE ISN'T EVEN GIRL! SHE'S A MONSTER.
I'M DISGUSTED. THAT'S WHAT I AM.
BUT IF I WAS JEALOUS, SO WHAT? I HAVE THAT RIGHT, DON'T I?
HOW DO YOU HAVE THAT RIGHT?
HELLO!
YOU CHEATED ON ME, YOU FUCKING JERK!
WHOA. I CHEATED?
WE...WE BROKE UP SIX MONTHS AGO.
WHAT? WE STOPPED TALKING SIX MONTHS AGO! YOU THOUGHT WE BROKE UP?
W-WE HAD THAT FIGHT, REMEMBER? YOU MOVED OUT!
WE WERE TOGETHER FOR A YEAR, AND YOU THINK WE BROKE UP OVER A LITTLE SPAT?!
I THOUGHT WE WERE...TAKING A TIME-OUT!
NO WAY. THIS IS BULLSHIT. YOU MOVED ON, TAYLOR.
WHAT ABOUT YOU AND WES, YAKKING IT UP AT THE BAR EVERY DAMN NIGHT?
I'M THE BARTENDER!
I CAUGHT YOU BRINGING HIM APPLE PIE THE OTHER DAY.
OUR APPLE PIE, DAMMIT.
YOU REALLY DON'T UNDERSTAND, DO YOU?
AFTER YOUR LITTLE PSYCHOTIC BREAKDOWN FRIDAY NIGHT, WES WAS READY TO RUN YOU OUT OF TOWN THAT NEXT MORNING.
I BROUGHT HIM THAT PIE TO CALM HIM DOWN.
SO YOU COULD STAY.
ASSHOLE.

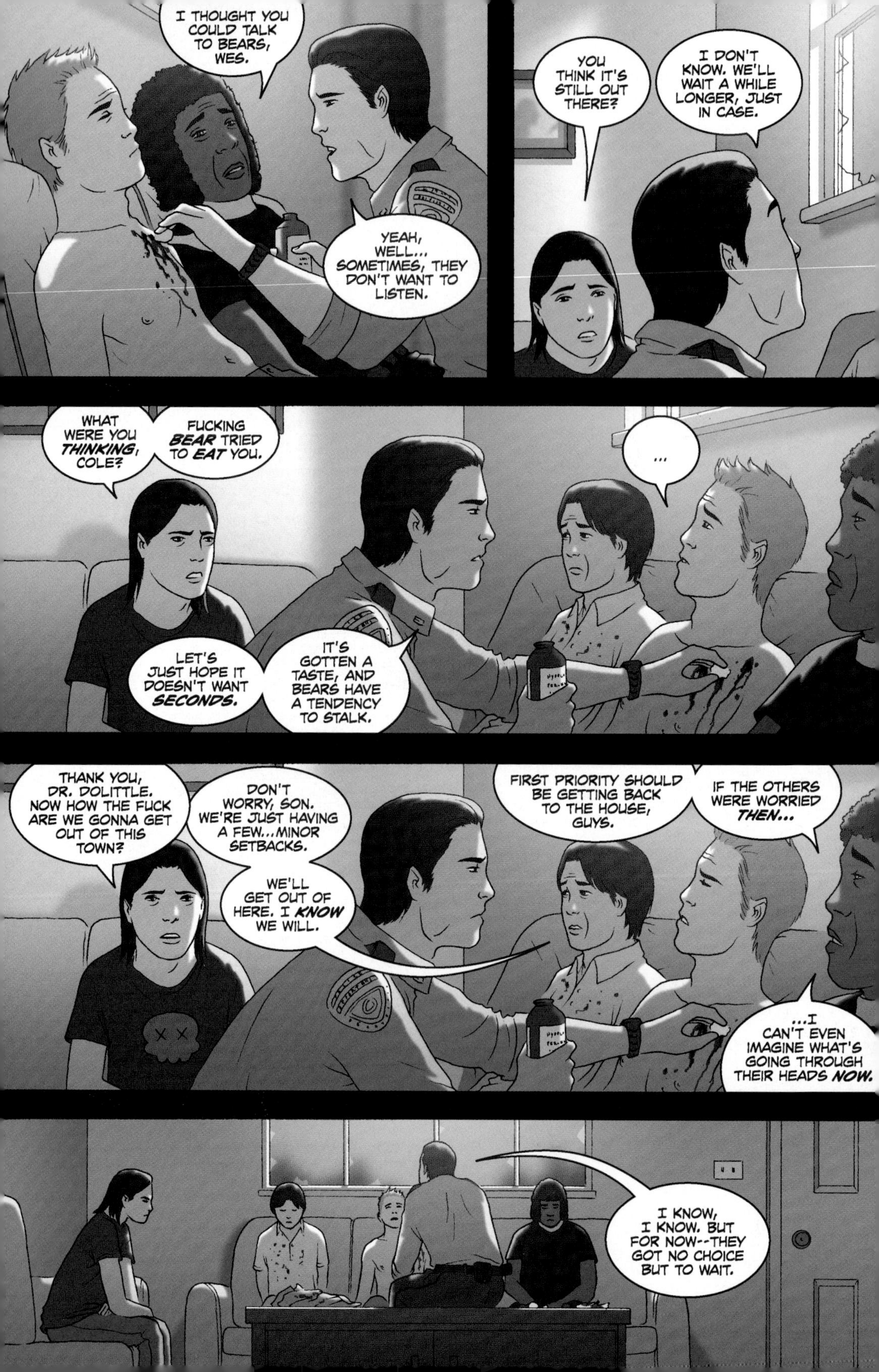
I THOUGHT YOU COULD TALK TO BEARS, WES.
YEAH, WELL... SOMETIMES, THEY DON'T WANT TO LISTEN.
YOU THINK IT'S STILL OUT THERE?
I DON'T KNOW. WE'LL WAIT A WHILE LONGER, JUST IN CASE.
WHAT WERE YOU THINKING, COLE?
FUCKING BEAR TRIED TO EAT YOU.
...
LET'S JUST HOPE IT DOESN'T WANT SECONDS.
IT'S GOTTEN A TASTE, AND BEARS HAVE A TENDENCY TO STALK.
THANK YOU, DR. DOLITTLE. NOW HOW THE FUCK ARE WE GONNA GET OUT OF THIS TOWN?
DON'T WORRY, SON. WE'RE JUST HAVING A FEW...MINOR SETBACKS.
WE'LL GET OUT OF HERE. I KNOW WE WILL.
FIRST PRIORITY SHOULD BE GETTING BACK TO THE HOUSE, GUYS.
IF THE OTHERS WERE WORRIED THEN...
...I CAN'T EVEN IMAGINE WHAT'S GOING THROUGH THEIR HEADS NOW.
I KNOW, I KNOW. BUT FOR NOW--THEY GOT NO CHOICE BUT TO WAIT.

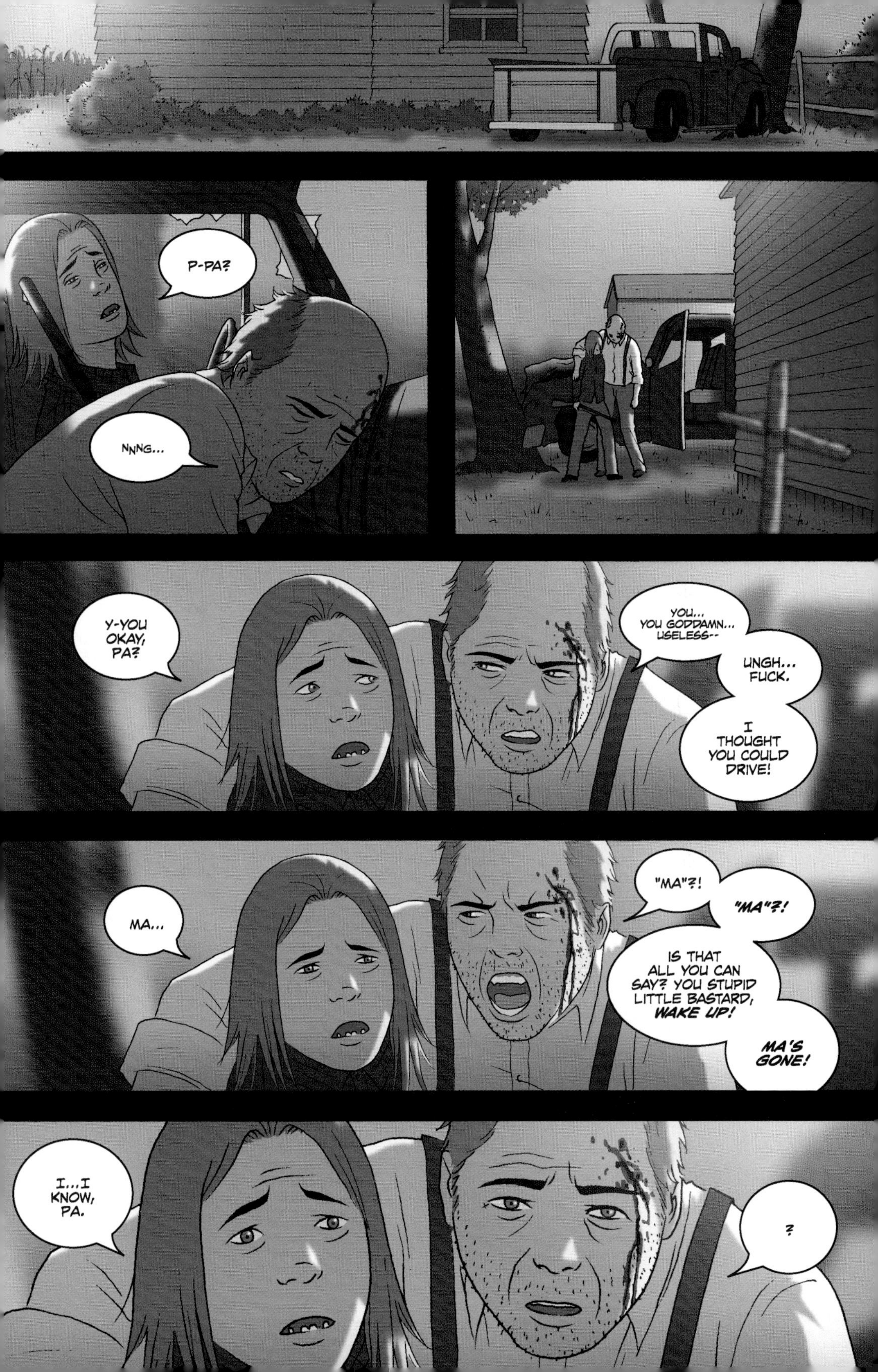
P-PA?
NNNG...
Y-YOU OKAY, PA?
YOU... YOU GODDAMN... USELESS--
UNGH... FUCK.
I THOUGHT YOU COULD DRIVE!
MA...
"MA"?!
"MA"?!
IS THAT ALL YOU CAN SAY? YOU STUPID LITTLE BASTARD, WAKE UP!
MA'S GONE!
I...I KNOW, PA.
?

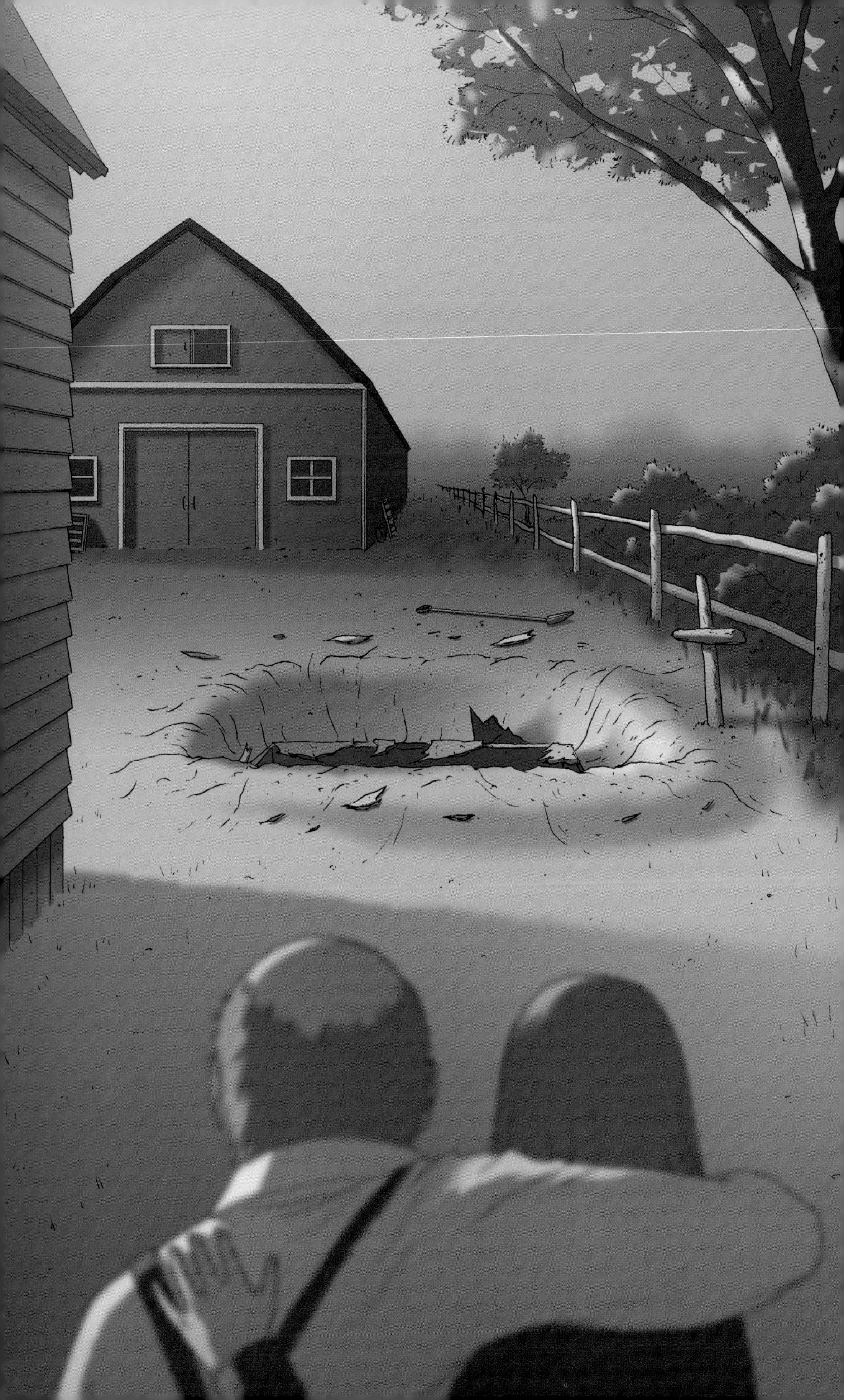

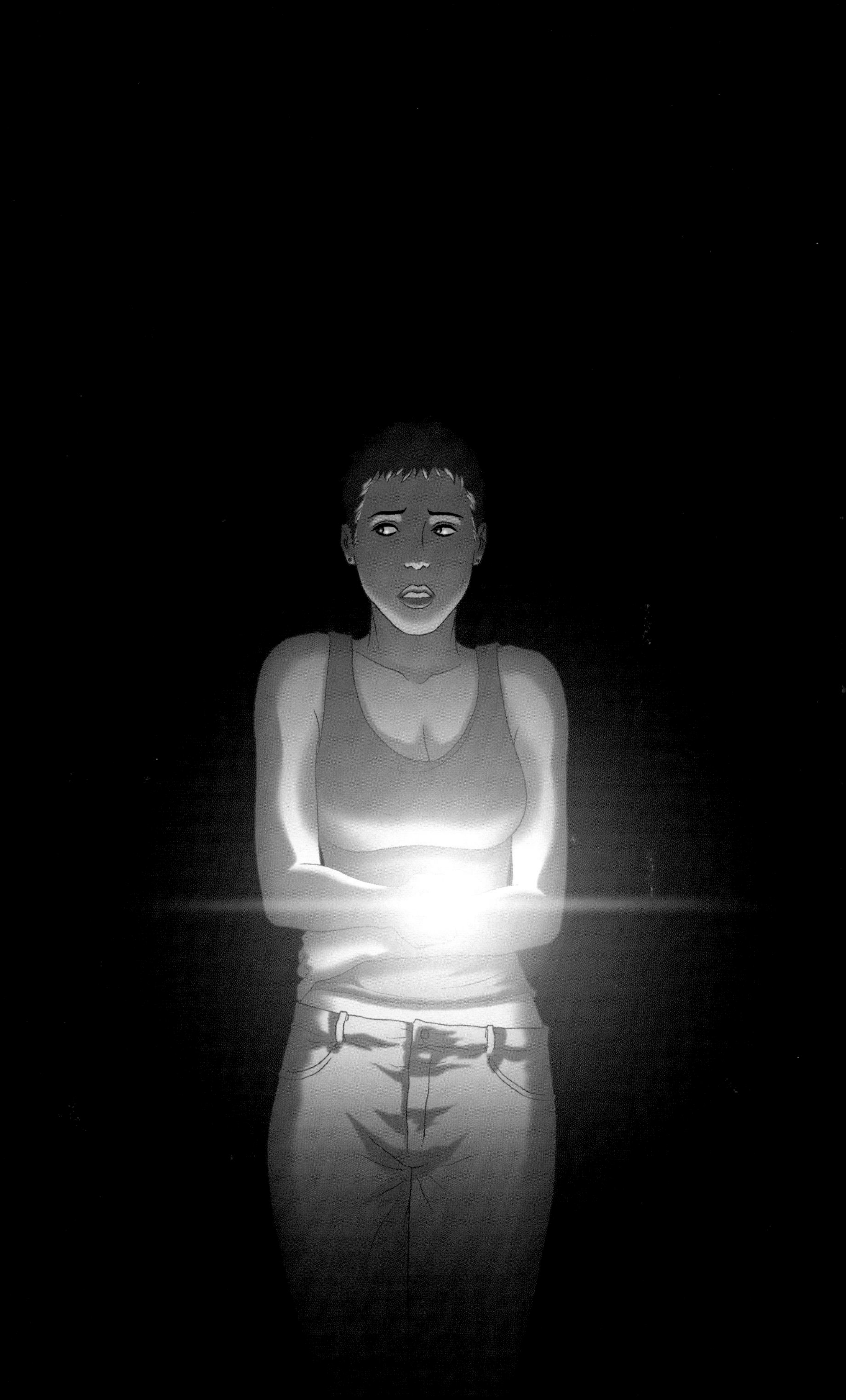

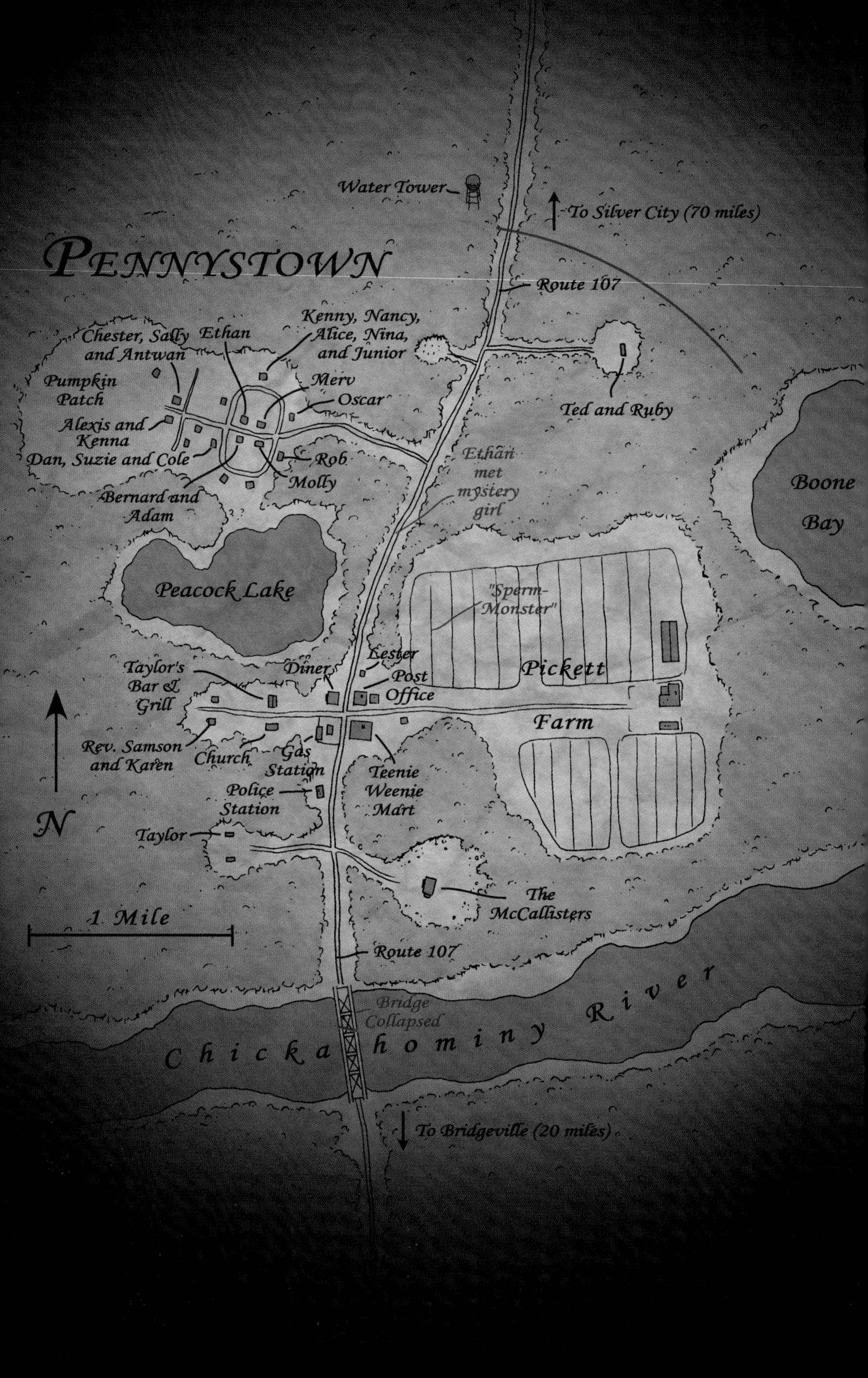

Pennystown
Water Tower
To Silver City (70 miles)
Route 107
Kenny, Nancy, Alice, Nina, and Junior
Chester, Sally and Antwan
Ethan
Pumpkin Patch
Merv
Oscar
Ted and Ruby
Alexis and Kenna
Dan, Suzie and Cole
Rob
Molly
Bernard and Adam
Ethan met mystery girl
Boone Bay
Peacock Lake
"Sperm-Monster"
Lester
Taylor's Bar & Grill
Diner
Post Office
Pickett Farm
Rev. Samson and Karen
Church
Gas Station
Teenie Weenie Mart
Police Station
N
Taylor
The McCallisters
1 Mile
Route 107
Bridge Collapsed
Chickahominy River
To Bridgeville (20 miles)

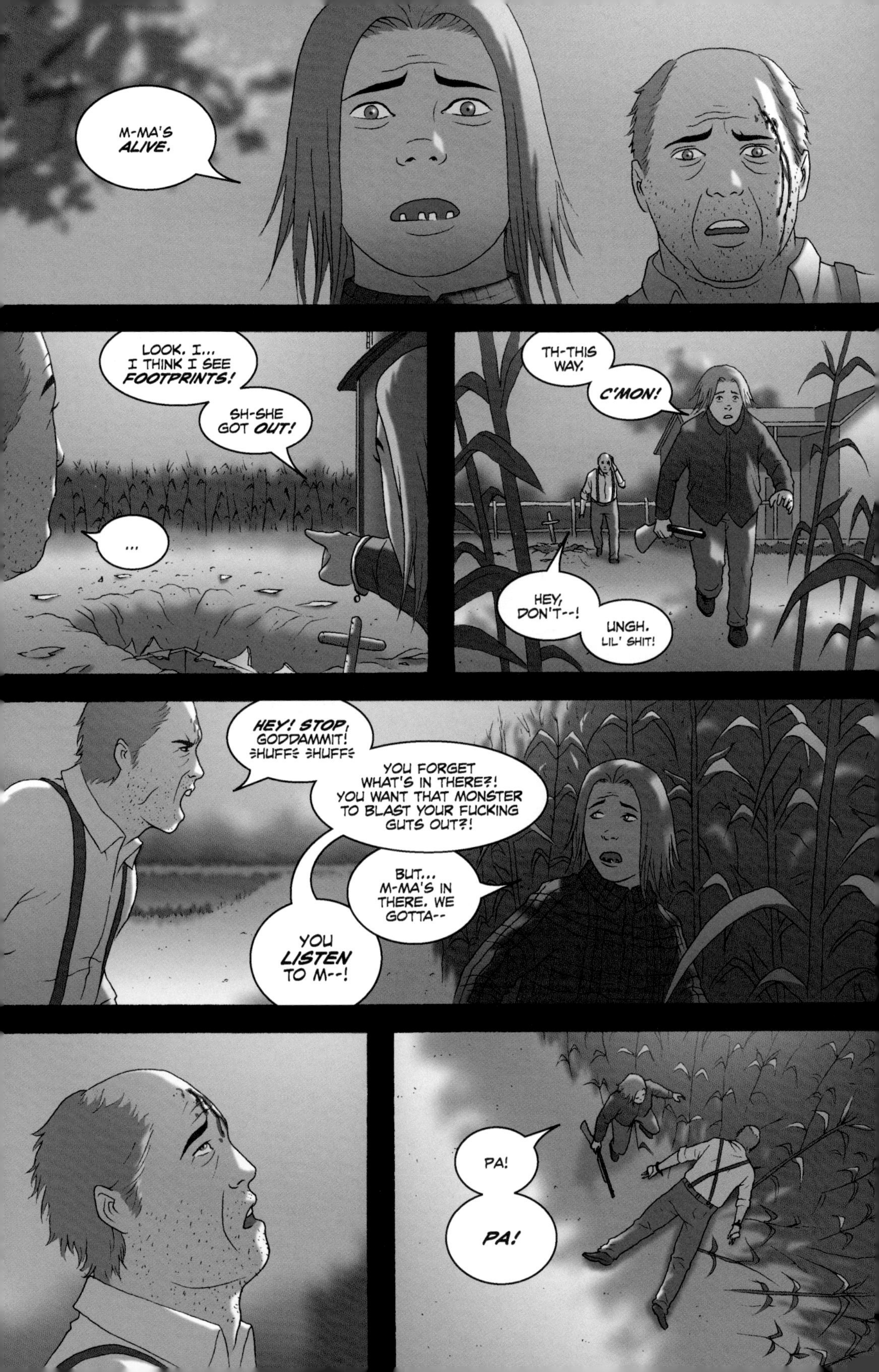
M-MA'S *ALIVE.*
LOOK. I... I THINK I SEE *FOOTPRINTS!*
SH-SHE GOT *OUT!*
...
TH-THIS WAY.
C'MON!
HEY, DON'T--!
UNGH. LIL' SHIT!
HEY! STOP! GODDAMMIT! HUFF HUFF
YOU FORGET WHAT'S IN THERE?! YOU WANT THAT MONSTER TO BLAST YOUR FUCKING GUTS OUT?!
BUT... M-MA'S IN THERE. WE GOTTA--
YOU *LISTEN* TO M--!
PA!
PA!

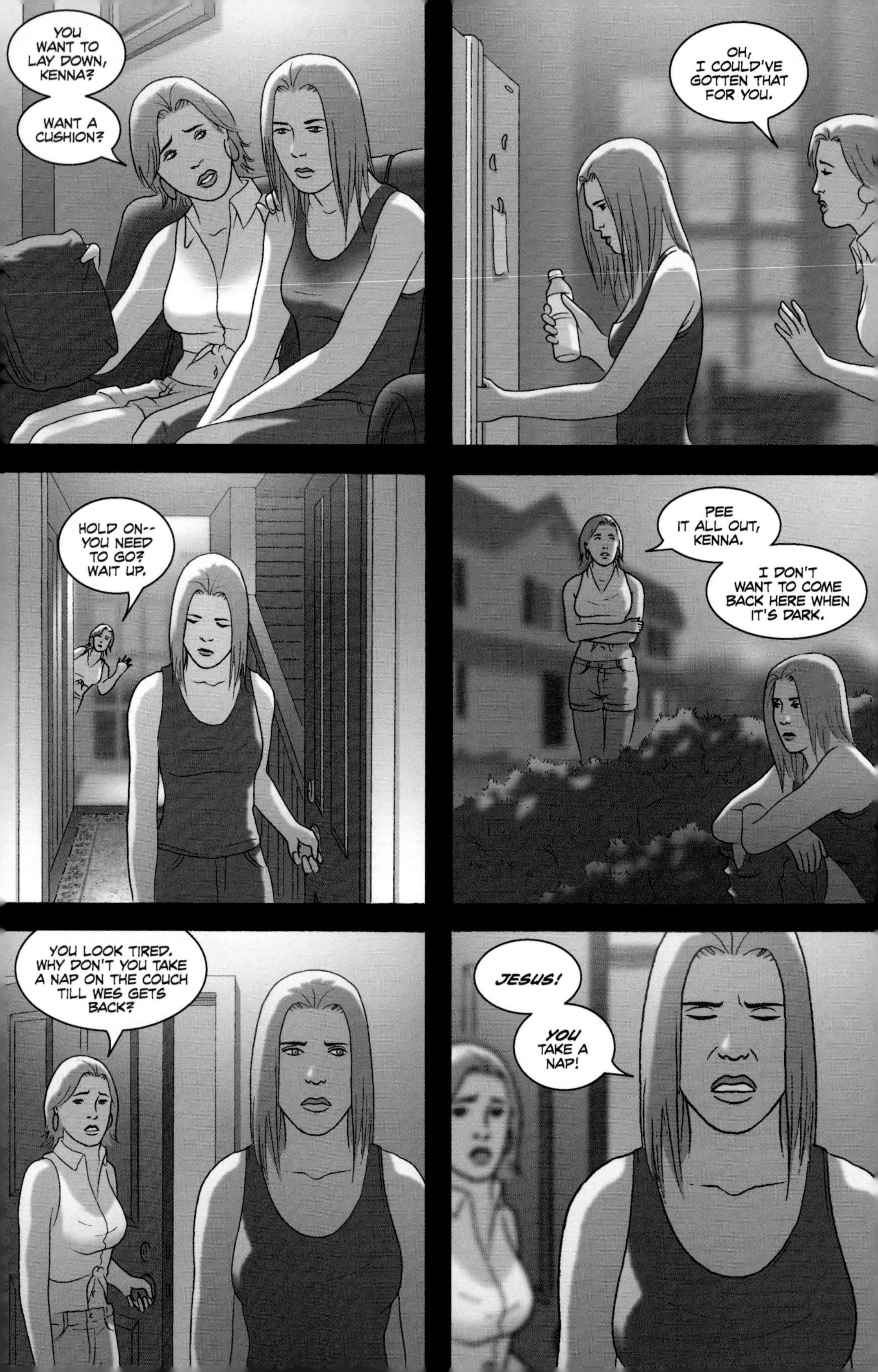
YOU WANT TO LAY DOWN, KENNA?
WANT A CUSHION?
OH, I COULD'VE GOTTEN THAT FOR YOU.
HOLD ON-- YOU NEED TO GO? WAIT UP.
PEE IT ALL OUT, KENNA.
I DON'T WANT TO COME BACK HERE WHEN IT'S DARK.
YOU LOOK TIRED. WHY DON'T YOU TAKE A NAP ON THE COUCH TILL WES GETS BACK?
JESUS!
YOU TAKE A NAP!

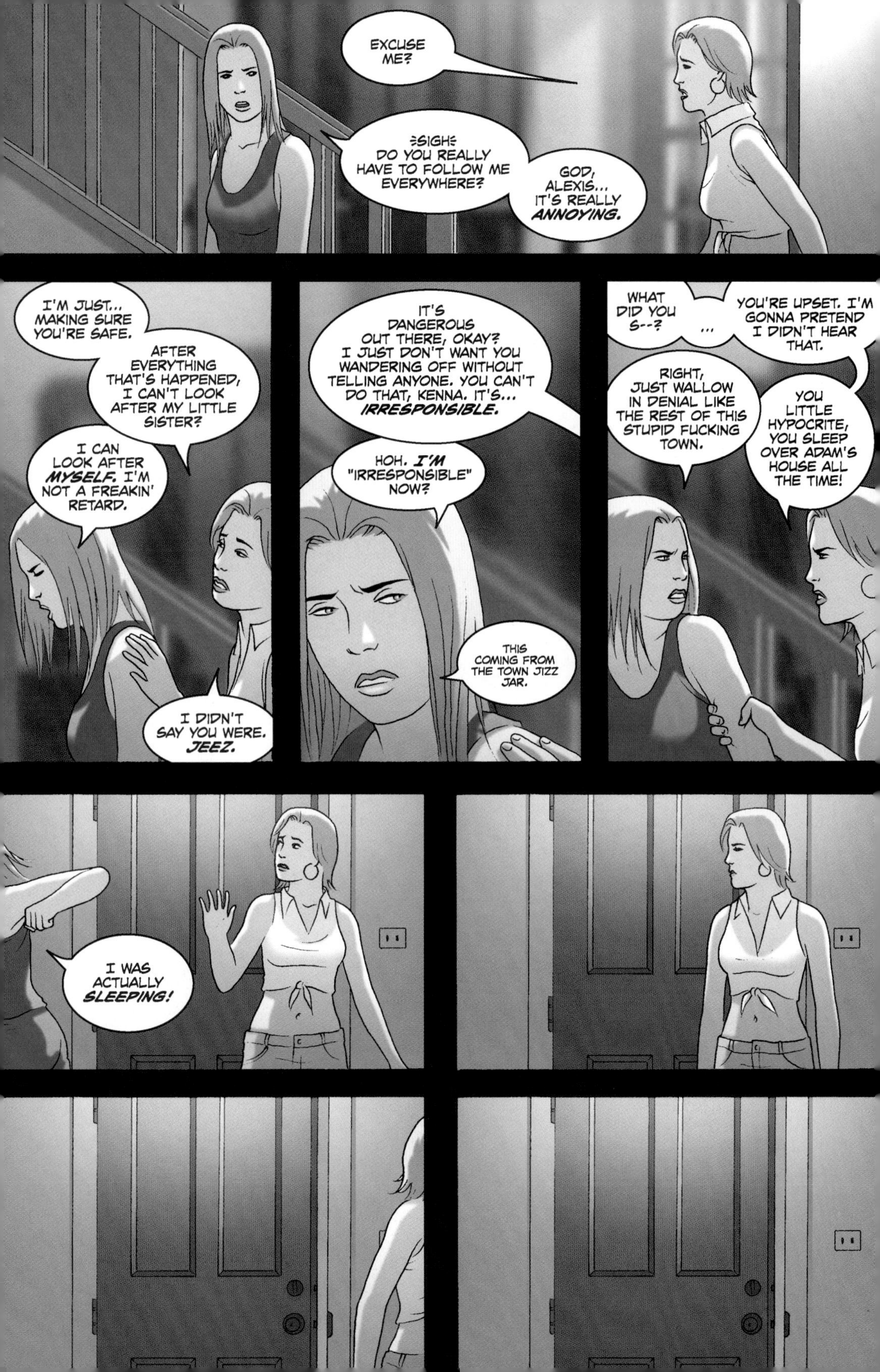

EXCUSE ME?
≈SIGH≈ DO YOU REALLY HAVE TO FOLLOW ME EVERYWHERE?
GOD, ALEXIS... IT'S REALLY ANNOYING.
I'M JUST... MAKING SURE YOU'RE SAFE.
AFTER EVERYTHING THAT'S HAPPENED, I CAN'T LOOK AFTER MY LITTLE SISTER?
I CAN LOOK AFTER MYSELF. I'M NOT A FREAKIN' RETARD.
I DIDN'T SAY YOU WERE. JEEZ.
IT'S DANGEROUS OUT THERE, OKAY? I JUST DON'T WANT YOU WANDERING OFF WITHOUT TELLING ANYONE. YOU CAN'T DO THAT, KENNA. IT'S... IRRESPONSIBLE.
HOH. I'M "IRRESPONSIBLE" NOW?
THIS COMING FROM THE TOWN JIZZ JAR.
WHAT DID YOU S--?
...
YOU'RE UPSET. I'M GONNA PRETEND I DIDN'T HEAR THAT.
RIGHT, JUST WALLOW IN DENIAL LIKE THE REST OF THIS STUPID FUCKING TOWN.
YOU LITTLE HYPOCRITE, YOU SLEEP OVER ADAM'S HOUSE ALL THE TIME!
I WAS ACTUALLY SLEEPING!

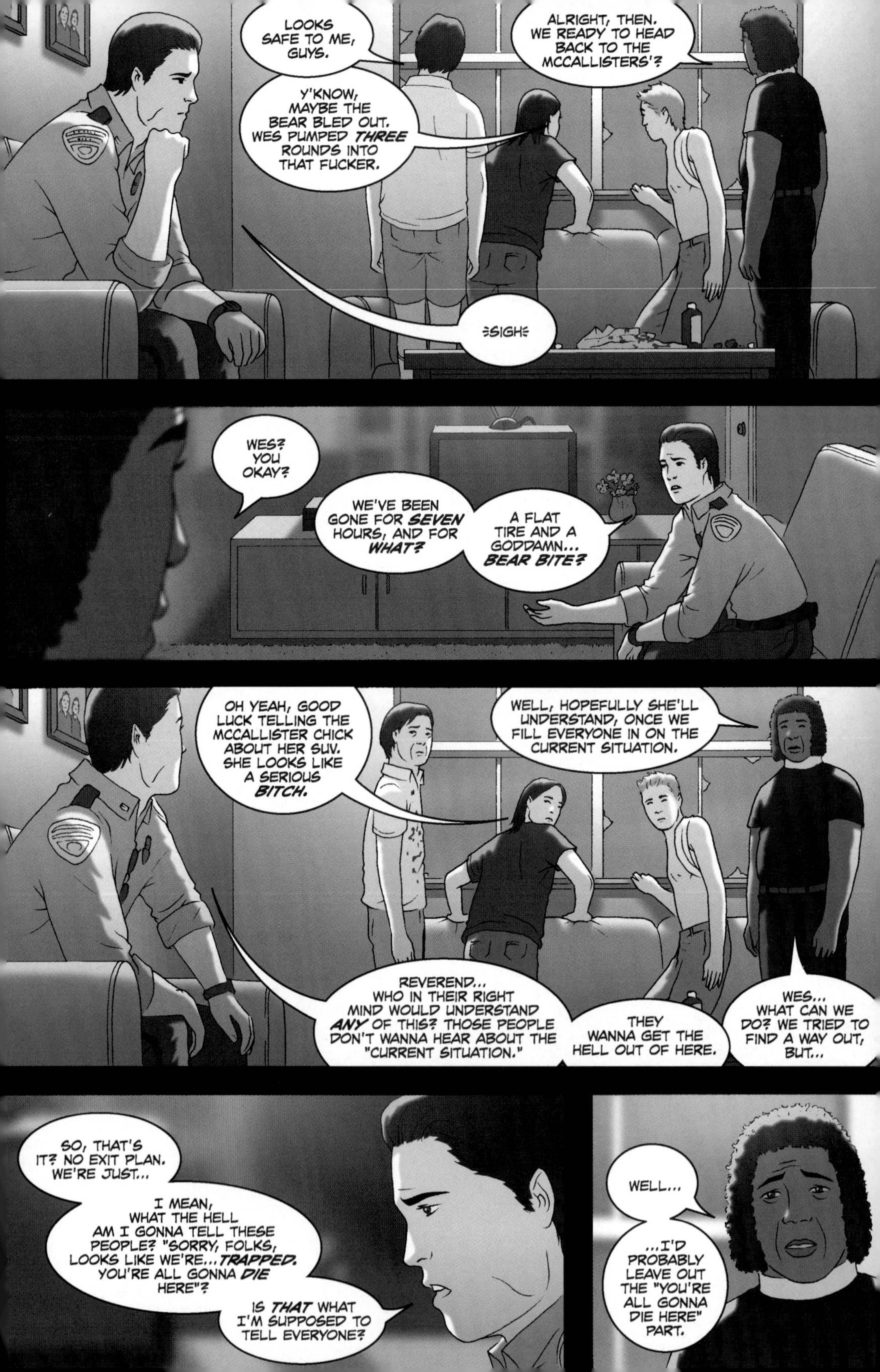
LOOKS SAFE TO ME, GUYS.
ALRIGHT, THEN. WE READY TO HEAD BACK TO THE MCCALLISTERS'?
Y'KNOW, MAYBE THE BEAR BLED OUT. WES PUMPED THREE ROUNDS INTO THAT FUCKER.
=SIGH=
WES? YOU OKAY?
WE'VE BEEN GONE FOR SEVEN HOURS, AND FOR WHAT?
A FLAT TIRE AND A GODDAMN... BEAR BITE?
OH YEAH, GOOD LUCK TELLING THE MCCALLISTER CHICK ABOUT HER SUV. SHE LOOKS LIKE A SERIOUS BITCH.
WELL, HOPEFULLY SHE'LL UNDERSTAND, ONCE WE FILL EVERYONE IN ON THE CURRENT SITUATION.
REVEREND... WHO IN THEIR RIGHT MIND WOULD UNDERSTAND ANY OF THIS? THOSE PEOPLE DON'T WANNA HEAR ABOUT THE "CURRENT SITUATION."
THEY WANNA GET THE HELL OUT OF HERE.
WES... WHAT CAN WE DO? WE TRIED TO FIND A WAY OUT, BUT...
SO, THAT'S IT? NO EXIT PLAN. WE'RE JUST...
I MEAN, WHAT THE HELL AM I GONNA TELL THESE PEOPLE? "SORRY, FOLKS, LOOKS LIKE WE'RE... TRAPPED. YOU'RE ALL GONNA DIE HERE"?
IS THAT WHAT I'M SUPPOSED TO TELL EVERYONE?
WELL...
...I'D PROBABLY LEAVE OUT THE "YOU'RE ALL GONNA DIE HERE" PART.

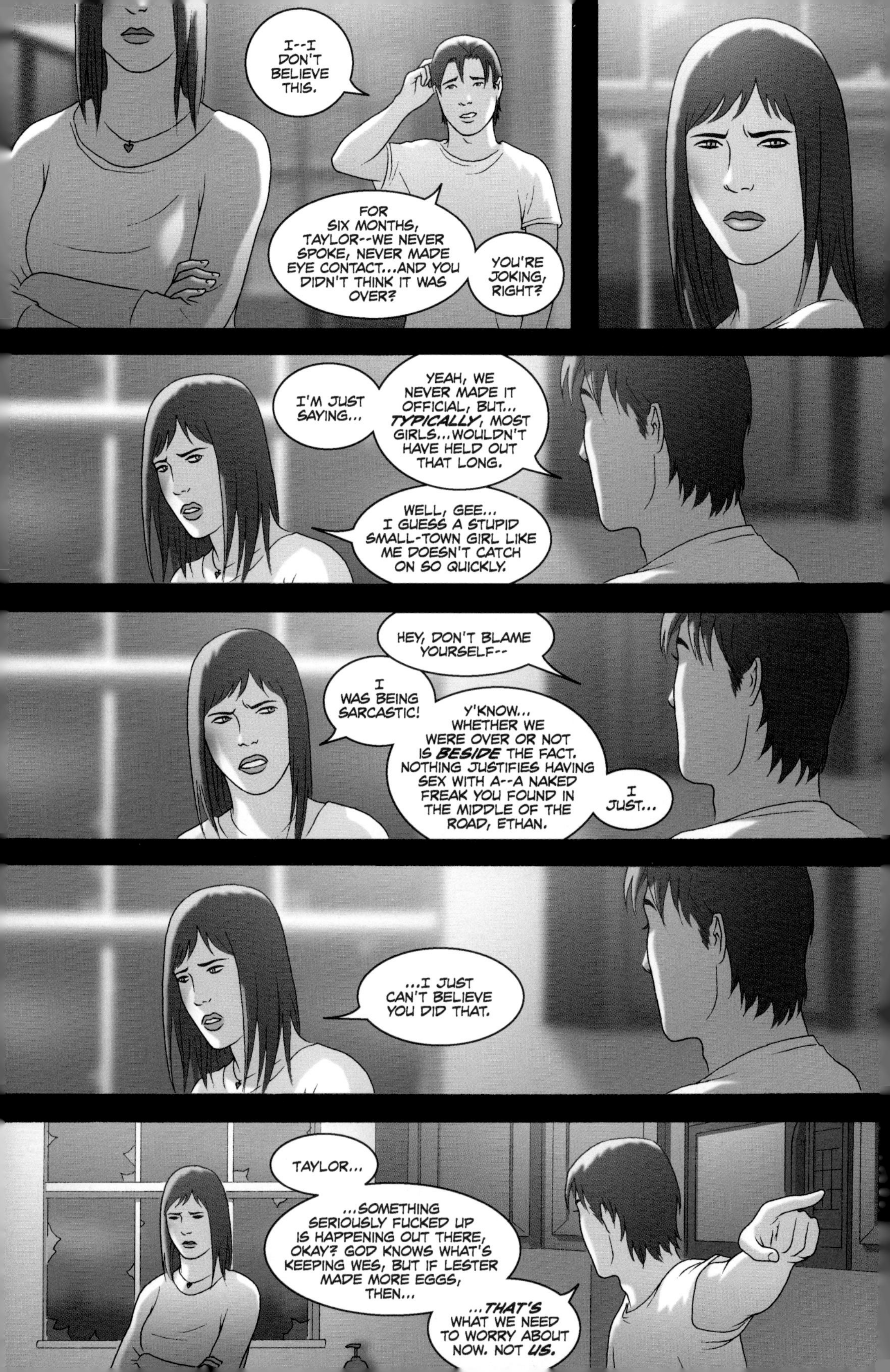

I--I DON'T BELIEVE THIS.
FOR SIX MONTHS, TAYLOR--WE NEVER SPOKE, NEVER MADE EYE CONTACT...AND YOU DIDN'T THINK IT WAS OVER?
YOU'RE JOKING, RIGHT?
I'M JUST SAYING...
YEAH, WE NEVER MADE IT OFFICIAL, BUT... *TYPICALLY*, MOST GIRLS...WOULDN'T HAVE HELD OUT THAT LONG.
WELL, GEE... I GUESS A STUPID SMALL-TOWN GIRL LIKE ME DOESN'T CATCH ON SO QUICKLY.
HEY, DON'T BLAME YOURSELF--
I WAS BEING SARCASTIC!
Y'KNOW... WHETHER WE WERE OVER OR NOT IS *BESIDE* THE FACT. NOTHING JUSTIFIES HAVING SEX WITH A--A NAKED FREAK YOU FOUND IN THE MIDDLE OF THE ROAD, ETHAN.
I JUST...
...I JUST CAN'T BELIEVE YOU DID THAT.
TAYLOR...
...SOMETHING SERIOUSLY FUCKED UP IS HAPPENING OUT THERE, OKAY? GOD KNOWS WHAT'S KEEPING WES, BUT IF LESTER MADE MORE EGGS, THEN...
...*THAT'S* WHAT WE NEED TO WORRY ABOUT NOW. NOT *US*.

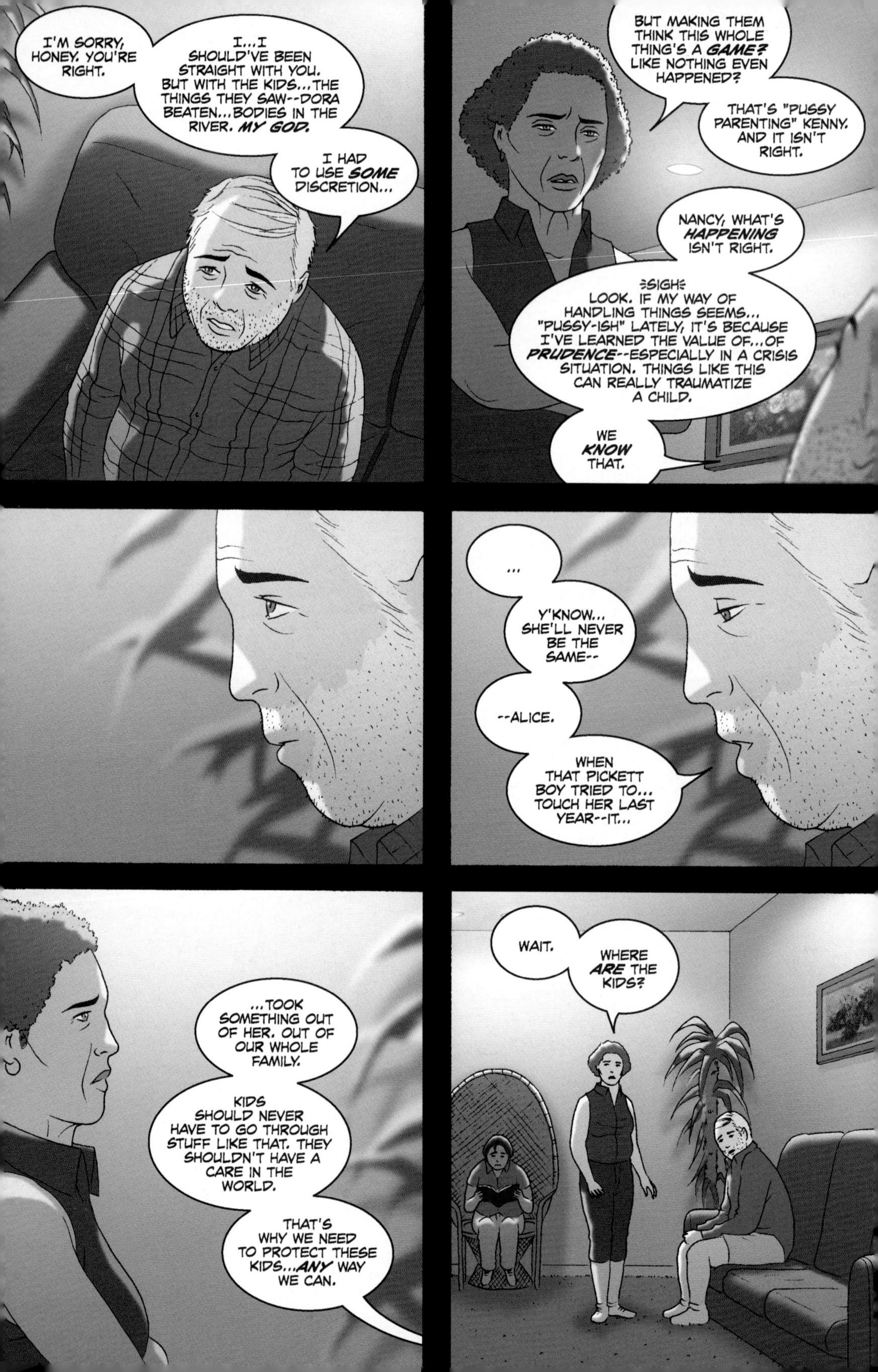
I'M SORRY, HONEY. YOU'RE RIGHT.
I...I SHOULD'VE BEEN STRAIGHT WITH YOU. BUT WITH THE KIDS...THE THINGS THEY SAW--DORA BEATEN...BODIES IN THE RIVER. MY GOD.
I HAD TO USE SOME DISCRETION...
BUT MAKING THEM THINK THIS WHOLE THING'S A GAME? LIKE NOTHING EVEN HAPPENED?
THAT'S "PUSSY PARENTING" KENNY. AND IT ISN'T RIGHT.
NANCY, WHAT'S HAPPENING ISN'T RIGHT.
SIGH
LOOK. IF MY WAY OF HANDLING THINGS SEEMS... "PUSSY-ISH" LATELY, IT'S BECAUSE I'VE LEARNED THE VALUE OF...OF PRUDENCE--ESPECIALLY IN A CRISIS SITUATION. THINGS LIKE THIS CAN REALLY TRAUMATIZE A CHILD.
WE KNOW THAT.
...
Y'KNOW... SHE'LL NEVER BE THE SAME--
--ALICE.
WHEN THAT PICKETT BOY TRIED TO... TOUCH HER LAST YEAR--IT...
...TOOK SOMETHING OUT OF HER. OUT OF OUR WHOLE FAMILY.
KIDS SHOULD NEVER HAVE TO GO THROUGH STUFF LIKE THAT. THEY SHOULDN'T HAVE A CARE IN THE WORLD.
THAT'S WHY WE NEED TO PROTECT THESE KIDS...ANY WAY WE CAN.
WAIT.
WHERE ARE THE KIDS?

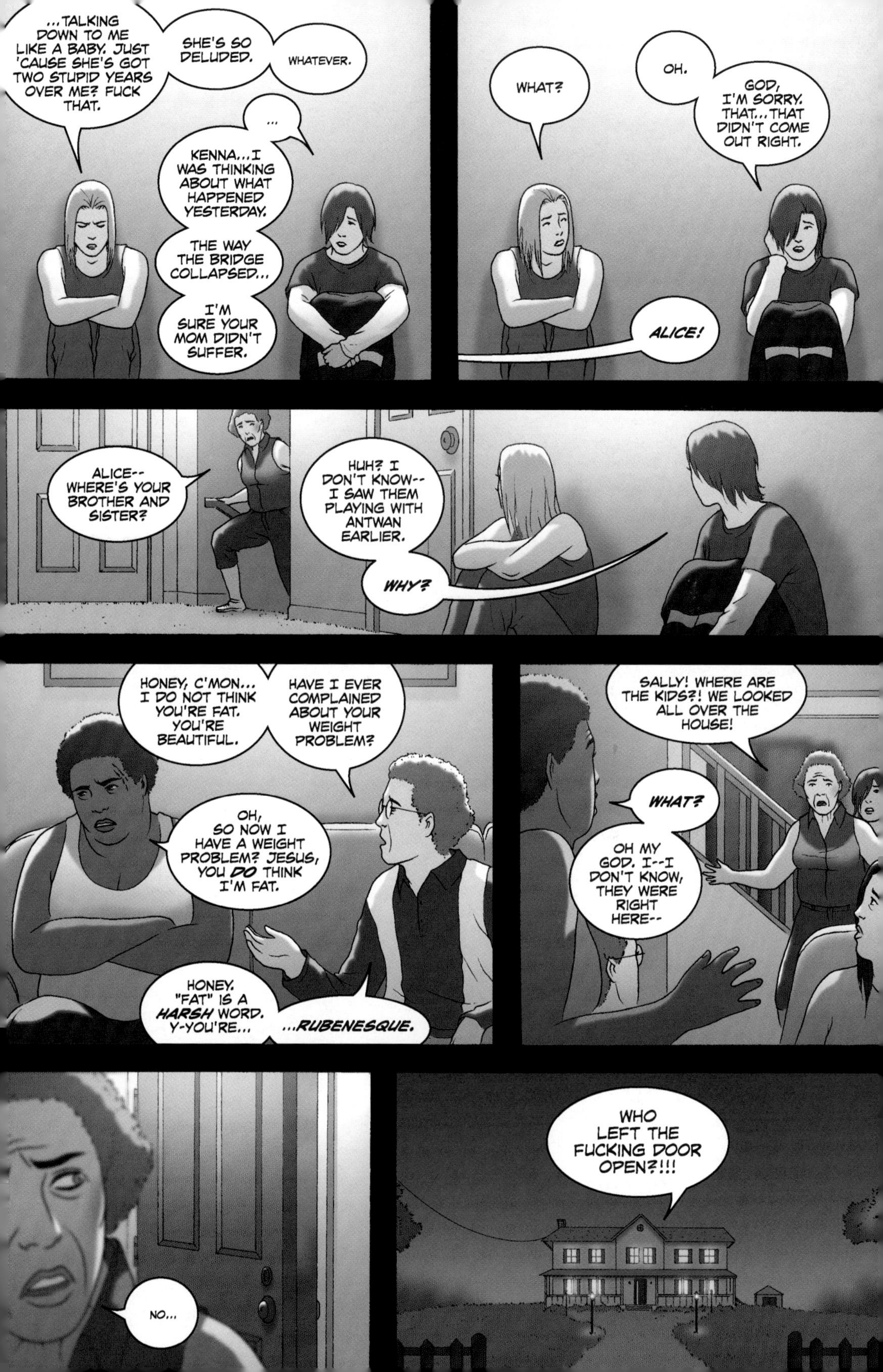
...TALKING DOWN TO ME LIKE A BABY. JUST 'CAUSE SHE'S GOT TWO STUPID YEARS OVER ME? FUCK THAT.
SHE'S SO DELUDED.
WHATEVER.
...
KENNA...I WAS THINKING ABOUT WHAT HAPPENED YESTERDAY.
THE WAY THE BRIDGE COLLAPSED...
I'M SURE YOUR MOM DIDN'T SUFFER.
WHAT?
OH.
GOD, I'M SORRY. THAT...THAT DIDN'T COME OUT RIGHT.
ALICE!
ALICE-- WHERE'S YOUR BROTHER AND SISTER?
HUH? I DON'T KNOW-- I SAW THEM PLAYING WITH ANTWAN EARLIER.
WHY?
HONEY, C'MON... I DO NOT THINK YOU'RE FAT. YOU'RE BEAUTIFUL.
HAVE I EVER COMPLAINED ABOUT YOUR WEIGHT PROBLEM?
OH, SO NOW I HAVE A WEIGHT PROBLEM? JESUS, YOU DO THINK I'M FAT.
HONEY. "FAT" IS A HARSH WORD. Y-YOU'RE...
...RUBENESQUE.
SALLY! WHERE ARE THE KIDS?! WE LOOKED ALL OVER THE HOUSE!
WHAT?
OH MY GOD. I--I DON'T KNOW, THEY WERE RIGHT HERE--
NO...
WHO LEFT THE FUCKING DOOR OPEN?!!!

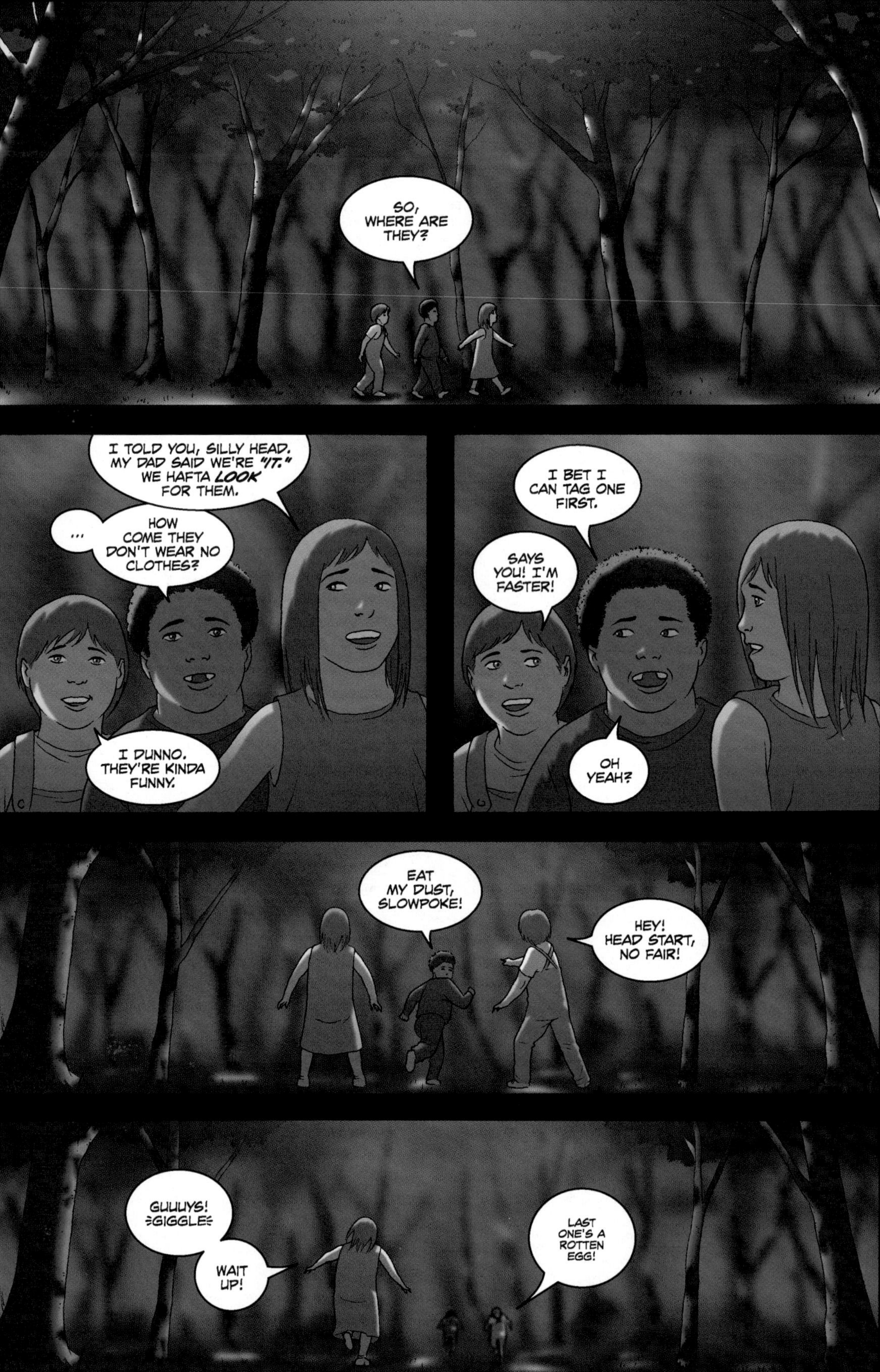
SO, WHERE ARE THEY?
I TOLD YOU, SILLY HEAD. MY DAD SAID WE'RE "IT." WE HAFTA LOOK FOR THEM.
...
HOW COME THEY DON'T WEAR NO CLOTHES?
I DUNNO. THEY'RE KINDA FUNNY.
I BET I CAN TAG ONE FIRST.
SAYS YOU! I'M FASTER!
OH YEAH?
EAT MY DUST, SLOWPOKE!
HEY! HEAD START, NO FAIR!
GUUUYS! GIGGLE
WAIT UP!
LAST ONE'S A ROTTEN EGG!

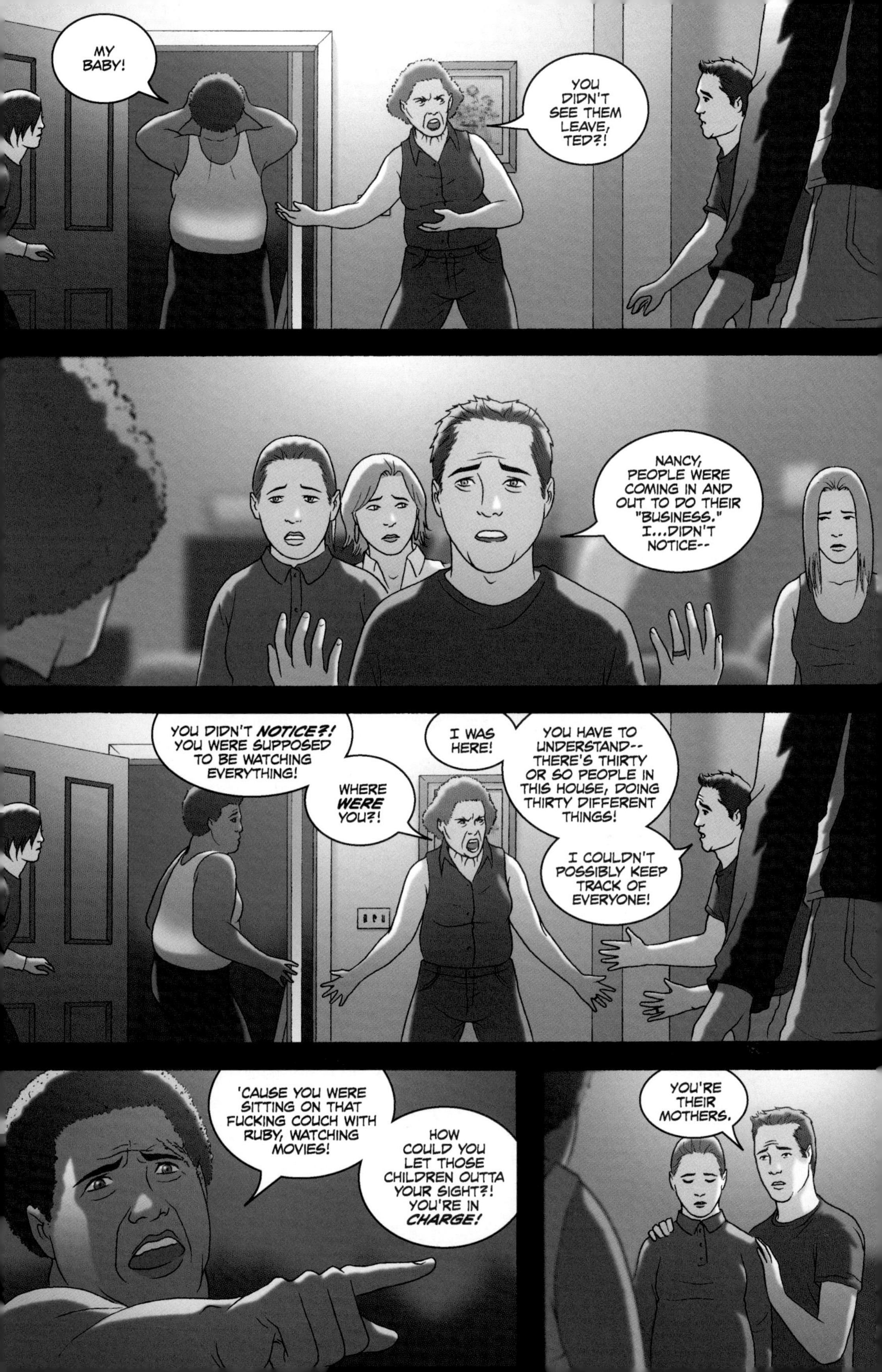
MY BABY!
YOU DIDN'T SEE THEM LEAVE, TED?!
NANCY, PEOPLE WERE COMING IN AND OUT TO DO THEIR "BUSINESS." I...DIDN'T NOTICE--
YOU DIDN'T *NOTICE?!* YOU WERE SUPPOSED TO BE WATCHING EVERYTHING!
WHERE *WERE* YOU?!
I WAS HERE!
YOU HAVE TO UNDERSTAND-- THERE'S THIRTY OR SO PEOPLE IN THIS HOUSE, DOING THIRTY DIFFERENT THINGS!
I COULDN'T POSSIBLY KEEP TRACK OF EVERYONE!
'CAUSE YOU WERE SITTING ON THAT FUCKING COUCH WITH RUBY, WATCHING MOVIES!
HOW COULD YOU LET THOSE CHILDREN OUTTA YOUR SIGHT?! YOU'RE IN *CHARGE!*
YOU'RE THEIR MOTHERS.

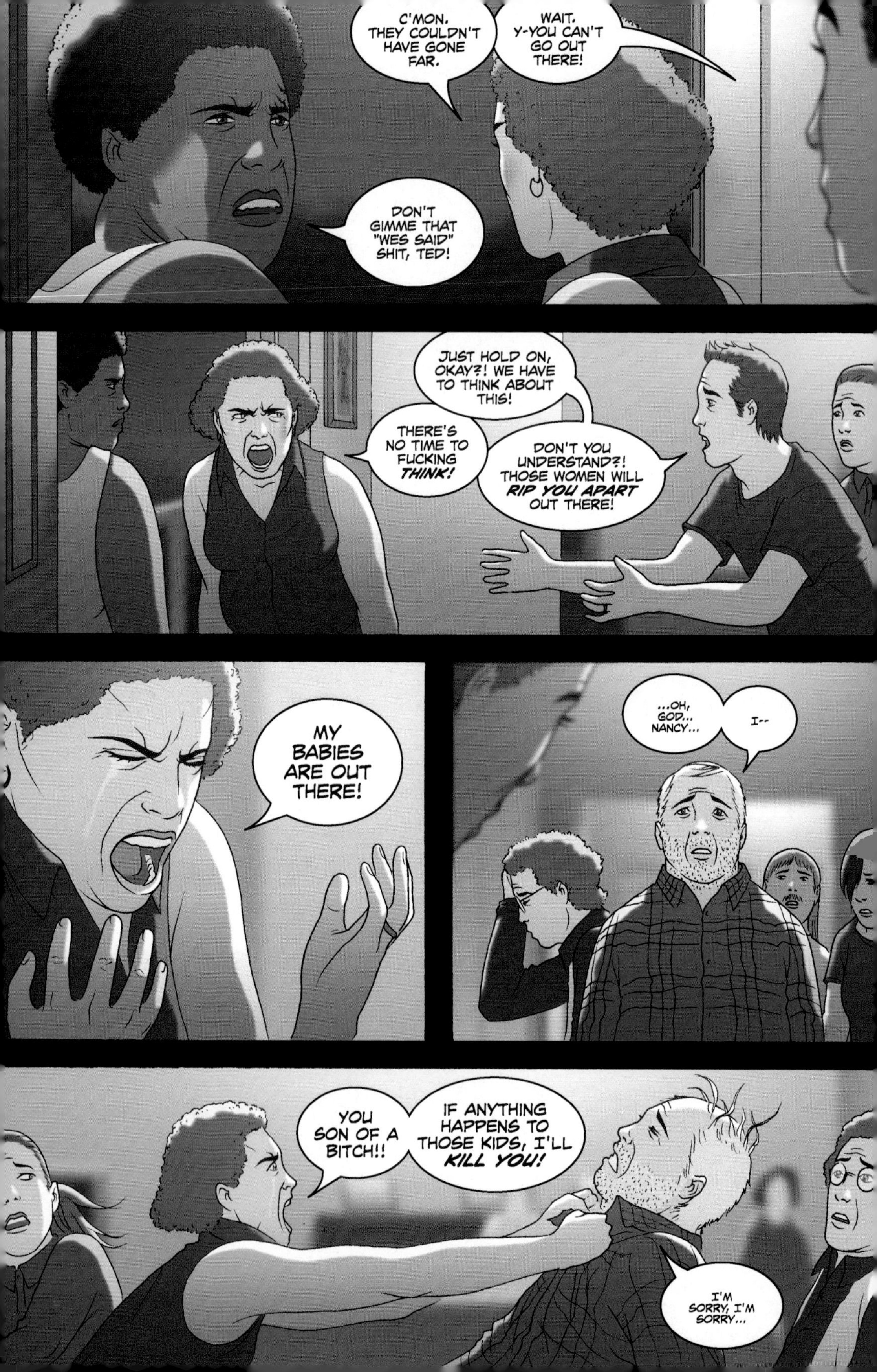
C'MON. THEY COULDN'T HAVE GONE FAR.
WAIT. Y-YOU CAN'T GO OUT THERE!
DON'T GIMME THAT "WES SAID" SHIT, TED!
JUST HOLD ON, OKAY?! WE HAVE TO THINK ABOUT THIS!
THERE'S NO TIME TO FUCKING *THINK!*
DON'T YOU UNDERSTAND?! THOSE WOMEN WILL *RIP YOU APART* OUT THERE!
MY BABIES ARE OUT THERE!
...OH, GOD... NANCY...
I--
YOU SON OF A BITCH!!
IF ANYTHING HAPPENS TO THOSE KIDS, I'LL *KILL YOU!*
I'M SORRY, I'M SORRY...

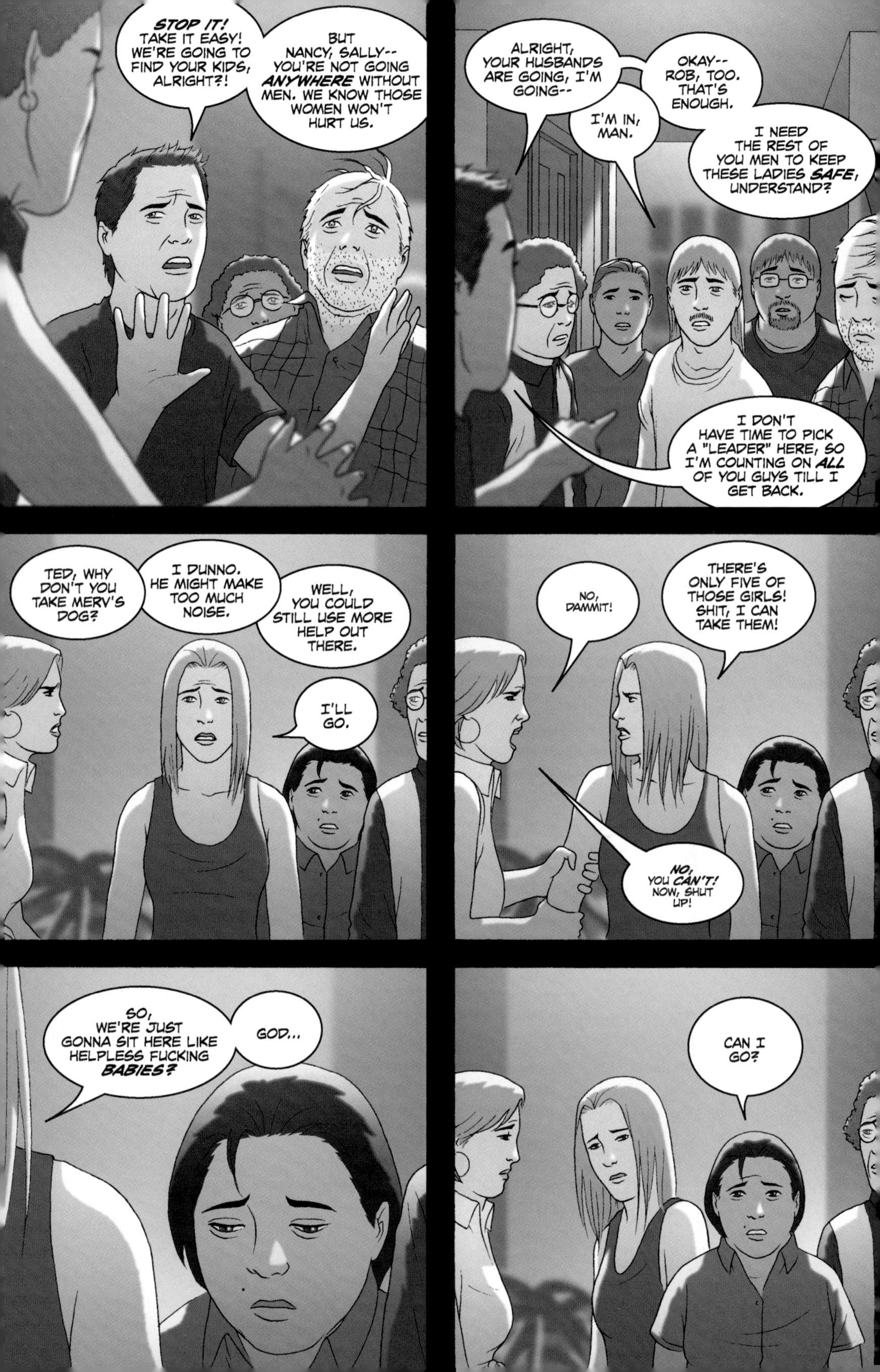
STOP IT! TAKE IT EASY! WE'RE GOING TO FIND YOUR KIDS, ALRIGHT?!
BUT NANCY, SALLY-- YOU'RE NOT GOING ANYWHERE WITHOUT MEN. WE KNOW THOSE WOMEN WON'T HURT US.
ALRIGHT, YOUR HUSBANDS ARE GOING, I'M GOING--
I'M IN, MAN.
OKAY-- ROB, TOO. THAT'S ENOUGH.
I NEED THE REST OF YOU MEN TO KEEP THESE LADIES SAFE, UNDERSTAND?
I DON'T HAVE TIME TO PICK A "LEADER" HERE, SO I'M COUNTING ON ALL OF YOU GUYS TILL I GET BACK.
TED, WHY DON'T YOU TAKE MERV'S DOG?
I DUNNO. HE MIGHT MAKE TOO MUCH NOISE.
WELL, YOU COULD STILL USE MORE HELP OUT THERE.
I'LL GO.
NO, DAMMIT!
THERE'S ONLY FIVE OF THOSE GIRLS! SHIT, I CAN TAKE THEM!
NO, YOU CAN'T! NOW, SHUT UP!
SO, WE'RE JUST GONNA SIT HERE LIKE HELPLESS FUCKING BABIES?
GOD...
CAN I GO?

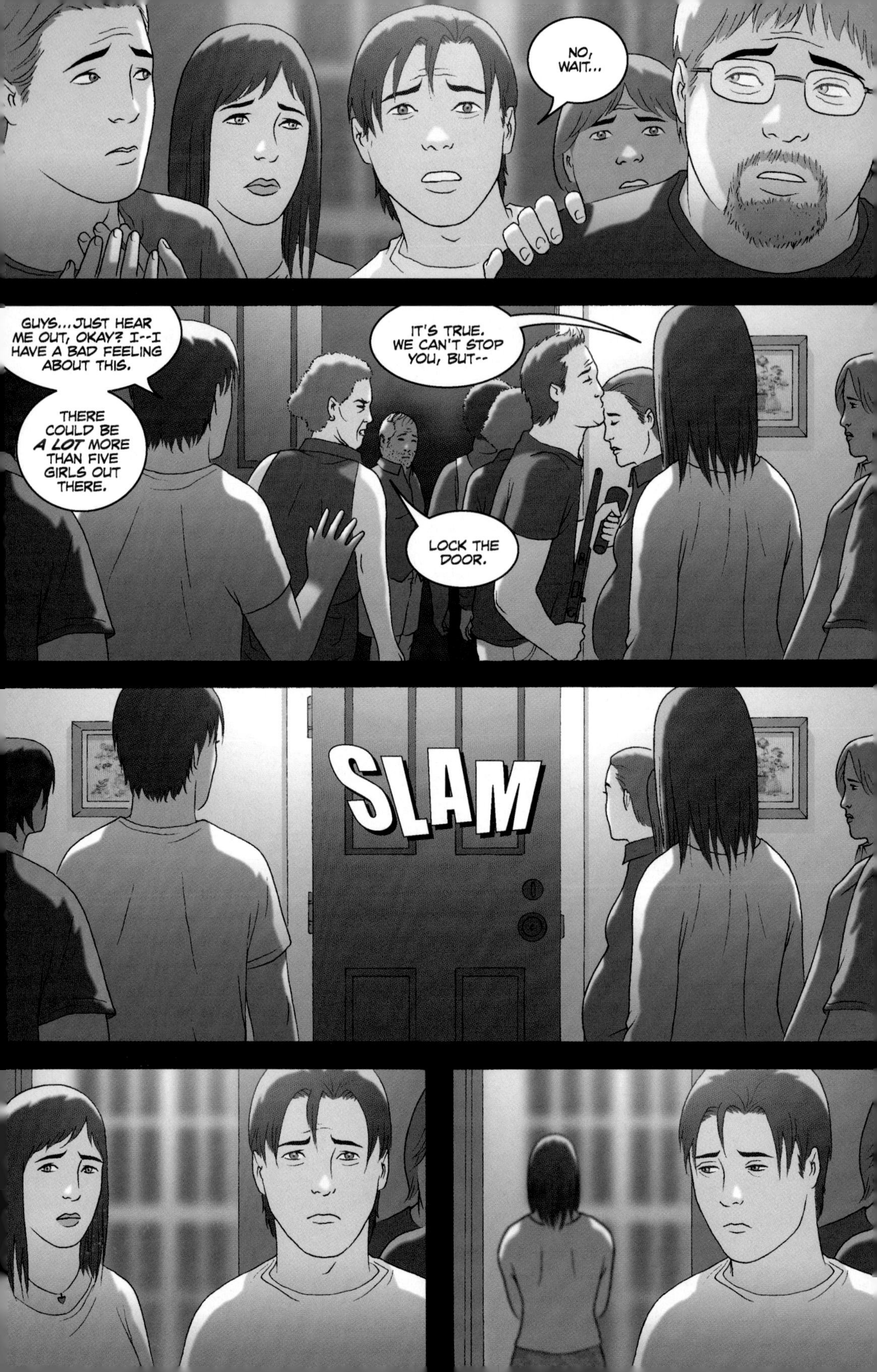
NO, WAIT...
GUYS... JUST HEAR ME OUT, OKAY? I--I HAVE A BAD FEELING ABOUT THIS.
THERE COULD BE *A LOT* MORE THAN FIVE GIRLS OUT THERE.
IT'S TRUE. WE CAN'T STOP YOU, BUT--
LOCK THE DOOR.
SLAM

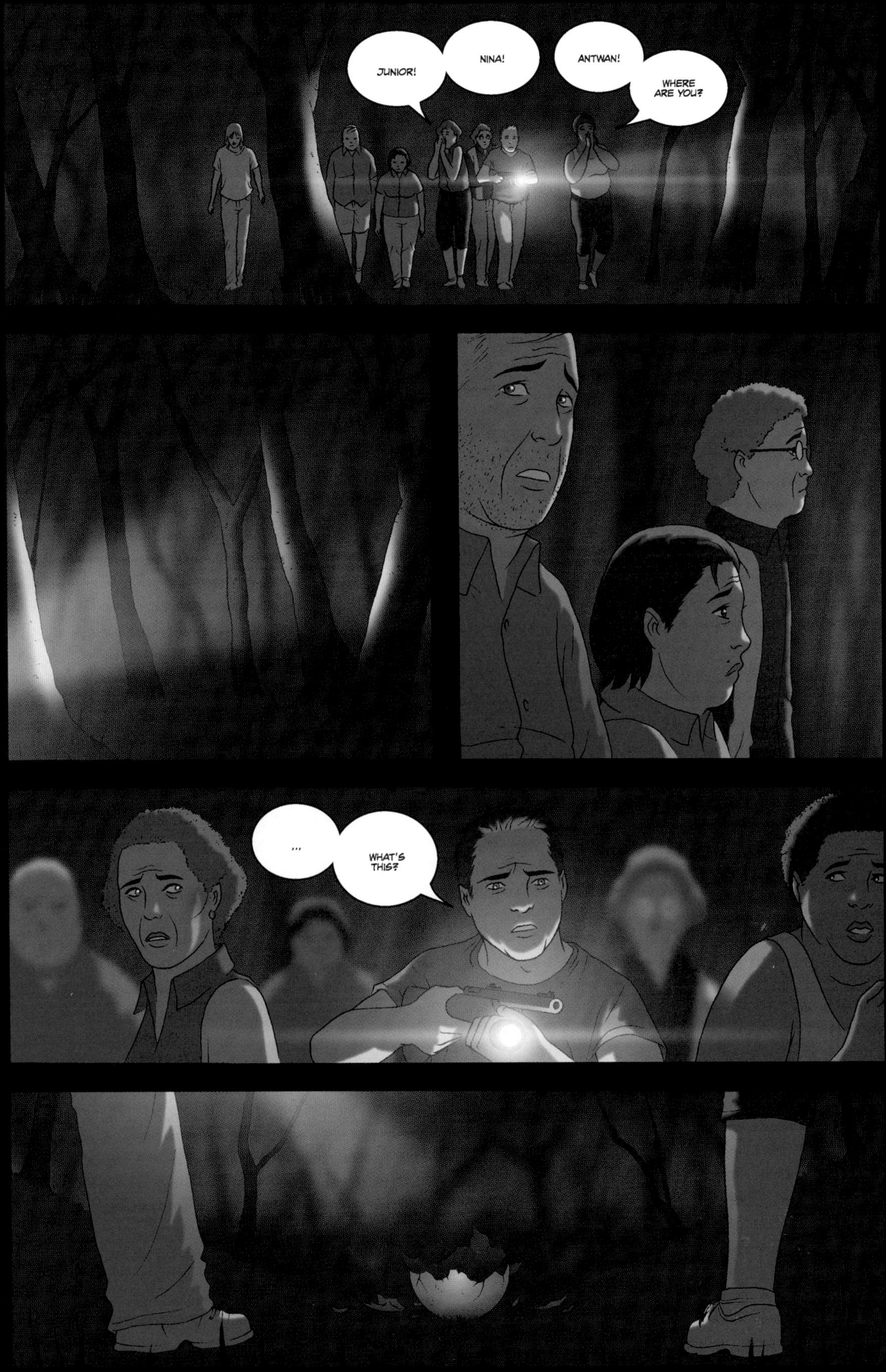
JUNIOR!
NINA!
ANTWAN!
WHERE ARE YOU?
...
WHAT'S THIS?

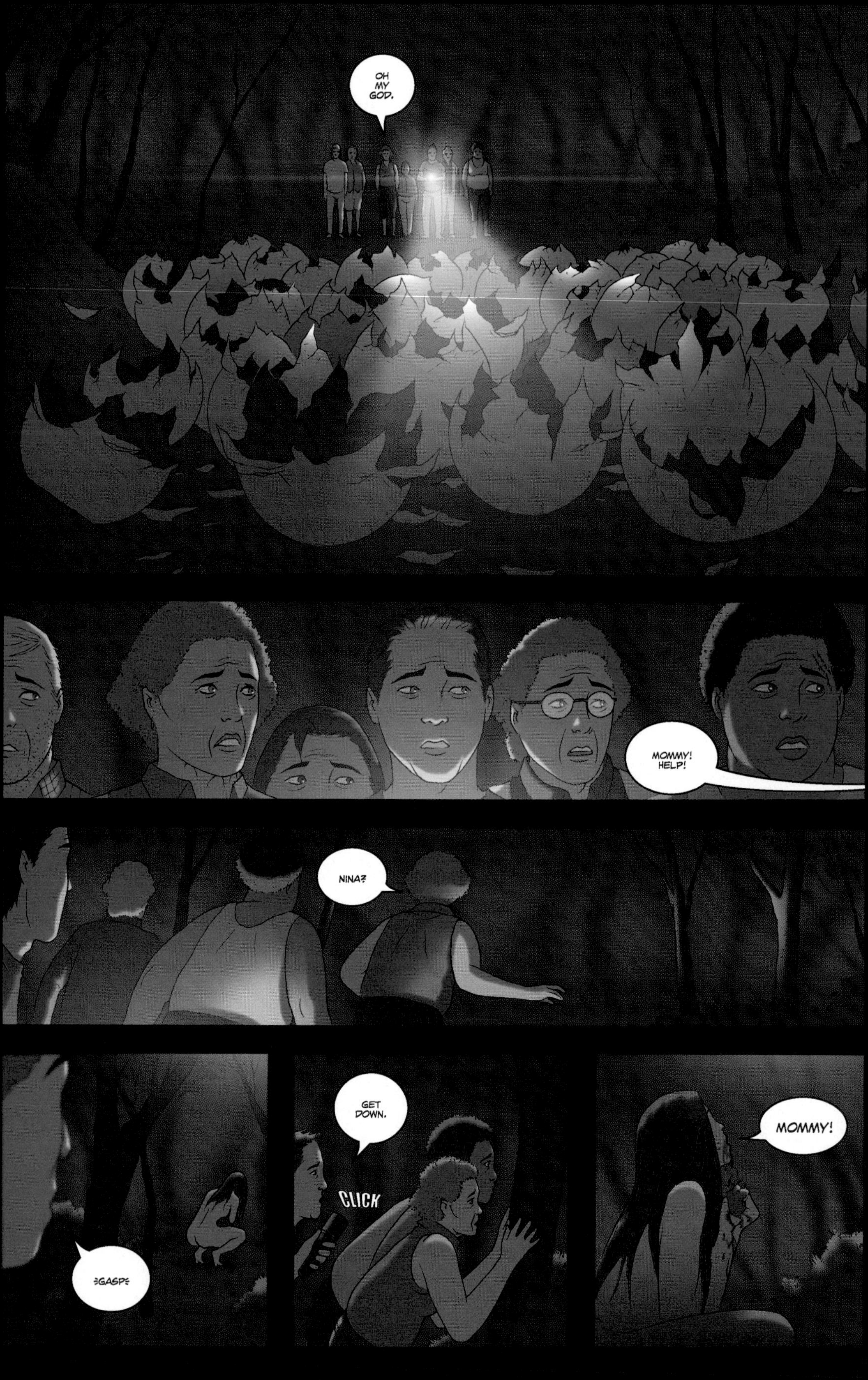
OH MY GOD.
MOMMY! HELP!
NINA?
≠GASP≠
GET DOWN.
CLICK
MOMMY!

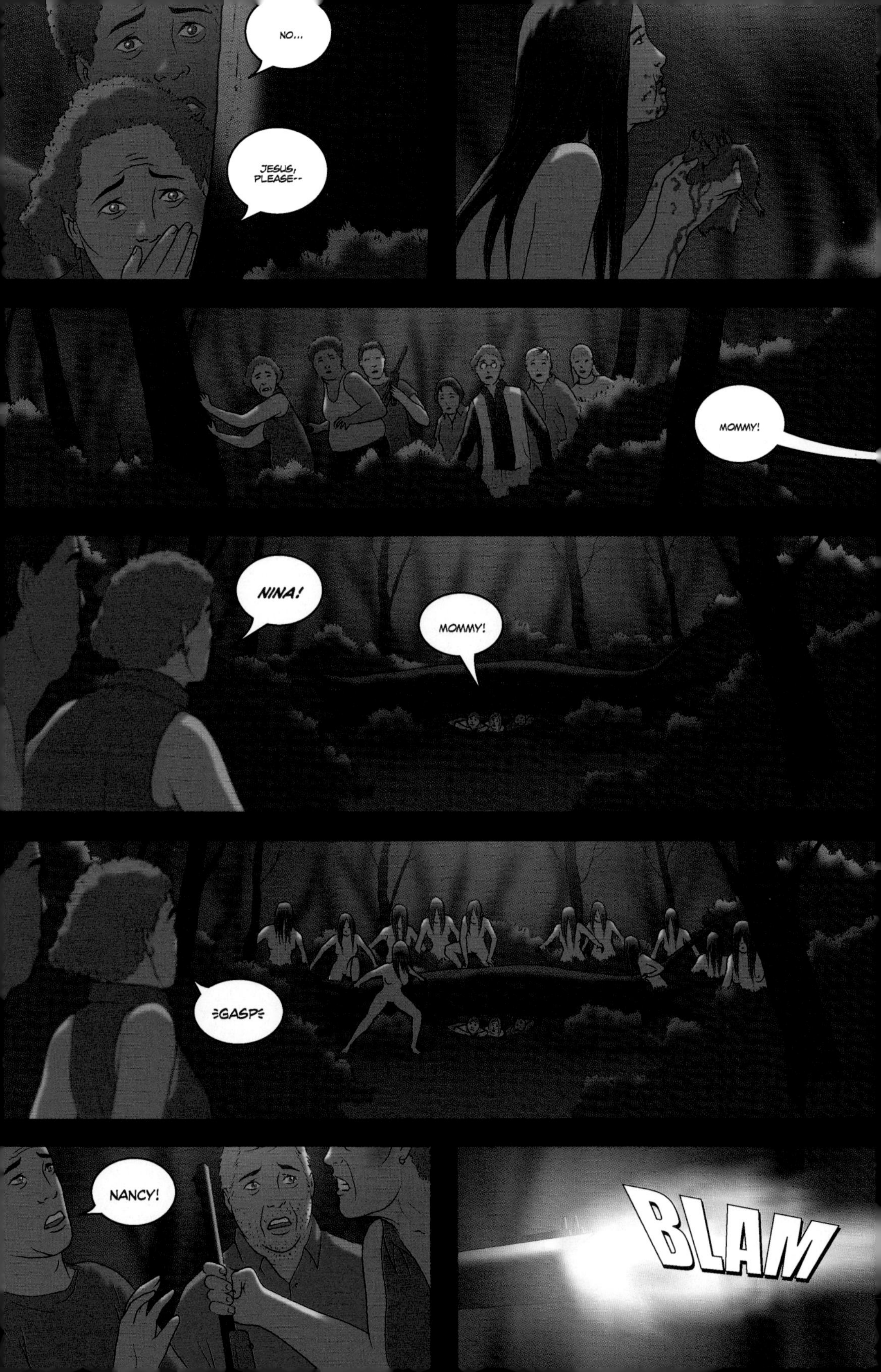

NO...
JESUS, PLEASE--
MOMMY!
NINA!
MOMMY!
GASP
NANCY!
BLAM

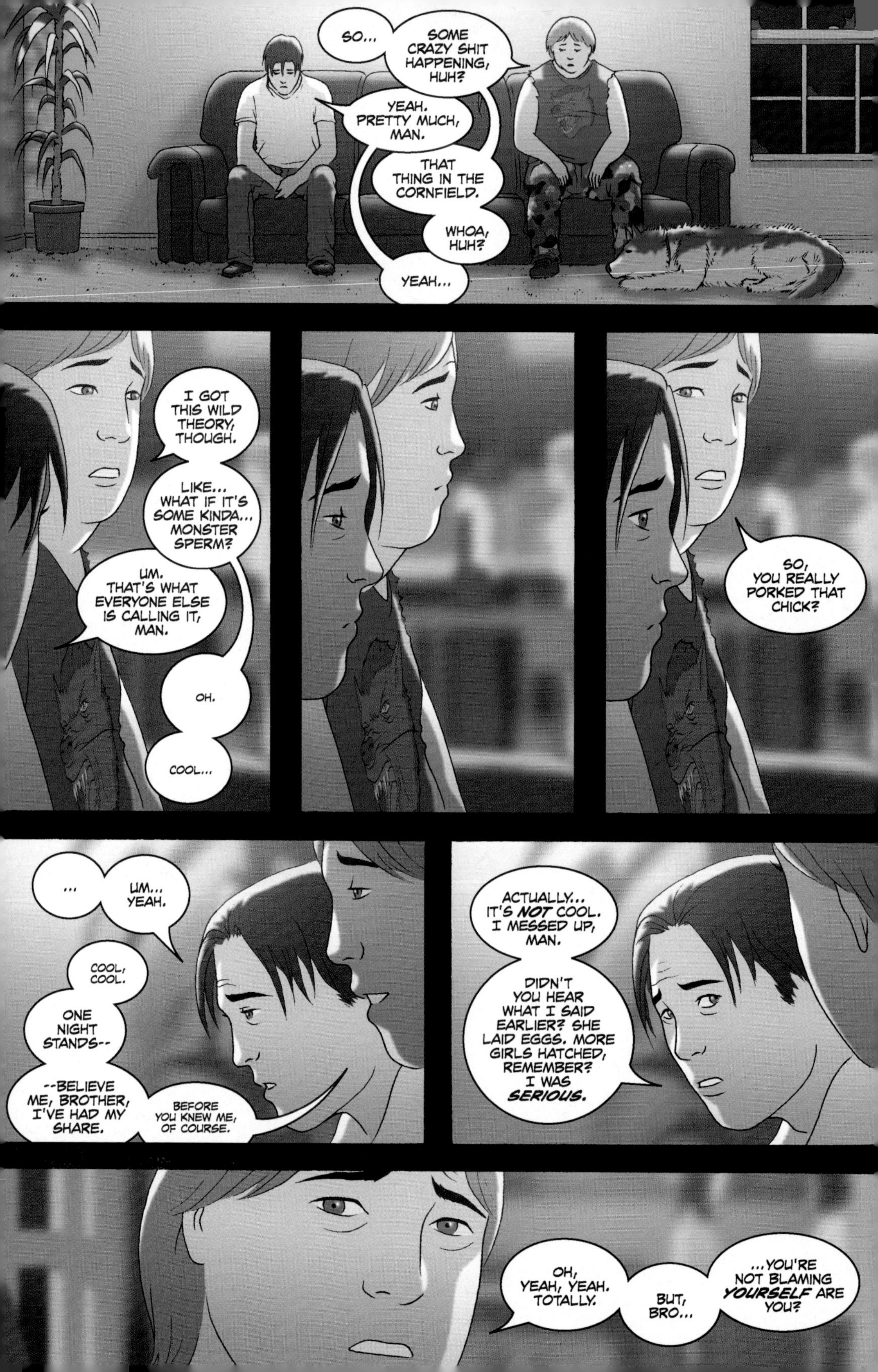
SO...
SOME CRAZY SHIT HAPPENING, HUH?
YEAH. PRETTY MUCH, MAN.
THAT THING IN THE CORNFIELD.
WHOA, HUH?
YEAH...
I GOT THIS WILD THEORY, THOUGH.
LIKE... WHAT IF IT'S SOME KINDA... MONSTER SPERM?
UM. THAT'S WHAT EVERYONE ELSE IS CALLING IT, MAN.
OH.
COOL...
SO, YOU REALLY PORKED THAT CHICK?
...
UM... YEAH.
COOL, COOL.
ONE NIGHT STANDS--
--BELIEVE ME, BROTHER, I'VE HAD MY SHARE.
BEFORE YOU KNEW ME, OF COURSE.
ACTUALLY... IT'S NOT COOL. I MESSED UP, MAN.
DIDN'T YOU HEAR WHAT I SAID EARLIER? SHE LAID EGGS. MORE GIRLS HATCHED, REMEMBER? I WAS SERIOUS.
OH, YEAH, YEAH. TOTALLY.
BUT, BRO...
...YOU'RE NOT BLAMING YOURSELF ARE YOU?

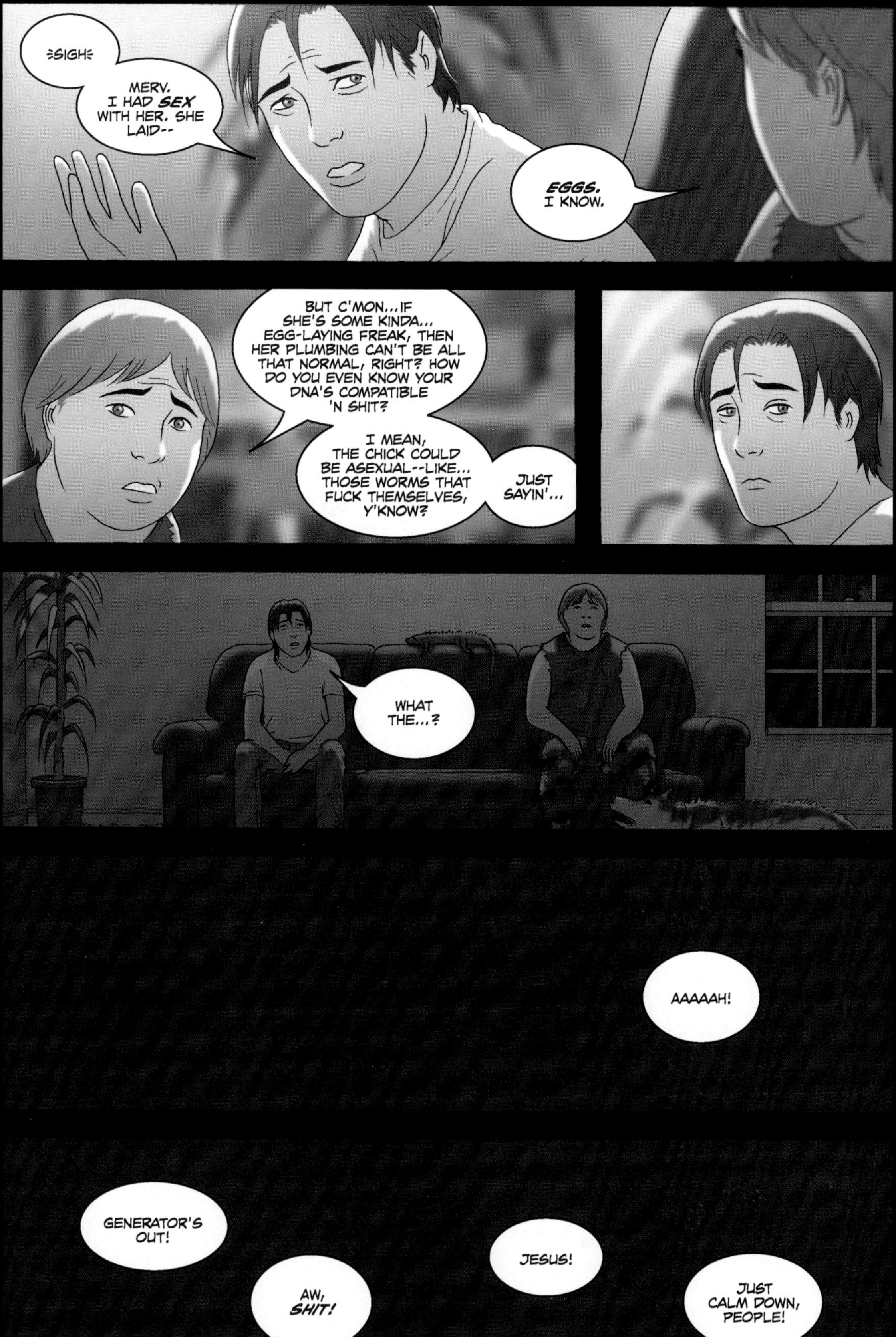
=SIGH=
MERV. I HAD SEX WITH HER. SHE LAID--
EGGS. I KNOW.
BUT C'MON...IF SHE'S SOME KINDA... EGG-LAYING FREAK, THEN HER PLUMBING CAN'T BE ALL THAT NORMAL, RIGHT? HOW DO YOU EVEN KNOW YOUR DNA'S COMPATIBLE 'N SHIT?
I MEAN, THE CHICK COULD BE ASEXUAL--LIKE... THOSE WORMS THAT FUCK THEMSELVES, Y'KNOW?
JUST SAYIN'...
WHAT THE...?
AAAAAH!
GENERATOR'S OUT!
AW, SHIT!
JESUS!
JUST CALM DOWN, PEOPLE!

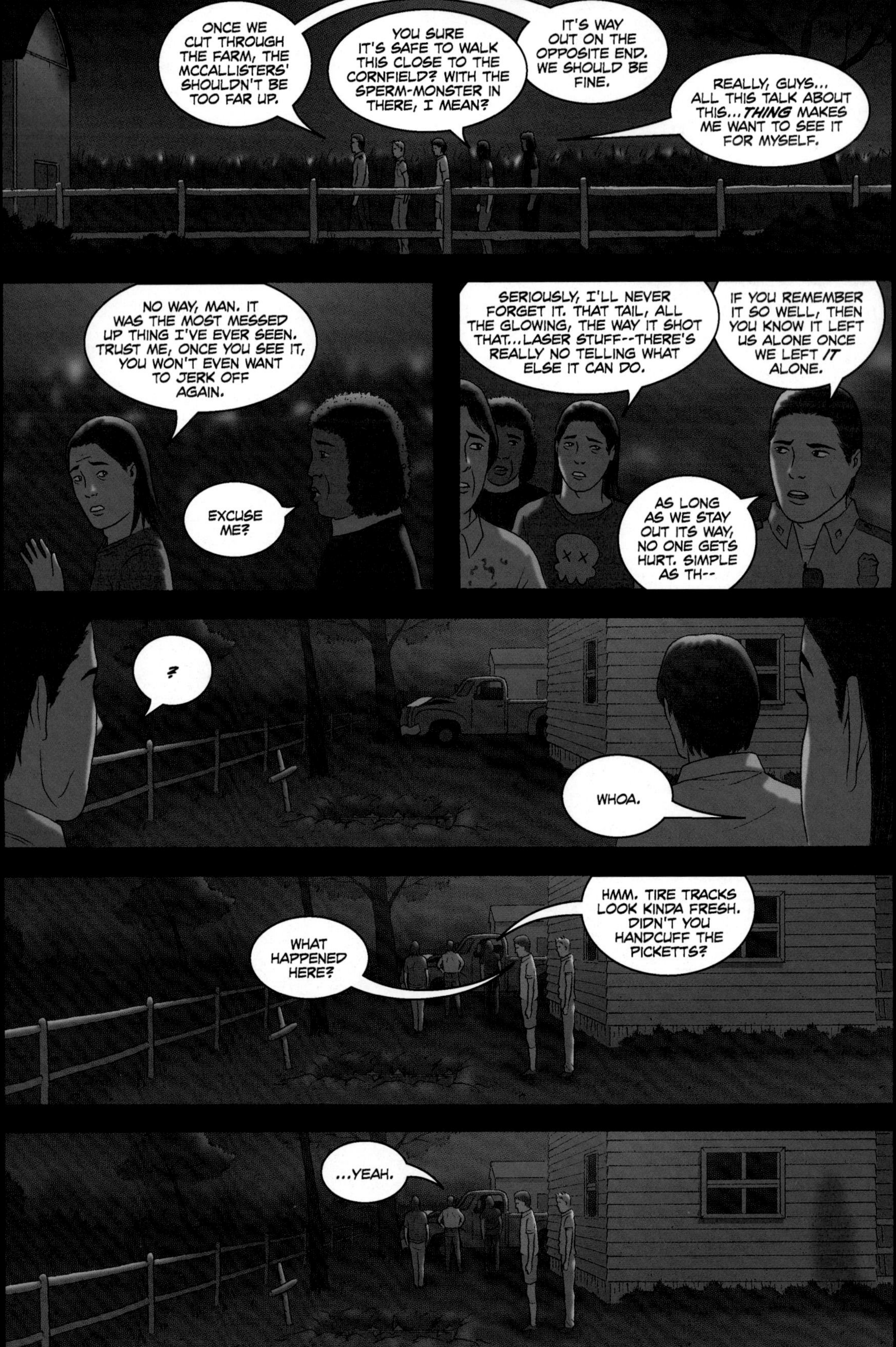
ONCE WE CUT THROUGH THE FARM, THE MCCALLISTERS' SHOULDN'T BE TOO FAR UP.
YOU SURE IT'S SAFE TO WALK THIS CLOSE TO THE CORNFIELD? WITH THE SPERM-MONSTER IN THERE, I MEAN?
IT'S WAY OUT ON THE OPPOSITE END. WE SHOULD BE FINE.
REALLY, GUYS... ALL THIS TALK ABOUT THIS...*THING* MAKES ME WANT TO SEE IT FOR MYSELF.
NO WAY, MAN. IT WAS THE MOST MESSED UP THING I'VE EVER SEEN. TRUST ME, ONCE YOU SEE IT, YOU WON'T EVEN WANT TO JERK OFF AGAIN.
EXCUSE ME?
SERIOUSLY, I'LL NEVER FORGET IT. THAT TAIL, ALL THE GLOWING, THE WAY IT SHOT THAT...LASER STUFF--THERE'S REALLY NO TELLING WHAT ELSE IT CAN DO.
IF YOU REMEMBER IT SO WELL, THEN YOU KNOW IT LEFT US ALONE ONCE WE LEFT *IT* ALONE.
AS LONG AS WE STAY OUT ITS WAY, NO ONE GETS HURT. SIMPLE AS TH--
?
WHOA.
WHAT HAPPENED HERE?
HMM. TIRE TRACKS LOOK KINDA FRESH. DIDN'T YOU HANDCUFF THE PICKETTS?
...YEAH.

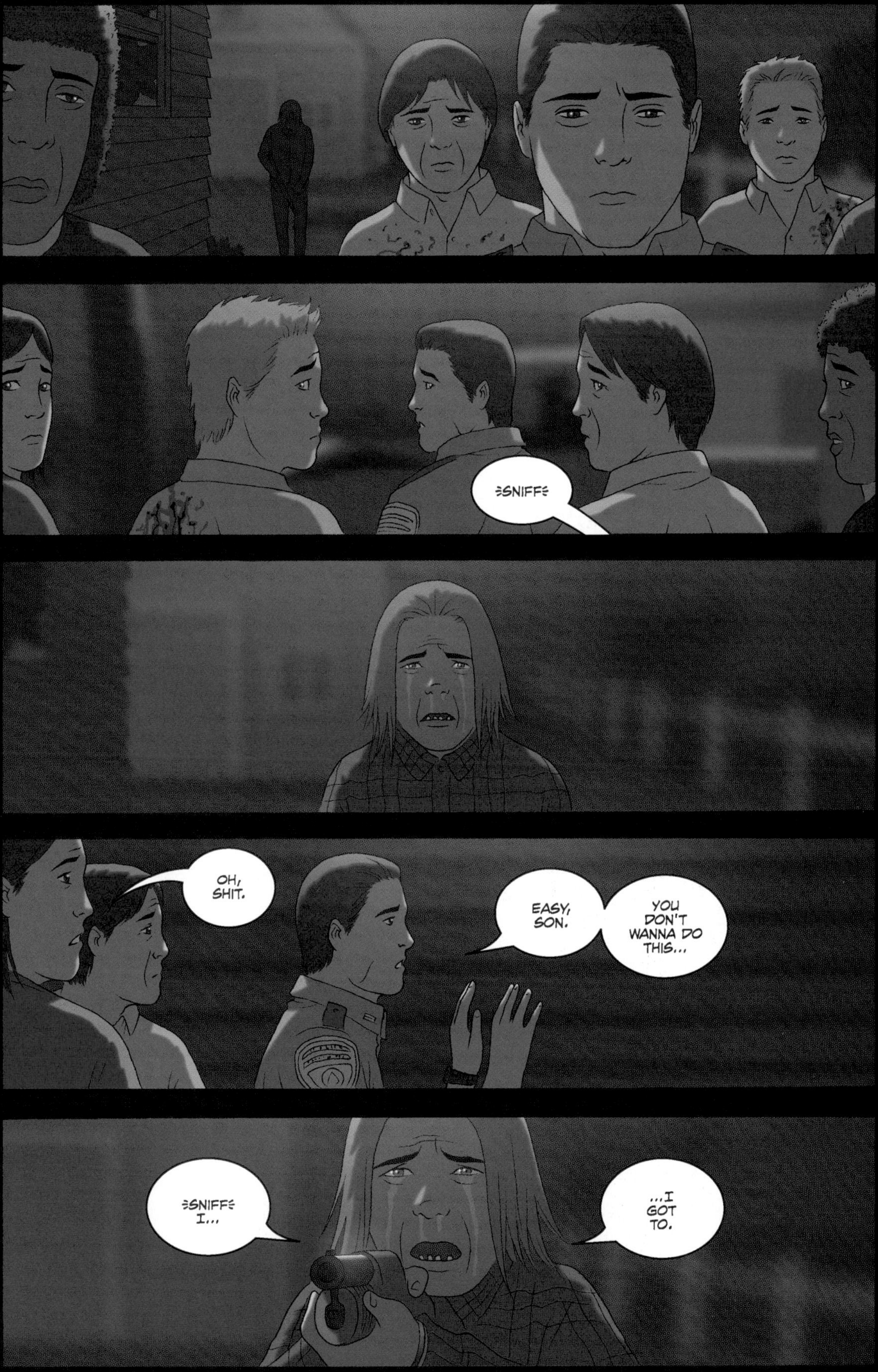

≈SNIFF≈
OH, SHIT.
EASY, SON.
YOU DON'T WANNA DO THIS...
≈SNIFF≈ I...
...I GOT TO.

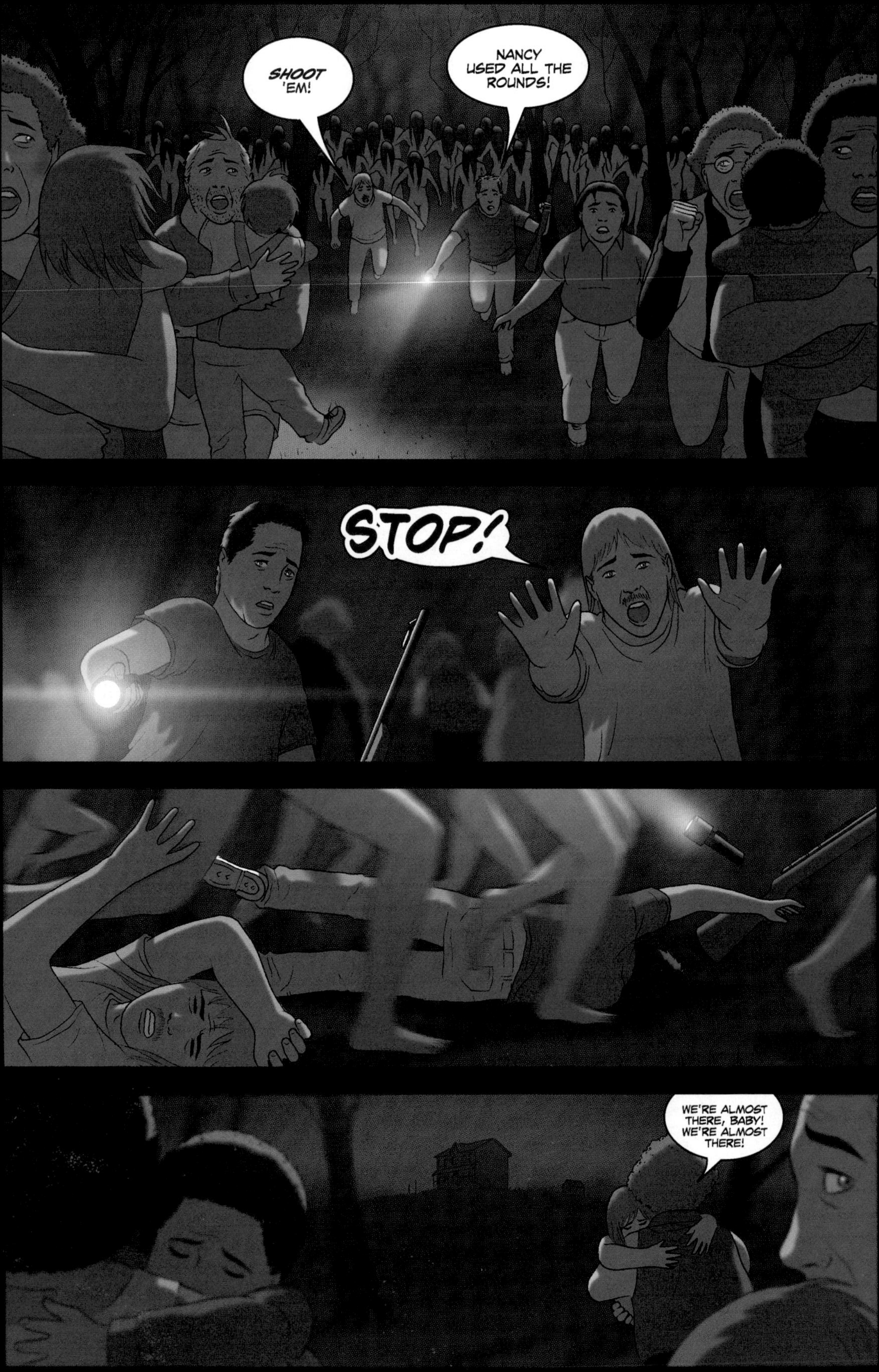
SHOOT 'EM!
NANCY USED ALL THE ROUNDS!
STOP!
WE'RE ALMOST THERE, BABY! WE'RE ALMOST THERE!

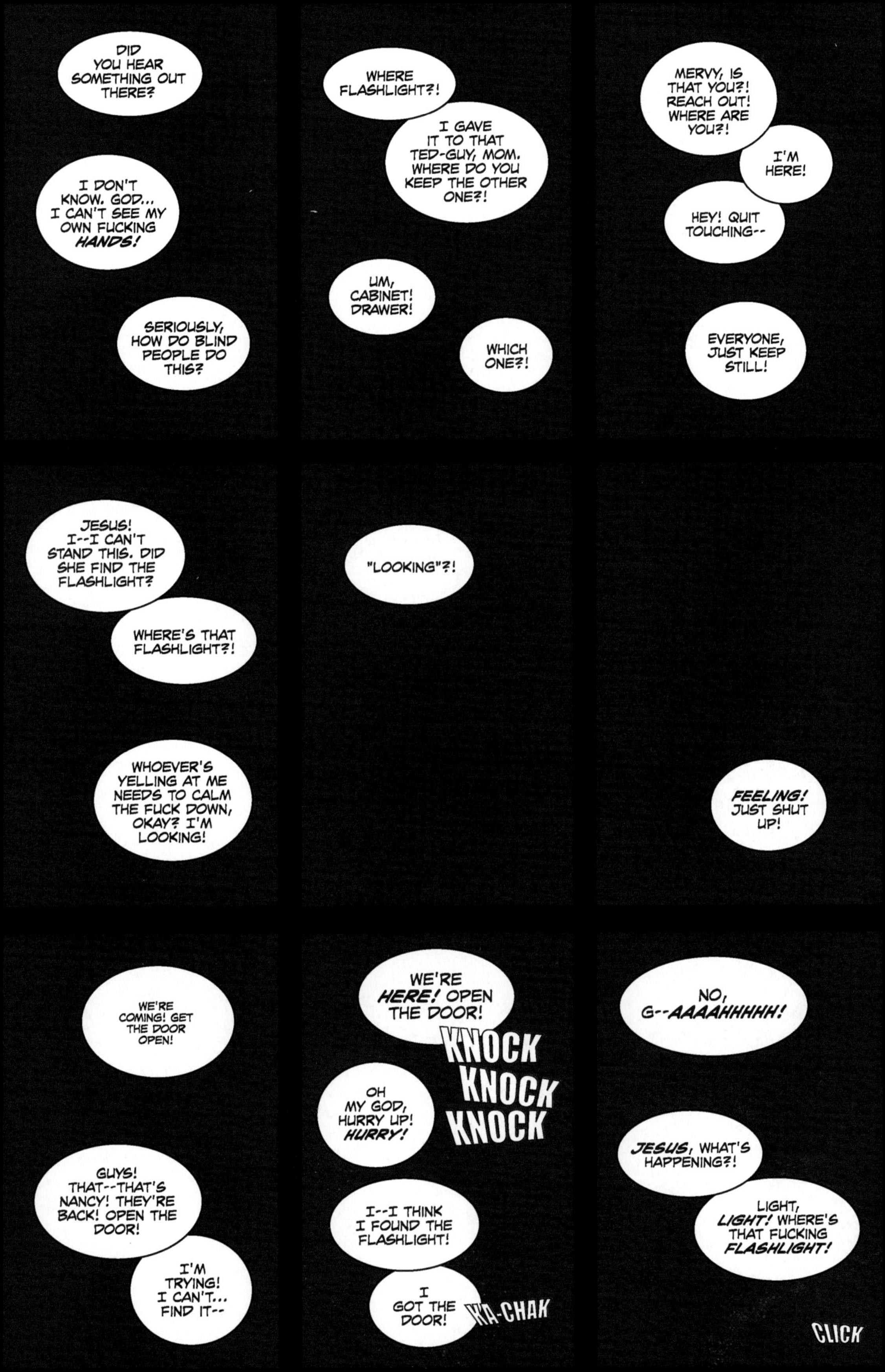
DID YOU HEAR SOMETHING OUT THERE?
I DON'T KNOW. GOD... I CAN'T SEE MY OWN FUCKING *HANDS!*
SERIOUSLY, HOW DO BLIND PEOPLE DO THIS?
WHERE FLASHLIGHT?!
I GAVE IT TO THAT TED-GUY, MOM. WHERE DO YOU KEEP THE OTHER ONE?!
UM, CABINET! DRAWER!
WHICH ONE?!
MERVY, IS THAT YOU?! REACH OUT! WHERE ARE YOU?!
I'M HERE!
HEY! QUIT TOUCHING--
EVERYONE, JUST KEEP STILL!
JESUS! I--I CAN'T STAND THIS. DID SHE FIND THE FLASHLIGHT?
WHERE'S THAT FLASHLIGHT?!
WHOEVER'S YELLING AT ME NEEDS TO CALM THE FUCK DOWN, OKAY? I'M LOOKING!
"LOOKING"?!
FEELING! JUST SHUT UP!
WE'RE COMING! GET THE DOOR OPEN!
GUYS! THAT--THAT'S NANCY! THEY'RE BACK! OPEN THE DOOR!
I'M TRYING! I CAN'T... FIND IT--
WE'RE *HERE!* OPEN THE DOOR!
KNOCK KNOCK KNOCK
OH MY GOD, HURRY UP! *HURRY!*
I--I THINK I FOUND THE FLASHLIGHT!
I GOT THE DOOR!
KA-CHAK
NO, G--*AAAAHHHHH!*
JESUS, WHAT'S HAPPENING?!
LIGHT, *LIGHT!* WHERE'S THAT FUCKING *FLASHLIGHT!*
CLICK

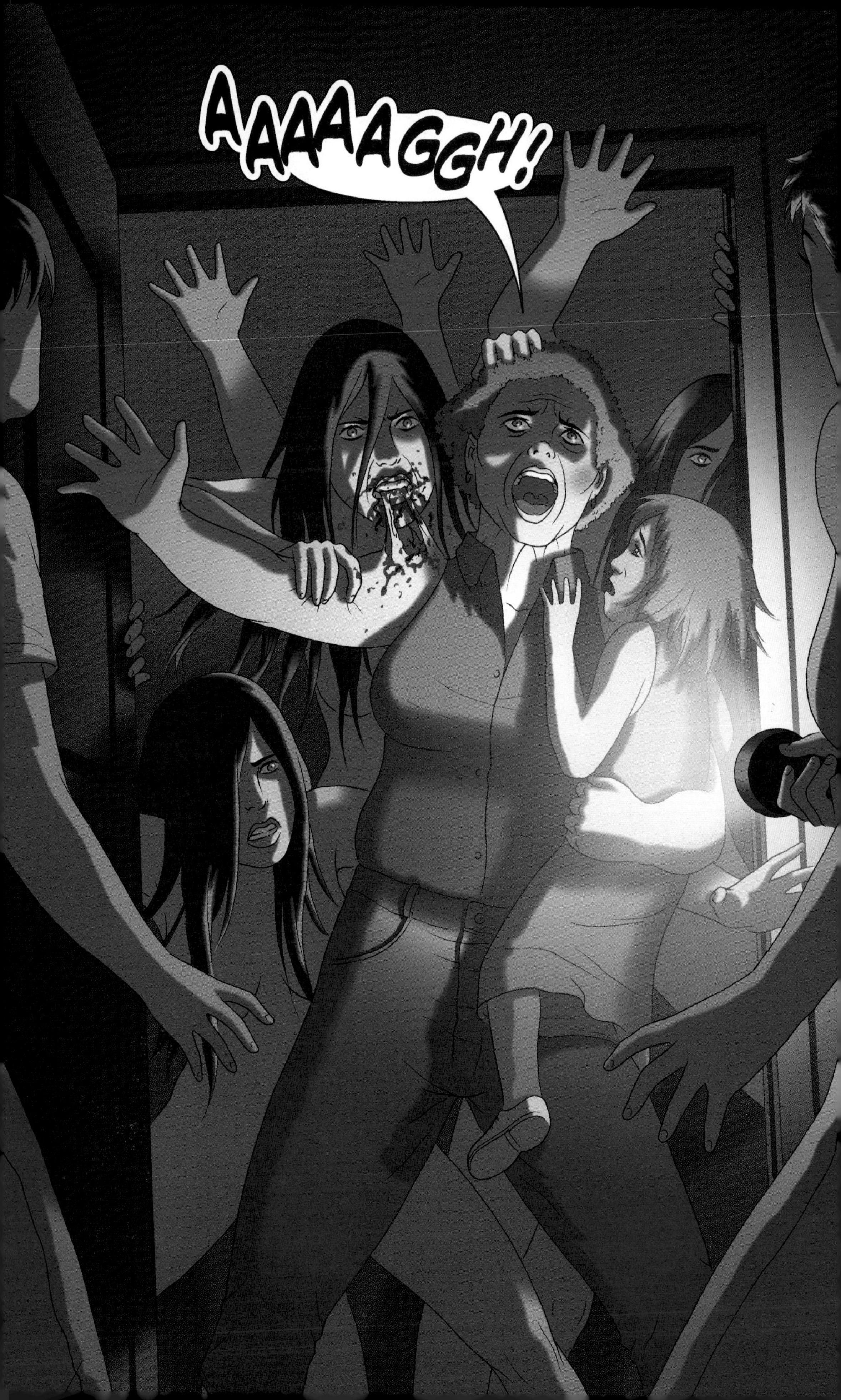
AAAAAGGH!

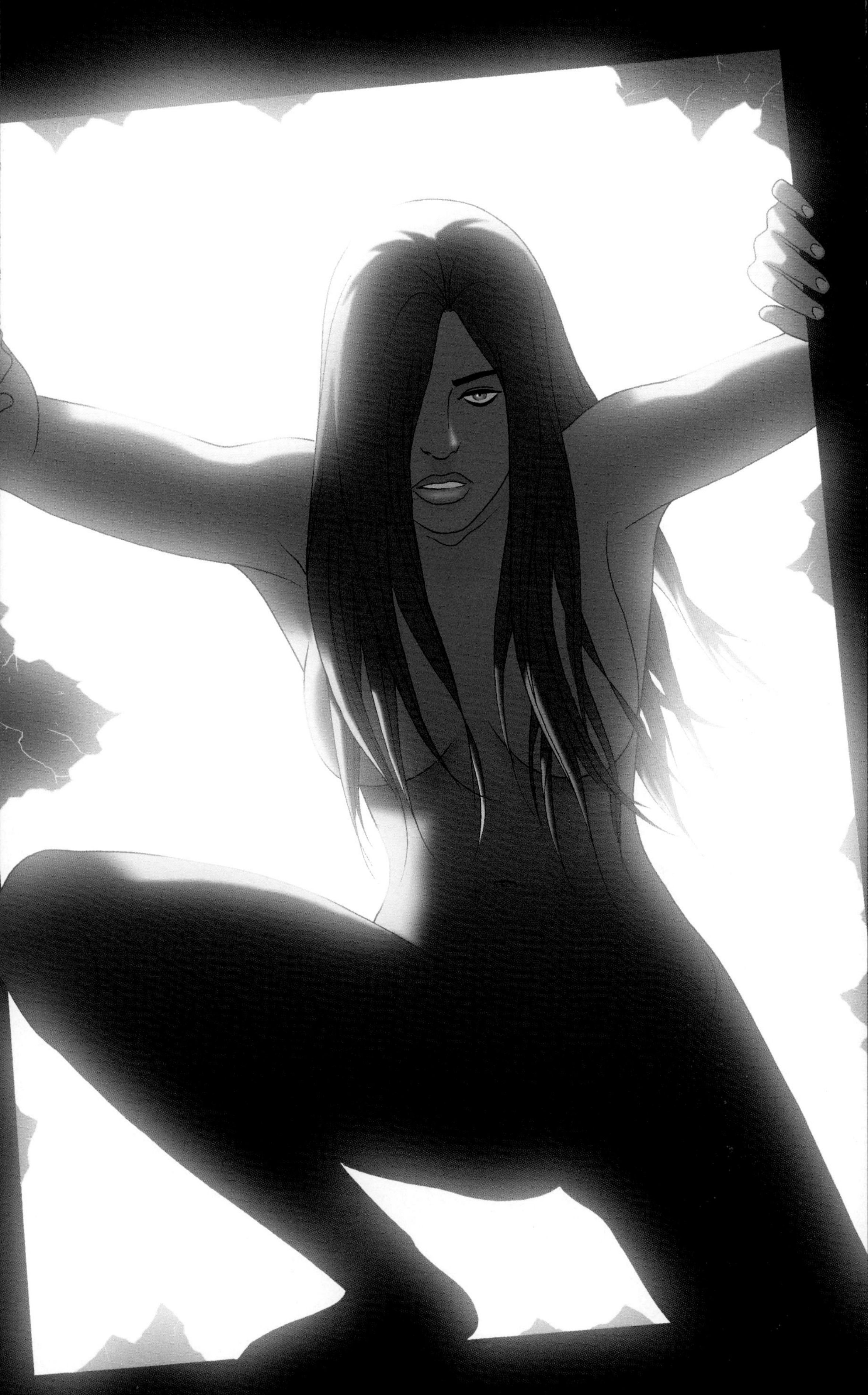

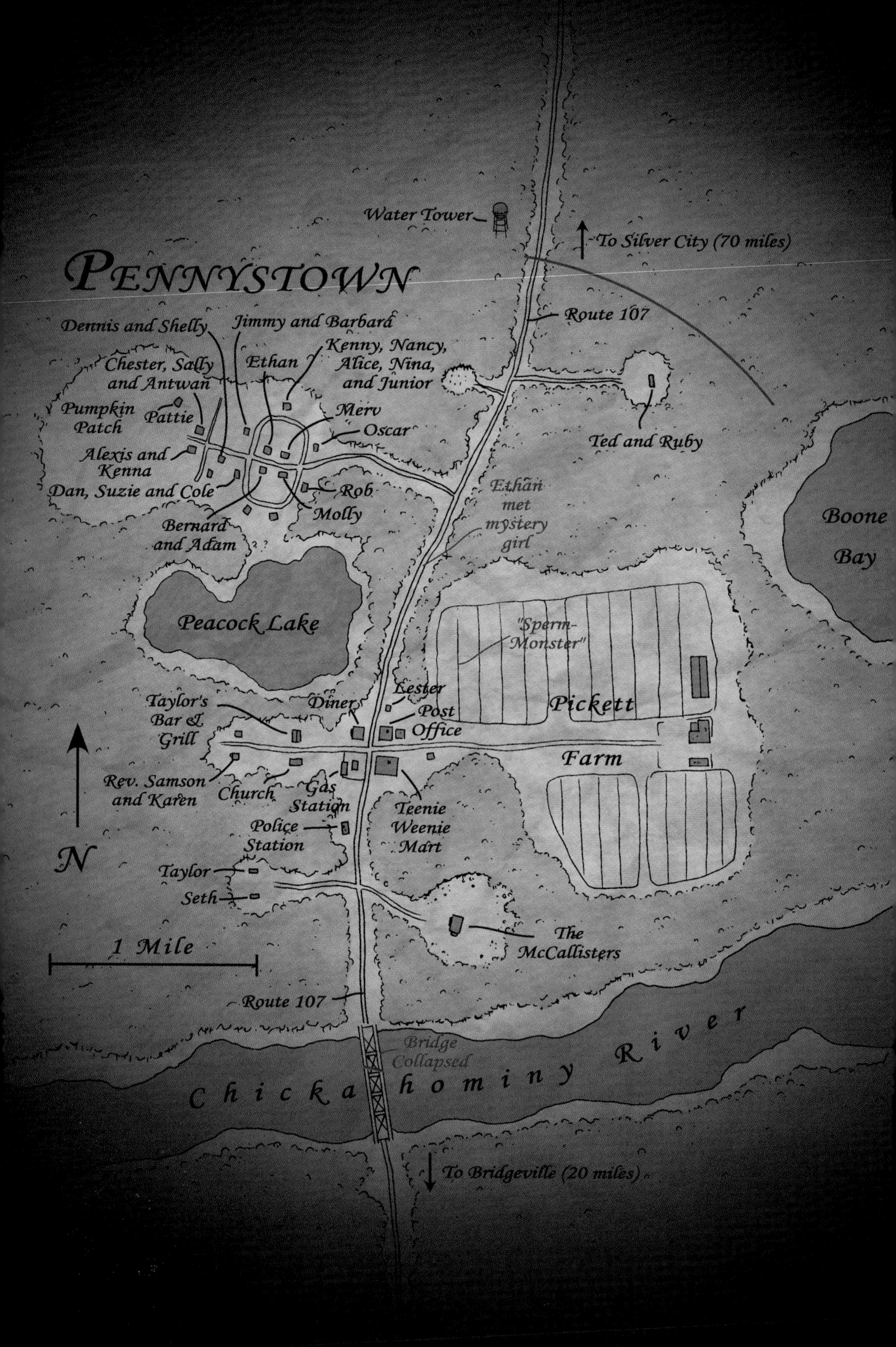
PENNYSTOWN
Water Tower
To Silver City (70 miles)
Route 107
Dennis and Shelly
Jimmy and Barbara
Chester, Sally and Antwan
Ethan
Kenny, Nancy, Alice, Nina, and Junior
Pumpkin Patch
Pattie
Merv
Oscar
Alexis and Kenna
Ted and Ruby
Dan, Suzie and Cole
Rob
Molly
Bernard and Adam
Ethan met mystery girl
Boone Bay
Peacock Lake
"Sperm-Monster"
Lester
Diner
Taylor's Bar & Grill
Post Office
Pickett
Farm
Rev. Samson and Karen
Church
Gas Station
Teenie Weenie Mart
Police Station
N
Taylor
Seth
The McCallisters
1 Mile
Route 107
Bridge Collapsed
Chickahominy River
To Bridgeville (20 miles)

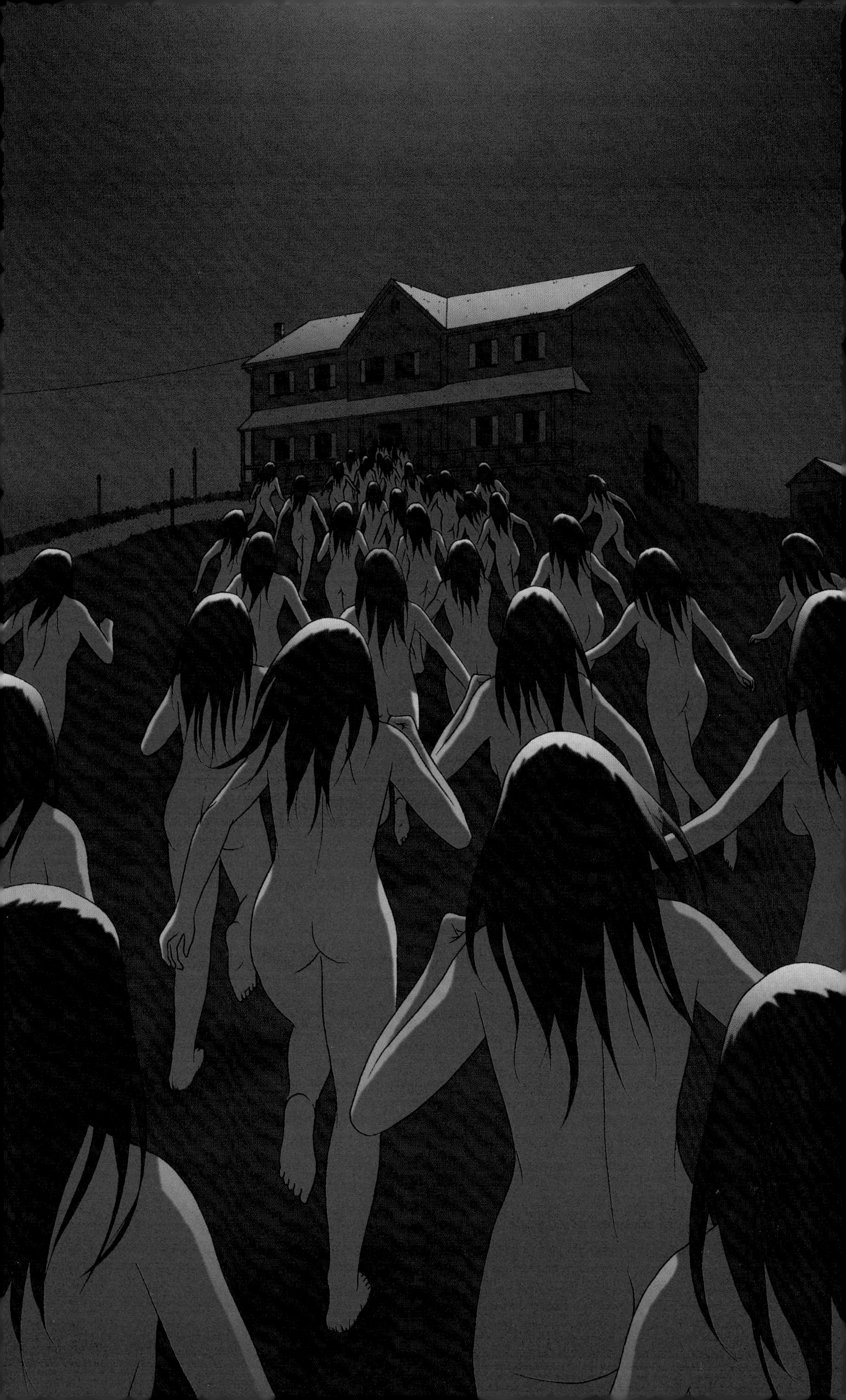

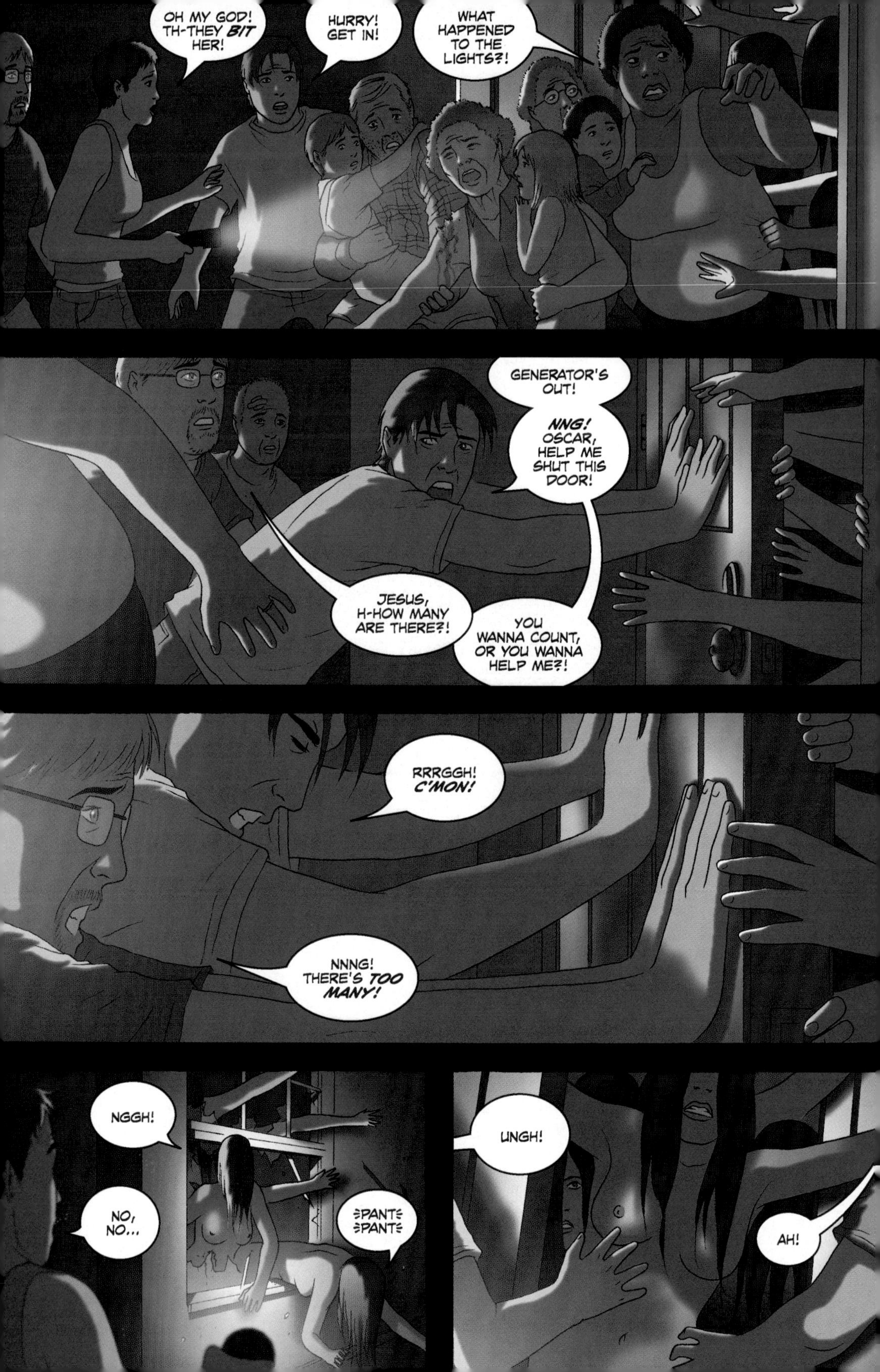

OH MY GOD! TH-THEY *BIT* HER!
HURRY! GET IN!
WHAT HAPPENED TO THE LIGHTS?!
GENERATOR'S OUT!
NNG! OSCAR, HELP ME SHUT THIS DOOR!
JESUS, H-HOW MANY ARE THERE?!
YOU WANNA COUNT, OR YOU WANNA HELP ME?!
RRRGGH! *C'MON!*
NNNG! THERE'S *TOO MANY!*
NGGH!
NO, NO...
PANT PANT
UNGH!
AH!

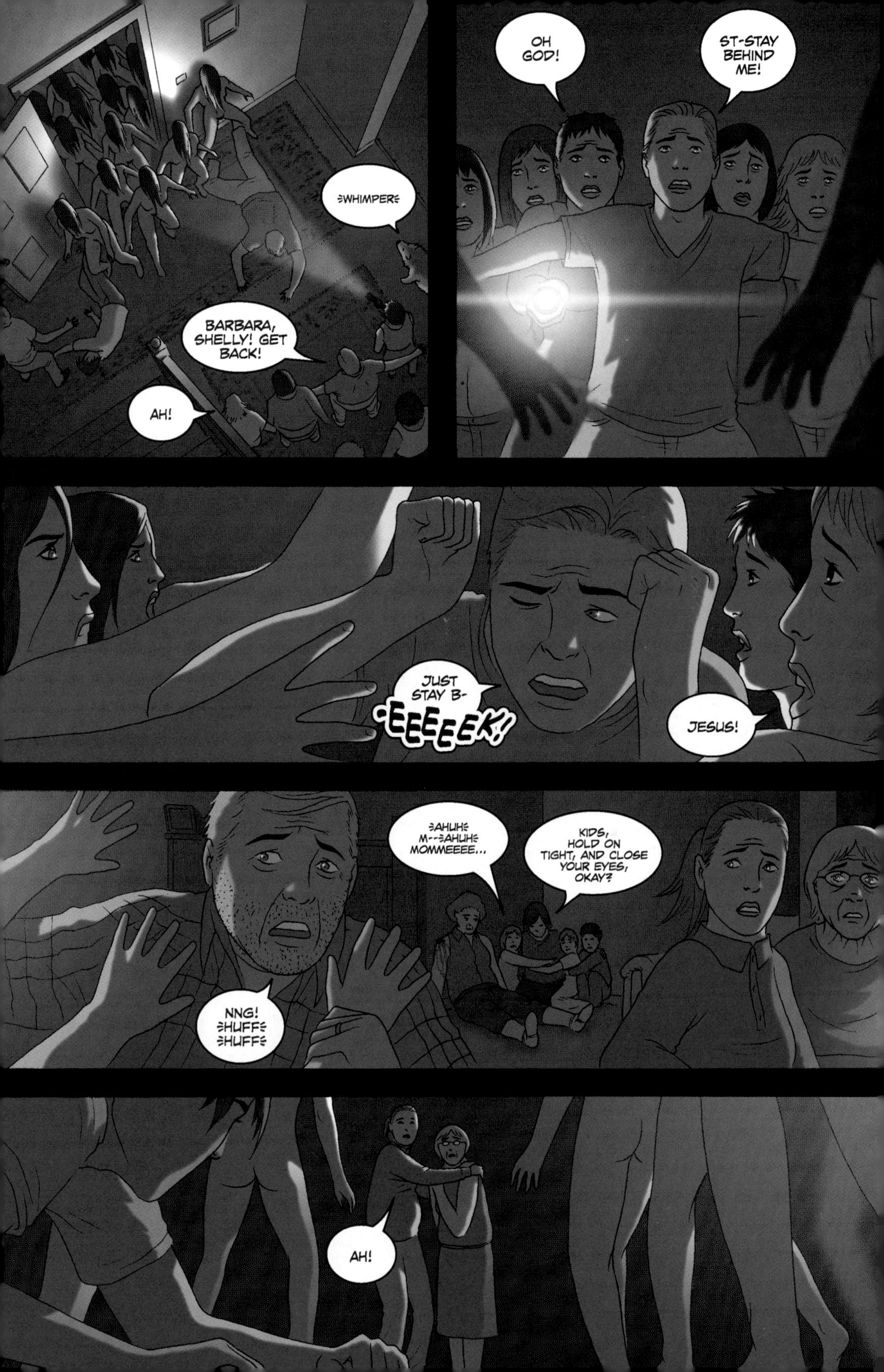

=WHIMPER=
BARBARA, SHELLY! GET BACK!
AH!
OH GOD!
ST-STAY BEHIND ME!
JUST STAY B-
-EEEEEK!
JESUS!
=AHUH= M--=AHUH= MOMMEEEE...
KIDS, HOLD ON TIGHT, AND CLOSE YOUR EYES, OKAY?
NNG! =HUFF= =HUFF=
AH!

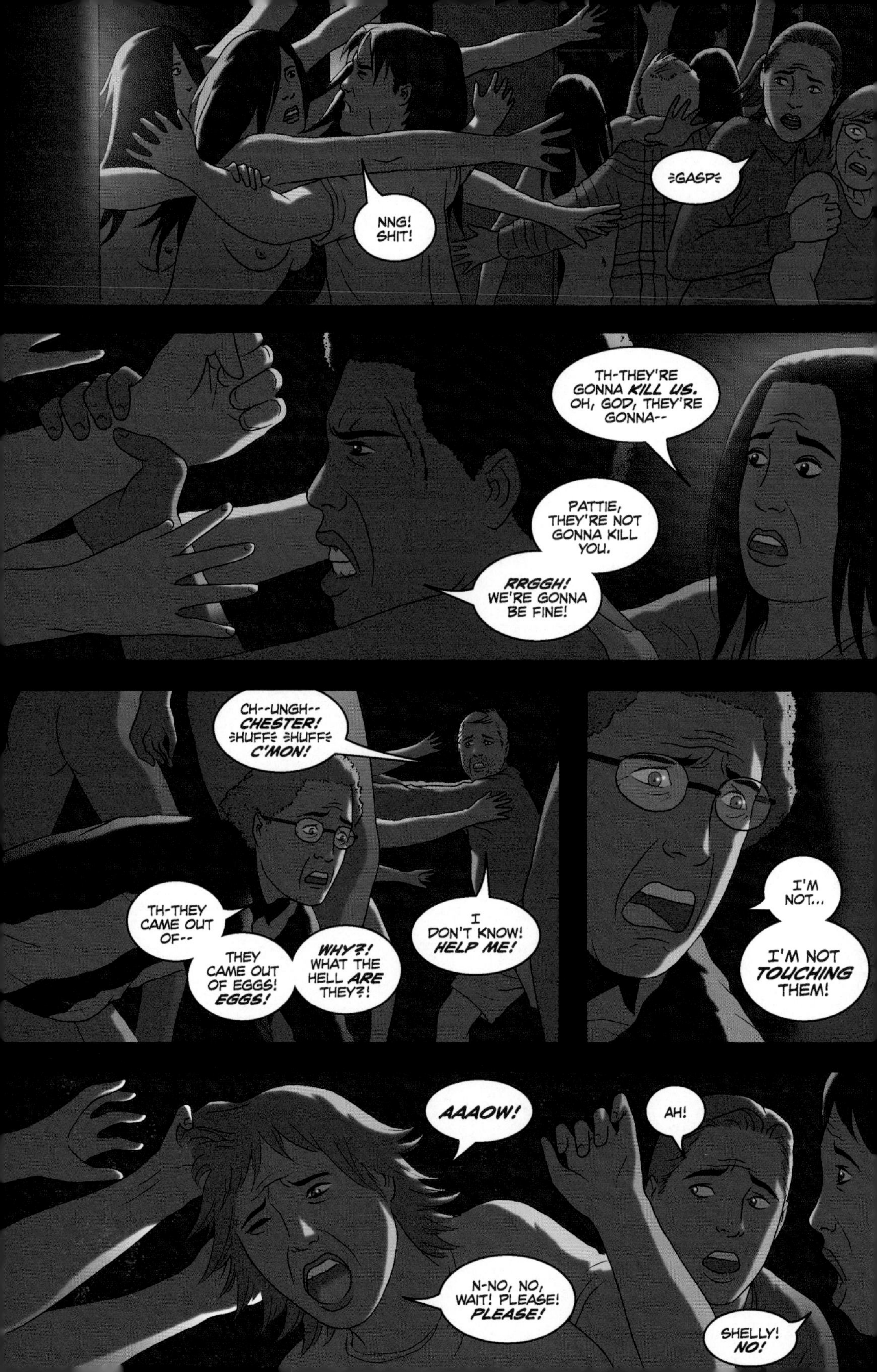
NNG! SHIT!
GASP
TH-THEY'RE GONNA *KILL US.* OH, GOD, THEY'RE GONNA--
PATTIE, THEY'RE NOT GONNA KILL YOU.
RRGGH! WE'RE GONNA BE FINE!
CH--UNGH-- *CHESTER!* HUFF HUFF *C'MON!*
TH-THEY CAME OUT OF--
THEY CAME OUT OF EGGS! *EGGS!*
WHY?! WHAT THE HELL *ARE* THEY?!
I DON'T KNOW! *HELP ME!*
I'M NOT...
I'M NOT *TOUCHING* THEM!
AAAOW!
AH!
N-NO, NO, WAIT! PLEASE! *PLEASE!*
SHELLY! *NO!*

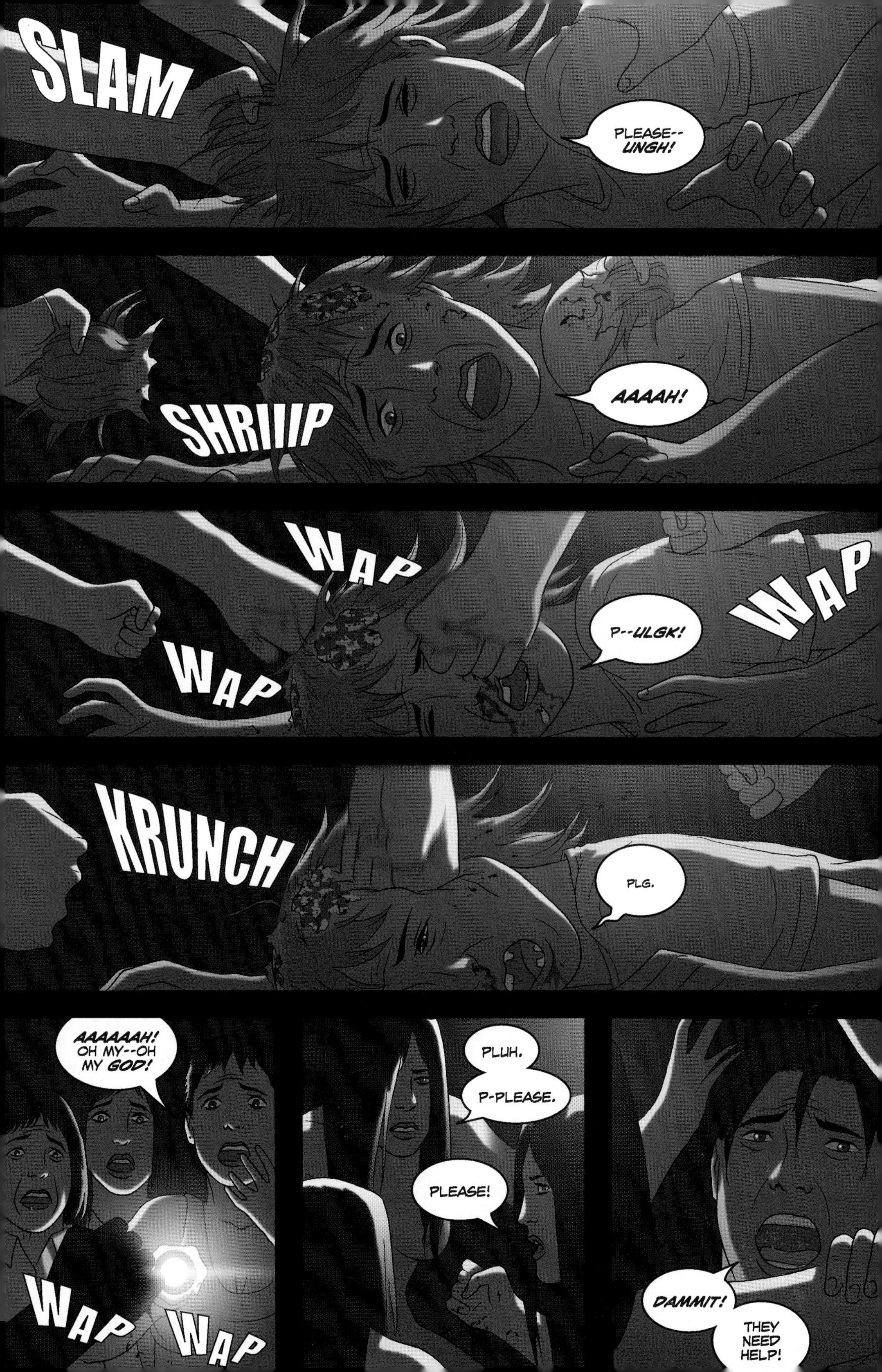
SLAM
PLEASE-- UNGH!
SHRIIIP
AAAAH!
WAP
WAP
P--ULGK!
WAP
KRUNCH
PLG.
AAAAAAH! OH MY--OH MY GOD!
WAP
WAP
PLUH.
P-PLEASE.
PLEASE!
DAMMIT!
THEY NEED HELP!

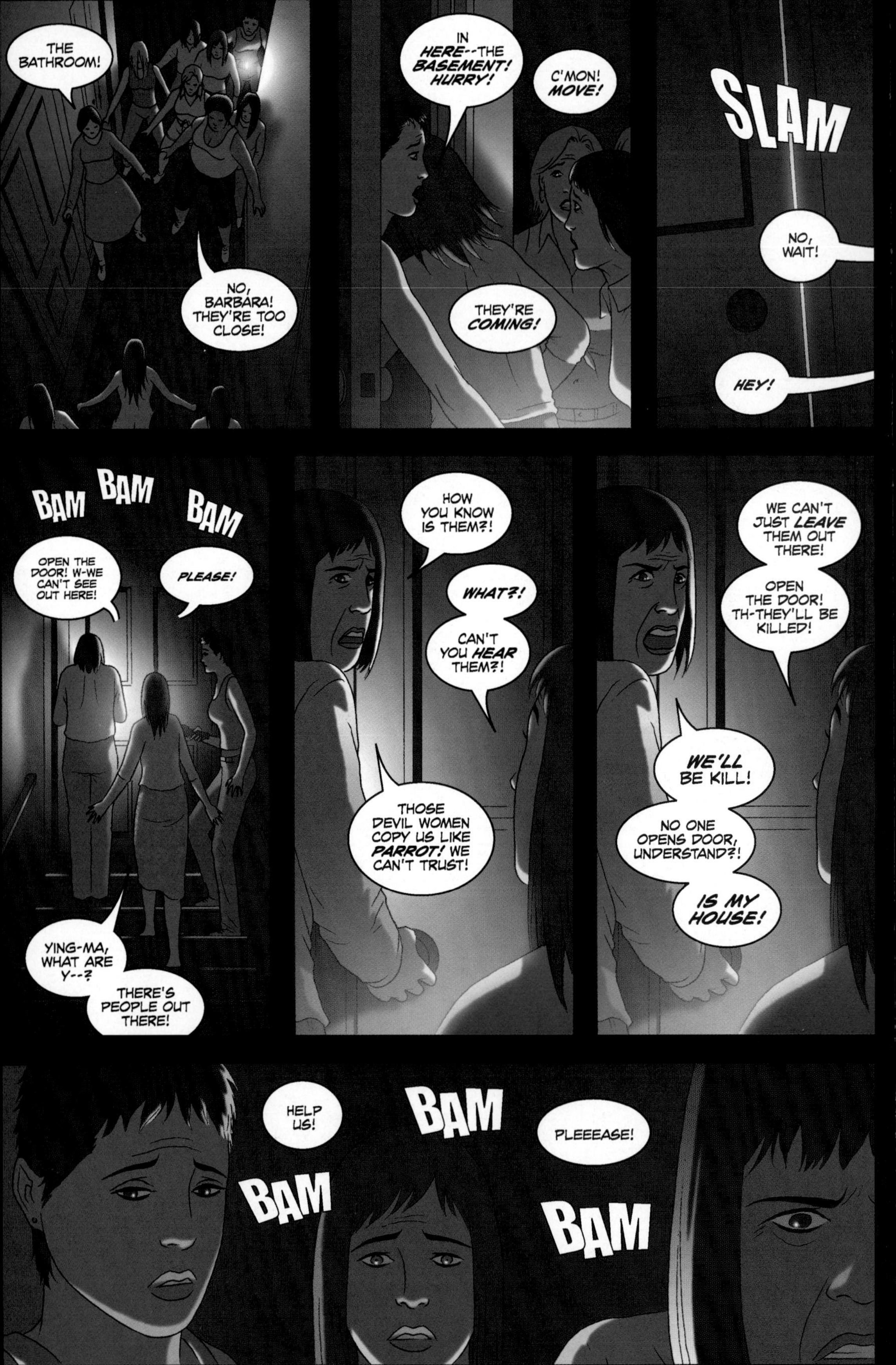
THE BATHROOM!
NO, BARBARA! THEY'RE TOO CLOSE!
IN HERE--THE BASEMENT! HURRY!
C'MON! MOVE!
THEY'RE COMING!
SLAM
NO, WAIT!
HEY!
BAM BAM BAM
OPEN THE DOOR! W-WE CAN'T SEE OUT HERE!
PLEASE!
YING-MA, WHAT ARE Y--?
THERE'S PEOPLE OUT THERE!
HOW YOU KNOW IS THEM?!
WHAT?!
CAN'T YOU HEAR THEM?!
THOSE DEVIL WOMEN COPY US LIKE PARROT! WE CAN'T TRUST!
WE CAN'T JUST LEAVE THEM OUT THERE!
OPEN THE DOOR! TH-THEY'LL BE KILLED!
WE'LL BE KILL!
NO ONE OPENS DOOR, UNDERSTAND?!
IS MY HOUSE!
HELP US!
BAM
PLEEEASE!
BAM
BAM

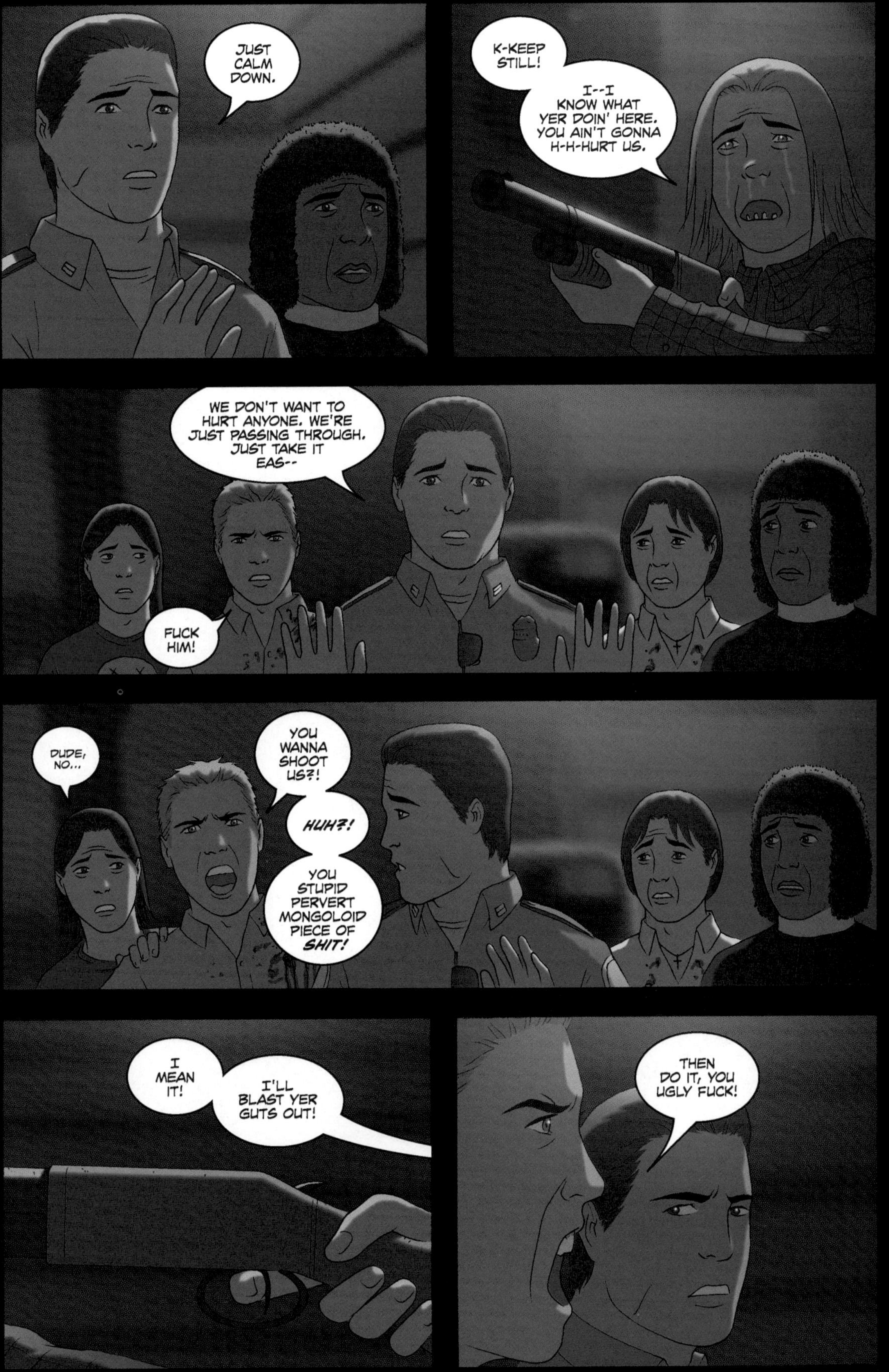
JUST CALM DOWN.
K-KEEP STILL!
I--I KNOW WHAT YER DOIN' HERE. YOU AIN'T GONNA H-H-HURT US.
WE DON'T WANT TO HURT ANYONE. WE'RE JUST PASSING THROUGH. JUST TAKE IT EAS--
FUCK HIM!
DUDE, NO...
YOU WANNA SHOOT US?!
HUH?!
YOU STUPID PERVERT MONGOLOID PIECE OF SHIT!
I MEAN IT!
I'LL BLAST YER GUTS OUT!
THEN DO IT, YOU UGLY FUCK!

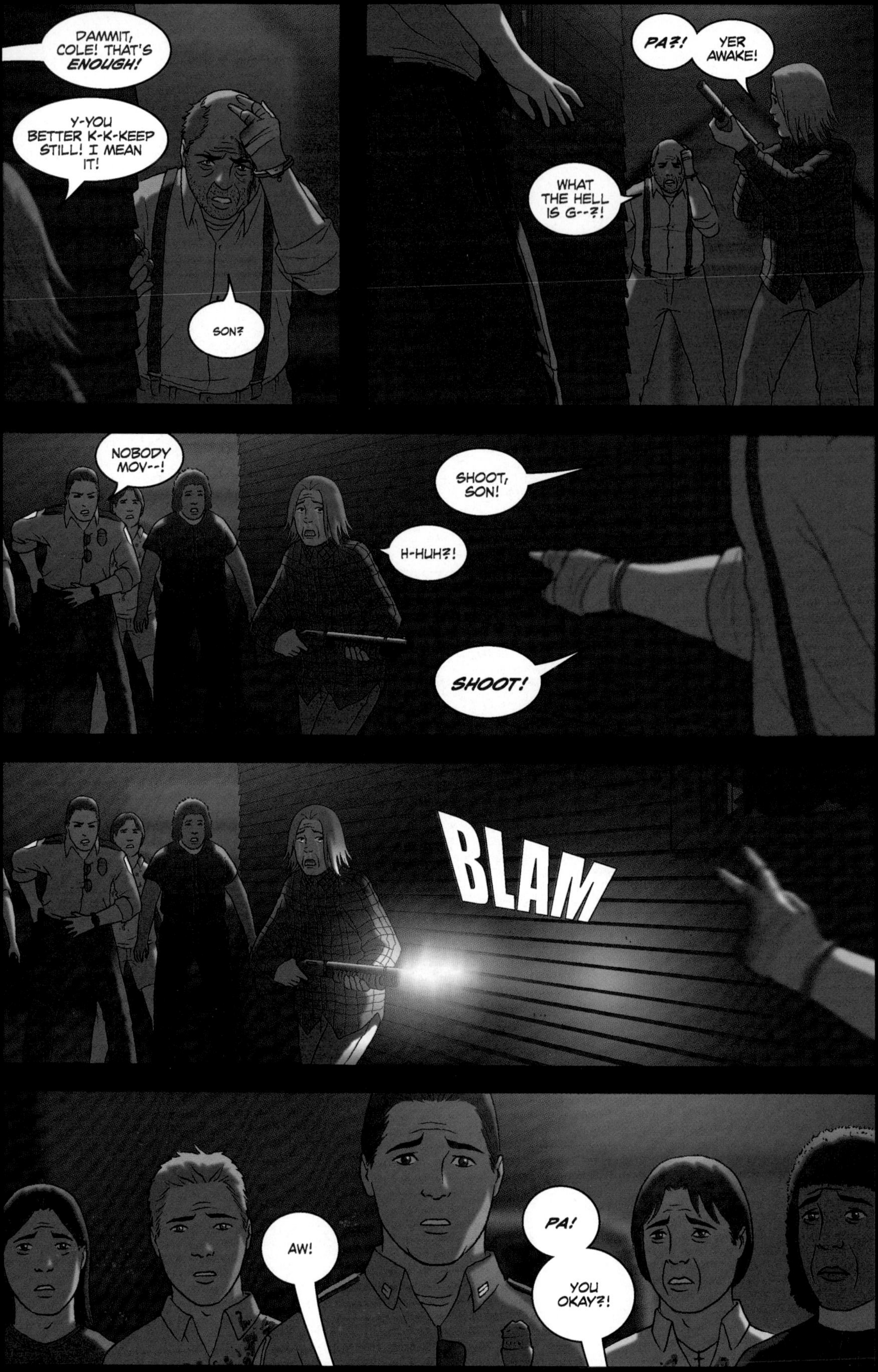
DAMMIT, COLE! THAT'S *ENOUGH!*
Y-YOU BETTER K-K-KEEP STILL! I MEAN IT!
SON?
PA?!
YER AWAKE!
WHAT THE HELL IS G--?!
NOBODY MOV--!
SHOOT, SON!
H-HUH?!
SHOOT!
BLAM
AW!
PA!
YOU OKAY?!

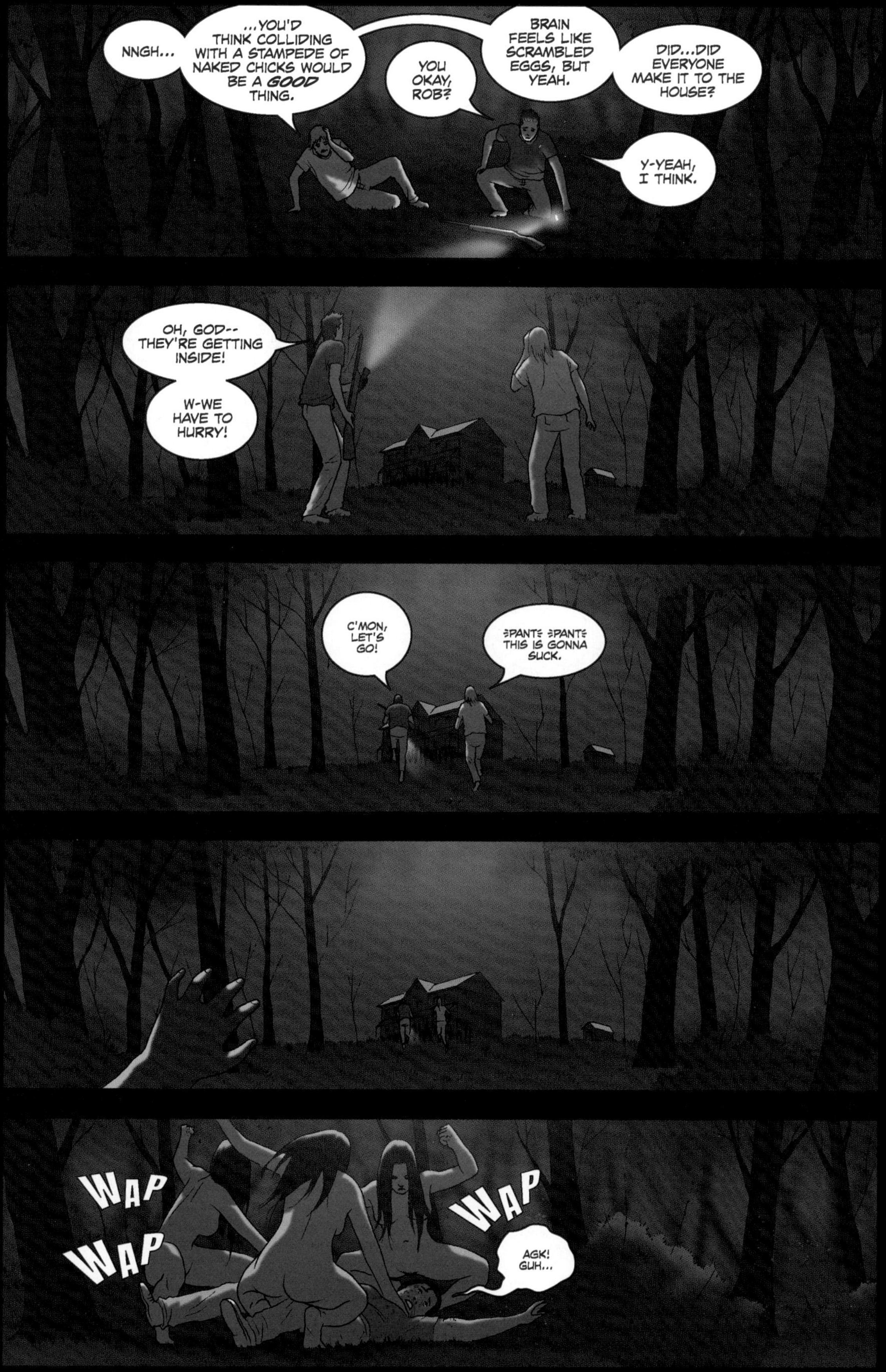
NNGH...
...YOU'D THINK COLLIDING WITH A STAMPEDE OF NAKED CHICKS WOULD BE A GOOD THING.
YOU OKAY, ROB?
BRAIN FEELS LIKE SCRAMBLED EGGS, BUT YEAH.
DID...DID EVERYONE MAKE IT TO THE HOUSE?
Y-YEAH, I THINK.
OH, GOD-- THEY'RE GETTING INSIDE!
W-WE HAVE TO HURRY!
C'MON, LET'S GO!
=PANT= =PANT= THIS IS GONNA SUCK.
WAP
WAP
WAP
AGK! GUH...

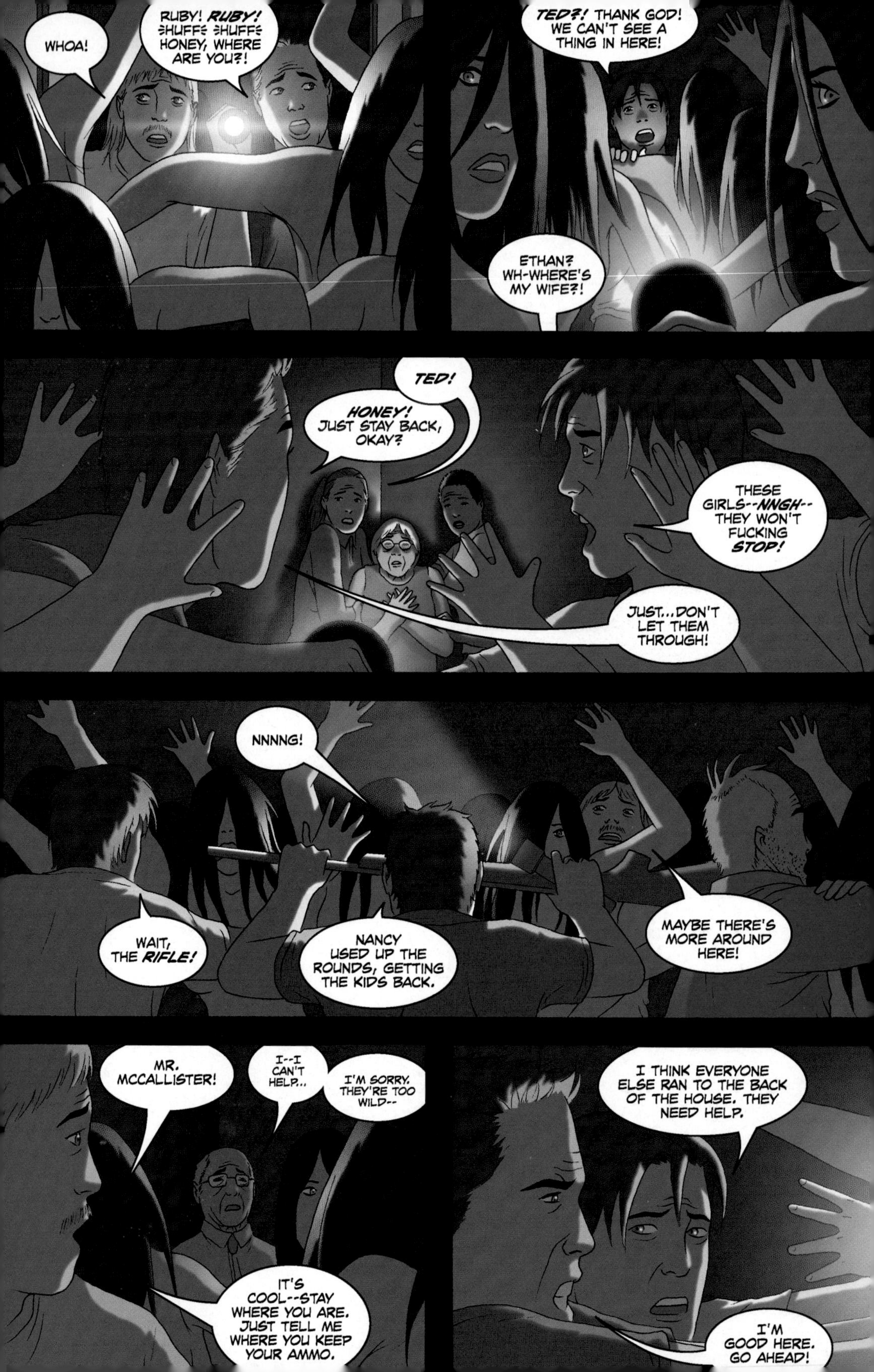
WHOA!
RUBY! RUBY! HUFF HUFF HONEY, WHERE ARE YOU?!
TED?! THANK GOD! WE CAN'T SEE A THING IN HERE!
ETHAN? WH-WHERE'S MY WIFE?!
TED!
HONEY! JUST STAY BACK, OKAY?
THESE GIRLS--NNGH--THEY WON'T FUCKING STOP!
JUST...DON'T LET THEM THROUGH!
NNNNG!
WAIT, THE RIFLE!
NANCY USED UP THE ROUNDS, GETTING THE KIDS BACK.
MAYBE THERE'S MORE AROUND HERE!
MR. MCCALLISTER!
I--I CAN'T HELP...
I'M SORRY. THEY'RE TOO WILD--
IT'S COOL--STAY WHERE YOU ARE. JUST TELL ME WHERE YOU KEEP YOUR AMMO.
I THINK EVERYONE ELSE RAN TO THE BACK OF THE HOUSE. THEY NEED HELP.
I'M GOOD HERE. GO AHEAD!

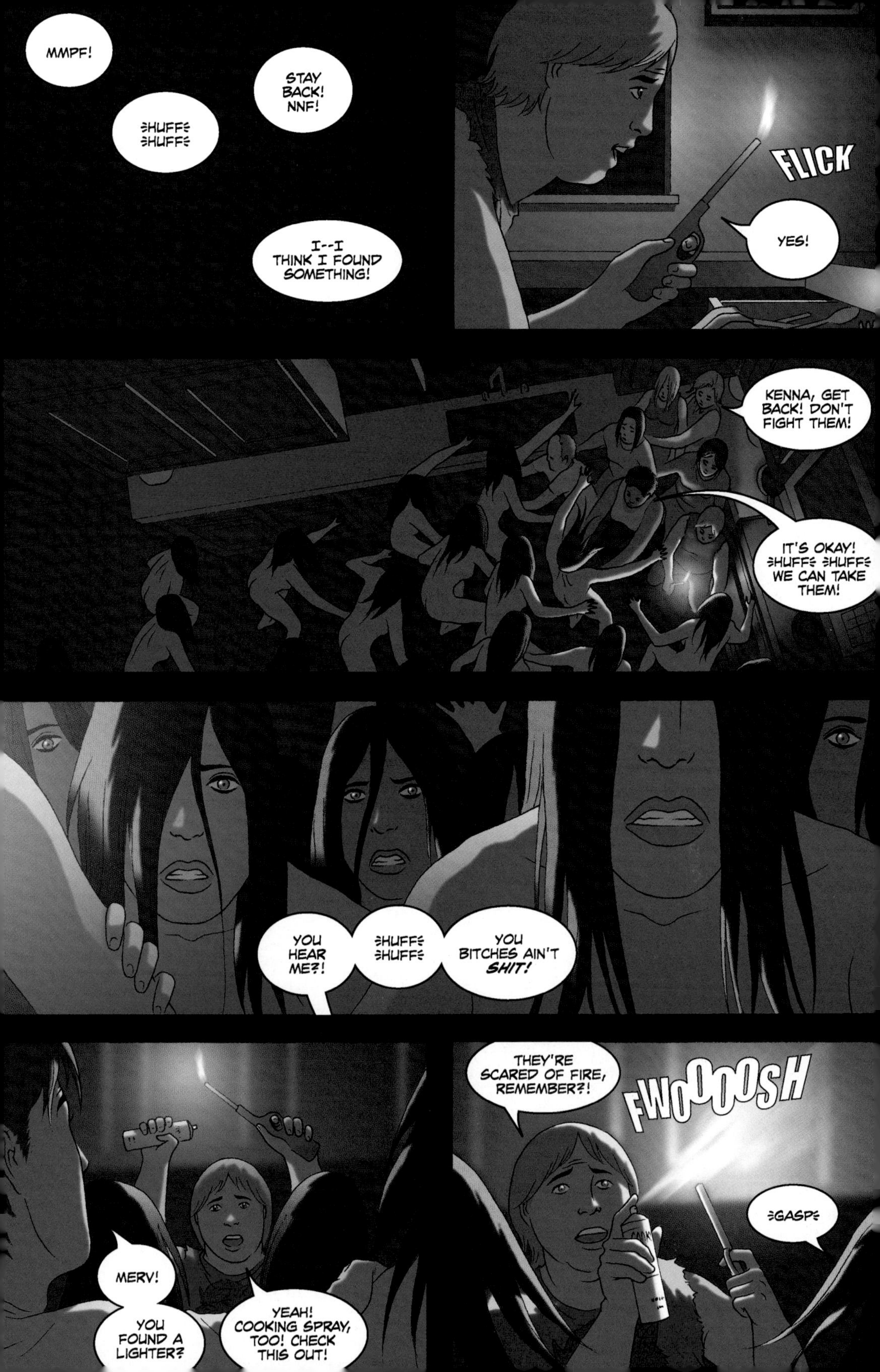
MMPF!
⁼HUFF⁼ ⁼HUFF⁼
STAY BACK! NNF!
I--I THINK I FOUND SOMETHING!
FLICK
YES!
KENNA, GET BACK! DON'T FIGHT THEM!
IT'S OKAY! ⁼HUFF⁼ ⁼HUFF⁼ WE CAN TAKE THEM!
YOU HEAR ME?!
⁼HUFF⁼ ⁼HUFF⁼
YOU BITCHES AIN'T *SHIT!*
MERV!
YOU FOUND A LIGHTER?
YEAH! COOKING SPRAY, TOO! CHECK THIS OUT!
THEY'RE SCARED OF FIRE, REMEMBER?!
FWOOOOSH
⁼GASP⁼

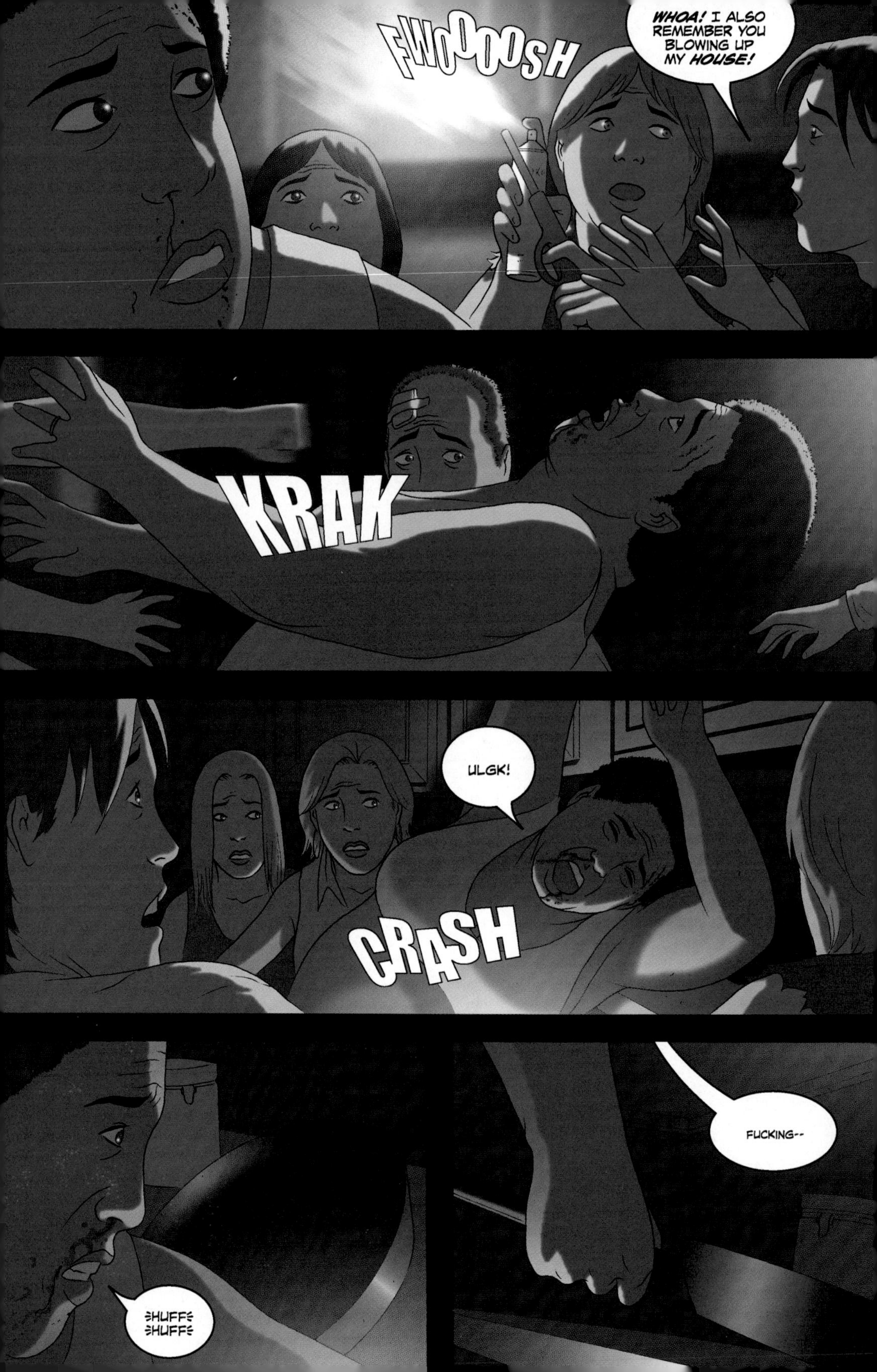
FWOOOOSH
WHOA! I ALSO REMEMBER YOU BLOWING UP MY HOUSE!
KRAK
ULGK!
CRASH
FUCKING--
HUFF HUFF

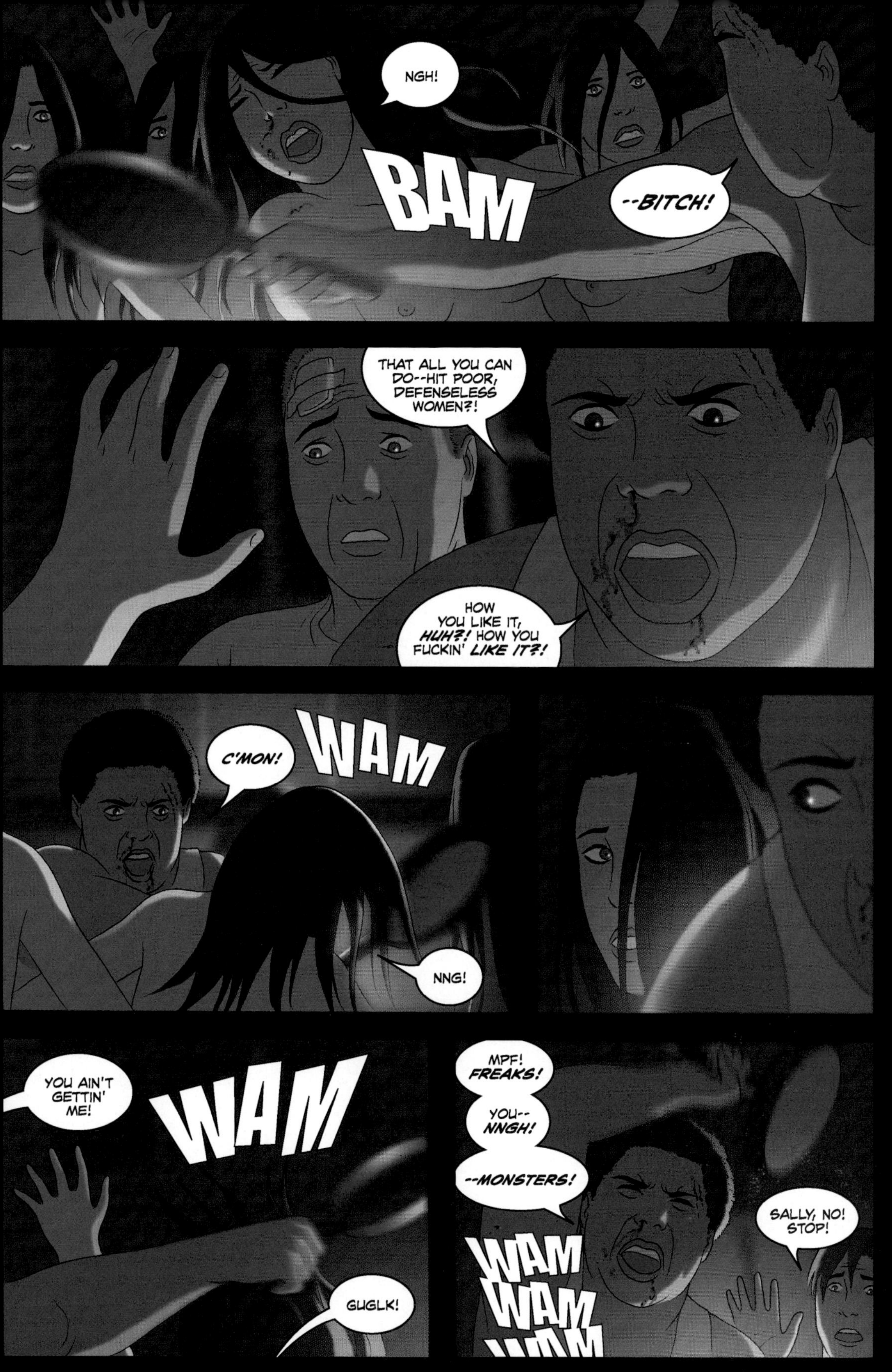
NGH!
BAM
--BITCH!
THAT ALL YOU CAN DO--HIT POOR, DEFENSELESS WOMEN?!
HOW YOU LIKE IT, HUH?! HOW YOU FUCKIN' LIKE IT?!
C'MON!
WAM
NNG!
YOU AIN'T GETTIN' ME!
WAM
GUGLK!
MPF! FREAKS!
YOU-- NNGH!
--MONSTERS!
WAM
WAM
SALLY, NO! STOP!

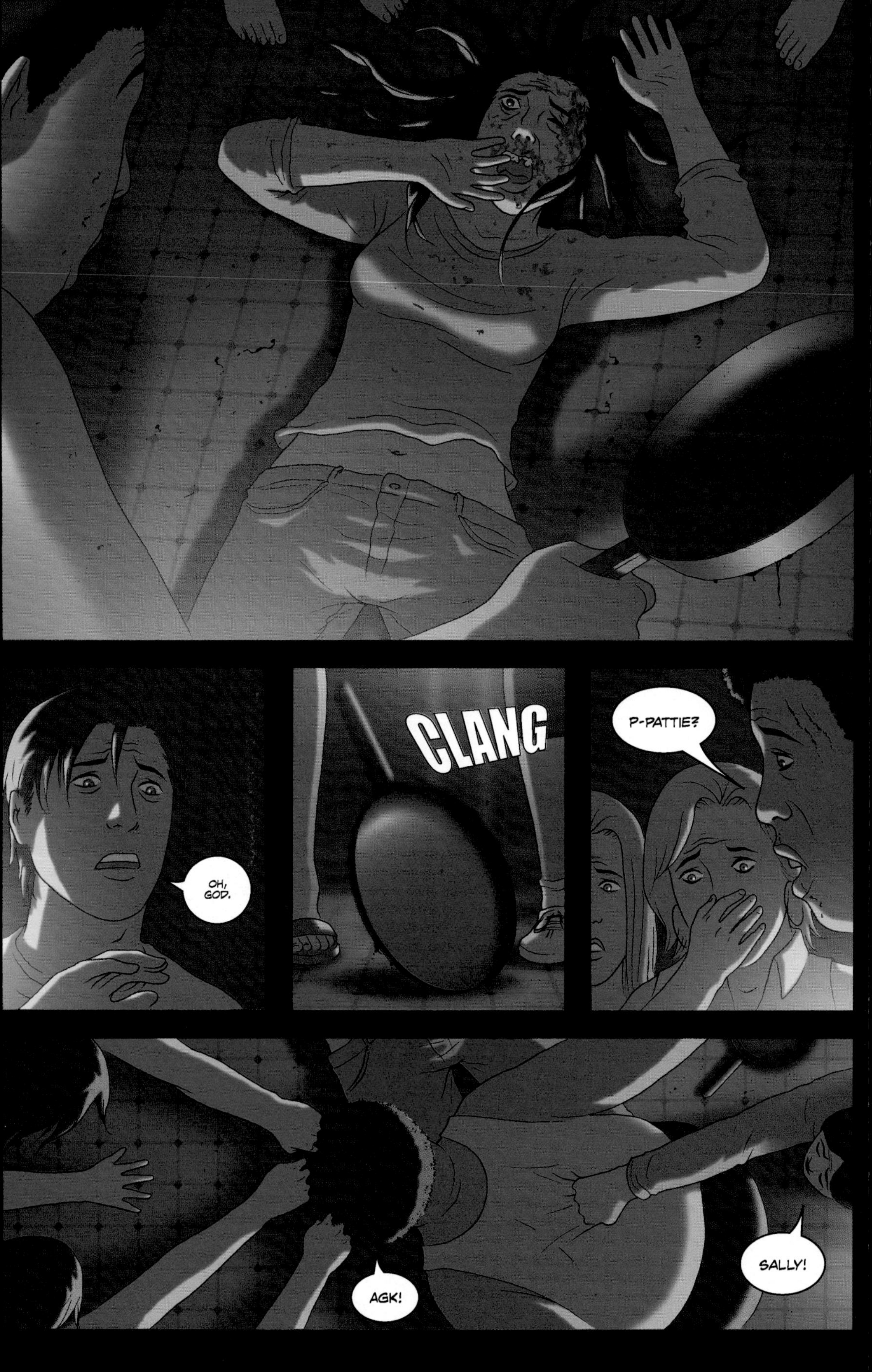
OH, GOD.
CLANG
P-PATTIE?
AGK!
SALLY!

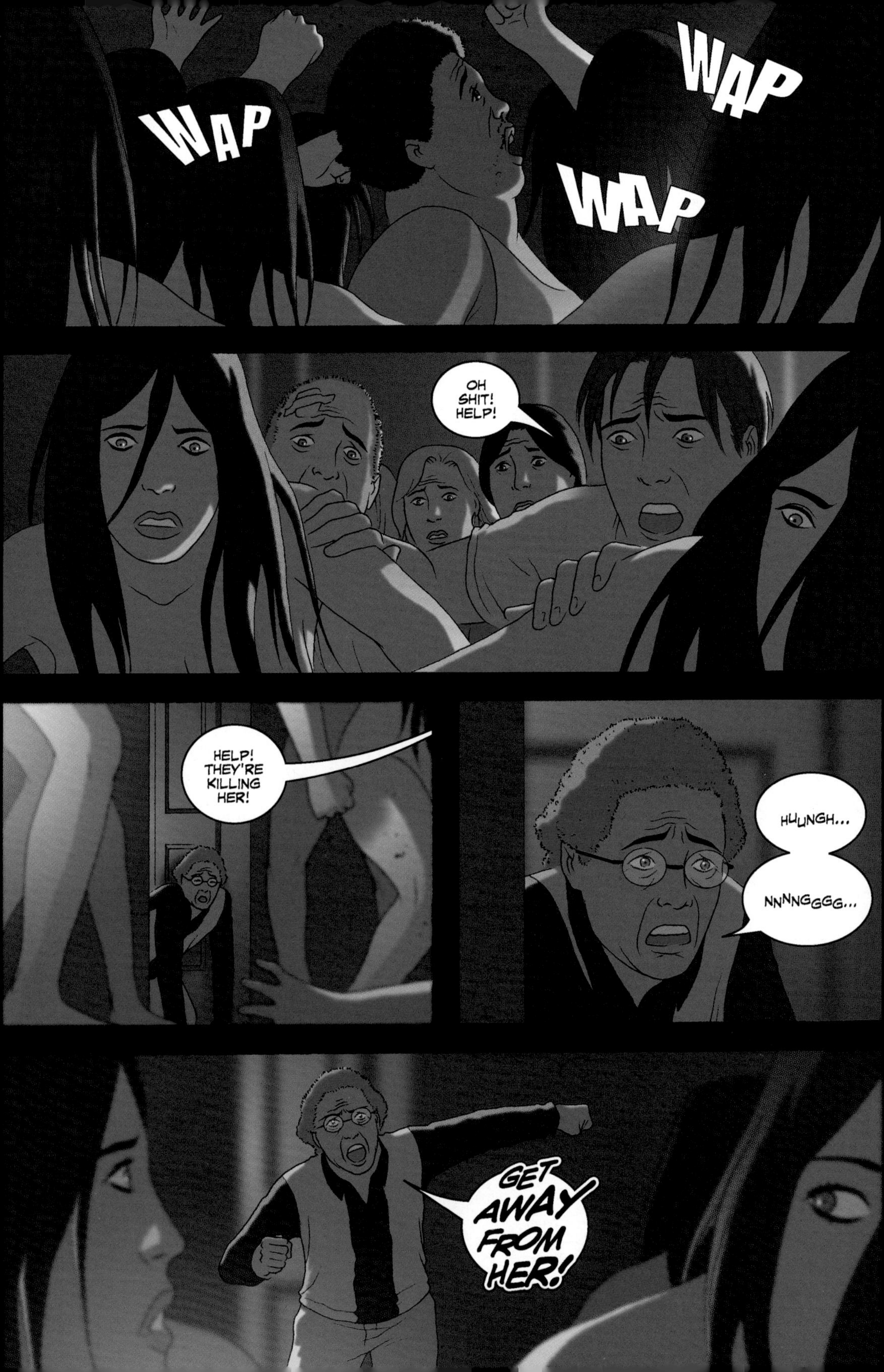
WAP
WAP
WAP
OH SHIT! HELP!
HELP! THEY'RE KILLING HER!
HUUNGH...
NNNNGGGG...
GET AWAY FROM HER!

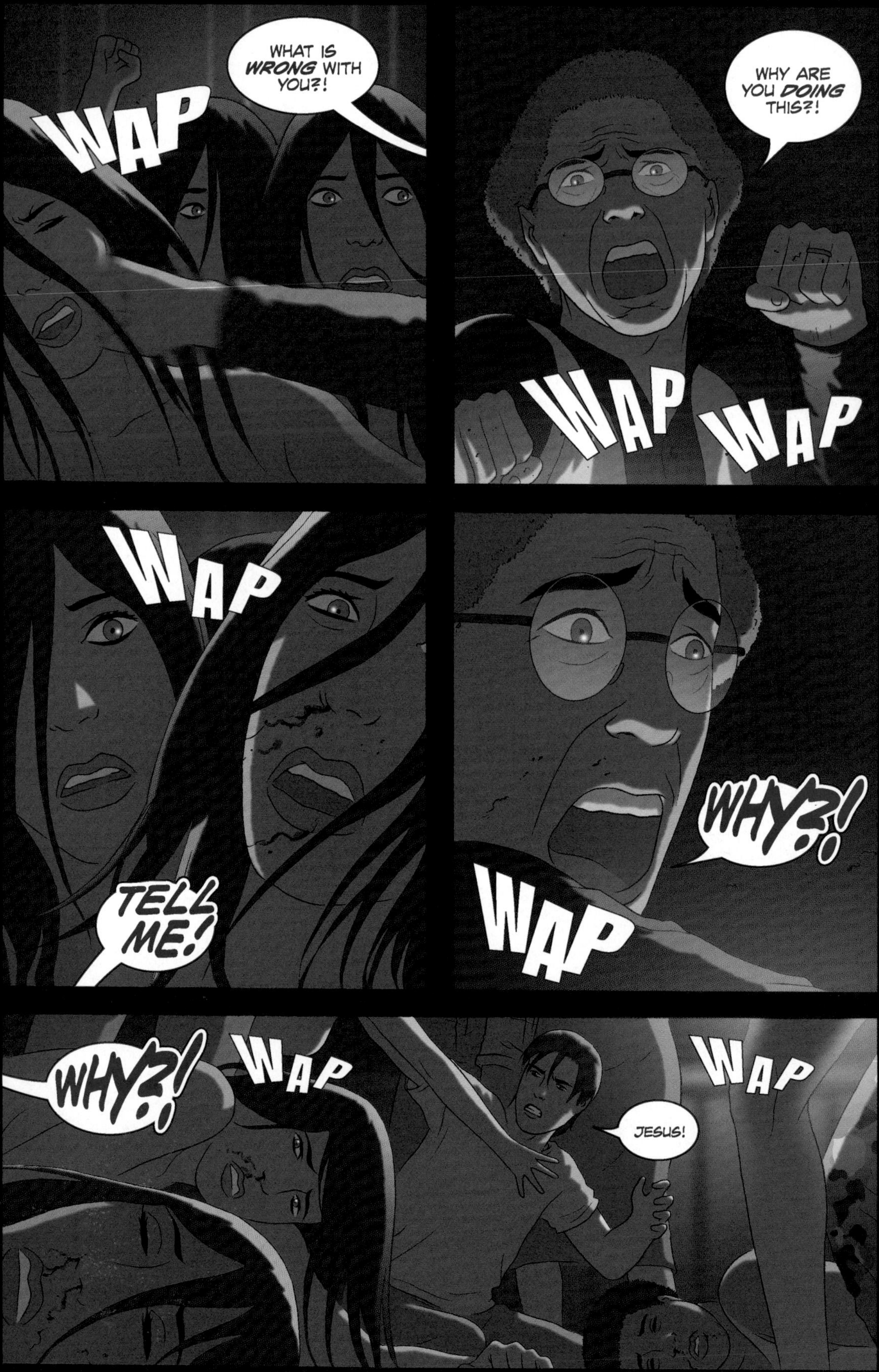
WHAT IS WRONG WITH YOU?!
WAP
WHY ARE YOU DOING THIS?!
WAP
WAP
WAP
TELL ME!
WHY?!
WAP
WHY?!
WAP
JESUS!
WAP

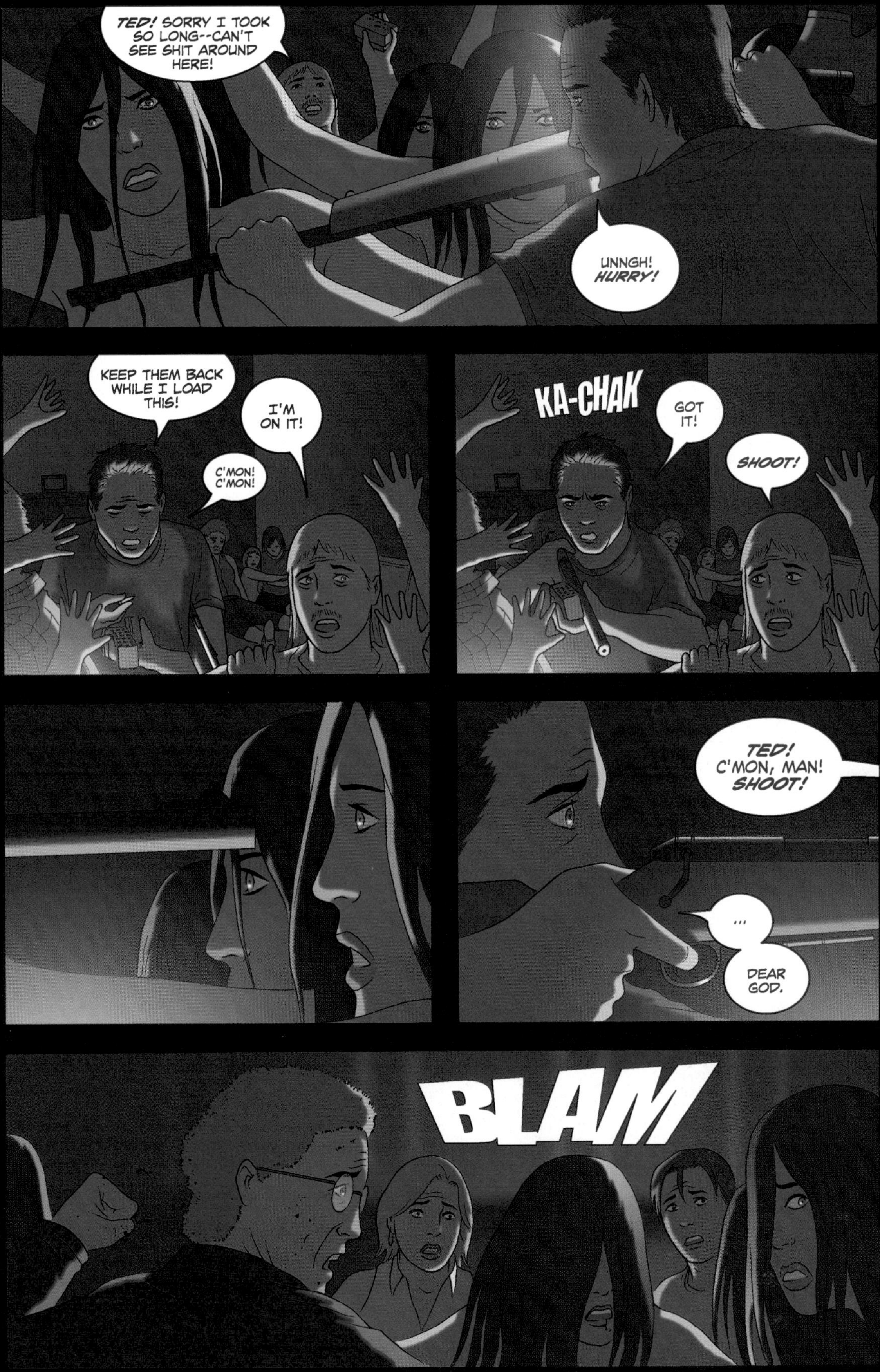
TED! SORRY I TOOK SO LONG--CAN'T SEE SHIT AROUND HERE!
UNNGH! HURRY!
KEEP THEM BACK WHILE I LOAD THIS!
I'M ON IT!
C'MON! C'MON!
KA-CHAK
GOT IT!
SHOOT!
TED! C'MON, MAN! SHOOT!
...
DEAR GOD.
BLAM

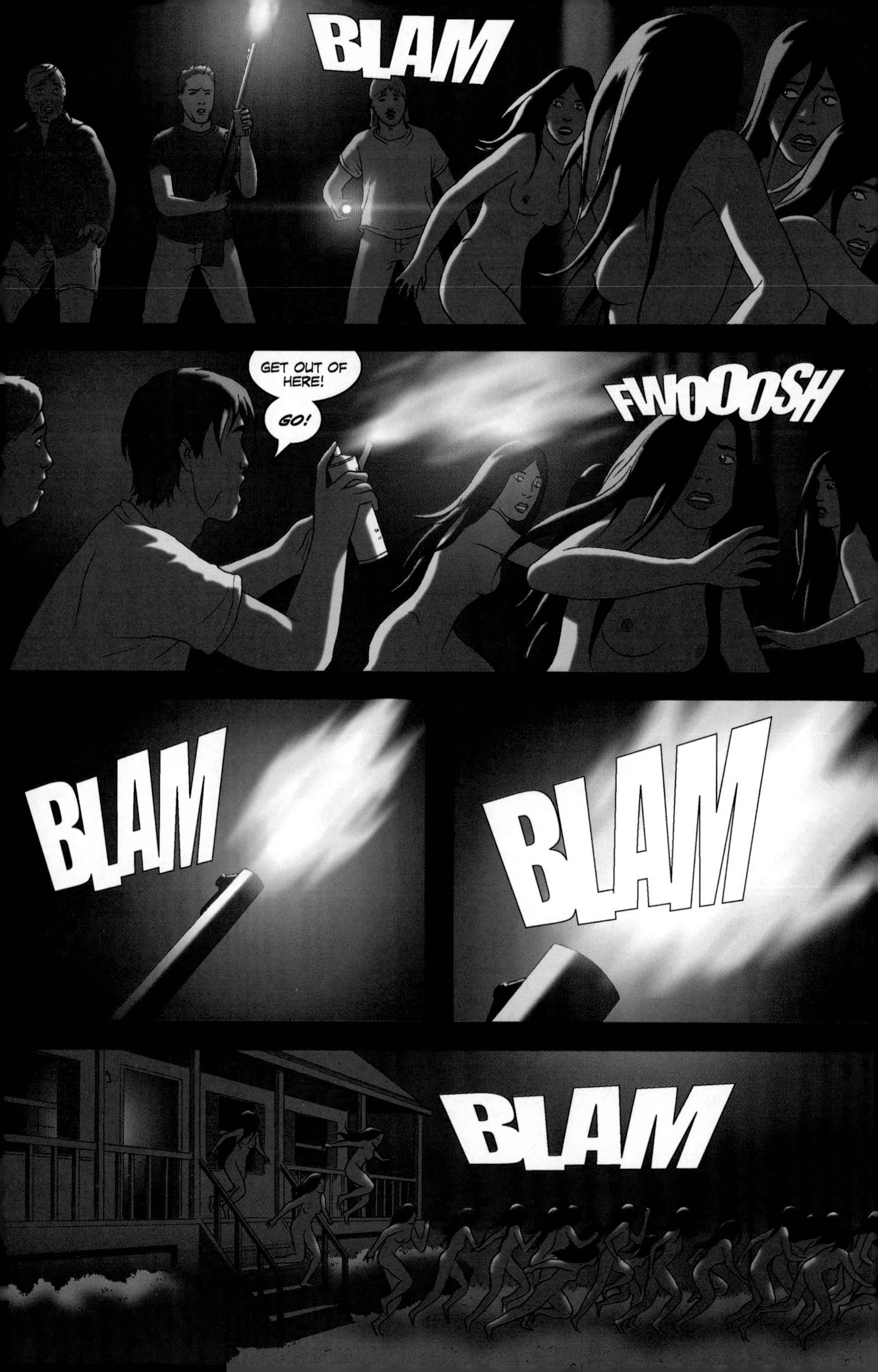
BLAM
GET OUT OF HERE!
GO!
FWOOOSH
BLAM
BLAM
BLAM

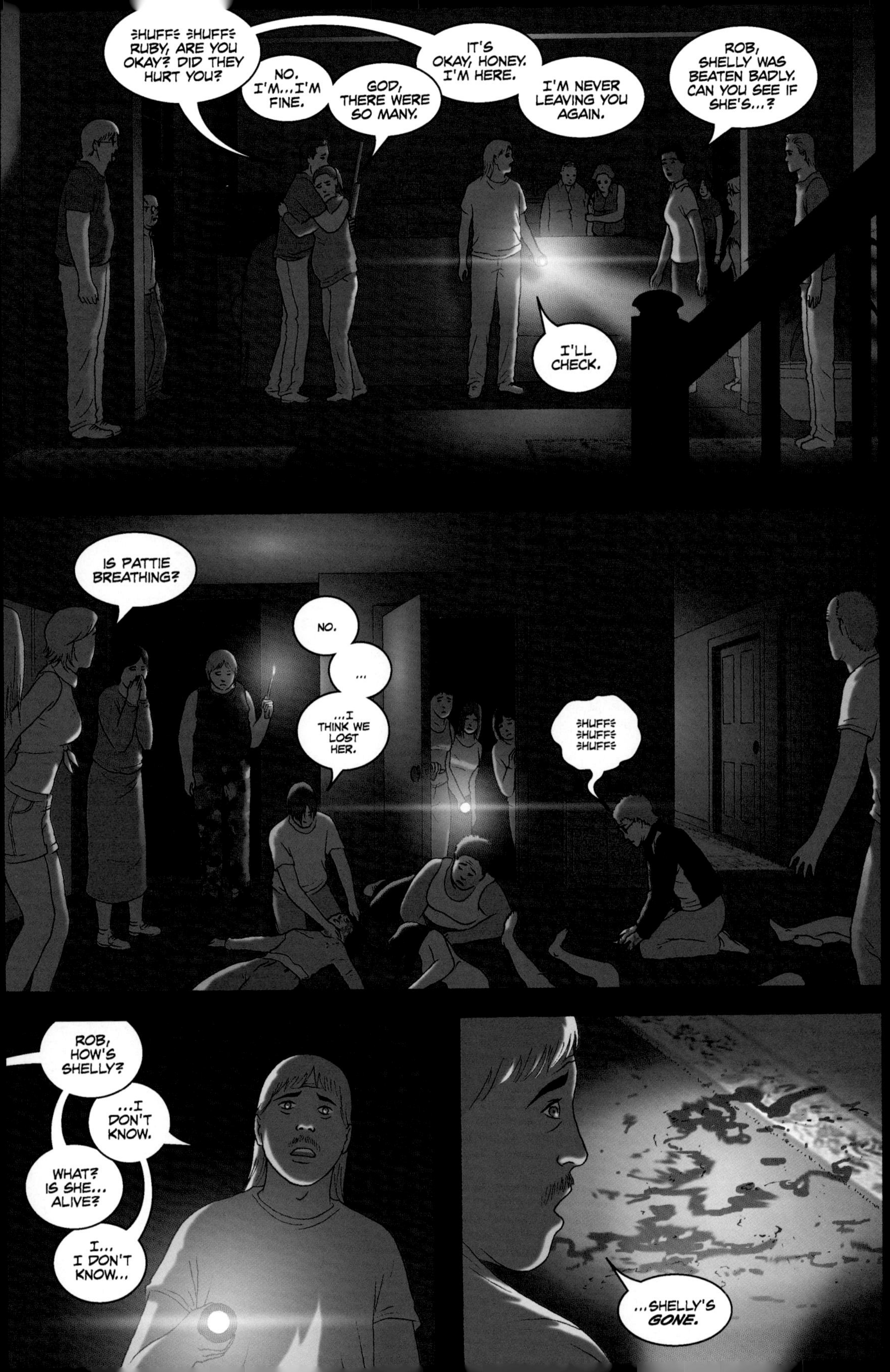

HUFF HUFF RUBY, ARE YOU OKAY? DID THEY HURT YOU?
NO. I'M...I'M FINE.
GOD, THERE WERE SO MANY.
IT'S OKAY, HONEY. I'M HERE.
I'M NEVER LEAVING YOU AGAIN.
ROB, SHELLY WAS BEATEN BADLY. CAN YOU SEE IF SHE'S...?
I'LL CHECK.
IS PATTIE BREATHING?
NO.
...
...I THINK WE LOST HER.
HUFF HUFF HUFF
ROB, HOW'S SHELLY?
...I DON'T KNOW.
WHAT? IS SHE... ALIVE?
I... I DON'T KNOW...
...SHELLY'S GONE.

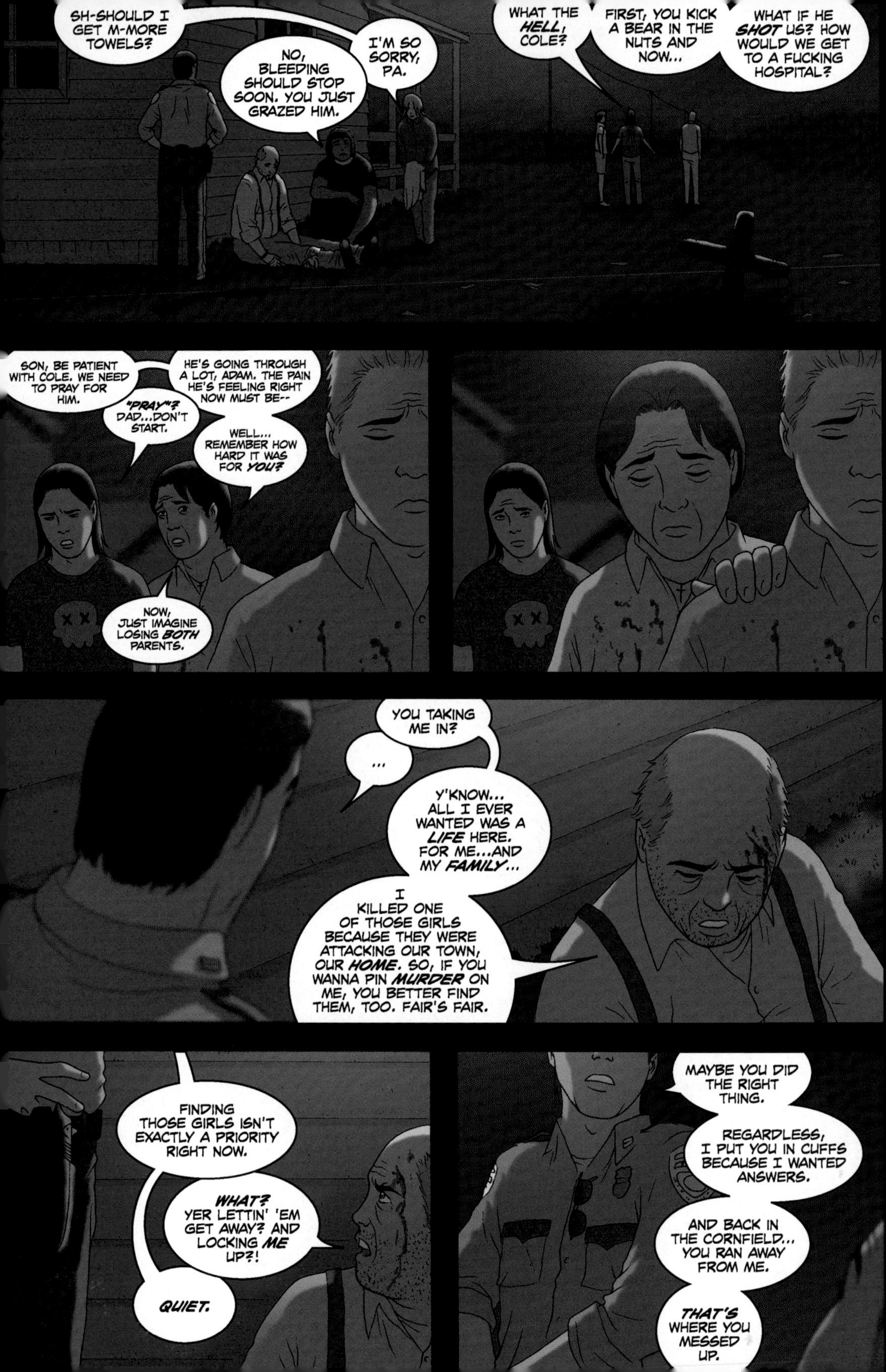
SH-SHOULD I GET M-MORE TOWELS?
I'M SO SORRY, PA.
NO, BLEEDING SHOULD STOP SOON. YOU JUST GRAZED HIM.
WHAT THE HELL, COLE?
FIRST, YOU KICK A BEAR IN THE NUTS AND NOW...
WHAT IF HE SHOT US? HOW WOULD WE GET TO A FUCKING HOSPITAL?
SON, BE PATIENT WITH COLE. WE NEED TO PRAY FOR HIM.
"PRAY"? DAD...DON'T START.
HE'S GOING THROUGH A LOT, ADAM. THE PAIN HE'S FEELING RIGHT NOW MUST BE--
WELL... REMEMBER HOW HARD IT WAS FOR YOU?
NOW, JUST IMAGINE LOSING BOTH PARENTS.
YOU TAKING ME IN?
...
Y'KNOW... ALL I EVER WANTED WAS A LIFE HERE. FOR ME...AND MY FAMILY...
I KILLED ONE OF THOSE GIRLS BECAUSE THEY WERE ATTACKING OUR TOWN, OUR HOME. SO, IF YOU WANNA PIN MURDER ON ME, YOU BETTER FIND THEM, TOO. FAIR'S FAIR.
FINDING THOSE GIRLS ISN'T EXACTLY A PRIORITY RIGHT NOW.
WHAT? YER LETTIN' 'EM GET AWAY? AND LOCKING ME UP?!
QUIET.
MAYBE YOU DID THE RIGHT THING.
REGARDLESS, I PUT YOU IN CUFFS BECAUSE I WANTED ANSWERS.
AND BACK IN THE CORNFIELD... YOU RAN AWAY FROM ME.
THAT'S WHERE YOU MESSED UP.

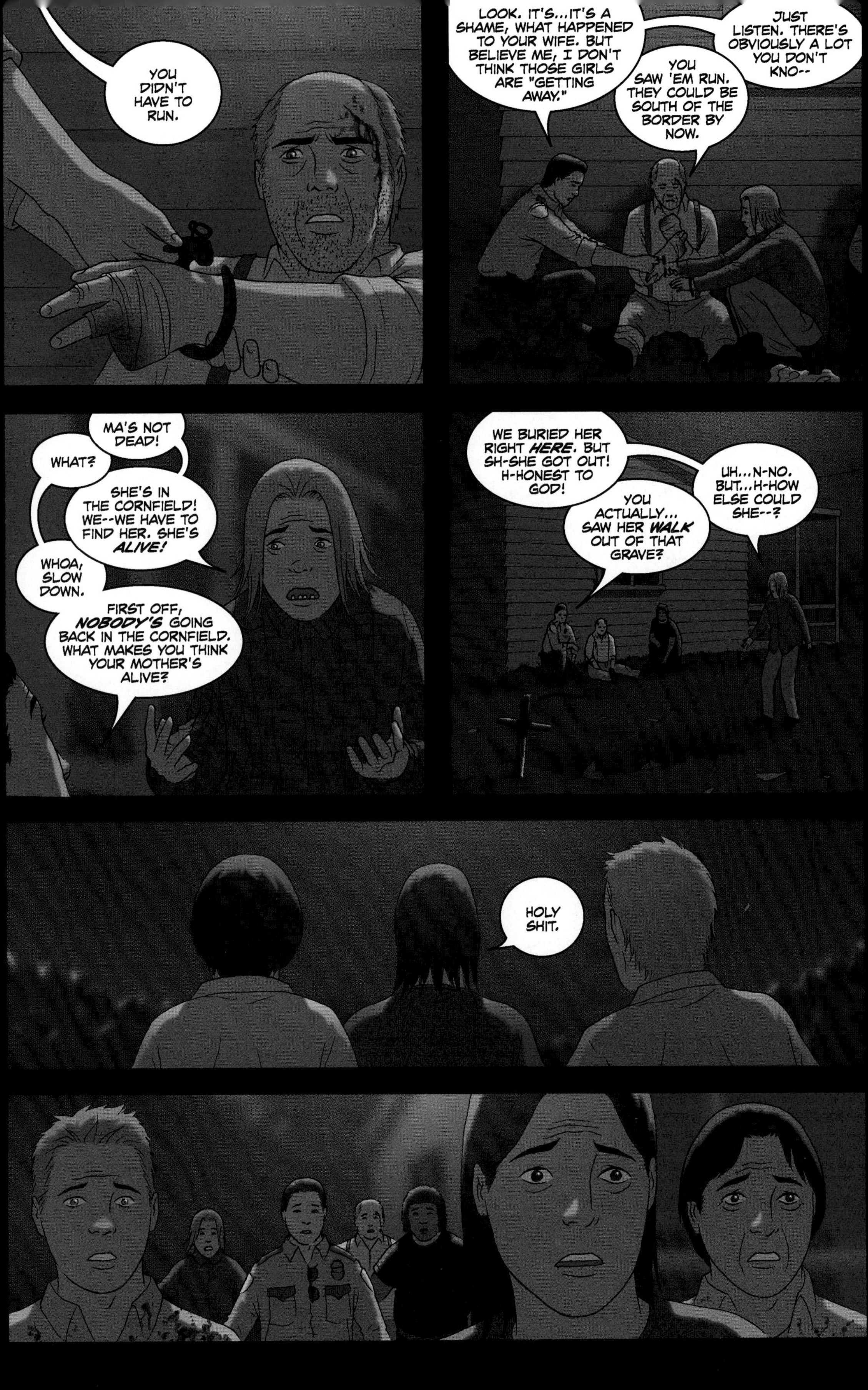
YOU DIDN'T HAVE TO RUN.
LOOK. IT'S...IT'S A SHAME, WHAT HAPPENED TO YOUR WIFE. BUT BELIEVE ME, I DON'T THINK THOSE GIRLS ARE "GETTING AWAY."
YOU SAW 'EM RUN. THEY COULD BE SOUTH OF THE BORDER BY NOW.
JUST LISTEN. THERE'S OBVIOUSLY A LOT YOU DON'T KNO--
MA'S NOT DEAD!
WHAT?
SHE'S IN THE CORNFIELD! WE--WE HAVE TO FIND HER. SHE'S ALIVE!
WHOA, SLOW DOWN.
FIRST OFF, NOBODY'S GOING BACK IN THE CORNFIELD. WHAT MAKES YOU THINK YOUR MOTHER'S ALIVE?
WE BURIED HER RIGHT HERE. BUT SH-SHE GOT OUT! H-HONEST TO GOD!
YOU ACTUALLY... SAW HER WALK OUT OF THAT GRAVE?
UH...N-NO. BUT...H-HOW ELSE COULD SHE--?
HOLY SHIT.

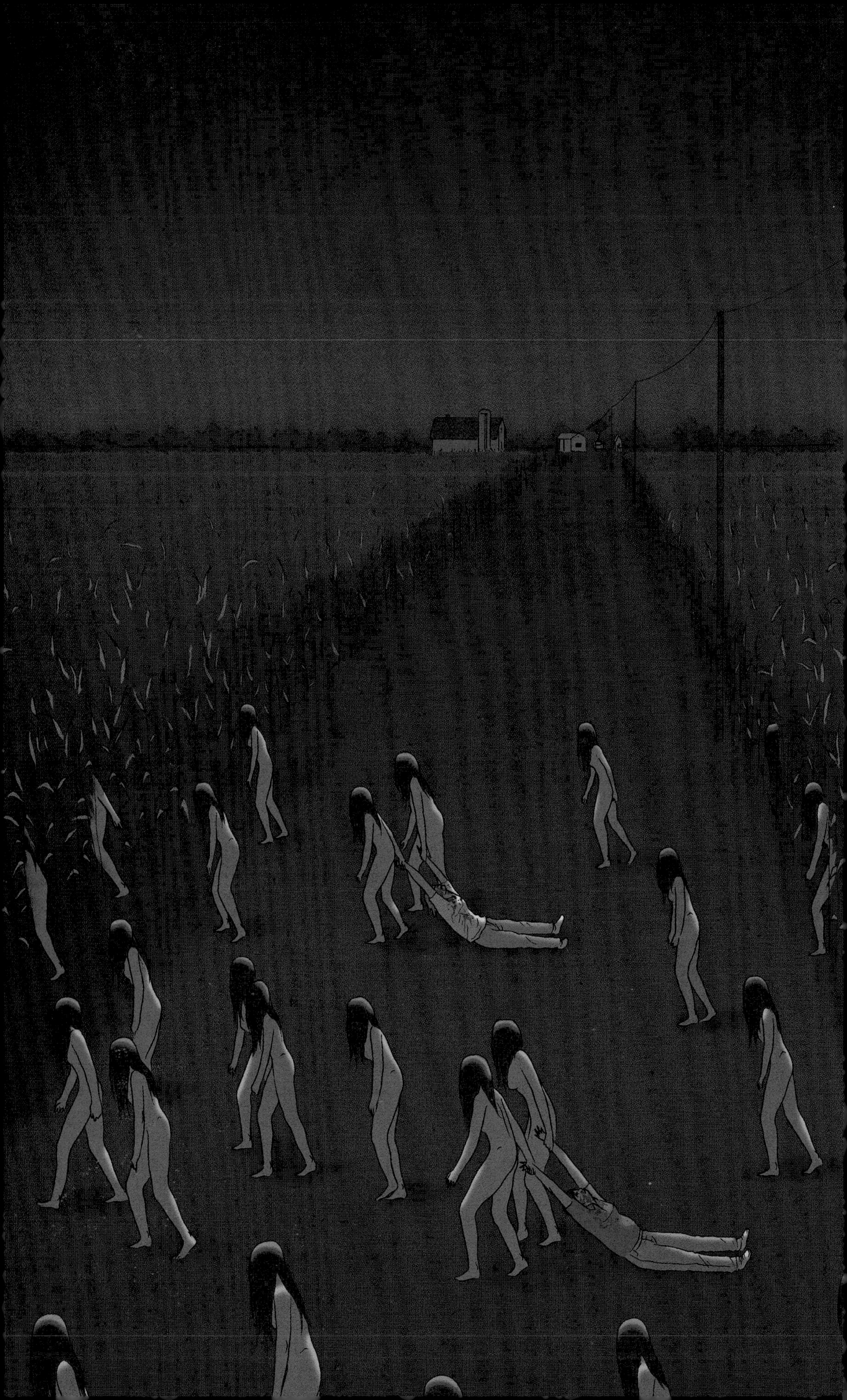

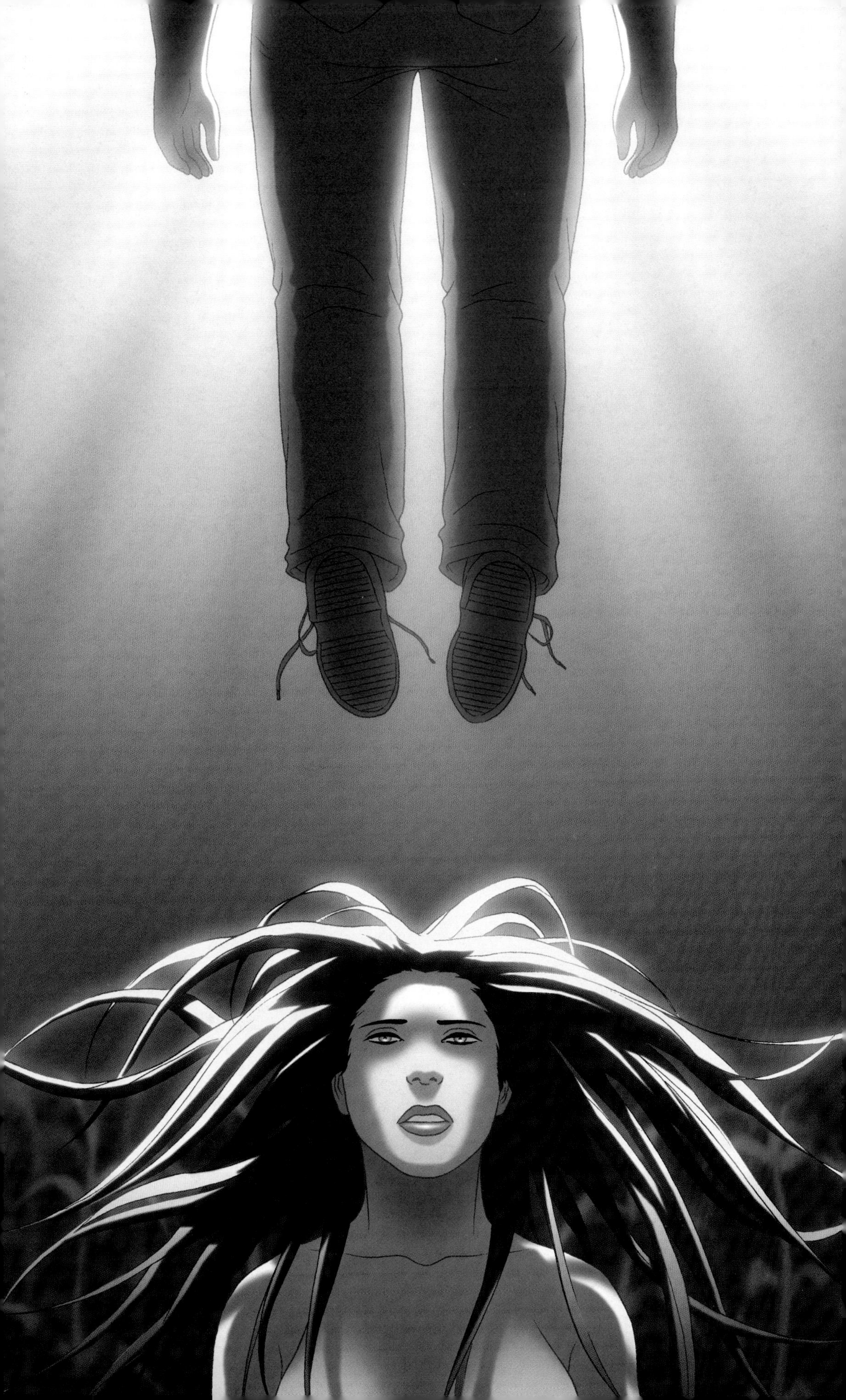

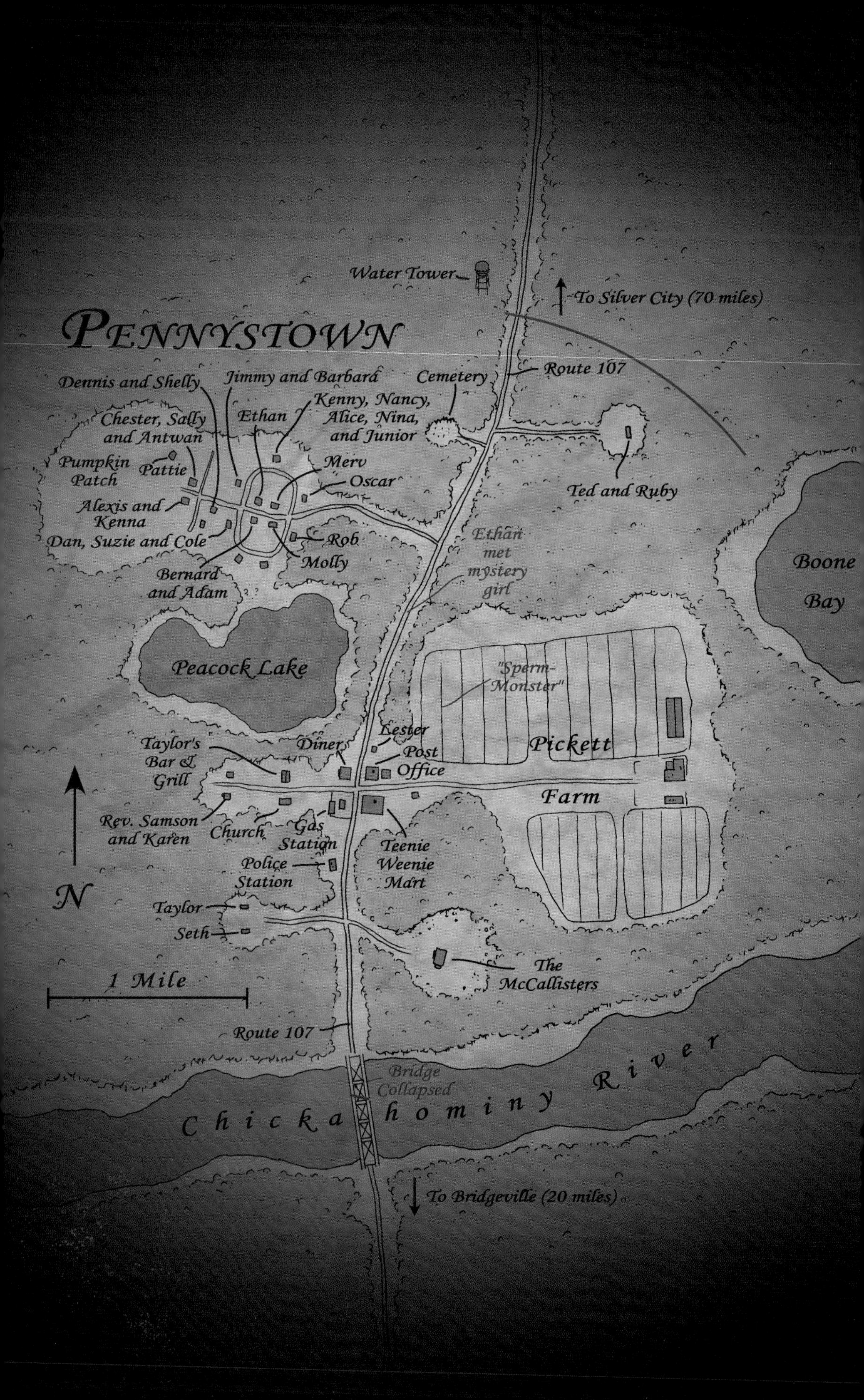

Water Tower

↑ To Silver City (70 miles)

PENNYSTOWN

Dennis and Shelly

Jimmy and Barbara

Cemetery

Route 107

Chester, Sally and Antwan

Ethan

Kenny, Nancy, Alice, Nina, and Junior

Pumpkin Patch

Pattie

Merv

Oscar

Alexis and Kenna

Dan, Suzie and Cole

Rob

Molly

Ted and Ruby

Bernard and Adam

Ethan met mystery girl

Boone Bay

Peacock Lake

"Sperm-Monster"

Pickett

Taylor's Bar & Grill

Diner

Lester

Post Office

Farm

Rev. Samson and Karen

Church

Gas Station

Police Station

Teenie Weenie Mart

Taylor

Seth

N

The McCallisters

1 Mile

Route 107

Bridge Collapsed

C h i c k a h o m i n y   R i v e r

↓ To Bridgeville (20 miles)

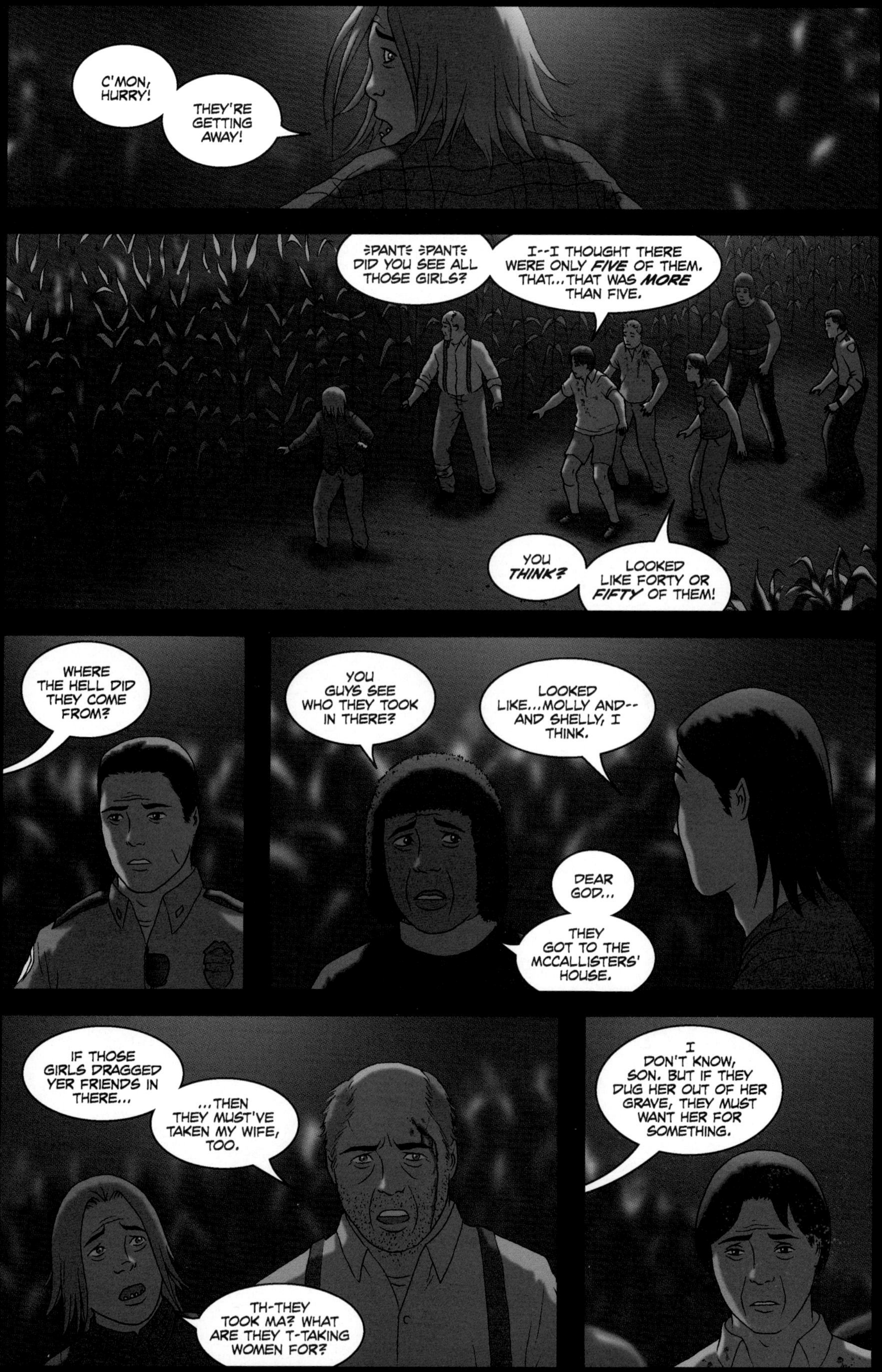
C'MON, HURRY!
THEY'RE GETTING AWAY!
=PANT= =PANT= DID YOU SEE ALL THOSE GIRLS?
I--I THOUGHT THERE WERE ONLY *FIVE* OF THEM. THAT...THAT WAS *MORE* THAN FIVE.
YOU *THINK?*
LOOKED LIKE FORTY OR *FIFTY* OF THEM!
WHERE THE HELL DID THEY COME FROM?
YOU GUYS SEE WHO THEY TOOK IN THERE?
LOOKED LIKE...MOLLY AND--AND SHELLY, I THINK.
DEAR GOD...
THEY GOT TO THE MCCALLISTERS' HOUSE.
IF THOSE GIRLS DRAGGED YER FRIENDS IN THERE...
...THEN THEY MUST'VE TAKEN MY WIFE, TOO.
TH-THEY TOOK MA? WHAT ARE THEY T-TAKING WOMEN FOR?
I DON'T KNOW, SON. BUT IF THEY DUG HER OUT OF HER GRAVE, THEY MUST WANT HER FOR SOMETHING.

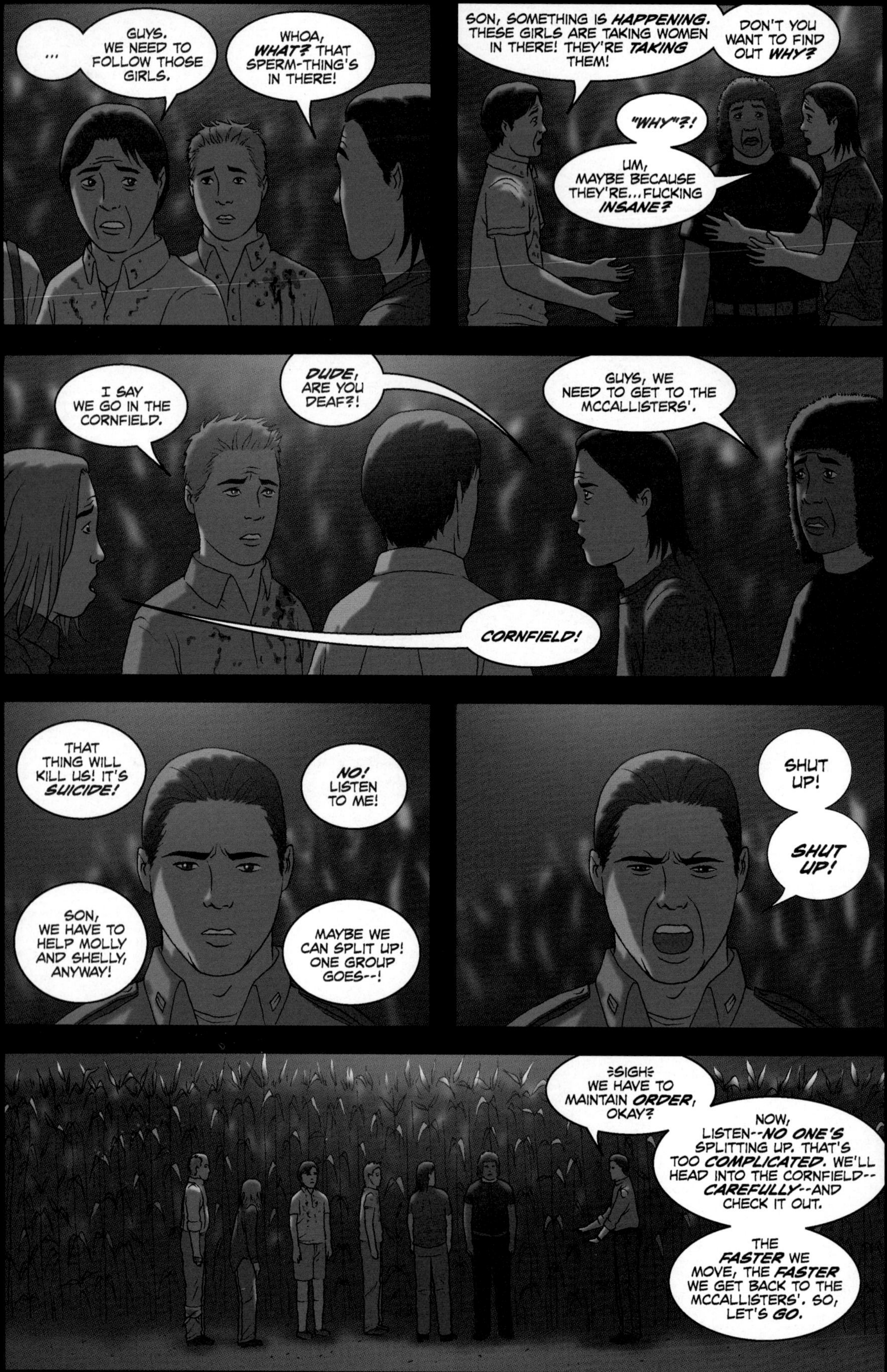
...
GUYS. WE NEED TO FOLLOW THOSE GIRLS.
WHOA, WHAT? THAT SPERM-THING'S IN THERE!
SON, SOMETHING IS HAPPENING. THESE GIRLS ARE TAKING WOMEN IN THERE! THEY'RE TAKING THEM!
DON'T YOU WANT TO FIND OUT WHY?
"WHY"?!
UM, MAYBE BECAUSE THEY'RE...FUCKING INSANE?
I SAY WE GO IN THE CORNFIELD.
DUDE, ARE YOU DEAF?!
CORNFIELD!
GUYS, WE NEED TO GET TO THE MCCALLISTERS'.
THAT THING WILL KILL US! IT'S SUICIDE!
NO! LISTEN TO ME!
SON, WE HAVE TO HELP MOLLY AND SHELLY, ANYWAY!
MAYBE WE CAN SPLIT UP! ONE GROUP GOES--!
SHUT UP!
SHUT UP!
SIGH
WE HAVE TO MAINTAIN ORDER, OKAY?
NOW, LISTEN--NO ONE'S SPLITTING UP. THAT'S TOO COMPLICATED. WE'LL HEAD INTO THE CORNFIELD--CAREFULLY--AND CHECK IT OUT.
THE FASTER WE MOVE, THE FASTER WE GET BACK TO THE MCCALLISTERS'. SO, LET'S GO.

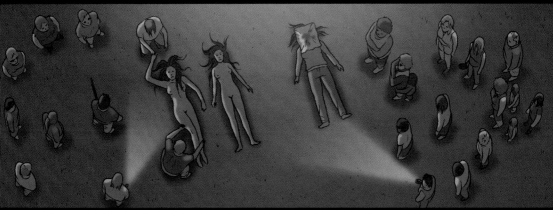

WELL, GUYS...IT SEEMS LIKE THE RIFLE SHOTS SCARED THOSE WOMEN OFF PRETTY GOOD.

BUT WHILE WE'RE STILL WAITING FOR WES, WE SHOULD PROBABLY FORTIFY THIS PLACE SOMEHOW. JUST IN CASE OF ANOTHER ATTACK.

WE CAN BUILD SOME BONFIRES.

WHAT?

≋AHEM≋ THOSE GIRLS ARE REALLY AFRAID OF FIRE, TOO. WE CAN SET UP A PERIMETER OR SOMETHING.

WE KEEP FIREWOOD IN THE SHED.

OKAY, ALRIGHT...THAT SOUNDS LIKE A PLAN.

I NEED TWO GROUPS. ONE TO GATHER UP THE WOOD AND PILE THEM AROUND THE HOUSE--

--AND THE OTHER TO KEEP REMOVING BODIES FROM THE HOUSE.

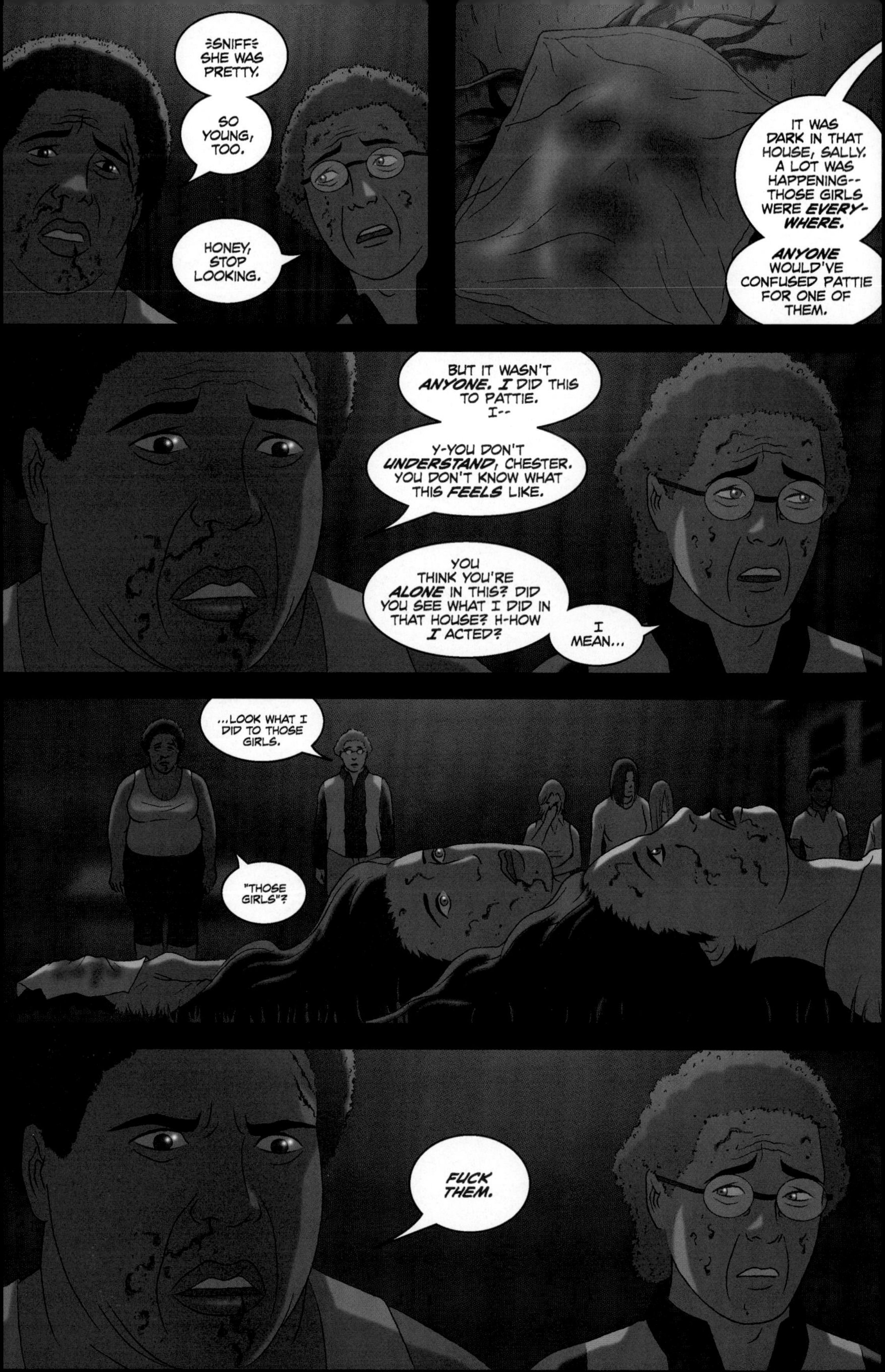

≡SNIFF≡ SHE WAS PRETTY.
SO YOUNG, TOO.
HONEY, STOP LOOKING.
IT WAS DARK IN THAT HOUSE, SALLY. A LOT WAS HAPPENING-- THOSE GIRLS WERE EVERY-WHERE.
ANYONE WOULD'VE CONFUSED PATTIE FOR ONE OF THEM.
BUT IT WASN'T ANYONE. I DID THIS TO PATTIE. I--
Y-YOU DON'T UNDERSTAND, CHESTER. YOU DON'T KNOW WHAT THIS FEELS LIKE.
YOU THINK YOU'RE ALONE IN THIS? DID YOU SEE WHAT I DID IN THAT HOUSE? H-HOW I ACTED?
I MEAN...
...LOOK WHAT I DID TO THOSE GIRLS.
"THOSE GIRLS"?
FUCK THEM.

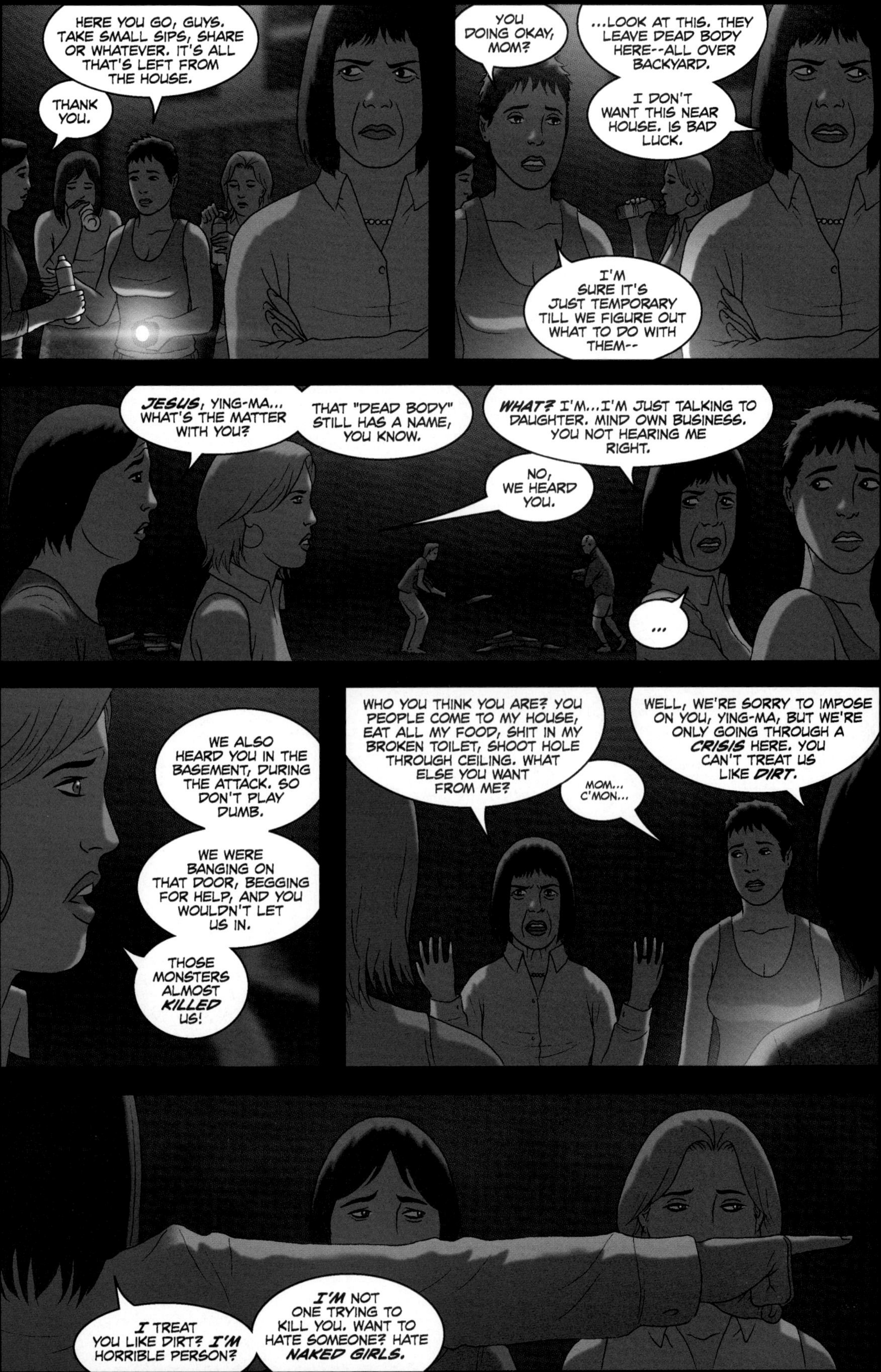
HERE YOU GO, GUYS. TAKE SMALL SIPS, SHARE OR WHATEVER. IT'S ALL THAT'S LEFT FROM THE HOUSE.
THANK YOU.
YOU DOING OKAY, MOM?
...LOOK AT THIS. THEY LEAVE DEAD BODY HERE--ALL OVER BACKYARD.
I DON'T WANT THIS NEAR HOUSE. IS BAD LUCK.
I'M SURE IT'S JUST TEMPORARY TILL WE FIGURE OUT WHAT TO DO WITH THEM--
JESUS, YING-MA... WHAT'S THE MATTER WITH YOU?
THAT "DEAD BODY" STILL HAS A NAME, YOU KNOW.
WHAT? I'M...I'M JUST TALKING TO DAUGHTER. MIND OWN BUSINESS. YOU NOT HEARING ME RIGHT.
NO, WE HEARD YOU.
...
WE ALSO HEARD YOU IN THE BASEMENT, DURING THE ATTACK. SO DON'T PLAY DUMB.
WE WERE BANGING ON THAT DOOR, BEGGING FOR HELP, AND YOU WOULDN'T LET US IN.
THOSE MONSTERS ALMOST KILLED US!
WHO YOU THINK YOU ARE? YOU PEOPLE COME TO MY HOUSE, EAT ALL MY FOOD, SHIT IN MY BROKEN TOILET, SHOOT HOLE THROUGH CEILING. WHAT ELSE YOU WANT FROM ME?
MOM... C'MON...
WELL, WE'RE SORRY TO IMPOSE ON YOU, YING-MA, BUT WE'RE ONLY GOING THROUGH A CRISIS HERE. YOU CAN'T TREAT US LIKE DIRT.
I TREAT YOU LIKE DIRT? I'M HORRIBLE PERSON?
I'M NOT ONE TRYING TO KILL YOU. WANT TO HATE SOMEONE? HATE NAKED GIRLS.

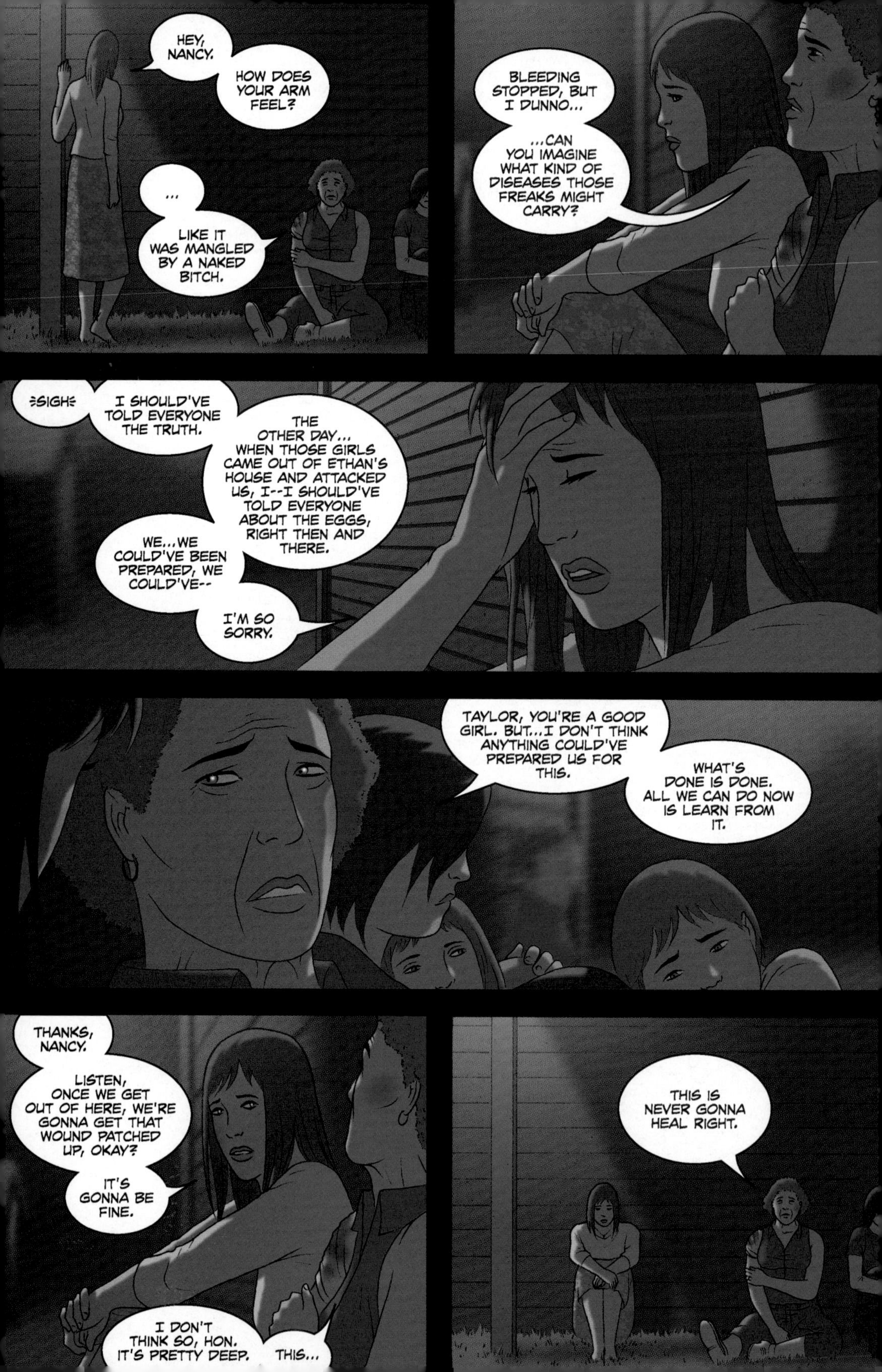
HEY, NANCY.
HOW DOES YOUR ARM FEEL?
...
LIKE IT WAS MANGLED BY A NAKED BITCH.
BLEEDING STOPPED, BUT I DUNNO...
...CAN YOU IMAGINE WHAT KIND OF DISEASES THOSE FREAKS MIGHT CARRY?
SIGH
I SHOULD'VE TOLD EVERYONE THE TRUTH.
THE OTHER DAY... WHEN THOSE GIRLS CAME OUT OF ETHAN'S HOUSE AND ATTACKED US, I--I SHOULD'VE TOLD EVERYONE ABOUT THE EGGS, RIGHT THEN AND THERE.
WE...WE COULD'VE BEEN PREPARED, WE COULD'VE--
I'M SO SORRY.
TAYLOR, YOU'RE A GOOD GIRL. BUT...I DON'T THINK ANYTHING COULD'VE PREPARED US FOR THIS.
WHAT'S DONE IS DONE. ALL WE CAN DO NOW IS LEARN FROM IT.
THANKS, NANCY.
LISTEN, ONCE WE GET OUT OF HERE, WE'RE GONNA GET THAT WOUND PATCHED UP, OKAY?
IT'S GONNA BE FINE.
I DON'T THINK SO, HON. IT'S PRETTY DEEP.
THIS...
THIS IS NEVER GONNA HEAL RIGHT.

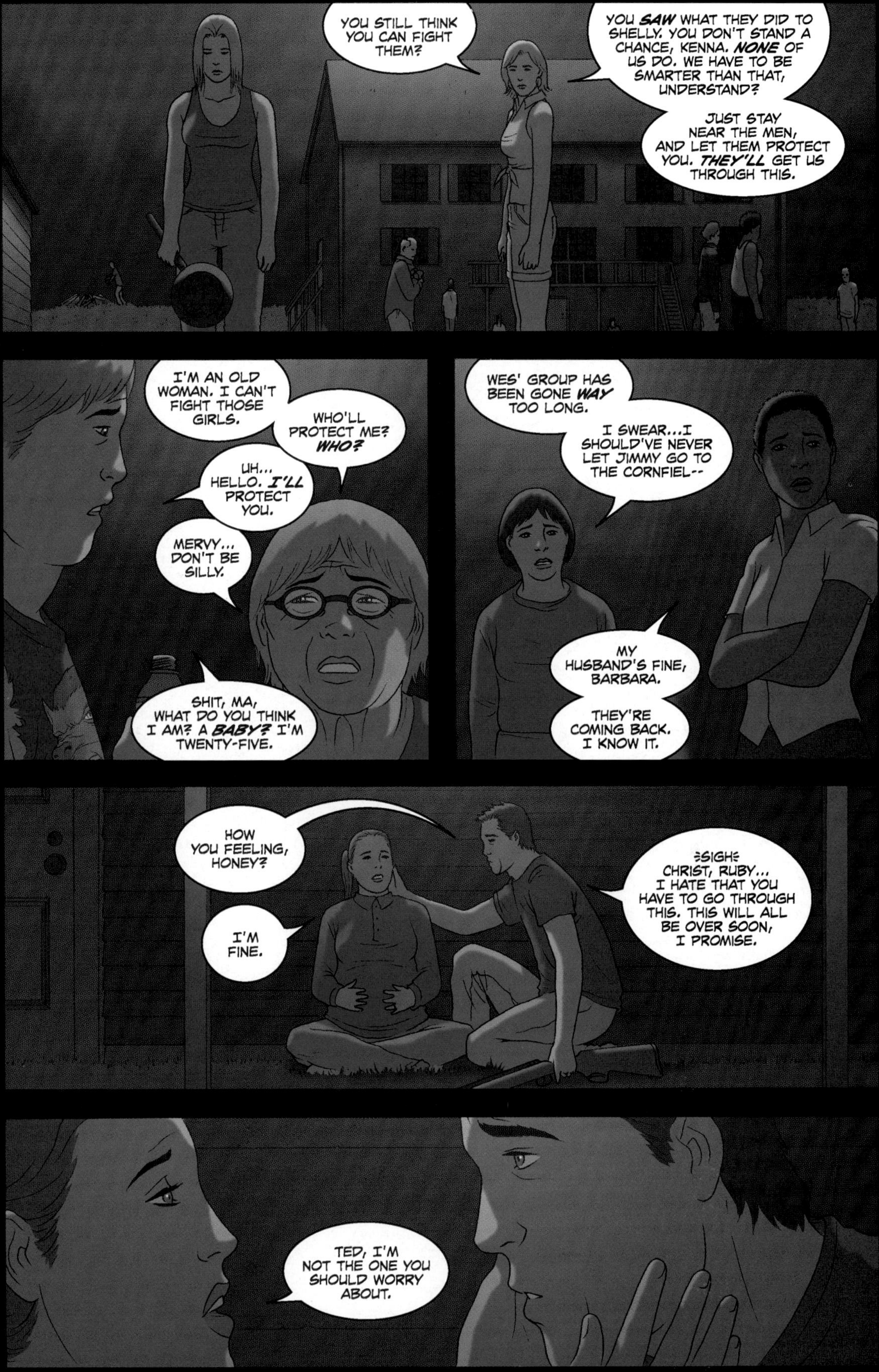
YOU STILL THINK YOU CAN FIGHT THEM?
YOU SAW WHAT THEY DID TO SHELLY. YOU DON'T STAND A CHANCE, KENNA. NONE OF US DO. WE HAVE TO BE SMARTER THAN THAT, UNDERSTAND?
JUST STAY NEAR THE MEN, AND LET THEM PROTECT YOU. THEY'LL GET US THROUGH THIS.
I'M AN OLD WOMAN. I CAN'T FIGHT THOSE GIRLS.
WHO'LL PROTECT ME? WHO?
UH... HELLO. I'LL PROTECT YOU.
MERVY... DON'T BE SILLY.
SHIT, MA, WHAT DO YOU THINK I AM? A BABY? I'M TWENTY-FIVE.
WES' GROUP HAS BEEN GONE WAY TOO LONG.
I SWEAR...I SHOULD'VE NEVER LET JIMMY GO TO THE CORNFIEL--
MY HUSBAND'S FINE, BARBARA.
THEY'RE COMING BACK. I KNOW IT.
HOW YOU FEELING, HONEY?
I'M FINE.
SIGH CHRIST, RUBY... I HATE THAT YOU HAVE TO GO THROUGH THIS. THIS WILL ALL BE OVER SOON, I PROMISE.
TED, I'M NOT THE ONE YOU SHOULD WORRY ABOUT.

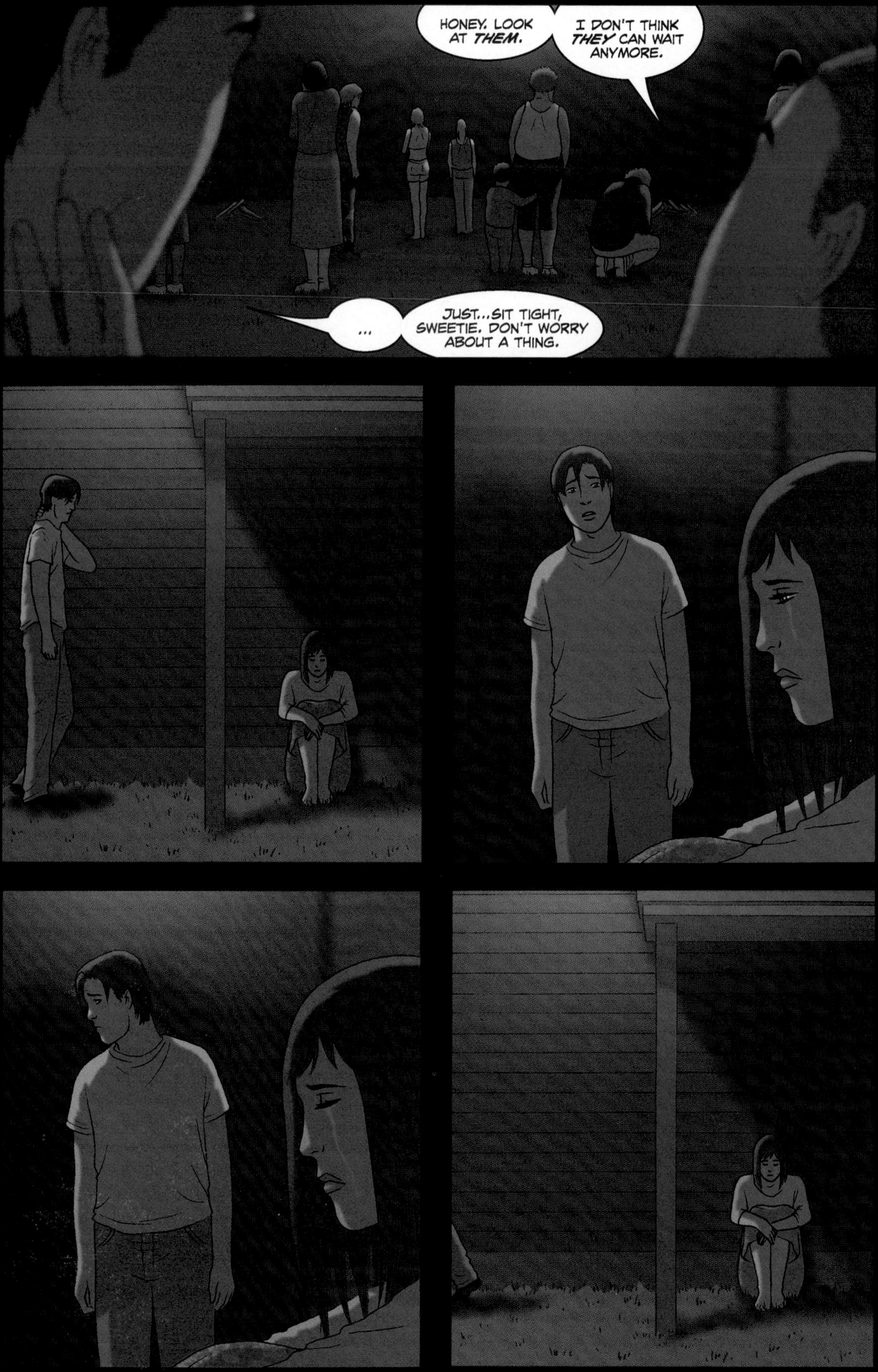
HONEY. LOOK AT *THEM*.
I DON'T THINK *THEY* CAN WAIT ANYMORE.
...
JUST...SIT TIGHT, SWEETIE. DON'T WORRY ABOUT A THING.

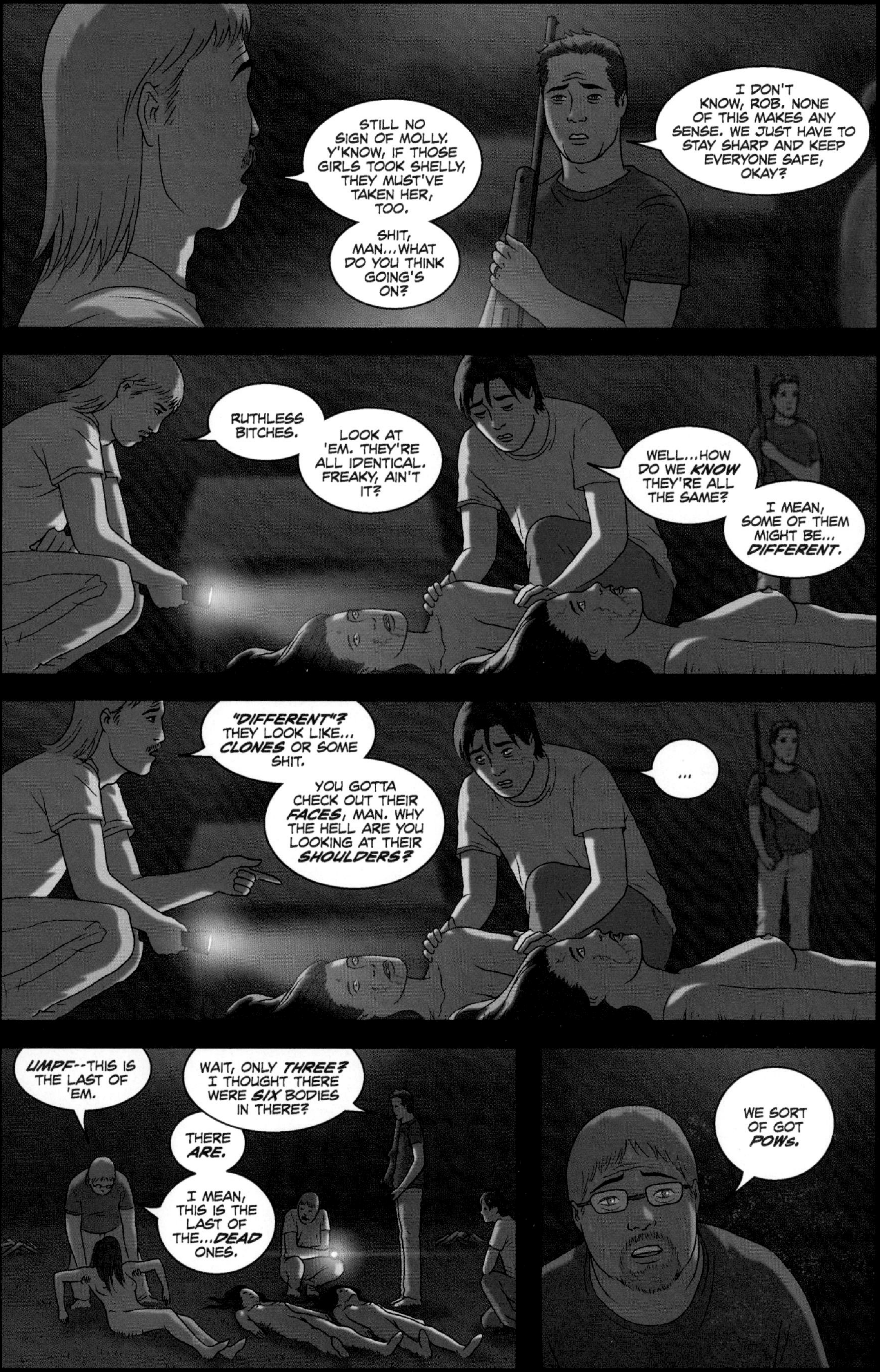
STILL NO SIGN OF MOLLY. Y'KNOW, IF THOSE GIRLS TOOK SHELLY, THEY MUST'VE TAKEN HER, TOO.
SHIT, MAN...WHAT DO YOU THINK GOING'S ON?
I DON'T KNOW, ROB. NONE OF THIS MAKES ANY SENSE. WE JUST HAVE TO STAY SHARP AND KEEP EVERYONE SAFE, OKAY?
RUTHLESS BITCHES.
LOOK AT 'EM. THEY'RE ALL IDENTICAL. FREAKY, AIN'T IT?
WELL...HOW DO WE KNOW THEY'RE ALL THE SAME?
I MEAN, SOME OF THEM MIGHT BE... DIFFERENT.
"DIFFERENT"? THEY LOOK LIKE... CLONES OR SOME SHIT.
YOU GOTTA CHECK OUT THEIR FACES, MAN. WHY THE HELL ARE YOU LOOKING AT THEIR SHOULDERS?
...
UMPF--THIS IS THE LAST OF 'EM.
WAIT, ONLY THREE? I THOUGHT THERE WERE SIX BODIES IN THERE?
THERE ARE.
I MEAN, THIS IS THE LAST OF THE...DEAD ONES.
WE SORT OF GOT POWS.

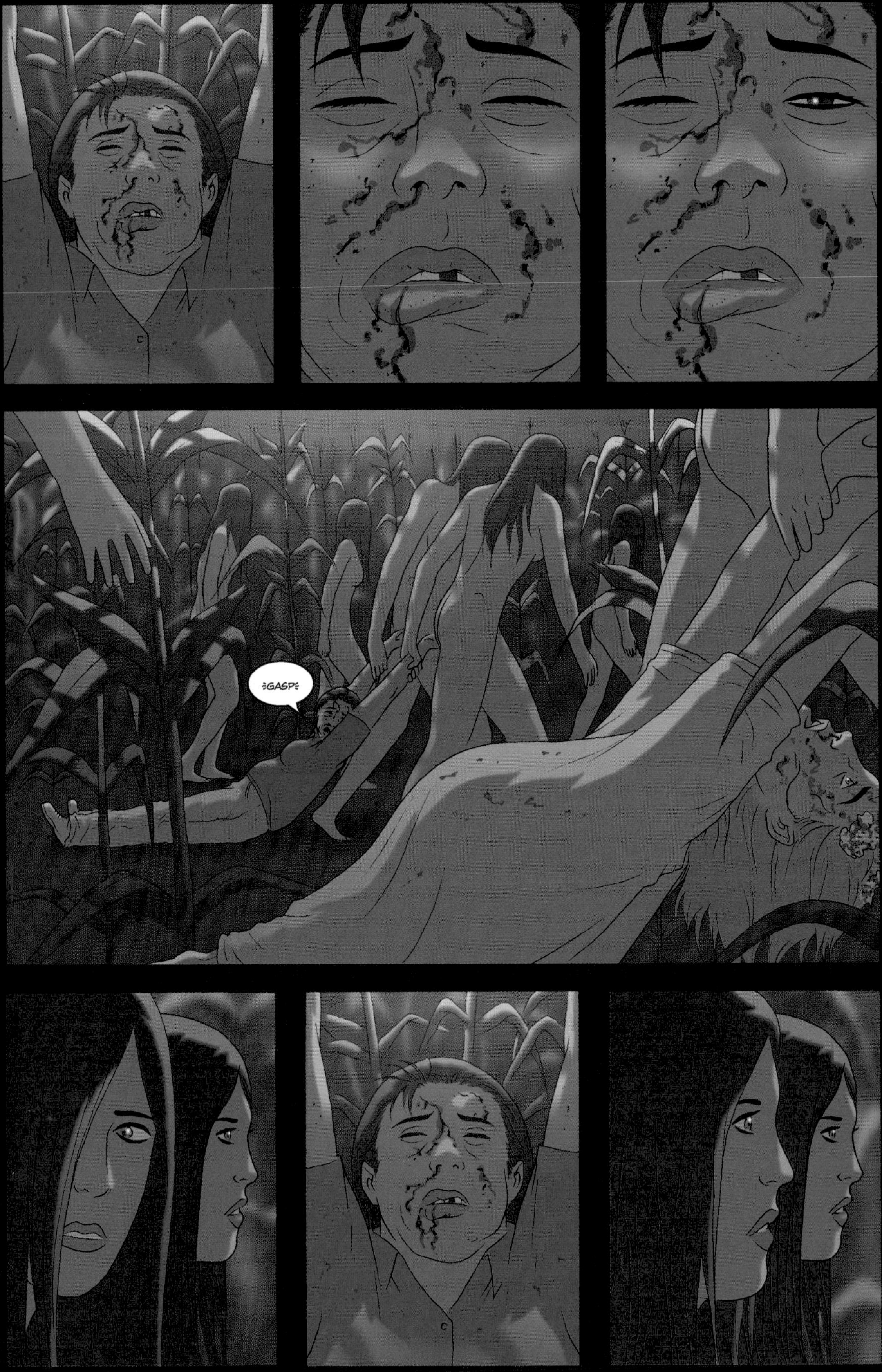
GASP

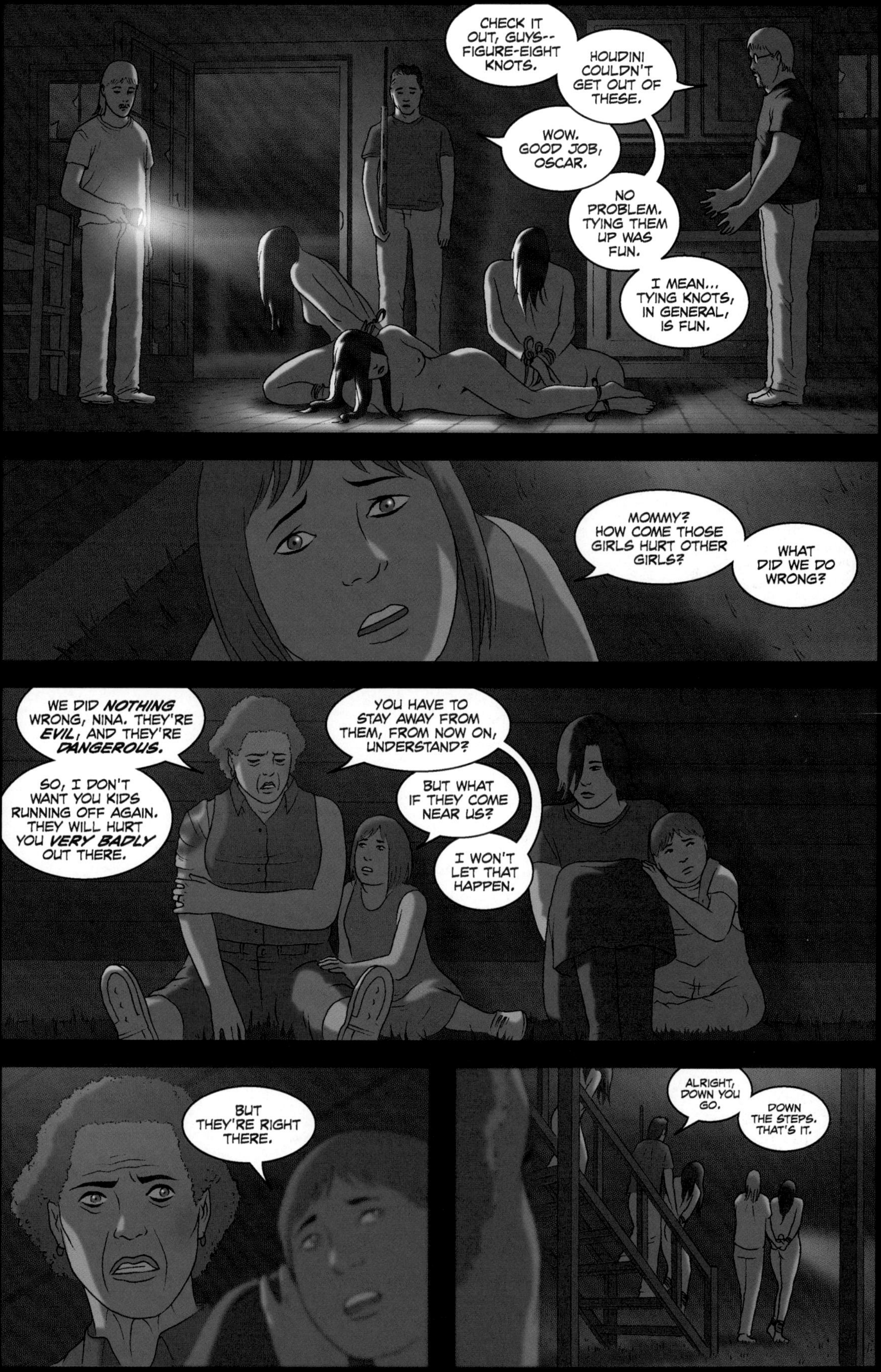
CHECK IT OUT, GUYS-- FIGURE-EIGHT KNOTS.
HOUDINI COULDN'T GET OUT OF THESE.
WOW. GOOD JOB, OSCAR.
NO PROBLEM. TYING THEM UP WAS FUN.
I MEAN... TYING KNOTS, IN GENERAL, IS FUN.
MOMMY? HOW COME THOSE GIRLS HURT OTHER GIRLS?
WHAT DID WE DO WRONG?
WE DID *NOTHING* WRONG, NINA. THEY'RE *EVIL*, AND THEY'RE *DANGEROUS.*
SO, I DON'T WANT YOU KIDS RUNNING OFF AGAIN. THEY WILL HURT YOU *VERY BADLY* OUT THERE.
YOU HAVE TO STAY AWAY FROM THEM, FROM NOW ON, UNDERSTAND?
BUT WHAT IF THEY COME NEAR US?
I WON'T LET THAT HAPPEN.
BUT THEY'RE RIGHT THERE.
ALRIGHT, DOWN YOU GO.
DOWN THE STEPS. THAT'S IT.

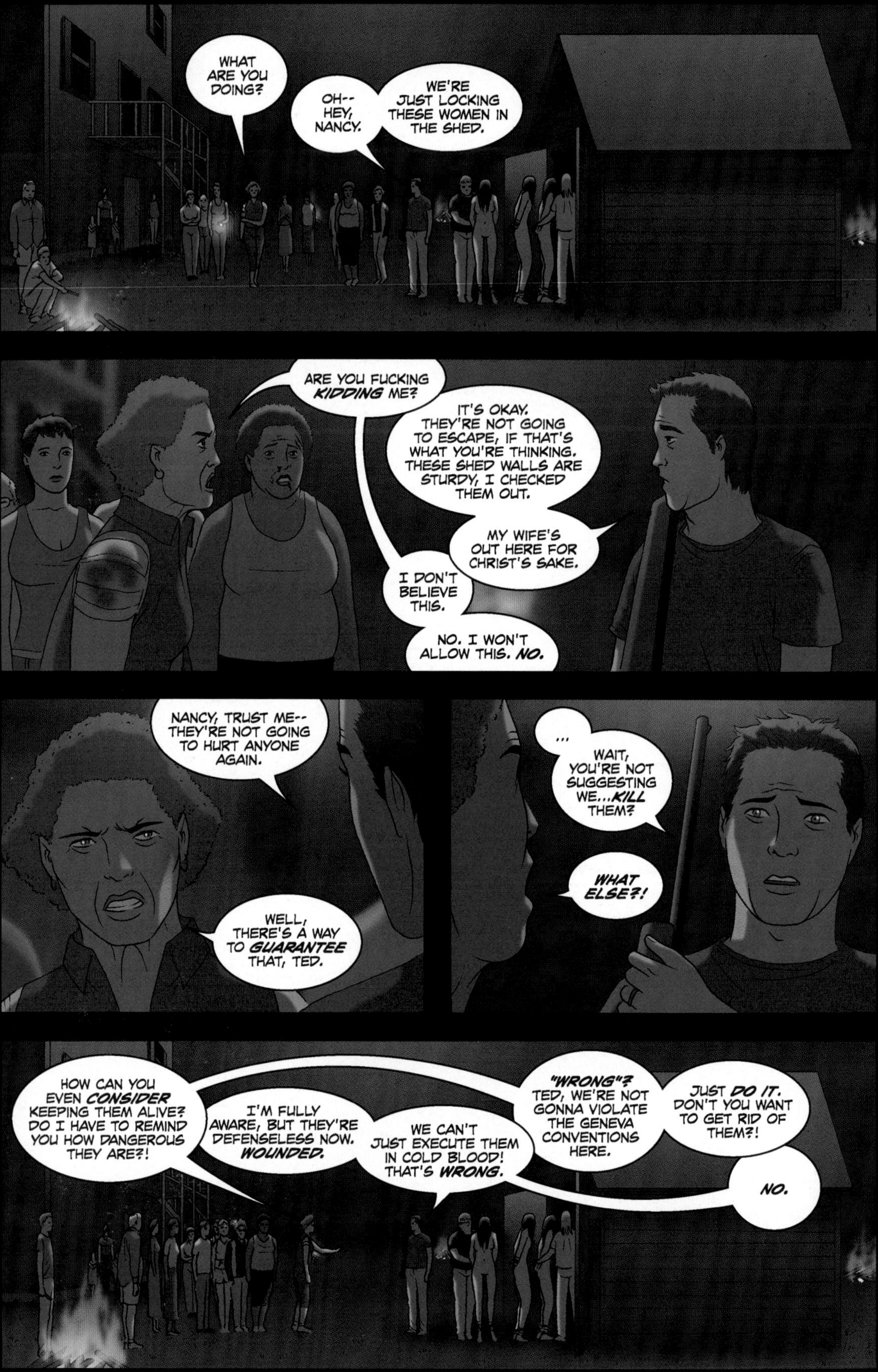
WHAT ARE YOU DOING?
OH-- HEY, NANCY.
WE'RE JUST LOCKING THESE WOMEN IN THE SHED.
ARE YOU FUCKING *KIDDING* ME?
IT'S OKAY. THEY'RE NOT GOING TO ESCAPE, IF THAT'S WHAT YOU'RE THINKING. THESE SHED WALLS ARE STURDY, I CHECKED THEM OUT.
MY WIFE'S OUT HERE FOR CHRIST'S SAKE.
I DON'T BELIEVE THIS.
NO. I WON'T ALLOW THIS. ***NO.***
NANCY, TRUST ME-- THEY'RE NOT GOING TO HURT ANYONE AGAIN.
WELL, THERE'S A WAY TO ***GUARANTEE*** THAT, TED.
...
WAIT, YOU'RE NOT SUGGESTING WE...***KILL*** THEM?
WHAT ELSE?!
HOW CAN YOU EVEN ***CONSIDER*** KEEPING THEM ALIVE? DO I HAVE TO REMIND YOU HOW DANGEROUS THEY ARE?!
I'M FULLY AWARE, BUT THEY'RE DEFENSELESS NOW. ***WOUNDED.***
WE CAN'T JUST EXECUTE THEM IN COLD BLOOD! THAT'S ***WRONG.***
"WRONG"? TED, WE'RE NOT GONNA VIOLATE THE GENEVA CONVENTIONS HERE.
JUST ***DO IT.*** DON'T YOU WANT TO GET RID OF THEM?!
NO.

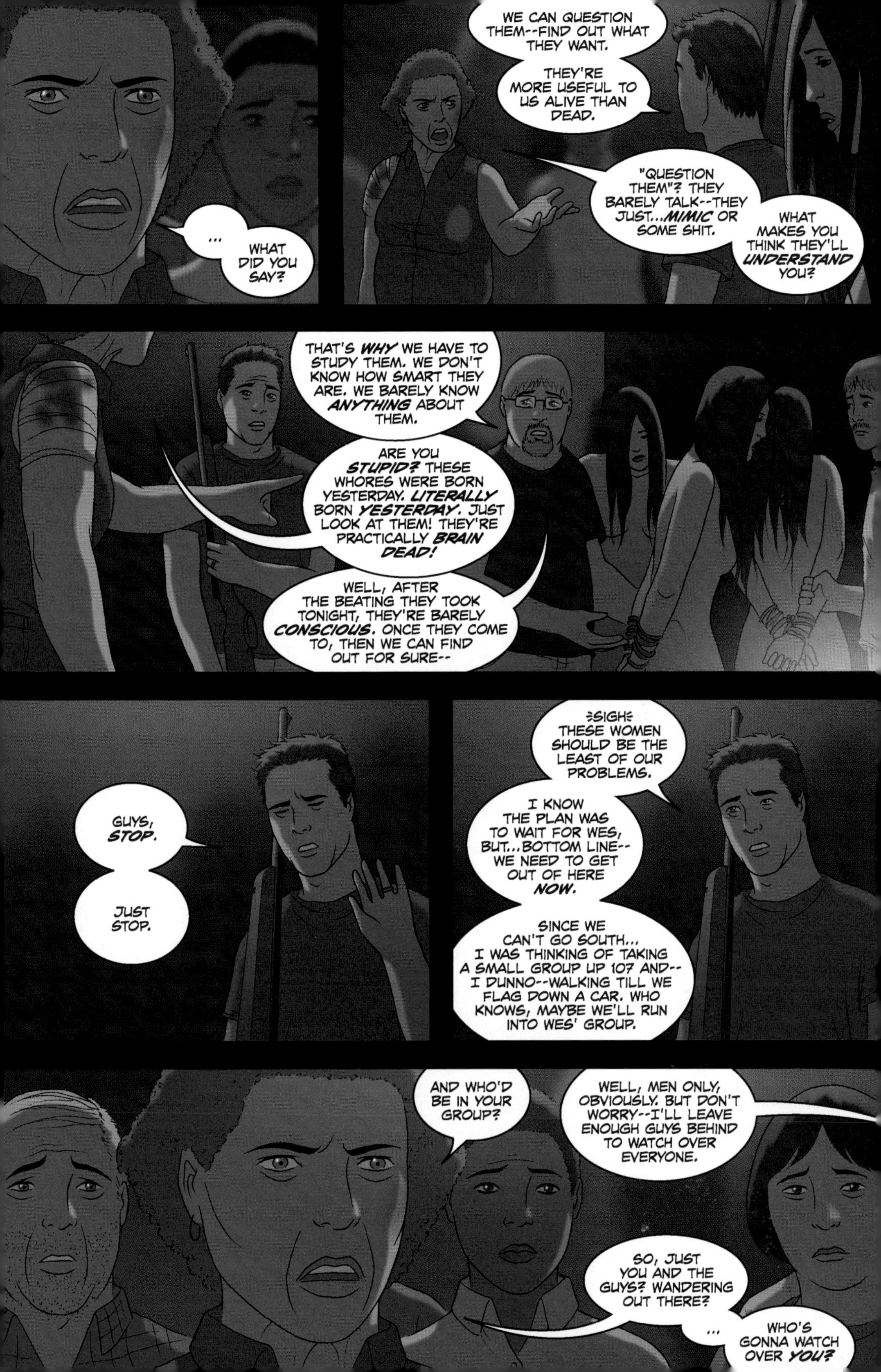
...
WHAT DID YOU SAY?
WE CAN QUESTION THEM--FIND OUT WHAT THEY WANT.
THEY'RE MORE USEFUL TO US ALIVE THAN DEAD.
"QUESTION THEM"? THEY BARELY TALK--THEY JUST...MIMIC OR SOME SHIT.
WHAT MAKES YOU THINK THEY'LL UNDERSTAND YOU?
THAT'S WHY WE HAVE TO STUDY THEM. WE DON'T KNOW HOW SMART THEY ARE. WE BARELY KNOW ANYTHING ABOUT THEM.
ARE YOU STUPID? THESE WHORES WERE BORN YESTERDAY. LITERALLY BORN YESTERDAY. JUST LOOK AT THEM! THEY'RE PRACTICALLY BRAIN DEAD!
WELL, AFTER THE BEATING THEY TOOK TONIGHT, THEY'RE BARELY CONSCIOUS. ONCE THEY COME TO, THEN WE CAN FIND OUT FOR SURE--
GUYS, STOP.
JUST STOP.
≶SIGH≶ THESE WOMEN SHOULD BE THE LEAST OF OUR PROBLEMS.
I KNOW THE PLAN WAS TO WAIT FOR WES, BUT...BOTTOM LINE--WE NEED TO GET OUT OF HERE NOW.
SINCE WE CAN'T GO SOUTH... I WAS THINKING OF TAKING A SMALL GROUP UP 107 AND--I DUNNO--WALKING TILL WE FLAG DOWN A CAR. WHO KNOWS, MAYBE WE'LL RUN INTO WES' GROUP.
AND WHO'D BE IN YOUR GROUP?
WELL, MEN ONLY, OBVIOUSLY. BUT DON'T WORRY--I'LL LEAVE ENOUGH GUYS BEHIND TO WATCH OVER EVERYONE.
SO, JUST YOU AND THE GUYS? WANDERING OUT THERE?
...
WHO'S GONNA WATCH OVER YOU?

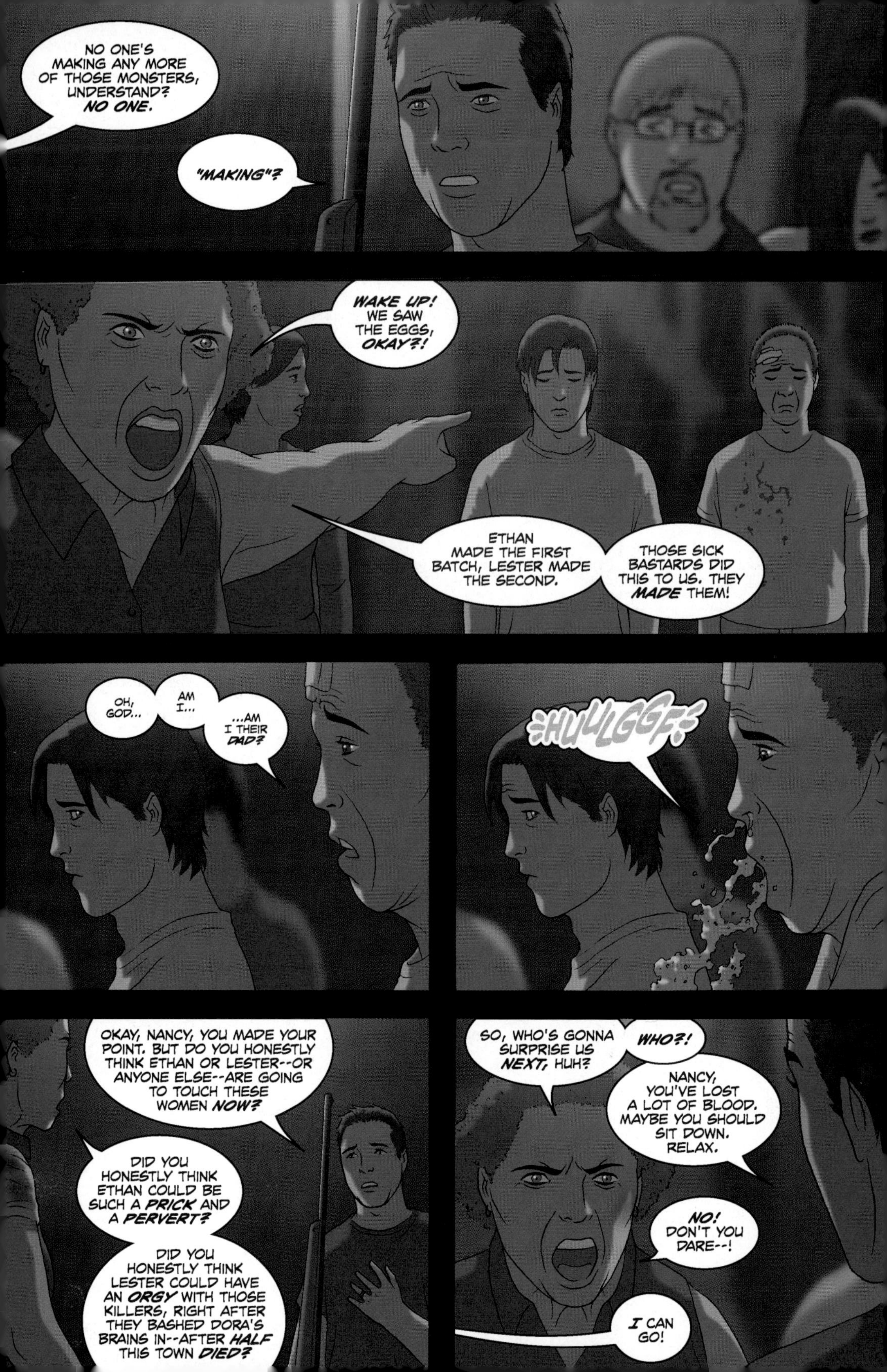
NO ONE'S MAKING ANY MORE OF THOSE MONSTERS, UNDERSTAND? NO ONE.
"MAKING"?
WAKE UP! WE SAW THE EGGS, OKAY?!
ETHAN MADE THE FIRST BATCH, LESTER MADE THE SECOND.
THOSE SICK BASTARDS DID THIS TO US. THEY MADE THEM!
OH, GOD...
AM I...
...AM I THEIR DAD?
HUULGGF!
OKAY, NANCY, YOU MADE YOUR POINT. BUT DO YOU HONESTLY THINK ETHAN OR LESTER--OR ANYONE ELSE--ARE GOING TO TOUCH THESE WOMEN NOW?
DID YOU HONESTLY THINK ETHAN COULD BE SUCH A PRICK AND A PERVERT?
DID YOU HONESTLY THINK LESTER COULD HAVE AN ORGY WITH THOSE KILLERS, RIGHT AFTER THEY BASHED DORA'S BRAINS IN--AFTER HALF THIS TOWN DIED?
SO, WHO'S GONNA SURPRISE US NEXT, HUH?
WHO?!
NANCY, YOU'VE LOST A LOT OF BLOOD. MAYBE YOU SHOULD SIT DOWN. RELAX.
NO! DON'T YOU DARE--!
I CAN GO!

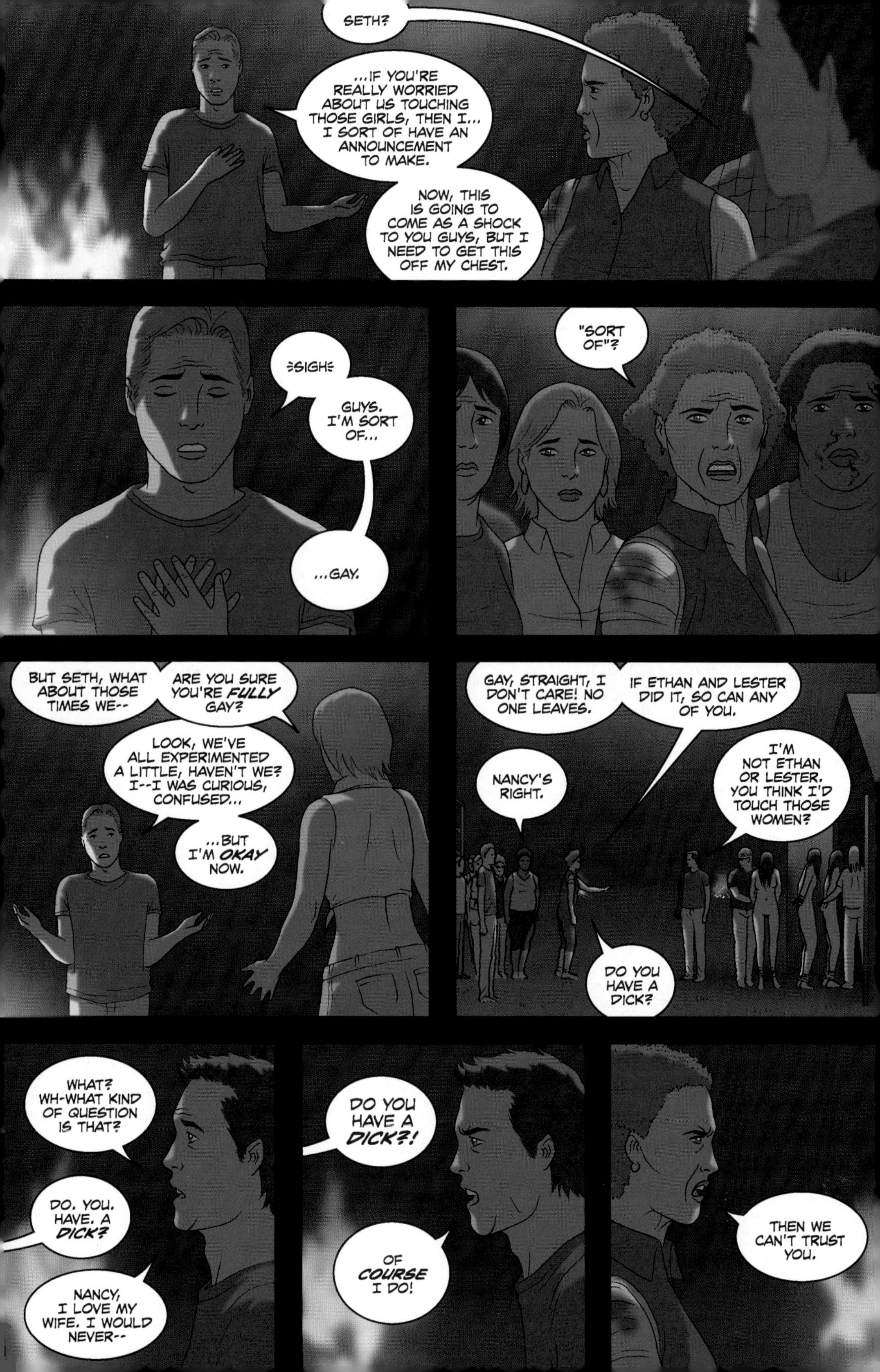
SETH?
...IF YOU'RE REALLY WORRIED ABOUT US TOUCHING THOSE GIRLS, THEN I... I SORT OF HAVE AN ANNOUNCEMENT TO MAKE.
NOW, THIS IS GOING TO COME AS A SHOCK TO YOU GUYS, BUT I NEED TO GET THIS OFF MY CHEST.
=SIGH=
GUYS. I'M SORT OF...
...GAY.
"SORT OF"?
BUT SETH, WHAT ABOUT THOSE TIMES WE--
ARE YOU SURE YOU'RE FULLY GAY?
LOOK, WE'VE ALL EXPERIMENTED A LITTLE, HAVEN'T WE? I--I WAS CURIOUS, CONFUSED...
...BUT I'M OKAY NOW.
GAY, STRAIGHT, I DON'T CARE! NO ONE LEAVES.
IF ETHAN AND LESTER DID IT, SO CAN ANY OF YOU.
NANCY'S RIGHT.
I'M NOT ETHAN OR LESTER. YOU THINK I'D TOUCH THOSE WOMEN?
DO YOU HAVE A DICK?
WHAT? WH-WHAT KIND OF QUESTION IS THAT?
DO. YOU. HAVE. A DICK?
NANCY, I LOVE MY WIFE. I WOULD NEVER--
DO YOU HAVE A DICK?!
OF COURSE I DO!
THEN WE CAN'T TRUST YOU.

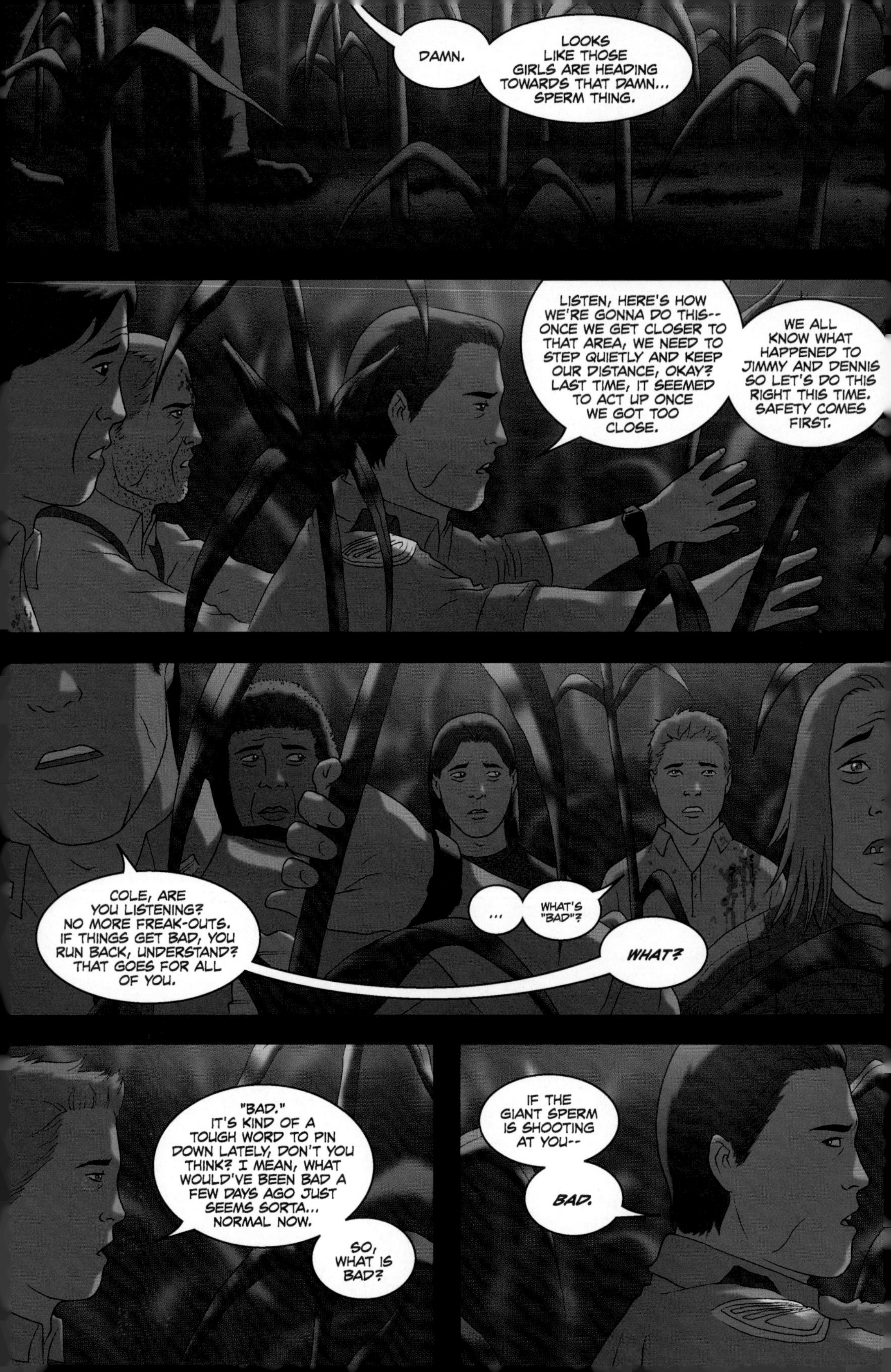
DAMN.
LOOKS LIKE THOSE GIRLS ARE HEADING TOWARDS THAT DAMN... SPERM THING.
LISTEN, HERE'S HOW WE'RE GONNA DO THIS-- ONCE WE GET CLOSER TO THAT AREA, WE NEED TO STEP QUIETLY AND KEEP OUR DISTANCE, OKAY? LAST TIME, IT SEEMED TO ACT UP ONCE WE GOT TOO CLOSE.
WE ALL KNOW WHAT HAPPENED TO JIMMY AND DENNIS SO LET'S DO THIS RIGHT THIS TIME. SAFETY COMES FIRST.
COLE, ARE YOU LISTENING? NO MORE FREAK-OUTS. IF THINGS GET BAD, YOU RUN BACK, UNDERSTAND? THAT GOES FOR ALL OF YOU.
...
WHAT'S "BAD"?
WHAT?
"BAD." IT'S KIND OF A TOUGH WORD TO PIN DOWN LATELY, DON'T YOU THINK? I MEAN, WHAT WOULD'VE BEEN BAD A FEW DAYS AGO JUST SEEMS SORTA... NORMAL NOW.
SO, WHAT IS BAD?
IF THE GIANT SPERM IS SHOOTING AT YOU--
BAD.

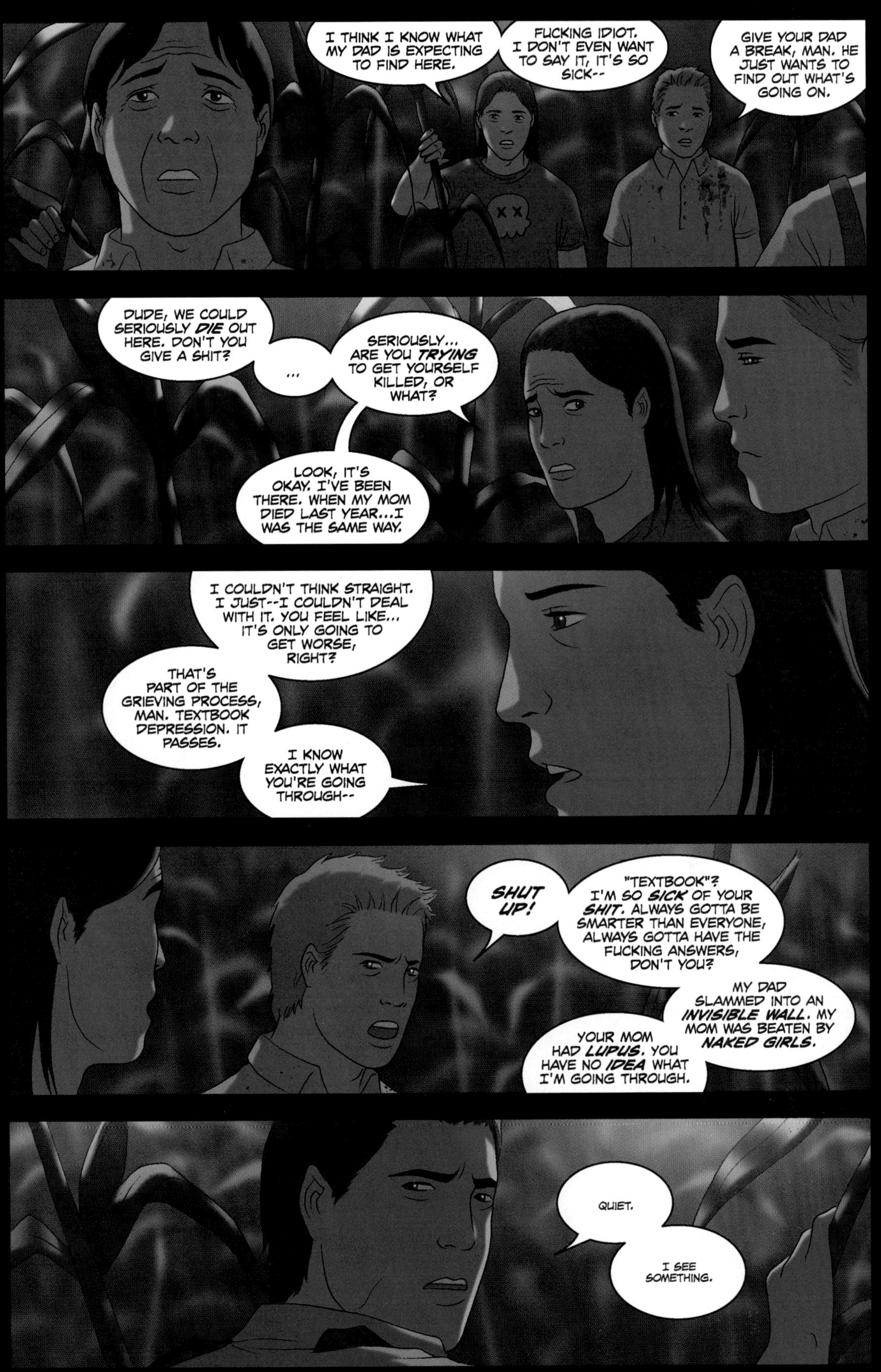
I THINK I KNOW WHAT MY DAD IS EXPECTING TO FIND HERE.
FUCKING IDIOT. I DON'T EVEN WANT TO SAY IT, IT'S SO SICK--
GIVE YOUR DAD A BREAK, MAN. HE JUST WANTS TO FIND OUT WHAT'S GOING ON.
DUDE, WE COULD SERIOUSLY *DIE* OUT HERE. DON'T YOU GIVE A SHIT?
...
SERIOUSLY... ARE YOU *TRYING* TO GET YOURSELF KILLED, OR WHAT?
LOOK, IT'S OKAY. I'VE BEEN THERE. WHEN MY MOM DIED LAST YEAR...I WAS THE SAME WAY.
I COULDN'T THINK STRAIGHT. I JUST--I COULDN'T DEAL WITH IT. YOU FEEL LIKE... IT'S ONLY GOING TO GET WORSE, RIGHT?
THAT'S PART OF THE GRIEVING PROCESS, MAN. TEXTBOOK DEPRESSION. IT PASSES.
I KNOW EXACTLY WHAT YOU'RE GOING THROUGH--
SHUT UP!
"TEXTBOOK"? I'M SO *SICK* OF YOUR *SHIT*. ALWAYS GOTTA BE SMARTER THAN EVERYONE, ALWAYS GOTTA HAVE THE FUCKING ANSWERS, DON'T YOU?
MY DAD SLAMMED INTO AN *INVISIBLE WALL*. MY MOM WAS BEATEN BY *NAKED GIRLS*.
YOUR MOM HAD *LUPUS*. YOU HAVE NO *IDEA* WHAT I'M GOING THROUGH.
QUIET.
I SEE SOMETHING.

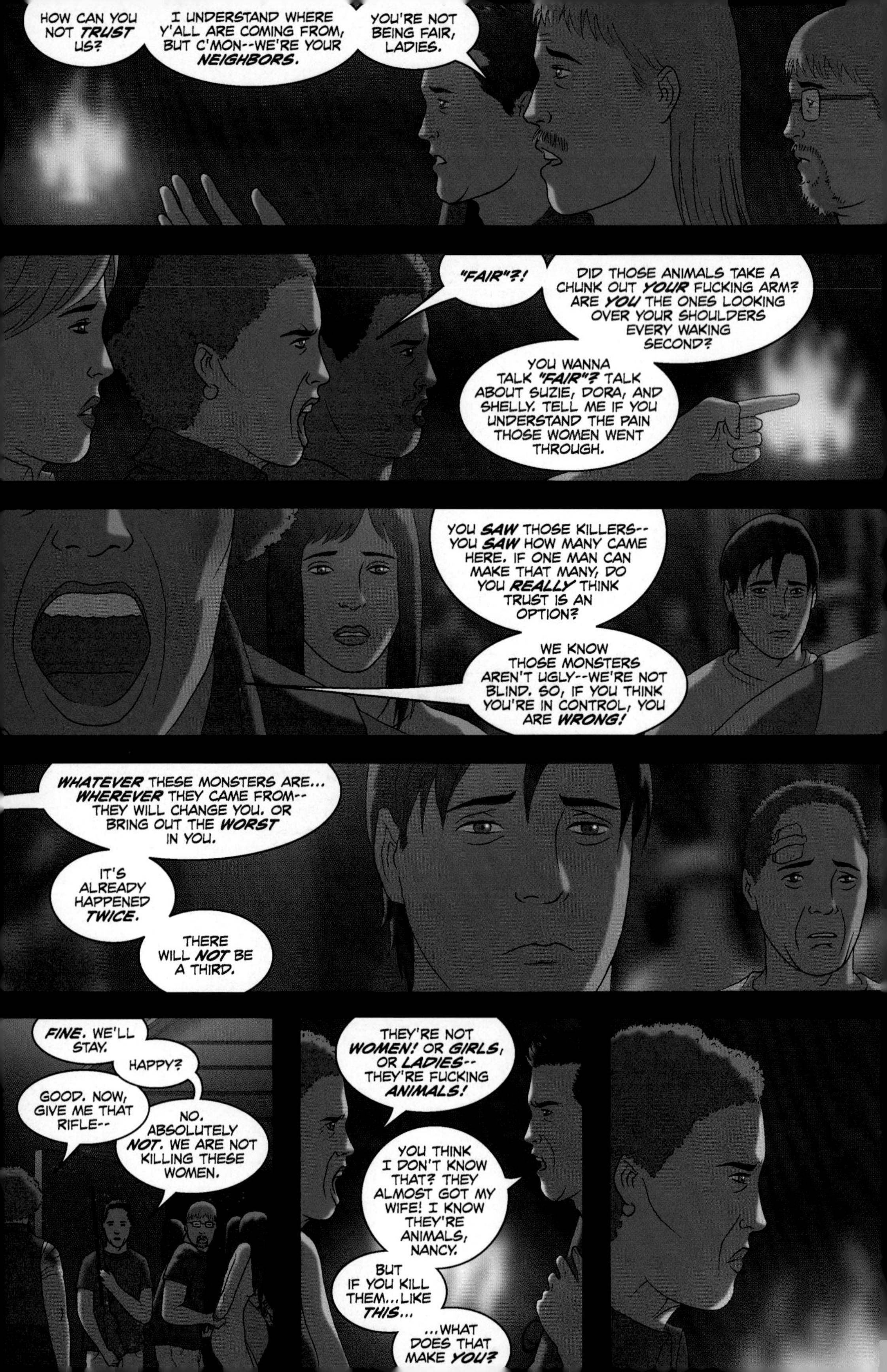
HOW CAN YOU NOT TRUST US?
I UNDERSTAND WHERE Y'ALL ARE COMING FROM, BUT C'MON--WE'RE YOUR NEIGHBORS.
YOU'RE NOT BEING FAIR, LADIES.
"FAIR"?!
DID THOSE ANIMALS TAKE A CHUNK OUT YOUR FUCKING ARM? ARE YOU THE ONES LOOKING OVER YOUR SHOULDERS EVERY WAKING SECOND?
YOU WANNA TALK "FAIR"? TALK ABOUT SUZIE, DORA, AND SHELLY. TELL ME IF YOU UNDERSTAND THE PAIN THOSE WOMEN WENT THROUGH.
YOU SAW THOSE KILLERS--YOU SAW HOW MANY CAME HERE. IF ONE MAN CAN MAKE THAT MANY, DO YOU REALLY THINK TRUST IS AN OPTION?
WE KNOW THOSE MONSTERS AREN'T UGLY--WE'RE NOT BLIND. SO, IF YOU THINK YOU'RE IN CONTROL, YOU ARE WRONG!
WHATEVER THESE MONSTERS ARE... WHEREVER THEY CAME FROM--THEY WILL CHANGE YOU. OR BRING OUT THE WORST IN YOU.
IT'S ALREADY HAPPENED TWICE.
THERE WILL NOT BE A THIRD.
FINE. WE'LL STAY.
HAPPY?
GOOD. NOW, GIVE ME THAT RIFLE--
NO. ABSOLUTELY NOT. WE ARE NOT KILLING THESE WOMEN.
THEY'RE NOT WOMEN! OR GIRLS, OR LADIES--THEY'RE FUCKING ANIMALS!
YOU THINK I DON'T KNOW THAT? THEY ALMOST GOT MY WIFE! I KNOW THEY'RE ANIMALS, NANCY.
BUT IF YOU KILL THEM...LIKE THIS...
...WHAT DOES THAT MAKE YOU?

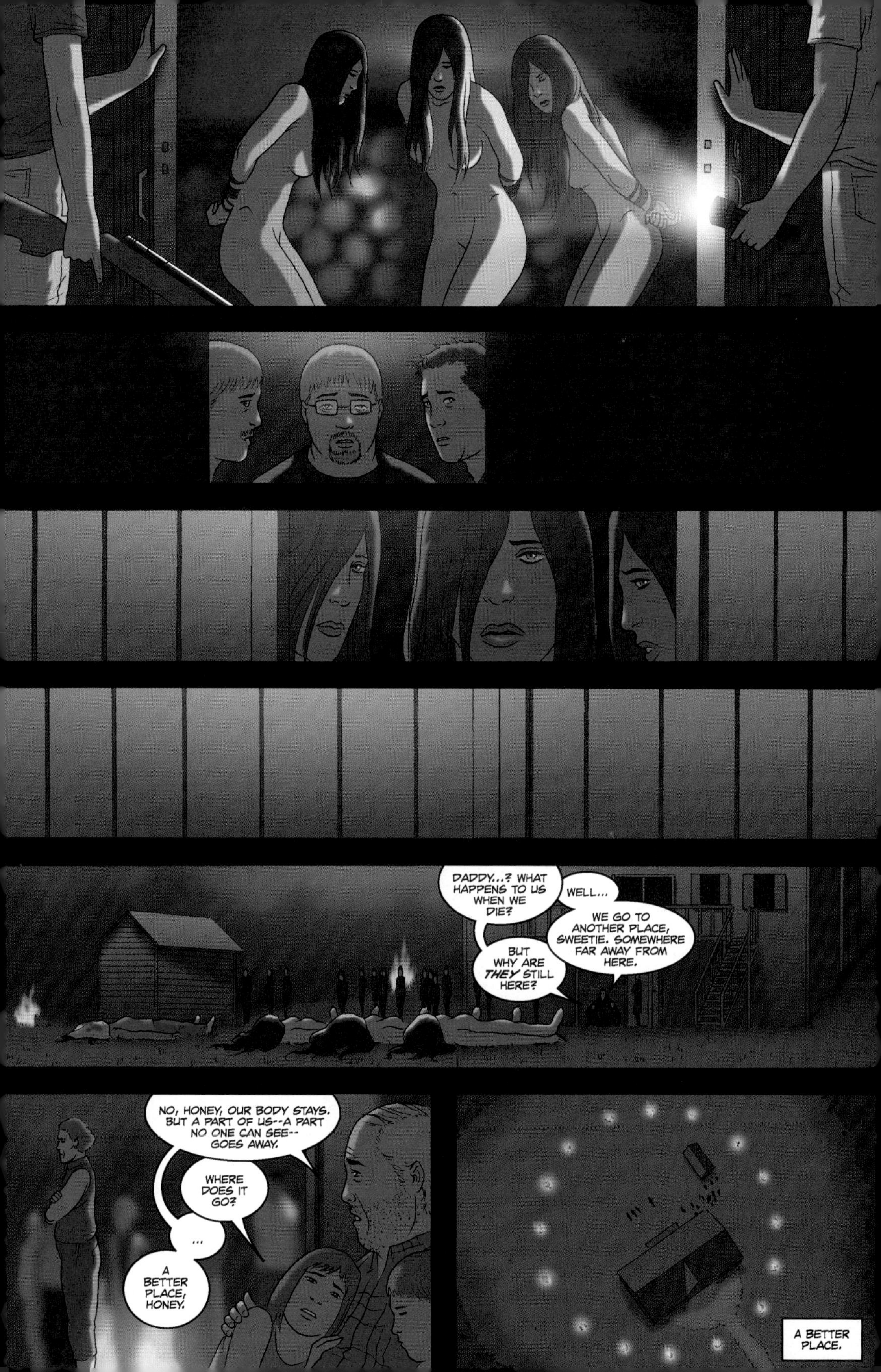

DADDY...? WHAT HAPPENS TO US WHEN WE DIE?
WELL...
WE GO TO ANOTHER PLACE, SWEETIE. SOMEWHERE FAR AWAY FROM HERE.
BUT WHY ARE *THEY* STILL HERE?
NO, HONEY, OUR BODY STAYS. BUT A PART OF US--A PART NO ONE CAN SEE--GOES AWAY.
WHERE DOES IT GO?
...
A BETTER PLACE, HONEY.
A BETTER PLACE.

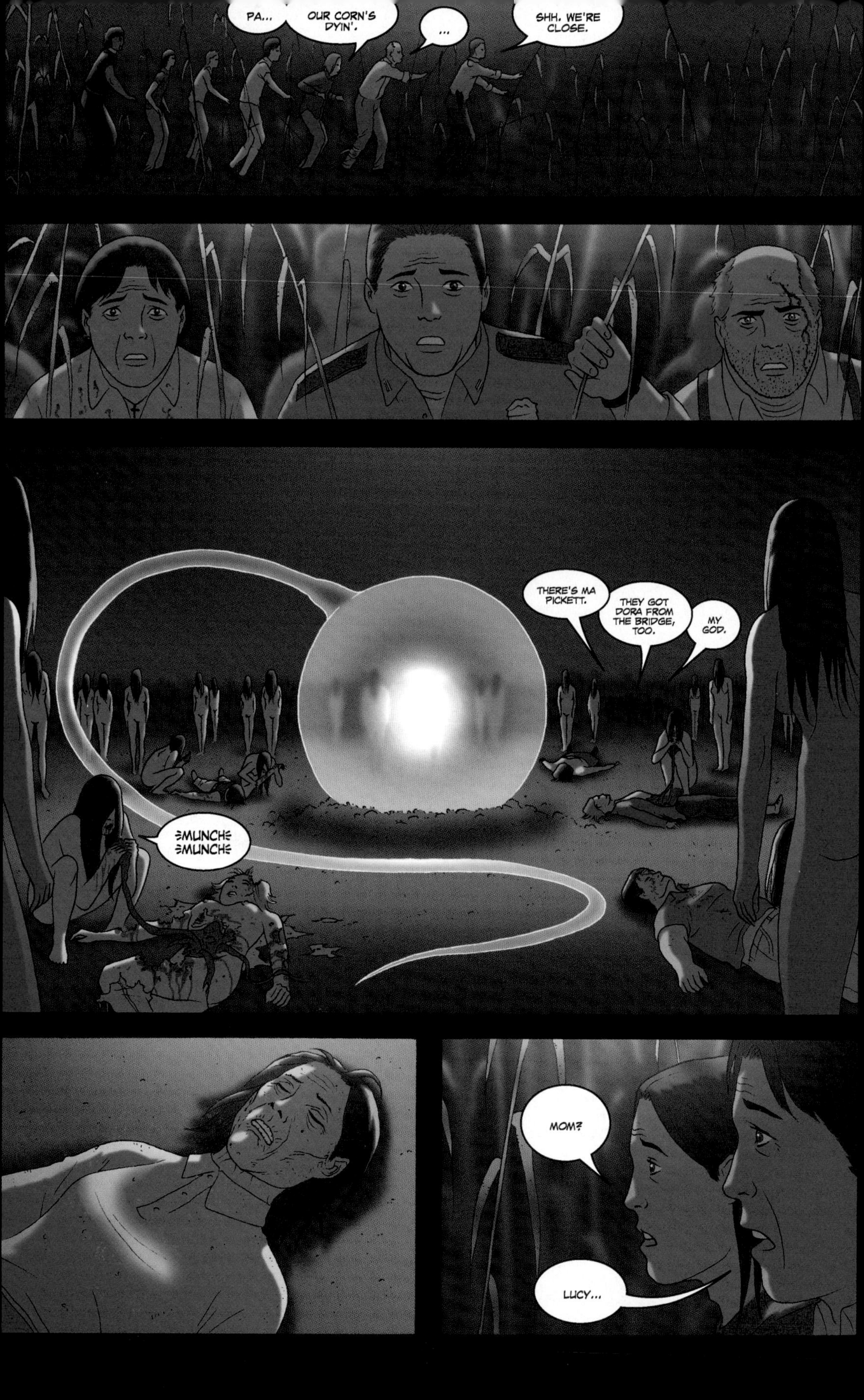
PA...
OUR CORN'S DYIN'.
...
SHH. WE'RE CLOSE.
THERE'S MA PICKETT.
THEY GOT DORA FROM THE BRIDGE, TOO.
MY GOD.
MUNCH MUNCH
MOM?
LUCY...

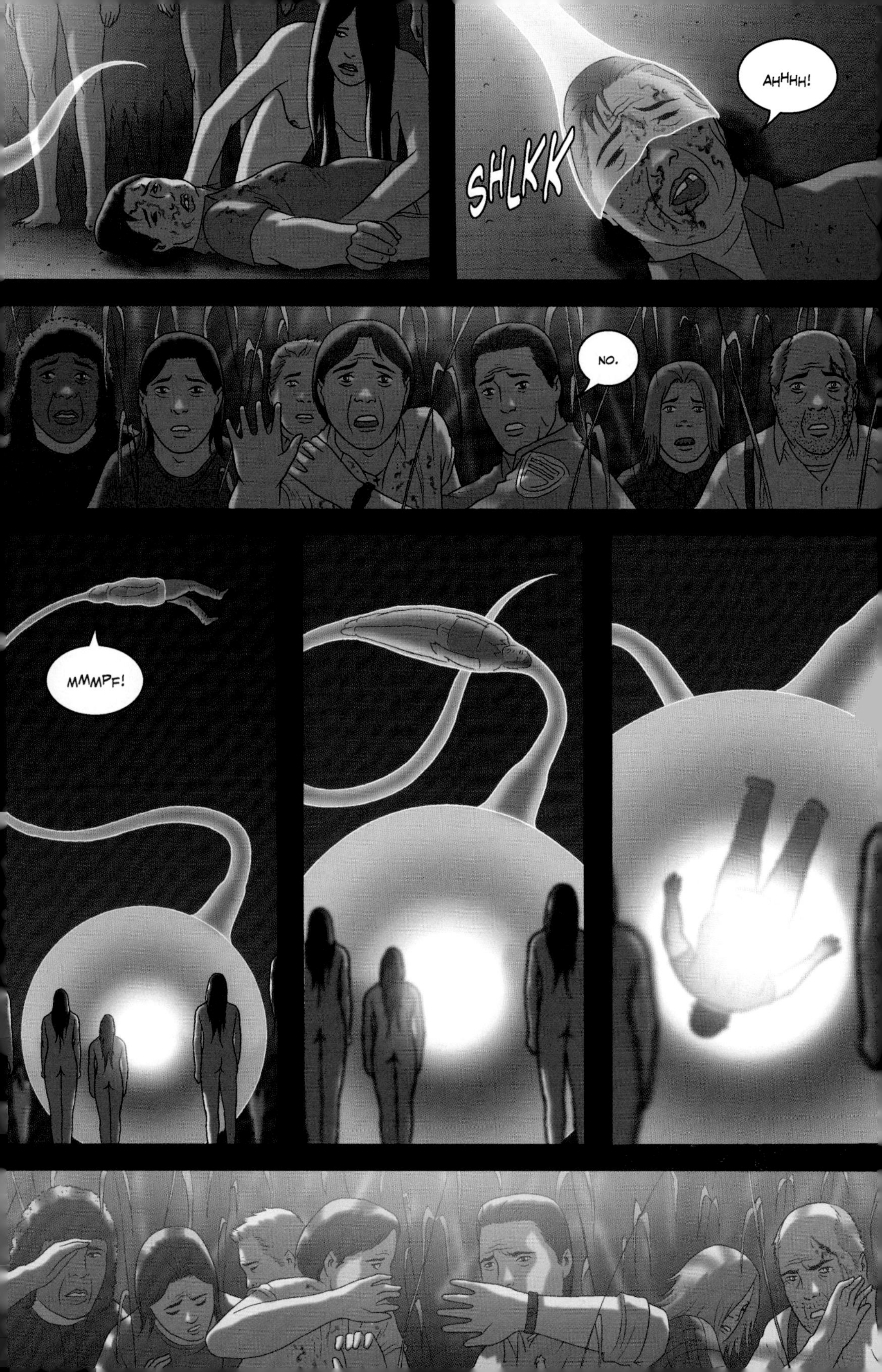
SHLKK
AHHHH!
NO.
MMMPF!

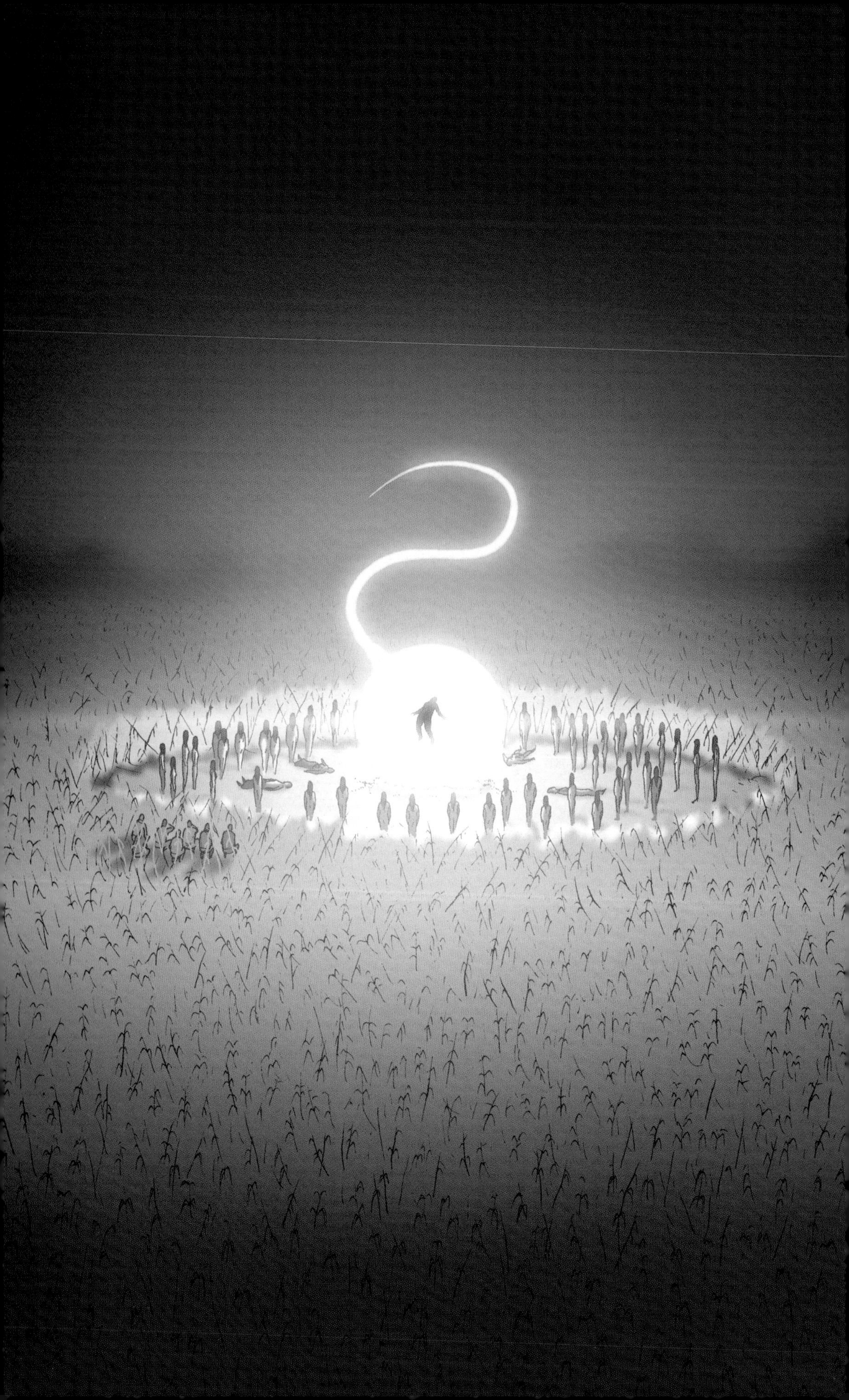

MORE GREAT IMAGE BOOKS FROM
THE LUNA BROTHERS

ULTRA

SEVEN DAYS
Trade Paperback

$17.95
ISBN: 1-58240-483-6
Collects ULTRA #1-8
248 Pages

In Spring City, where superheroes blur the lines between law enforcement and celebrity, Pearl Penalosa, a.k.a. Ultra, is a workaholic. At the prestigious agency, Heroine Inc., she has earned a legion of fans, a nomination for "Best Heroine of the Year" and a perfect life. Well, almost perfect. A chance encounter with a mysterious fortune teller prophesizes true love for Pearl within seven days.

DIRECTED BY THE LUNA BROTHERS
ULTRA
SEVEN DAYS
CRESCENT PICTURES

GIRLS

Vol.1: CONCEPTION
Trade Paperback

$14.99
ISBN: 1-58240-529-8
Collects GIRLS #1-6
152 Pages

Ethan Daniels is a small town bachelor who suffers from one, infallible truth: dealing with the opposite sex can be complicated. One night, he bumps into a mysterious woman who will change his life... and maybe even the world.

THE LUNA BROTHERS
GIRLS
Volume 1
CONCEPTION

For a comic shop near you carrying graphic novels from Image Comics, please call toll free: 1-888-COMIC-BOOK

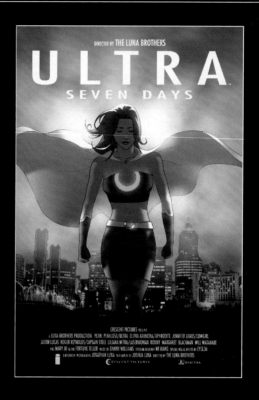

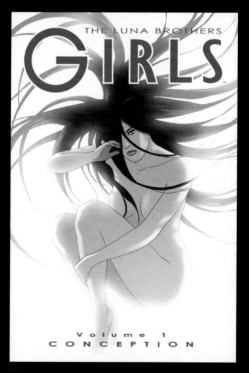